THE CRISIS OF
DEMOCRATIC THEORY

Published for the
Organization of American Historians

THE CRISIS OF
DEMOCRATIC THEORY

Scientific Naturalism & the Problem of Value

Edward A. Purcell, Jr.

The UNIVERSITY PRESS *of* KENTUCKY

ISBN: 0–8131–1282–6

Library of Congress Catalog Card Number: 72–91669

Copyright © 1973 by The University Press of Kentucky

A statewide cooperative scholarly publishing agency
serving Berea College, Centre College of Kentucky,
Eastern Kentucky University, Georgetown College,
Kentucky Historical Society, Kentucky State University,
Morehead State University, Murray State University,
Northern Kentucky State College, Transylvania University,
University of Kentucky, University of Louisville, and
Western Kentucky University.

Editorial and Sales Offices: Lexington, Kentucky 40506

for Sallee
for every reason

Contents

Preface

Although this book does not discuss the problems of racial conflict in the United States, it grew out of a commitment to what in the early sixties was called the Civil Rights Movement. Engaged in debate and action that assumed certain fundamental and democratic moral beliefs, I became increasingly curious about their rational foundations as ethical propositions. That philosophical concern gradually directed my historical interest toward the period of the thirties, when Americans confronted the moral and intellectual challenge that European "totalitarianism" posed to traditional democratic ideals. Slowly the study's center of gravity shifted from a philosophical examination of political theory itself to a wider analysis of certain major ideas and attitudes that many twentieth century intellectuals shared. The problem of the rational, ethical foundation of democracy remained the central issue, but the scope broadened to become more specifically historical. Still, for those who find the distinction meaningful, the study is perhaps more a history of ideas than an intellectual history. It is, as one of my teachers would have called it, a work on a "rarefied" level; unfortunately, he would not necessarily have meant rare in the sense of valuable, but only in the sense of theoretical.

I should hasten to add at this point that I am not assuming that by themselves either ideas or their logical implications are determinative historical forces. The present work does assume, however, that ideas have practical significance as they subtly interplay with human hopes and values, social institutions, and important historical events. Just as those things help create and color ideas, the ideas help interpret them and give them their human meaning.

The present study deals with social scientists and legal scholars especially, with philosophers and educators, and to a lesser extent with mathematicians, scientists, and historians. Conspicuous by their absence are literary figures, artists, and radical or Marxist intellectuals. There are two reasons for their absence. First, historians have already studied them in great detail and often with great insight. In fact, historians have largely written the intellectual history of twentieth century America through the study of one or more of those groups. Important as they are, they are only parts of a larger whole, which demands a certain rebalancing. Second, perhaps the most significant social development that impinges on the intellectual life in contemporary America has been the academic institutionalization of men of ideas. During the period encompassed by this work, from the second to the seventh decades of the present century, the recognized leaders of thought have increasingly been professionally trained university graduates, most of whom retained some close connection with the academies. Though my concern is not primarily to study institutionalization and professionalization as such, it nevertheless seems useful and necessary in examining American thought in the twentieth century to focus in large part on the attitudes and assumptions of professional scholars.

Concerned with the theoretical problem of the rational, ethical basis of democracy—a problem that does not draw the attention of everyone—, I have assumed that anyone who dealt in any "coherent" (and written) way with relevant ideas was an "intellectual." More specifically, examining the attitudes of academic scholars, I have assumed that anyone who wrote for any professional journal was an "intellectual." In short, I have used the term in a very broad sense, often merely as a convenient collective label, but have retained the implicit and subjective qualitative judgment that "intellectuals" as a group meet some minimum standard of serious and critical thought. I doubt whether any sharper definition is possible or useful, at least for the present purposes.

As my subject matter broadened from philosophy to include law and the social sciences, so too the chronological period unavoidably expanded. The conflicts of the thirties seemed to point back to the years around 1910, though obviously the "origins" of the intellectual issues could be traced to the nineteenth century or even as far back as the early seventeenth century. Practically, however, the end of the first decade of the present century appeared the most relevant place to start. First of all, most of the detailed historical writing on law, philosophy, and social science tails off somewhere during the decade between 1910 and 1920, with World War I often serving as the stopping point. Profiting from that work it was possible to start where previous scholarship had tended to finish. Second, and more important, gradually between about 1900 and 1920 there was a significant change in the attitudes of philosophers, social scientists, and legal scholars. Clearly growing out of the ideas of the earlier period, but nevertheless quite distinct from them, a new intellectual orientation dominated the period from about 1910 through the middle thirties. It was with those new attitudes and assumptions that most American intellectuals confronted the theoretical problems raised in the late thirties.

Finally, my material forced me to go beyond what had originally seemed a logical stopping point, American entry into World War II. As my research reached the late thirties and early forties, it soon became obvious that the war changed the context of the dominant ideas but did not mark their end. Most of the assumptions that characterized the thirties remained vividly alive, though subtly altered. The historical result of the intellectual conflict of the thirties resided principally neither in the confused foreign policy debates at the end of that decade nor in the war fought at the beginning of the next. Instead it lay in the conceptual assumptions that came to pervade American thought in general and the social sciences in particular during the twenty-year period after the war. It was necessary then to move the concluding point from the mid-forties to the mid-sixties. Though the attitudes formed clearly did not disappear even then, the mid-sixties appear from the present vantage point to have ushered in a new set of conditions and a new cluster of ideas that distinguish the present period from the era that extends back to the mid-thirties.

Perhaps the most satisfying part of finishing such a study is the opportunity to thank the many people who helped to make it possible. E. David Cronon, Merle Curti, Lane Davis, Kenneth Dolbeare, J. Rogers Hollingsworth, and Samuel Mermin offered many valuable comments on an early version of the manuscript prepared at the University of Wisconsin. My fellow graduate students, Harry H. Dawson, Richard Magurno, Gregory Mueller, Walter Meyer, John Murray, and D. Harold Nelson provided a stimulating intellectual environment. I am deeply indebted to my colleagues at the University of California, Berkeley, and the University of Missouri, Columbia, for their generous and perceptive criticisms, especially to Gerard Clarfield, Samuel Haber, Richard S. Kirkendall, Paul C. Nagel, Hannah Pitkin, Walter V. Scholes, David P. Thelen, William M. Wiecek, and Ronald Yank, all of whom read parts of the manuscript and helped eliminate some of the more egregious errors. John J. Bricke's careful reading aided immeasurably in bringing a degree of logical clarity to the argument.

I owe a special debt of gratitude to two men, Clifford S. Griffin and Irvin G. Wyllie. With his ideal combination of a wry sense of humor and a keen sense for the jugular, Professor Griffin introduced me to the challenges of writing history and constantly forced me to try to meet them.

Professor Wyllie continued that process, broadening my more theoretical interests to encompass the social context in which ideas appear. His steady support and encouragement have been invaluable.

Portions of Chapters 5 and 9 originally appeared as "American Jurisprudence between the Wars: Legal Realism and the Crisis of Democratic Theory," published in the *American Historical Review*, 75 (December, 1969). Permission to incorporate this material is gratefully acknowledged.

I wish to thank the Faculty Research Council of the University of Missouri for two generous grants that helped defray the expenses involved in preparing this study, and express my appreciation to Mrs. Jeanette Dunn, Miss Cindy Ford, and Mrs. Ida Mae Wolff who liberally aided in typing innumerable drafts of the manuscript.

My greatest debt is to my wife, Sallee McNamara Purcell, who contributed to every phase of the research and writing. Words cannot convey the extent of her help.

Columbia, Missouri
September 21, 1972

I

The Problems
of Democratic Theory

1

Scientific Naturalism in
American Thought

In the spring of 1934 the hostility created by five decades of intellectual conflict erupted in a debate held on the campus of the University of Chicago. The renowned physiologist Anton J. Carlson, nicknamed "Ajax" by his opponents, glared across a platform at law professor Mortimer J. Adler before a divided and intensely partisan overflow crowd that had jammed itself into Mandel Hall, the university's largest auditorium. Although tickets had been free, the demand was so great that enterprising students were able to sell them for as much as a dollar apiece. The students and faculty in the audience reacted passionately and repeatedly interrupted the debate with thunderous applause whenever, in the words of one of the participants, "a punch landed on either side."[1]

The confrontation between Adler and Carlson climaxed a spirited battle at the University of Chicago, a struggle that saw students and faculty divide and enlist in one of two opposing camps. Adler, one of the leaders of a neo-Aristotelian revival in the thirties, stood for a philosophical rationalism holding that human reason could discover certain immutable metaphysical principles that explained the true nature of reality. Those principles were ultimates, Adler argued, and as such they were the foundation of the rationally true and the ethically good. Carlson, a convinced empiricist, spoke for a broad position best identified as scientific naturalism. Absolute rational principles did not govern or explain the universe. No a priori truths existed, and metaphysics was merely a cover for human ignorance and superstition. Only concrete, scientific investigations could yield true knowledge, Carlson maintained, and that knowledge was empirical, particular, and experimentally verifiable.

During the twenties the University of Chicago had established itself as the intellectual center of American academic life, especially in the rapidly growing social sciences. Scientific naturalism set the university's intellectual tone and dominated the faculty, which included some of the most prominent physical and social scientists in the country. During the early thirties, however, as the depression worsened and Nazism triumphed in Germany, a new group of scholars formed at Chicago who helped create an enthusiastic neo-Aristotelian revival. Conflict was unavoidable.

The university newspaper, the *Daily Maroon*, publicized the debate by printing numerous attacks and replies. The *Maroon* editor in 1933–34, John P. Barden, had become a convert to Adler's rationalism, and he devoted a series of editorials to defending the Aristotelian-Thomistic synthesis. After much arguing, both sides grew intemperate. "Persons who deny the validity of a truth that is self-evident," charged an editorial, "possess a kind of bigoted, emotional intolerance that any rational person may refuse to deal with." Debate with such persons was simply useless. "Rational men have a right, if they wish to save time," the editorial concluded, "to be intolerant of simple or intentional stupidity."[2] Critics both of Aristotelian rationalism and of the *Maroon*'s attitude answered in kind. "A peculiarly common disease of the juvenile has made its little stir on the midway in recent months," declared the economist Harry D. Gideonse in repudiating the rationalist revival.[3] At one point the *Daily Maroon* brought out a special supplement devoted exclusively to the controversy, an edition that sold 5,000 copies and brought requests for bulk shipments from colleges all over the country.[4]

The debate kept the campus in a turmoil, and even one of the inevitable results—a baseball game between the "Aristotelians" and the "social scientists"—resolved very little. The Aristotelians paraphrased the school song, "Wave the Flag," with the words

> Wave the flag for social science
> They stand for facts alone.
> Ever shall they be dogmatic
> John Dewey they enthrone.
> With the pragmatists to lead them
> Without a thought they stand
> So cheer again for social science
> For they're zeroes every man.

There were rumors that the social science departments would adopt their own song, which, though it did not rhyme, had more to recommend it on *ad hominem* grounds:

4

Everybody knows that Aquinas is dead,
Everybody knows but Adler.
Nobody knows what Adler knows,
Let's ask *The Daily Maroon*.

One student reported that Adler's classes had spent twenty-two meetings reading six pages of Aristotle's *Physics*, and a fortuneteller near the campus hung out a sign proclaiming "Licensed Metaphysician."[5]

The debate at Chicago was part of a broad and bitter confrontation in the thirties that aroused the partisanship of intellectuals across the nation. Naturalistic attitudes had spread into law, philosophy, and the social sciences between the end of the nineteenth century and the mid-thirties, and their implications raised fundamental questions about the validity of traditional democratic theory. At the same time the frightening rise of European totalitarianism, especially Nazism, directly challenged both the political security and theoretical validity of democracy. In the face of both those developments, rationalist philosophers and religious spokesmen sharply increased their attack on scientific naturalism, claiming that its skepticism and moral cynicism were largely responsible for the spread of totalitarianism. American intellectuals were forced to reevaluate their basic assumptions amid a continually deepening world crisis and an increasingly bitter domestic debate.

During the nineteenth century Americans had generally accepted the validity of democratic government with neither qualms nor qualifications. The democratic ideal was the unquestioned American ideal, and it was widely accepted as an axiom of life. Though Americans were unconcerned with elaborate theoretical justifications, they were nevertheless convinced that democracy was both rationally and morally the best possible form of government. Religious faith, national tradition, a moderate rationalism going back to the ideas of the Declaration of Independence, and the concrete experience of most Americans all testified to the validity and certainty of its ideals.

In the last third of the nineteenth century evolutionary Darwinism began to spread into American thought, and scholars freely applied its concepts to all fields of knowledge. William Graham Sumner and Lester Ward helped establish the new discipline of sociology on the basis of two different interpretations of Darwin's theory. Oliver Wendell Holmes, Jr., demonstrated how the common law had developed according to the pro-

5

cesses of natural selection. Thorstein Veblen examined the growth of economic institutions from the same viewpoint. Chauncey Wright, William James, Edward L. Thorndike, and John Dewey applied evolutionary methods to the study of human psychology, examining "mind" as an adaptive physiological function of the body rather than as a separate spiritual entity. Dewey, James, and Charles Sanders Peirce began their critique of traditional logic and philosophy under the inspiration of the new evolutionary naturalism. Truth, they argued, was not to be found in the abstract logic of ideas, but in their practical consequences. There were no absolute or a priori truths, only workable and nonworkable hypotheses.

Determined opposition to naturalism and especially to the doctrine of evolution mounted quickly. Most of the churches in America initially rejected Darwinism, especially after The Descent of Man appeared in 1871. By the end of the century, however, most of them had begun, warily, to accept Darwinism and use it to demonstrate the infinite creative wisdom of God. Many staunchly religious Americans continued to oppose the doctrine, and took refuge in a fundamentalism that led to such results as state laws prohibiting the teaching of evolution in public schools. Josiah Royce and William T. Harris were among the decreasing number of intellectuals who clung to philosophical idealism and rejected the newer approaches. Undoubtedly most Americans continued to believe in such traditional principles as the "higher law" and the moral equality of all men.

In spite of the opposition, however, naturalistic attitudes continued to win new adherents. More and more scientists, like the paleontologist O. C. Marsh and the botanist Luther Burbank, succeeded in producing solid evidence to support the claims of evolution, until continued rejection of the doctrine came to seem merely willful blindness. Rapid technological advance contributed further to the general faith in science and confirmed it as the most reliable method of attaining useful knowledge. The whole impact of vast social change—industrialization, urbanization, and new techniques of production—made it clear that science was also the way to power. What was good in the changes seemed the result of science; what was bad seemed eradicable only with the aid of more science. Fitting in with the general optimism and faith in progress that marked the nineteenth century, scientific method appeared the perfect instrument to bring about the continuous improvement of society.

Both the rapidly accumulating wealth and the new technical demands that industrialism created helped spur the great age of university expansion. Between 1868 and 1891 millionaires founded Cornell, Johns Hopkins, Vanderbilt, Clark, Chicago, and Stanford; between 1878 and 1898 private sources donated some $140 million to higher education. Under the Morrill Acts of 1862 and 1890 the federal government indirectly contributed tens of millions more, and by the 1890s the universities of Michigan, Wisconsin, and Minnesota were emerging as major academic institutions. In 1890 over $21 million was spent on higher education in the United States, and by 1910 that had grown to $76 million. Undergraduate enrollment jumped from 52,000 in 1870 to 355,000 in 1910, and graduate enrollment multiplied even more rapidly. American universities counted 198 graduate students in 1871. In 1910 there were 9,370.[6]

Even more important than the numerical growth was the new outlook of the universities: secular, scientific, and professional. The great academic organizers of the period, men such as Charles W. Eliot, Andrew Dixon White, G. Stanley Hall, William Rainey Harper, and Daniel Coit Gilman were deeply committed to the ideal of scholarship, specialized graduate training, and the achievement of intellectual excellence. In most cases, too, they were themselves evolutionists with a strong belief in the new science. The faculties they recruited reflected those same attitudes and devoted themselves to scholarly research and the broader task of raising the quality of American education generally. Wealthy donors, too, seemed willing in most cases to see their money spent in whatever ways the university administrations thought best. "I would found an institution," Ezra Cornell had declared, "in which any person can find instruction in any study."[7]

The expansion and transformation of American higher education coincided with the rise of the new science, and they reinforced one another. When Johns Hopkins, the first university in the United States devoted mainly to graduate education, opened its doors in 1876, thirty-six of its original fifty-four advanced students chose biology, chemistry, physics, or mathematics as their special fields. Although religious and Hegelian influences remained strong at Hopkins through the 1880s, Darwinism exerted a growing influence.[8] The new academic professions began to rival and then surpass the prestige of the ministry as a career choice, and clergymen were replaced as college presidents by a new generation of professional academic administrators. When Andrew Carnegie set up a pension plan for retired college professors in 1905, he specifically excluded denominational institutions from eligibility. Bowdoin, Wesleyan, Rochester, and Hanover were among the many schools that moved to break all denominational ties in an attempt to qualify.[9] In place of the older idea of piety, the new universities began to emphasize the ideal of scholarly competence as the criterion for judging faculty qualifications. Concurrently, the idea of academic freedom developed into a broad formula for tolerating heretical ideas and affirmed such freedom as a positive requirement for intellectual and social advance.[10] The universities provided the institutional base that gave scholars the freedom, opportunity, and encouragement to elaborate their new ideas, as well as furnishing a growing student body from which to draw new recruits. The faculties increasingly made the universities into centers of the new naturalism.

As the new science spread in the years between 1880 and 1910, American intellectuals began to outgrow their early fascination with Darwinism. Emphasis on evolution itself, and on the direct application of Darwin's hypotheses to nonbiological processes, gave way to a broader naturalism that saw Darwinism not as an analogy but as an example of both careful empirical methodology and a nonteleological, antimetaphysical approach to human knowledge. Although older attitudes—belief in nature as part of a comprehensive divine order and in science as part of a larger and morally oriented natural philosophy—continued to influence American thought into the twentieth century, intellectuals were moving through a transition stage toward a wholly naturalistic and empirically oriented world view.

William Graham Sumner, one of the earliest and most confident of the social interpreters of Darwin, himself exemplified the kinds of changes that were taking place. In the 1880s he conceived of social science as the wholesale application of the law of survival to human relations, viewing the laws of sociology and the laws of biology as "truly cognate." He accepted Darwinism, but placed it in a rationalistic and moralistic framework; his method remained deductive. "The essential elements of political economy," he emphasized, "are only corollaries or special cases of sociological principles." Sumner still thought in terms of rationally demonstrable ethical principles even though he saw their source not in religion or metaphysics but in scientific laws. The practical utility of sociology, he maintained in 1881, "consists in deriving the rules of right social living from the facts and laws which prevail by nature in the constitution and functions of society."[11]

8

During the next decades, however, Sumner increasingly concerned himself with actual human behavior, employed a less deductive and more empirical methodology, and began to downplay the idea of scientific, moral absolutes. In his classic *Folkways*, published in 1906, he was ready to argue that all institutions and moral standards were the product of slowly changing and deeply ingrained customs—the mores of the folk. "The morality of a group at a time is the sum of the taboos and prescriptions in the folkways by which right conduct is defined," he concluded. "Therefore morals can never be intuitive. They are historical, institutional, and empirical."[12] Sumner remained an elitist, a determinist, and a secular preacher throughout his life, and he continued to emphasize the law of the survival of the fittest. By 1906, however, he made the latter concept part of a largely empirical study of social and cultural change, and not the basis of a rigid, deductive, and morally absolutistic theory of society.

In the 1880s many intellectuals still placed Darwinian terms in an essentially static conceptual framework, one that assumed a comprehensive religious or rationalistic ordering principle, but by the beginning of the twentieth century they increasingly interpreted Darwinism in light of a fully naturalistic world view. They saw change as given, order as accidental, process as nonteleological, behavior as adaptive, values as experiential, and absolutes of any kind as superstitions. "The influence of Darwin on philosophy," John Dewey commented perceptively in 1910, "resides in his having conquered the phenomena of life for the principle of transition, and thereby freed the new logic for application to mind and morals and life."[13] In that slow but profound change lay the broader intellectual significance of Darwinism.

From the 1890s onward, educated discussion concerned not the basic validity of evolution but the human meaning of the new science. While investigators refined and largely confirmed Darwin's original hypotheses, social theorists argued over the implications of evolution for the study of human society. Some, like Sumner, had interpreted the survival of the fittest in harsh terms and believed that biology disproved human equality. Competition should flourish so that the stronger could eliminate the weaker, thereby strengthening the race and ensuring social progress. Sumner pointedly rejected such ideas as natural rights, declaring that man's only right was the opportunity to fight for survival.[14] The new evolutionary science thus appeared hostile to certain traditional demo-

9

cratic beliefs. If the struggle for survival was the law of life, humanitarian morals were merely unwarranted handicaps in the fight. If a harsh and relentless nature determined his fate, then man was helpless to create a more just society. And finally, if men were divided into the fit and the unfit, then the ideal of equality was an unattainable illusion.

The depth and pervasiveness of democratic ideals was apparent in the discussion over the meaning of the new science, however, for neither Sumner's view of evolution nor the harsh, deterministic interpretation of man's place in the universe won general acceptance. Instead, Americans turned the new ideas to the support of the old. Led by James, Dewey, and Ward, social thinkers defined empiricism and evolution as broadly humanitarian and democratic. First, they interpreted the struggle for survival in terms of the species against its environment, pointing out that nature revealed mutual aid among all members of the same species. Sympathetic unity of the species implied equality and cooperation. Second, they destroyed fatalistic determinism by insisting that evolution had produced human intelligence, which enabled man to control his environment for the benefit of all members of the species. Intelligence suggested the possibility of the conscious creation of a more just social order. Pragmatism and instrumentalism thus commandeered evolutionary naturalism and argued that it was egalitarian in theory and humanitarian in practice. Even after World War I "there was no tendency to abandon democratic theories of government," the distinguished political scientist Charles E. Merriam concluded in 1920; "on the contrary, the general faith in the ultimate triumph of democratic principles and institutions was never stronger."[15]

As naturalistic attitudes moved from a focus on evolution itself to a broader empirical approach to problems of social process and human knowledge, however, they raised yet another and different challenge to democratic theory. What was the relationship between scientific naturalism as a philosophical world view and the moral and political ideals traditionally associated with democracy? Centering around the nature and implications of scientific naturalism itself, the second challenge was initially much less obvious and ultimately much more difficult to resolve. Although many intellectuals had moved from evolutionary naturalism to scientific naturalism in large part to avoid the antidemocratic implications of Sumner's biological determinism, the reconciliation they made between democracy and science was not as easy or as obvious as it appeared in 1910.

Between the first decade of the twentieth century and the mid-thirties the methods and assumptions of scientific naturalism helped expose major weaknesses in traditional democratic theory. First, it destroyed rational justifications of ethical ideals, such as a "higher law," which had provided democratic theory with its moral foundation. In the years after 1910 scientific naturalists strictly confined induction to observable, concrete phenomena and ruled it out as a method of proving the validity of any moral principles. At the same time they sharply redefined the nature of deductive logic, always closely allied with rational ethical systems. By demonstrating its wholly abstract and formal nature, scientific naturalists denied it any authority in questions concerning the legitimacy of moral values. Rejecting the possibility of demonstrating the truth of ethical propositions by either induction or deduction, they left moral ideals without a rational, theoretical basis. Second, in empirically examining human behavior and the actual process of American politics, scientific naturalists came to question and often reject three cardinal principles of democratic government: the possibility of a government of laws rather than of men, the rationality of human behavior, and the practical possibility of popular government itself. Legal scholars began to argue that judicial decisions were not the results of impartial logic but of the personal values of judges. There was no such thing as "established" law. Psychologists found that human behavior was largely irrational, especially in the complicated and emotional arena of politics. Most individuals, they maintained, were unable to fulfill the traditional democratic obligations of the citizen. Students of politics learned that in practice small groups of insiders dominated the government and that popular control was an illusion. Democratic government simply did not work as its theory claimed it should. By the early thirties traditional democratic theory seemed largely untenable.

Most scientific naturalists continued to believe in the desirability of democracy, and some tried to reformulate its theory. But the rise of European totalitarianism and the international political tensions of the late thirties transformed the problem of the validity of democratic theory into an unavoidable and essential question. The disillusionment of some intellectuals with naturalism, the hostility of church groups, and the frus-

11

trations created by the depression combined with the rise of Nazism to galvanize many Americans into a renewed attack on scientific naturalism as a destructive and inadequate world view. Out of the confrontation a new democratic theory emerged that would dominate American thought for two decades after World War II. The crisis of the thirties ultimately strengthened scientific naturalism rather than destroyed it, but the dominant scientific naturalism of the postwar decades would be significantly different from its prewar form.

II

The Undermining
of Democratic Theory

2

Naturalism & Objectivism
in the Social Sciences

By the second decade of the twentieth century the ideal of a science of society was firmly entrenched in American thought. Its roots lay deep in the history of Western civilization, especially in eighteenth century rationalism and nineteenth century positivism. In America Darwin had served as the great intellectual catalyst in producing the formal "social sciences," which by the beginning of the twentieth century were embarking on a period of astonishing growth. There were many lines of continuity, and yet both intellectually and institutionally a wide gulf separated those early years beginning in the 1870s from the established years after 1910.

The prestige associated with the idea of "science" represented the major element of continuity. Physics and biology still represented models of scientific achievement and continued to serve as inspirations—if no longer as rigid guides—to those studying human society. Though there remained disagreement on what exactly the concept "science of society" implied, most educated Americans came to believe that it was a desirable goal and that the scientific method should be employed as far as appropriate. As usual the word appropriate concealed problems rather than resolved them.

By the second decade of the twentieth century the social sciences—principally economics, sociology, political science, psychology, and anthropology—had become clearly distinguished and their research fields generally delimited. Fewer and fewer scholars attempted to study society as a whole or to propound the kinds of all-encompassing syntheses many of their predecessors had gloried in. Instead disciplinary lines grew sharper, and scholars focused on smaller and more manageable areas in their investigations.

Indeed, by the 1920s the age of the founders was clearly over. William James and William Graham Sumner had died in 1910, Lester Ward in 1913, and during the twenties such pathbreakers as G. Stanley Hall, Albion Small, Thorstein Veblen, E. B. Titchener, and Charles Horton Cooley all ended their long careers. Those of the earlier generation who lived through the twenties, men such as Edward A. Ross, James Mark Baldwin, and W. W. Willoughby, usually found their influence steadily declining and their works rapidly disappearing from footnotes and bibliographies. An ever increasing number of scholars took their places, scholars who often learned from their experiences but who in most cases rejected their methods.

The rapid growth and institutionalization of the social sciences also marked the two periods off from one another. In 1890 only a handful of social scientists held positions in American universities; by the twenties, thousands of them taught courses in hundreds of institutions, and Ph.D. programs had been established at several dozen universities. The long recognized field of economics began its period of most rapid growth somewhat earlier than the others, increasing course offerings by almost nine times between 1892 and 1910. James and Hall had started their primitive psychological laboratories during the 1880s, but it was not until 1892 that Chicago and Cornell established their departments of psychology, which largely dominated the field for the next quarter century. In 1889 only four universities in the United States offered courses in sociology, a figure that grew to 132 by 1901 and then to 337 during the next eight years. Although Columbia University established a graduate program in political science in 1880, the field did not generally become independent until after the turn of the century. The University of Wisconsin set up a separate department in 1901, Harvard followed in 1909, and by 1914 almost forty colleges and universities had independent departments. Anthropology, the last of the major five to arrive institutionally, was largely an esoteric, museum-oriented field through the first decade of the twentieth century. Not until after the war did it begin its rapid spread through the universities. By 1928 anthropology had four major scholarly journals, economics eleven, political science six, sociology nine, and psychology thirteen.[1]

As most advocates of a science of society had done during the preceding century, those after 1910 tended to look back and see how "unscientific" their predecessors had been. "Until quite recently," two sociologists charged in 1930, "social thinking has been predominantly metaphysical."[2] The earlier practitioners had bequeathed them the ideal, but few satisfactory techniques to make the ideal a reality. While admitting some occasional accomplishments of real significance, such as Sumner's study of folkways and E. L. Thorndike's work on learning behavior, social scientists after 1910 viewed most previous scholarship as metaphorical, value-laden, deductive, and too often based on written documents rather than on the actual observation of social events. "At the end of the first decade of the current century functional psychology was still speculative and literary," declared Horace M. Kallen, a philosopher at the New School for Social Research, "and animal psychology had only begun to turn from anecdote and anthropomorphism to scientifically controlled investigation."[3] Convinced that earlier attempts had failed to produce a true science of society, scholars in the years after 1910 blamed that deficiency on the lack of objective methodological rigor and unbiased factual observation.

By the end of the first decade of the twentieth century a new orientation was clearly developing in the study of politics. The American Political Science Association had been founded in 1904, and the organization's leadership emphasized that political science dealt not with philosophical categories but with practical politics. "One of the most salutary results of this vast accumulation of data on politics," announced Charles A. Beard in 1908, "has been to discredit the older speculative theorists and utopia makers."[4] In the same year Arthur F. Bentley published *The Process of Government*, emphasizing process over structure and pointing to group conflict as the central reality of politics. Frank J. Goodnow, A. Lawrence Lowell, and Albert Bushnell Hart all joined in bringing an increasingly pragmatic and empirical tone to political science, and in replacing the older structural and juristic emphasis with a new focus on process and conflict.

By the early twenties the University of Chicago had emerged as the most influential center of the new political science. In a survey conducted among political scientists to determine what scholars had had the greatest impact on the profession before 1945, the top three places went to Charles E. Merriam, Harold D. Lasswell, and Leonard D. White—all at Chicago.[5] Merriam, the guiding light of the Chicago department, established himself as the most influential political scientist in the country. Though he produced a large number of scholarly works, his major impact was as an organizer and exhorter. Urging his colleagues to use the latest discoveries of modern psychology and precise empirical observation, he

17

continually emphasized "the importance and possibility of scientific study of mankind on the political and social sides."[6] In 1925 he published his *New Aspects of Politics*, which served as the manifesto of empiricism and objective methodology in his discipline. Lasswell, White, and many others agreed with Merriam that, though a start had been made, a true science of politics still lay in the future.

Between 1913 and 1919 John Watson published his major path-breaking work outlining the behaviorist position in psychology. Though such scholars as John Dewey, Thorndike, Ivan Pavlov, and Lloyd Morgan had helped prepare the way, it was Watson who attempted to make the study of psychology a wholly observational, physical, and empirical science. His influence and method profoundly altered his own field and had a major impact on most of the social sciences after World War I. The aim of psychology, indeed the aim of any natural science, Watson declared, was complete objectivity. Psychologists should abandon the method of introspection, abjure the concept of consciousness, study only overt behavior guided by the stimulus-response relationship between the individual and his environment, and reduce all mental phenomena to observable physical processes.[7]

Numerous rival theories continued to compete among American psychologists, but by the twenties behaviorism was the most dynamic and broadly influential approach to the field. Such scholars as W. S. Hunter, Morris A. Copeland, K. S. Lashley, and E. R. Guthrie elaborated and applied the behaviorist approach for a growing professional and lay audience. In 1925 Albert Paul Weiss of Ohio State University attempted one of the first broad behaviorist syntheses in *A Theoretical Basis of Human Behavior*, a book that remained for the next decade one of the most elaborate formulations of the new approach. Behaviorism, Weiss declared, "assumes that man's educational, vocational, and social activities can be completely described or explained as the result of the same (and no other) forces used in the natural sciences."[8] By the thirties Edwin C. Tolman, B. F. Skinner, and Clark L. Hull emerged as leading spokesmen and devoted their careers to expanding and refining behaviorism in a systematic manner.

Following the rich suggestiveness of Veblen and the thorough research of the Columbia University economist Wesley C. Mitchell, Walton Hamilton announced the institutional approach to economic theory in 1918. "Institutions, seemingly such rigid and material things," he explained, "are merely conventional methods of behavior on the part of various groups or of persons in various situations."[9] Rather than relying on abstract theory or a *priori* conceptual schemes, economics could best become scientific by studying the actual operations of organized economic groups. What was the use of the classical concept of the free market mechanism in an economy dominated by huge corporations that restricted production and arbitrarily set prices?

Throughout the inter-war decades institutionalists of such varied stripes as Hamilton, Mitchell, Rexford G. Tugwell, John M. Clark, John R. Commons, A. A. Berle, Jr., and Lionel D. Edie contributed devastating attacks on the psychological abstractions and empirical inadequacies of the classical and marginal utility theories. Mitchell, the most influential economist in the United States during the inter-war years, proudly acknowledged his "predilection for the concrete." Scorning most earlier economics as arid metaphysics, he insisted that the only road toward intellectual progress was "the way of natural science."[10] Mitchell's quantitative studies of business cycles, Hamilton's historical analysis of the coal industry, and Commons' detailed examinations of the economic role of labor organizations and legal doctrines best represented the new direction of the institutional approach.[11]

In 1921 Robert E. Park and Ernest W. Burgess of the University of Chicago published their *Introduction to the Science of Sociology*, perhaps one of the most influential books ever written in the field.[12] Their major commitment was to a directly observational methodology that was designed to construct a science of society from the bottom up and end premature system building. "Sociology seems now, however, in a way to become, in some fashion or other, an experimental science," the authors declared.[13] Tentative and empirical, the book provided advice to younger scholars and an organized framework that proved immensely useful for directing empirical investigations. By the end of the decade it had become the most widely used sociology textbook in the country and had stimulated a massive outpouring of research along the lines it had suggested.

As in political science, the University of Chicago remained throughout the twenties the intellectual leader of American sociology as well as its largest producer of new Ph.D.'s, including such prominent scholars as Louis Wirth, Floyd N. House, Herbert Blumer, Howard Becker, and E. Franklin Frazier.[14] Together with William Fielding Ogburn, Luther L. Bernard, George A. Lundberg, and Read Bain, they led the profession toward an increasingly empirical emphasis focusing on group processes, organizations, and functions. Reflecting the growing absorption with empirical techniques that characterized many sociologists, Lundberg in 1929 published his *Social Research*, a book length analysis of the various methods of data collection available to the social scientist. The new techniques, he proclaimed, promised the birth of "exact social sciences and a consequent transformation of the social world comparable to that which the physical sciences have wrought in the physical world."[15]

Although anthropology came of age in America during the same years, its development was somewhat different from that of the other social sciences. Under the brilliant leadership of Franz Boas, American anthropologists since the last decade of the nineteenth century had been vigorously reacting against the rigid laws of the evolutionary school exemplified by scholars such as Lewis Henry Morgan.[16] That experience together with the distinct nature of their subject matter forced them into a greater skepticism about the applicability of an experimental method in their field. Though often doubting the possibility of discovering strict scientific "laws," American anthropologists still shared the growing belief in the necessity for a precise empiricism as well as for the uselessness of a *priori* theorizing and system building. "Anthropologists are, in the broad sense, behaviorists, and so stand shoulder to shoulder with those psychologists to whom the same term applies," declared Clark Wissler, the curator-in-chief in the division of anthropology of the American Museum of Natural History. "As we have said over and over again, anthropologists, in respect to culture, deal with objective phenomena."[17]

Drawn to North America as a rich research field, the German-born Boas began teaching at Columbia University in 1896 and continued as the discipline's grand figure until his death in 1943. In addition to his voluminous and influential writings, he trained most of the major scholars who were active in the field throughout the first half of the twentieth century: Wissler, Albert L. Kroeber, Robert H. Lowie, Alexander Goldenweiser, Ruth Benedict, Margaret Mead, Edwin Sapir, Melville Herskovits, Paul Radin, and M. F. Ashley Montagu among the most prominent. Boas and his remarkably talented students came to dominate American anthropology, building up a wealth of material in the richly diverse field of American Indian culture. In the early twenties the detailed work blossomed into major syntheses. Lowie's *Primitive Society* (1920), Goldenweiser's *Early Civilization* (1922), Wissler's *Man and Culture* (1923), and Kroeber's *Anthropology* (1923) distilled much of the work of the past twenty-five years and announced the full coming of age of American anthropology. By the twenties the field moved more fully out of the museums and began to take its place in the universities as an equal academic discipline. At the same time comparative anthropological material began appearing more and more frequently in the writings of other social scientists. By the early thirties Boasian anthropology was a dominant element in social science theory.[18]

Though rich diversity continued, certain common assumptions and attitudes united the often scattered research of a large number of scholars. Accepting a broadly naturalistic world view, they held that the only real knowledge available about both man and society was empirical and experimental. Theological dogmas and philosophical absolutes were at worst totally fraudulent and at best merely symbolic of deep human aspirations. Metaphysical questions, dealing with such nonempirical concepts as essence or soul, were simply meaningless. "As a naturalist I cannot express an opinion," declared the psychologist C. Judson Herrick, "for the essential nature of things is not a scientific problem."[19]

The intellectual distinctiveness of the twenty-five-year period after 1910 arose from the rapid spread and general acceptance of that basically naturalistic attitude and the positivist emphasis given it by a large number of social scientists. Keenly aware of the moral assumptions and personal value judgments of their predecessors, many scholars insisted that scientific knowledge must be wholly objective and based on concrete, universally verifiable data. Sharply skeptical of all nonempirical concepts and theories, they accepted a highly particularistic, nominalistic epistemology. Exasperated with a *priori* systems and rationalistic schematizations, they declared that knowledge must be based on empirical functions, not on logical necessities. Those assumptions of objectivism, particularism, and functionalism uniquely characterized the social science that blossomed after 1910.

Social scientists interpreted the concept of scientific objectivity in different ways, but most of them agreed heartily that objectivity was the goal of their research. "Objectivity in science is manifested generally in the minimizing and elimination of the personal factor," summarized one anthropologist. "Methods of collecting and treating data are devised which will as far as possible rule out errors due to individual variability in subjective attitude."[20] The only way they could build a scientific body of knowledge, many scholars argued, was by dealing with observable, physical phenomena that could be restudied, remanipulated, or remeasured by anyone who wished to test the conclusions offered. "What we need," declared Luther L. Bernard, "is objectively-tested fact to replace our venerable traditions."[21]

Such objectivity placed two severe restrictions on social scientists. Most came to believe that values and moral assumptions had no place in their work and had to be completely expunged. "If the sociologist wishes to be a scientist in fact as well as name, as it is to be presumed he does," argued Howard Becker, "he too must avoid the mixture of value-judgments and science."[22] The two were completely incompatible. "One cannot emphasize too strongly the necessity for keeping scientific procedure separated from all moralistic preconceptions," warned the sociologist Read Bain.[23] The unavoidable failure that faced those who ignored that warning echoed through the pages of every major social science journal of the period.

Second, objectivity demanded that rationalist speculations and system building be equally abjured in favor of empirical techniques that placed the criteria of judgment beyond the scientist's subjective evaluation. Intellectualism, the elaboration of various relationships of ideas, was one of the major threats to true science, Ogburn explained. "These ideas are only in rare cases statements of knowledge that can be safely relied upon by others."[24] The human mind by itself could not avoid a continually self-defeating subjectivism, Lundberg said. Hence scientific progress necessitated "objectifying devices outside of our organic equipment."[25] Precise techniques of measurement and description, operating on universally observable phenomena, thus became the *sine qua non* of objectivity and therefore of truth. The scientist's role was to develop, refine, and use such "objectifying devices" in order to eliminate his own values and preconceptions.

Emphasizing the goal of objectivity, many social scientists began to view "facts" in a highly particularistic manner, attempting to reduce observed phenomena to a series of separate and individual units. "The scrutiny of alleged facts, to determine whether or not they are facts, is the fundamental *systematic* work of science," declared the sociologist Franklin H. Giddings. A fact existed and could be observed, and it was the social scientist's function to separate the verifiable, objective facts from the confused and subjectively colored interpretations that men habitually gave them. "The structure of scientific knowledge is built up fact by fact," Giddings asserted.[26] The covert brick metaphor was apt, for facts, like bricks, were thought of as individual, separate, solid, and measurable. "Particularity in space and time and process with respect to human culture," another sociologist noted, "is the fundamental criterion for us to hold to as we readjust ourselves to a more fruitful study of man."[27]

That particularist assumption implied a philosophical nominalism that by 1930 many social scientists shared. Ideas were legitimate only insofar as they referred directly to specific, observable things. "The number of valid scientific concepts," Bain pointed out, "would equal the number of such activities exhibiting enough repetitive uniformity to permit prediction of sufficient accuracy to be useful in making societal adjustments."[28] Any concept that claimed to go beyond empirical particulars was unfounded and dangerous. "Conceptualism is the particular bugbear of the social sciences," wrote Rexford G. Tugwell, an economist at Columbia University, "as, a century or two ago, it was the bugbear of the natural sciences."[29] As long as the social sciences dealt only with individual, concrete units, so the assumption ran, they would finally be able to enjoy progress comparable to that of the physical sciences. "Most of the improper usage of the concept in science," summarized Herbert Blumer of the University of Chicago, "comes when the concept is set apart from the world of experience, when it is divorced from the perception from which it has arisen and into which it ordinarily ties."[30]

The third complementary but distinct characteristic of the social sciences after 1910 was its general functionalist orientation. Growing from the Darwinian emphasis on process over essence and drawing on Dewey's instrumentalism, the functionalist approach insisted that the meaning and significance of anything lay in the manner in which it operated in practice. Meaning and importance lay in practical consequences, not in the logic of any rationalist system. Indeed, Bernard insisted, "in the long run logic, if it is sound, must be determined by functions rather than functions being determined by logic."[31] People, customs, institutions, laws, and beliefs were what they did in practice, not what they were shown to be logically or what they ought to be morally.

Functionalism underlay most social science thought and helped give currency and meaning to the related ideas of behavior, institution, and culture. The concept of behavior not only implied empirical observability but was also a variety of functionalism—the things men actually did in

23

society. By 1934 the psychologist Joseph Jastrow could acknowledge that "substantially all current psychology is functional in scope and purpose."[32] Similarly, social scientists interpreted the concept of institution functionally, as describing the different ways men behaved together in groups operating through time. "The thing that gives a community the character of a society is not its structure," Robert E. Park pointed out, "but its capacity for concerted action." Sociology, therefore, could be defined institutionally as "the science of collective behavior."[33] Such functional institutions were in turn made parts of a more general concept, that of culture. Though the word had been used since ancient times in varying ways, usually implying a certain "advanced" state of civilization, it was only around 1910 that Boas and his first generation of students began to use it in its modern anthropological sense.[34] Culture, Wissler explained, was "the psychic functional history of the group."[35] Assuming that all men possessed a culture, regardless of the nature of their society, anthropologists made the term descriptive instead of prescriptive and emphasized the universality of culture as a social determinant and the diversity of its particular forms. Culture represented the sum total of ways that all past human activities operated on and influenced the subsequent behavior of human beings, individually and collectively. It was the molding function of the total social environment. Though differences remained, by the end of the twenties particularist, functionalist objectivism was the dominant tone of the social sciences.

The concerted drive toward the new objectivism came from several sources, including the ever-present tendency of social science to recognize in retrospect the peculiar value orientations of past generations. Ironically, in fact, the enthusiastic prewar reform movements, to which many social scientists owed allegiance, helped ultimately to foster the new objectivism. By the turn of the century many reformers had become deeply suspicious of "politics," which to them implied bosses, corruption, and the supremacy of partisan interests. Only an enlightened and selfless concern with the public interest could achieve true reform. Believing in the ultimately rational nature of the universe, they viewed science as the method that could lead to a full understanding of the social process and in turn persuade men to an intelligent reordering of American institutions in a spirit of social harmony. By the second decade of the twentieth century many were increasingly emphasizing the need for scientific expertise and administrative efficiency as the essential means to bring about ordered, benevolent

24

change. Suspicion of politics, belief in a rational social universe, and commitment to expertise and efficiency provided a fertile soil for the growth of an objectivist science.

Gradually methodology replaced moralism in the minds of many younger reformers and social scientists, and the instrument of social research came to overwhelm the goal of social reform. Whereas in the 1890s young people came to the flourishing social settlement houses saying "we must do something about the social disorder," Jane Addams remarked in 1911, by the next decade they flocked in with equal enthusiasm declaring "we want to investigate something."[36] The Eastern Rate Case of 1910–1911 provoked widespread interest in the "scientific management" ideas of Frederick W. Taylor. Many came to view political reform not in terms of good against evil but in terms of knowledge, efficiency, and scientific planning against ignorance, error, and economic waste. Moralistic rhetoric and faith in popular democracy had dominated prewar reform, but by the twenties the older reform movements had lost their political force and moral enthusiasm, and ideas of efficiency, administrative expertise, and scientific objectivity remained and rapidly grew.[37]

The experience of World War I accelerated the movement toward a new objectivism. First, many social scientists had served in the government during the war, helping to bring centralized control and orderly planning to the management of the nation's effort. That experience, both exhilarating and frustrating, inspired many with the possibilities for national progress and social reform through scientific planning. If they could build a social science equal to the challenge, one that could approach the reliability of the physical sciences, then, if the opportunity ever came again, they could accomplish truly amazing results.[38] Second, watching what many scholars regarded as the tragic failure of Wilsonian ideals in a world dominated by selfish political and economic interests, many social scientists assumed that they must adopt a more cynical and tough-minded attitude toward the study of social processes. Political scientists began to analyze power as a central element in politics and to deny the importance of less tangible phenomena. The striking use of propaganda during the war brought psychologists, political scientists, and sociologists to a new emphasis on human irrationality and the manipulative procedures employed by dominant social groups. Almost every scholar who had any connection with the war effort, declared the editors of the *Encyclopaedia of the Social Sciences* in 1930, emerged "with an unaccustomed richness of

realism added to his thinking."[39] Though World War I may have "dis-
illusioned" some American intellectuals, it helped open up vast new fields
of research for social scientists and suggested new insights and techniques
for understanding social processes. Those who moved toward the new
objectivism did so with the greatest intellectual optimism and enthusiasm.

The continuing desire for practicality and relevance helped further
stimulate the new objectivism. The idea of control had long fascinated
advocates of a science of society, and by the twenties many were convinced
that effective control was at last feasible. Though some of the objectivists,
such as Bain and Bernard, warned against corrupting science with re-
formism, most thought they could remain scientifically neutral while developing workable techniques of social control. "The anthropologist has
arrived at the table of the National Research Council, dropped thereon
his instrument case and announced that he is ready for the patient," Wissler proclaimed.[40] The new disciplines, Ogburn and Goldenweiser declared,
were "tools to be employed in the solution of the concrete practical problems of an existing and developing society."[41] Though the goal of science
was control, George E. G. Catlin, a political scientist at Cornell University, declared, he spoke for a large number of his colleagues when he
pointedly defined that control as morally neutral. "One of the tests of a
sound political science is that it is difficult to detect which social party its
conclusions favor, since they are formal results—results concerning what
one should do *if* one desires a given end."[42]

Since social scientists were not themselves in a position to exert any
meaningful institutional control in American society, many enthusiastically accepted the role of advisors and consultants to government and business. Such positions allowed social scientists to act practically, but also
raised the question of the values inherent in their practicality. "Objectivity" allowed them to avoid facing that problem and to continue their
useful roles.[43] If their findings were morally neutral, objective descriptions of institutional and human functions, then they were obviously
neither being used nor being partisan. Hence a belief in the new objectivity opened the way for a practical role in society and possible ultimate
realization of methods of control, while at the same time suppressing any
moral or social doubts about the actual consequences of their actions.

Objectivism, however, was a mask that covered a number of differences. Some social scientists clearly used it to hide the political implica-

tions of their work, whereas others believed that service on behalf of government or business was in itself a worthwhile endeavor. A third group used objectivism to give authority to approaches they hoped would eventually contribute to meaningful political reform. Especially in the context of the twenties, objectivism was a useful bulwark for some against the political pressures of a business dominated society. Thus a commitment to social reform remained among a number of social scientists, though it was muted and usually intimated in vague and antiseptic phrases. Additionally, in spite of those differences, social scientists almost unanimously believed in the ultimately benevolent consequences of their work. They could ignore the direct means of reform politics and the immediate results of their objective research because they were convinced that in the end all would prove useful and desirable. The belief in social progress through scientific advance rationalized in the minds of most the divorce between social science and the problems of political morality.

The increasing institutional growth and professionalization of the social sciences also reinforced the tendency toward objectivism. Since career patterns were no longer as fluid and amorphous as they had been in the nineteenth century, intellectuals who matured after the turn of the century found professional opportunities more sharply defined and more closely identified with both specific subject matter and institutional affiliation.[44] As younger intellectuals moved into the newly established professions, ideas that seemed to legitimize and magnify those careers exerted a powerful appeal. The claim of scientific objectivity was just such an ideal. With the establishment of the various new disciplines as independent departments and the accelerating growth of university enrollments, the scholarly accoutrements of national professional associations, journals, research committees, and specialized graduate programs quickly multiplied. To justify and protect their new place in the rapidly expanding academy, social scientists enthusiastically maintained that their disciplines were truly scientific. Sociologists and psychologists, especially sensitive to the charge that their fields were merely conglomerations of opinion, were among the most dedicated advocates of the new objectivism.

The growing availability of research funds from such institutions as the John Simon Guggenheim and Laura Spelman Rockefeller foundations created additional pressure for objective studies. In its first report the Spelman Foundation emphasized that the "Spelman Fund has no political objectives; it is interested only in helping to provide experience and wisdom in executing public programs which have already been adopted and which are no longer matters of political controversy."[45] Such openly acknowledged limits not only encouraged but demanded a commitment to "objective" studies. It seemed clear to scholars that only the promise of such scientific results would be likely to gain the desired support. The various foundations, the chairman of the Carnegie Corporation of New York acknowledged in the thirties, "have, I fear, been the chief offenders in forcing the techniques of research which developed in the natural sciences" onto the social sciences.[46] In 1921 one hundred foundations granted slightly over $180,000 for research and advanced education in the social sciences and history. By 1927 that benevolence had burgeoned to almost $8 million.[47]

In 1923 under the spur of Merriam and Beardsley Ruml, the director of the Spelman Fund, the American Economic Association, the American Sociological Society, and the American Political Science Association helped found the Social Science Research Council.[48] The organization's guiding spirits, Ruml, Merriam, and Wesley Mitchell, tended strongly toward the new objectivism and used the council and its growing resources to further its spread. In addition to helping plan cooperative research, Mitchell declared, its major goal was to act "as an informed general staff studying the larger possibilities of scientific method applied to the understanding of man and his institutions."[49]

As a final inspiration to the new objectivism there remained the traditional, fascinating ideal of equaling or at least approximating the achievements of the natural sciences. Rather than attempting to apply borrowed concepts, such as "the struggle for survival," to men and society, most social scientists began interpreting the idea of science in a more flexible and independent manner. They moved away from the analogical approach that had characterized many earlier versions of social science and accepted instead the idea of science as the practice of a general method rather than as the source of seminal metaphors. "The progressive character of science shows that its essence is to be sought not in the content of its specific conclusions," declared the philosopher Morris R. Cohen, "but rather in the method whereby its findings are made and constantly corrected."[50] Merriam insisted that the problems social scientists confronted were different from those presented to the natural sciences. True scientific method, he explained, required that scholars recognize those differences and develop their own special techniques of empirical investigation.[51]

The belief that they had uncovered the cause of earlier failures and the conviction that specific new techniques were forthcoming persuaded many that they were finally on the verge of establishing a true science of society. Though John Dewey had rejected the idea of complete objectivity, his continued insistence on the need for a scientific study of social problems lent much of his prestige to the new confidence. Dewey had after all emphasized "the supremacy of method."[52] The belief that they now understood the real nature of the scientific method—the key to understanding the social universe—was a heady inspiration.

The concept of science as method was crucial. Not only did it promise social scientists ultimate success, but it also explained in a reassuring way why no real social science had developed up to their time. Additionally, in an intellectual environment that rejected a priori principles and categories, method provided the one certainty that was needed. Any system of knowledge had to start somewhere, to have some foundation. Confidence in the utility of their new method provided that foundation. Finally, as with Peirce and Dewey a quarter of a century earlier, method appealed to social scientists as a way of bringing agreement and community into strife-torn human society. "The scientists above all others have won agreement," wrote the social science popularizer Stuart Chase. "With it has come an incomparable advance in knowledge, an incomparable opportunity to provide material well-being for every member of the race."[53] By analyzing social problems in an objective and scientific manner, they assumed, tendentious political disputes could be minimized and men could advance toward a more satisfying social order.

After 1929, facing the misery of the depression on one side and the challenge of Marxism on the other, social scientists embraced their new methodology even more firmly. It was not only intellectually appealing, but, in the thirties, socially necessary. Most believed implicitly or explicitly that their new methods provided a practical way to resolve social problems as well as a convincing answer to the inevitability of Marxian class conflict. The great majority of social scientists confidently ignored the upsurge in Marxist thought and rhetoric because of their faith in both the social and scientific power of the new methodology. That faith helps to explain why Marxism made so little headway in American social science during the thirties, just as it helps to explain why the assumptions behind naturalistic social science continued to dominate American thought well after World War II. Though the fervent adherence to the ideal of complete objectivity declined somewhat under the pressures of economic chaos, the commitment to a scientific analysis of social problems remained unshakeable.

3

Methodology & Morals

"The social sciences," declared Leonard White, "have now reached the point where it is open to them to use laboratory methods."[1] In 1923 White, together with representatives of a number of departments at the University of Chicago, including Merriam, Lasswell, Park, Thomas Vernor Smith, Ellsworth Faris, and L. L. Thurstone, joined to undertake extensive studies of human behavior in their city. Supported generously by the Laura Spelman Rockefeller Foundation, the group sponsored empirical research into the social processes of the city of Chicago, ranging from population movements to the formation of political factions. Although they could not control the conditions of their experiments, they believed that accurate observation of specific processes would, as Park said, "make the city in some more real sense than it has been hitherto a social laboratory."[2] The enthusiasm that the Chicago project generated led to an additional grant for the construction of a new social science building, completed in 1929, which symbolized the unbounded hopes of the new objectivists. Innumerable science buildings constructed on American campuses at the turn of the century had the names of Darwin and Tyndall carved on their walls; inscribed in stone over the entryway of Chicago's new social science building were the words: "When you cannot measure your knowledge is meager and unsatisfactory."

Quantification became one of the hallmarks of the new social science, for it symbolized the precision of the physical sciences and at the same time seemed flexible enough to be adapted to the unique problems of studying human behavior. "Whatever exists at all exists in some amount," E. L. Thorndike declared in 1918. "To know it thoroughly involves knowing its quantity as well as its quality." The belief in the possibility and necessity of measuring social phenomena, Thorndike declared, was part of his "general *Credo*."[3] In the next decade that belief spread into every area of American social science and eventually led many to deny the importance or even existence of what Thorndike had termed "quality."

During the 1890s social scientists and reformers had begun to use quantitative surveys to chart the rapid social changes they saw about them, and by 1900 such a preliminary research project was commonly the first step in a new reform push.[4] Supported by a grant from the Russell Sage Foundation, Paul U. Kellogg and Edward T. Devine directed the Pittsburgh survey of 1909, the first attempt to bring together diverse experts for a comprehensive quantitative summary of economic and social conditions in an American city. Compiling masses of data on wages, hours of work, health and sanitation, housing, public schools, and dozens of other topics, the Pittsburgh survey indicated the range of social phenomena that could be dealt with statistically. During the next dozen years the survey approach spread widely, while the techniques became increasingly specialized. By 1928 researchers could draw on the results of over 2,700 such compilations.[5]

The idea of measurement began winning converts in psychology and education after Theodore Simon and Alfred Binet developed their scale for measuring human intelligence in 1908. Thorndike and a number of his students began elaborating a wide series of such measuring tests during the following decade, and in 1916 Lewis M. Terman popularized the Stanford Revision of the Binet Scale, which seemed to place the testing concept on a much firmer technical basis.[6] By 1917 its advocates were sufficiently organized and confident to win a major victory, authorization from the United States Army for an extensive testing program for all inductees. The testers promised the army that they could rapidly evaluate its vast new manpower resources and identify the type of position in which each inductee could serve most ably and efficiently. The Army program, declared the psychologist Robert M. Yerkes, one of its chief organizers, offered the opportunity to "do much more for our science, as well as for national defense."[7] Though Yerkes was wholeheartedly committed to military success, it was not surprising that he mentioned his science first.

As the general commitment to quantification and measurement intensified, statistical techniques were growing more sophisticated and opening up exciting new possibilities for social analysis. Modern statistical theory had originated in the late seventeenth century and followed a somewhat erratic course until the late nineteenth century when many of its early techniques were established on sound mathematical bases. Working with a group of quantitative biologists, the Englishman Karl Pearson developed probability calculus into the principal tool of statistical theory. By the nineties Pearson's influence was beginning to spread, and by the twenties he enjoyed a great vogue among social scientists in the United States. Insisting on the logical unity of all scientific knowledge—a doctrine that won the heartfelt approval of American social scientists—Pearson defined that unity in terms of quantification and probability. "Proof in the field of perceptions is the demonstration of overwhelming probability."[8] Accepting a basically Humean epistemology, Pearson denied causality and established measurement, correlation, and probability as the central concepts of scientific method.

Because of its congenial subject matter economics became the first of the social sciences to make wide use of the more sophisticated statistical techniques. Irving Fischer's *Nature of Capital and Income* (1906) explicitly attempted to develop techniques for strict economic accounting, and Wesley Mitchell's work beginning in 1913 made extensive use of statistical correlations in analyzing economic fluctuations. His *Business Cycles and Unemployment* (1925) proved an impressive example of the possibilities for a new and refined statistical economics.[9] As director of the National Bureau of Economic Research, Mitchell helped develop wide ranges of reliable statistical material that further stimulated new quantitative research. By the early thirties Simon Kuznets, Warren M. Persons, and Henry L. Moore had added technical and theoretical contributions that made statistics a major tool of economic analysis.[10]

Shortly after World War I new techniques became available that greatly facilitated multiple correlation analysis and promoted its more general use throughout the other social sciences.[11] Robert E. Chaddock's *Principles and Methods of Statistics* (1925) and P. Sargent Florence's *The Statistical Method in Economics and Political Science* (1929) were only two of the more popular among dozens of books on statistical method that directed their attention toward application to social science.[12] In 1926 the American Statistical Association established its Committee on Social Statistics to act as liaison between the parent group and other social science organizations.[13] Under the leadership of Ralph G. Hurlin, the committee's first chairman, and Stuart A. Rice of the University of Pennsylvania, the group published *Statistics in Social Studies* (1930), an attempt to demonstrate the use of statistics in studying a variety of social phenomena.

Rice's *Quantitative Methods in Politics* (1928) was one of the first systematic attempts to apply statistics to political behavior, from attitude formation to voting habits. "There can be no doubt of the prestige possessed by quantitative methods in the minds of social scientists of the present generation," he declared. In his persistent search for quantitative objectivity, Rice attempted to work out techniques to measure subjective classifications as well as the statistical probabilities of degrees of subjective deviation in the observations of social scientists themselves.[14]

Such scholars as Mitchell, Merriam, Ogburn, Bain, F. Stuart Chapin, L. L. Thurstone, and John Candler Cobb enthusiastically supported Rice's stand. "I am not prepared to admit that there is any problem which cannot be solved by quantitative methods," Cobb declared in 1927.[15] By careful analysis and restatement the social scientist could break any problem into a series of empirical questions which he could then answer with statistical correlations. "The outstanding trend in American sociology," Bain announced, was "the use of statistical analysis with the implication that sociology is a natural science departing from its philosophico-moralistic antecedents as rapidly as chemistry and astronomy departed from alchemy and astrology during the seventeenth and eighteenth centuries."[16]

As many social scientists seized on the statistical method as a widely applicable tool to develop a precise social empiricism, so they turned to contemporary scientific psychology for a solution to their central problem, the human element. "The importance of the rapid rise of psychology in recent years," proclaimed the psychologist Edward S. Robinson of the Yale Law School, "is that it supplies a background for a natural science of society which has hitherto been lacking."[17] Like so many other social scientists, he was convinced that his discipline offered students of society the scientific tool they had so long needed. By explaining the sources and nature of human behavior, psychology would bring the elusive human factor under control and enable social scientists to make their work completely objective.

That optimistic belief helped create an intense interest in psychology throughout the social sciences during the interwar decades. The institutional economists focused much of their critique on what they considered the outmoded and overly rationalistic psychology underlying classical theory. Veblen had devoted much of his early work to undermining those assumptions, and during the second decade of the twentieth century Mitchell, Carleton H. Parker, and F. A. Fetter further elaborated that

34

critique. "A theory of motives must be used which is in harmony with the conclusions of modern social psychology," Walton Hamilton declared.[18] In political science Merriam, Lasswell, and many others repeatedly urged their colleagues to apply the insights of contemporary psychology to their work. Even in the more cautious profession of history a few scholars such as Arthur M. Schlesinger and Andrew Fish tentatively pointed out the relevance of new advances to their colleagues.[19]

Social scientists turned their attention to innumerable psychological theories, but behaviorism enjoyed the widest circulation. The "dominant psychology" of the day, summarized the editors of the *Encyclopaedia of the Social Sciences*, was "an experimental behaviorism which took nothing for granted except the primary significance of overt behavior."[20] It was objective, functional, and easily adapted to the study of social processes. "What the behaviorist sees in his laboratory," Tugwell remarked, "the economist meets in the fields and factories and is under an obligation to understand."[21] Though interpreting behaviorist theory in diverse ways, many social scientists saw it as the key to producing a unified, objective science. "It is only when opinions and attitudes find expression in conduct that they yield to exact analysis," Rice declared. If social scientists adopted a behaviorist approach, they would then be able to develop statistical techniques to deal with all aspects of human life. "Politics and sociology," Rice explained, "must be behavioristic if they are to be quantitative in method."[22] To focus solely on overt actions meant complete measurability, and thus behaviorism and statistics emerged as complementary methodologies. The behavior of all individuals and groups "must be considered a mechanically formulable resultant of the stimulus-response circle," summarized Horace M. Kallen in 1930. "All social sciences using quantitative methods, statistics and the like, may be said, whether explicitly or not, to rest on this premise."[23]

The behavioral-statistical methodology was an obvious corollary of the broader particularist, functionalist objectivism that underlay much of the social sciences. Behavior itself was a functional concept. As a readily identified phenomenon external to the observer's mind it was objective. Additionally the concept of behavior provided social scientists with what they considered a precise way to apply a pragmatic analysis to their subject. "The temper of the present generation is against recognizing any meaning in statements which cannot be translated into terms of some sort of behavior and so verified," explained John M. Clark, "and against recognizing

35

any difference of meaning in statements which call for identical behavior."[24] In spite of the differences that would develop between the extreme behaviorists and some pragmatists, the general behaviorism in the social sciences was clearly an extension of pragmatism based on a narrowed and wholly physical concept of human functionalism.

Assuming the existence of objective behavioral facts, and rejecting the use of a priori conceptual tools, statistical method logically became the most useful way to deal with social phenomena. Quantification directly implied particularism and nominalism; the use of statistics assumed that social processes could be broken into identifiable, concrete units. Though Rice and others maintained that no two phenomena were ever alike—an extreme form of particularism—he explained that science artificially grouped a part of the infinite number of physical phenomena to attain some practical predictive goal.[25] Scientific results were valid only to the extent that the correlation succeeded in allowing men to predict the future with sufficient accuracy to achieve the desired practical consequences.

Some who moved toward the behavioral-statistical approach still doubted whether it could attain complete objectivity or whether it would ever totally explain social phenomena. Most, however, agreed that it was the most promising approach and that wherever applicable it would provide the most reliable results. "As the sociologist adopts the numerical symbol of description in the definition of his concepts," Chapin explained, probably speaking for most of his colleagues, "they will become more precise and he will approach the position of the physicist in the precision of his work."[26] The extent of its applicability was uncertain, but the widespread utility of the method and the advance it indicated were generally accepted.

Luther L. Bernard, a professor of sociology at the University of Minnesota and later at Washington University, was one of the most outspoken of the new objectivists. "The contention is that the scientific sociologist must abandon the old subjective terminology," Bernard declared in 1919, and replace it with "a description of the objective act—both overtly and neurally expressed—thus following the newer behavior psychologists into the realm of biophysics and biochemistry."[27] Like such contemporaries as Rice and Mitchell, Bernard emphasized the necessary connection between behaviorism and quantitative method, the one the sine qua non of the other. "Science begins when man learns to measure his world or any part of it by definite objective standards." Through its application on an ever increasing scale "sociology is now beginning to emerge from the limbo of affective attitudes and emotional values into the measurement of causes and consequences, or of quantitative correlations."[28]

In the early twenties Bernard devoted himself to the destruction of the instinct psychology that had enjoyed a widespread circulation in the decade after William McDougall's *Introduction to Social Psychology* appeared in 1908. Though the sharp critique began immediately after World War I, led by J. R. Kantor, Knight Dunlap, and John Dewey, it was Bernard's *Instinct*, published in 1924, that drew the various critiques together and helped demonstrate the infinitely malleable and practically useless nature of the concept. The most damaging difficulty, he explained, was that various human activities were "not distinguished as to origin, any relatively fixed or definite action-pattern being pronounced an instinct whether it is acquired or inherited."[29]

Destruction of instinct psychology was a necessary step on the road to establishing a behavioral social science, since the former emphasized the central importance of innate human drives as opposed to the molding power of the external environment. Additionally, of course, an innate instinct offered obvious difficulties to any attempt at measurement, and hence would prove far too elusive for the kind of quantification that Bernard hoped to develop. The rapid decline of instinct psychology after World War I was thus closely related to the triumph of behaviorism in the same years.

Instead of any internal drives, then, the external environment was the central influence on the development of human behavior patterns. "The uniformities and similarities of behavior patterns in the protoplasms of the individual organisms," Bernard summarized, "derive immediately or ultimately from the conditioning environment."[30] Projecting the stimulus-response concept onto the relationship between the social system and individual human beings, Bernard explained human behavior in all its aspects by external pressures instead of internal drives. Social scientists could observe and measure physical actions and, by various techniques, could quantify and correlate varying environmental factors, thus establishing a wholly objective and quantitative social psychology. Such an approach enabled Bernard and other behaviorists to reduce psychology to wholly naturalistic and observable terms. Nothing unseen, nothing unquantifiable, would enter into the terms of analysis. "Knowledge or data arise through a purely naturalistic process of the conditioning of behavior processes originating in the adjustment behavior of individuals and perceived through the sensory and the internal behavior elaborating process."[31]

Behaviorists were torn between developing a wholly externalized, observational psychology on the one hand and somehow bringing an internalized thought process back into their theory. Bernard's internal "elaborating process" was a perfect example of that ambiguity. In spite of the vagueness, however, the crucial import of Bernard's behaviorism was clear. The environment was the determinant of human action, and ideas were the result of external pressure. "Mind," he explained, "is primarily the product of social pressures."[32]

By the mid-thirties several of the behavioral quantifiers were beginning to push their approach toward its most extreme objectivist position by attempting to introduce an operational theory of meaning into the social sciences. Stemming from the quantum-relativity revolution that transformed physics in the first thirty years of the twentieth century, operationalism had developed out of the work of Percy W. Bridgman, Hollis Professor of Mathematics and Natural History at Harvard. In *The Logic of Modern Physics* (1927) Bridgman suggested that scientific objectivity depended on the use of an operational definition of meaning. For any concept to be empirically valid it had to be defined in terms of a specific physical operation, just as the concept of length was defined in terms of an operation performed with a yardstick. "We mean by any concept nothing more than a set of operations," he declared, "*the concept is synonymous with the corresponding set of operations.*"[33] The objectivist social scientists had defined the criteria of a concept's validity as external to the human mind, but Bridgman defined the concept itself as external and literally embodied in a physical act.

In addition to the functionalist and objectivist nature of Bridgman's theory, it also implied a clear form of philosophical nominalism. "Operations," Bridgman asserted, "are performed by human beings in time and are subject to the essential limitations of the time of our experience—the full meaning of any term involves the addition of a date."[34] Thus although operations were repeatable, they could never be identical. Every operation, and hence every concept, was a distinct and particular phenomenon.

Enjoying the prestige of the new physics, and sharing the basic assumptions of particularist, functionalist objectivism, operationalism began to win adherents in the social sciences, especially in sociology and psychology. Chapin, Harry Pelle Hartkemeier, Arthur F. Bentley, S. C. Dodd, and S. S. Stevens all attempted to introduce operationalist definitions into their disciplines during the thirties.[35] Perhaps the most confident advocate was the sociologist George A. Lundberg. "I define the concept in terms of the operations by which I arrive at it, in conformity with the accepted requirement of science," he announced to his colleagues.[36] Operationalism had been implicit in his behavioral-quantitative theory before he knew of Bridgman's work, and after his discovery he enthusiastically proclaimed operationalism as the conceptual basis of "true" scientific method.[37] Theoretically operationalism was fully consistent with the views of the extreme behaviorists and, most important, it seemed the ideal methodology for achieving complete objectivity. Operationalism claimed to remove both verifying criteria and concepts themselves from the mind, and thus to finally eliminate the remaining element that tarnished the social sciences—the "mental" nature of concepts themselves.

Only a small number of scholars went so far as to embrace a full-fledged operationalism, but probably half of the active social scientists of the period accepted the outlines of the broader quantitative behaviorism. The still more widespread particularist, functionalist objectivism underlay the work of a large majority. Certainly there were few who did not implicitly reflect those basic theoretical assumptions, and fewer still who did not subscribe to that most general scientific naturalism that dominated the social sciences by 1930 and had given birth to those more specific approaches.

As the new methodologies, especially quantitative behaviorism, became dominant during the twenties, they spurred a broad and bitter debate that raged throughout the social sciences. The all-encompassing objectivism of such scholars as Lundberg, Rice, and Bernard provoked a heated critical response from some social scientists. The advent in the middle thirties of operationalism, the most extreme form of the new objectivism, only intensified the disagreement.

The lines of battle were drawn in jumbled and irregular ways in the different disciplines. Many social scientists who shared a general functionalist approach, such as Ogburn and Hamilton, criticized what they considered an excessive concern with measurement and an abuse of statistical techniques.[38] Under the spur of the depression, the reform goals of Merriam, Berle, and others broke more fully into the open as they

39

increasingly attacked "mere" fact-collecting unrelated to practical problem-solving.[39] Philosophical pragmatists such as John Dewey and Charner M. Perry argued that the quantitative-behaviorists distorted the scientific method in their desire to reduce social science to purely "factual" data.[40] Scholars as dissimilar as the philosophical relativist Charles A. Beard and the religiously oriented sociologist Charles A. Ellwood joined in rejecting the ethical neutralism which the strict objectivists claimed.[41] Even Boas's school of historical anthropology split, with Kroeber attacking Boas himself, Goldenweiser attacking Wissler, and Radin attacking everyone.[42]

While the debate was all-encompassing, at the center stood the crucial problem of the nature of scientific knowledge and its relationship to human value judgments. The majority of social scientists, accepting a wholly naturalistic world view and the broad assumptions of the new objectivism, denied the possibility of any "absolute" system of values and rejected the idea that science could ever produce a set of rational ethical norms. Until the middle thirties, however, that attitude received little careful attention, and most considered the whole problem unimportant and, in any case, intellectually futile.

Popular belief in ethical ideals was, of course, an empirical fact. The social scientist could be legitimately concerned with values, as Rice explained in 1932, "if by 'concern' is meant that he may regard the content of such topics as data for examination, analysis, comparison and generalization." As anything beyond "data," however, ethical values could only be considered subjective opinion.[43] Until the late thirties most social scientists refused to acknowledge any significant theoretical problem and simply accepted with varying degrees of awareness the values of their own society. "In the field of moral judgment or ethical discrimination," declared two attitude-quantifiers in 1931, "there seems to be more promise of finding suitable measures because there is no attempt to determine the magnitude of any trait, but rather to discover how far an individual has developed in relation to the moral and ethical standards of the society in which he lives."[44] Commonly accepted moral values thus provided the practical guidelines for quantitative research, just as they provided most social scientists in an unreflective way with their own personal values.

In applying his behavioral psychology to the problem of human values, Bernard was typical. Like ideas, values were the result of environmental stimuli, and differed from those ideas "only in the complexity of the functional neural organization."[45] His social behaviorism placed all values on a wholly naturalistic basis and dismissed any question of their rational worth. Disregarding the ethical questions his approach raised, he simply assumed the legitimacy of traditional humanitarian values, the type of assumption he would have pounced on in the writings of an a priori philosopher. Not only were behaviorism and traditional values consistent, they were also mutually complementary. "The philosophers and theologians," he argued, "did not realize that these very systems of values were being strengthened by the substitution of accurate methods of measuring such values for the old inaccurate and traditional methods."[46] He saw no theoretical problem concerning the intellectual validity of conflicting ethical ideals, therefore, but only a methodological, quantitative one.

Bernard, in fact, specifically defended behaviorism against the charge that it undermined moral values by claiming that its followers were "in the van of the idealists and projective thinkers." Such was the case because behaviorists fully grasped the possibilities an objective social science offered for a reordered and morally improved social structure. "Those who regard the behaviorists as without moral convictions, and therefore dangerous," he explained, "mistake the objectivity of their theory of knowledge and scientific technique for the personalities of the men."[47] By the rigid bifurcation between objective science and personal conviction Bernard demonstrated the obvious fact that behaviorists were human beings too, but he was unable to explain how their moral beliefs were anything but subjective and environmentally determined prejudices. The point was not whether behaviorists had moral values, but how they could justify them in light of their theory of knowledge. The most significant part of his argument, then, was not its logical failure, but the fact that it did not even recognize the nature of a major problem that was practical as well as theoretical.

A sweeping ethical relativism was implicit in the basic assumptions of most social science thought throughout the twenties and early thirties. The broadly characteristic scientific naturalism implied such relativism in two ways. First, social scientists recognized ideas validly based on empirical data as relative and changing. New facts, new theories, new viewpoints were all constantly intruding themselves upon previously accepted formulations. Such constant change and modification, undeniable in theory and common in practice, clearly meant that any scientific conclusions relating to ethical judgments were also relative and changing. Since most scholars considered the scientific method the most reliable method of attaining truth, there seemed to be no way of overcoming such uncertainty in the area of moral understanding.

Equally important, as Bernard indicated, scientific naturalism assumed a social and environmental explanation for the origin of all values. Sociology, declared Harry Elmer Barnes, "has emphasized the group basis and secular origins of all ethical guides and criteria, however dogmatic a social group may be with respect to the allegation of the divinely revealed nature of its ethical concepts and practices."[48] Without a basis in the supernatural, in revealed religion, or in a rationally authoritative philosophy, value systems could only be the products of social, economic, and psychological pressures operating on individuals and groups. As such, no values could be called "higher" in any meaningful sense. Some obviously had greater social support, but none had any greater "validity." "The naturalistic account of both the genesis and the nature of values," proclaimed Thomas Vernor Smith of the University of Chicago, "has won the day."[49]

Even more clearly did ethical relativism and, in a sense, ethical nihilism flow from the new objectivism. Particularism held that for a concept to be valid and meaningful it had to refer directly to an individual, concrete thing. Thus, nominalistic particularism denied even the possibility of a criterion or norm, since by its definition a norm implies something above or beyond any particular object. Functionalism held that knowledge was based on and confined to practical operations, which denied the possibility of a further standard for the worth of the function itself. The practical consequences of Christianity could, for example, be studied functionally; but a functional analysis could never establish the goodness, truth, or validity of its beliefs. Objectivism assumed from the very start that ethical beliefs had no place in scientific inquiry and only served to distort its conclusions. Not only could science not deal with problems of ethical justification, but ethical purposes would destroy the method itself.

In spite of the dominance of those ideas and the inclination of most to avoid theoretical ethical analyses, a few scholars took pointed exception to that failing. John Dewey, though a thoroughgoing naturalist and wholehearted antagonist of all absolutism, rejected strict objectivism and during the twenties attempted to develop a convincing naturalistic method of value criticism and justification.[50] Though he concluded that values were subject to scientific investigation and evaluation, he convinced only a minority. Many naturalists and objectivists, as well as their rationalist critics, thought his attempt a failure. There was no way, most agreed, that an empirical "is" could produce an ethical "ought."

Perhaps the two most prominent and persistent early critics of the ethical implications of the objectivists were Frank H. Knight, an economist at the University of Chicago, and the sociologist Charles A. Ellwood. Together with Paul T. Homan of Cornell and Thomas Nixon Carver of Harvard, Knight became one of the most influential critics of institutionalism and behaviorism in economics.[51] "Social science cannot, like the natural sciences, be restricted to the problem of means for achieving objectives taken for granted," he declared. "Not the winning of power, but its use is, and must be, the leading question."[52] However social scientists tried to disguise the matter, Knight insisted, they were in fact constantly and necessarily dealing with ethical problems. Their denial meant that they had "in general merely worked in terms of unformulated, unconscious ethical standards, and hence, in the literal sense, unintelligently."[53]

Although Knight rejected the ideal of objectivism, he agreed with most of his contemporaries that the scientific method was incapable of establishing a rationally convincing ethical system. He was thus left in a somewhat awkward position, insisting on both the unavoidability of value judgments and at the same time their necessarily subjective nature. Knight argued for a kind of esthetic humanism that would abandon absolute standards and make ethical judgments a matter of cultivated taste. "There are no rules for judging values," he declared, "and it is the worst of errors to attempt to make rules—beyond the rule to 'use good judgment.' "[54] Knight perceptively pointed to unacknowledged moral assumptions in objectivist social science, but the vagueness of his own ethical theory undercut much of the force of his argument. That weakness, together with his own acceptance of the belief that science could never establish moral standards, prevented his approach from growing into a clear alternative to the new objectivism. Though he was a Socratic gadfly to the objectivists, he remained within the naturalist camp.

Ellwood, who taught at the University of Missouri and then at Duke University, seemed somewhat more successful than Knight in gathering a sizeable academic following. He served for many years as the president of Pi Gamma Mu, a social science honorary society oriented toward social work and practical Christianity. Organized in late 1924, and drawing its strength from a number of smaller colleges and universities in the midwest and south, Pi Gamma Mu began publishing its journal *Social Science* in November, 1925.[55] Provocatively, the journal's first issue contained an essay attributed to a professor named Mann, but which, as the editors pointed out in a subsequent correction, had actually been written by a professor named Christ.

Utilizing both his national reputation and the forum provided by the new journal, Ellwood emerged by the early thirties as the most determined opponent of behaviorist sociology. Joining such prominent scholars as Robert M. MacIver and Pitirim Sorokin, the latter of whom had himself been a quantitative enthusiast until the late twenties, Ellwood called for a social science based on conscious values and aimed at practical social reform.[56] The sciences, especially the social sciences, were largely responsible for the problems of the twentieth century, he argued, for they had destroyed traditional religious beliefs without finding an adequate substitute.[57] The completely objectivist orientation that scientists adopted dehumanized their work. "It takes away all meaning from the higher values of life and of culture."[58] Such an orientation had proved relatively successful in dealing with physical nature, but it would simply not work for problems of society. In eliminating consciousness, purpose, and values the behaviorist was eliminating the most important parts of his subject, and hence his science was bound to fail.[59]

"The very nature of human society," Ellwood insisted, "makes a qualitative approach necessary to understand social problems."[60] He consistently rejected wholesale *a priori* speculation and insisted on the use of empirical evidence, but he also emphasized the fundamental similarities between sociology and philosophy. Deduction, synthesis, imagination, and logical criticism were all necessary methods. Though empirically based, sociology was fundamentally rational and imaginative rather than physical and quantitative. "The social sciences resemble philosophy in that they both deal with moral values."[61]

Like Knight, Ellwood believed that an understanding of human society was inextricably tied to an understanding of problems of value and purpose. A social science that examined human society qualitatively could establish a normative scientific ethics. All valid knowledge, Ellwood insisted, "is busy establishing norms or standards by which processes may be measured or judged."[62] The biological sciences, for example, established norms that clearly indicated what things were harmful to man's health and what were helpful. Though he emphasized the scientific nature of ethics, he acknowledged that "metaphysics must be the court of last resort for ethics as for all the sciences."[63] It was wisest not to engage in metaphysical argument immediately, however, since the construction of a relative, scientific ethics was a necessary prerequisite. "Absolutistic or metaphysical ethics is, apparently, a final development in the construction of the science of ethics."[64]

In spite of the attention he devoted to it, Ellwood's resolution of the value problem was no more convincing than Knight's had been. His argument ignored the fundamental distinction between the concepts of empirical consequence and ethical normality, while it contradictorily claimed that metaphysics was both the ultimate standard for, and the theoretical consequence of, a scientific ethics. Additionally Ellwood's assertion that values arose through the social process seemed to place his value theory on the same basis as that of the scientific naturalists.[65]

Thus by the early thirties several things were evident concerning the problem of ethical values in the world of American social science. First, the assumptions of the majority, from the general naturalist to the strict operationalist, denied the possibility of scientifically justifying or validating any ethical judgment. Many went even to the point of implicit ethical nihilism by maintaining that man could have no knowledge of the intellectual "validity" of any ethical proposition whatever.

Second, no established social scientist seemed capable of producing an intellectually convincing system of ethical evaluations. In spite of Dewey's great prestige, few thought his ethical theory completely successful. Knight left the problem in a vague esthetic state that did not provide any clear answers and even proclaimed the impossibility of clear answers. Ellwood based his claims theoretically on a metaphysics he would not specify and practically on a religious belief that most found unacceptable. The triumph of the empirical naturalist world view was clearly evident in those three theorists, for they were themselves naturalists—Dewey and Knight completely, and Ellwood, in his scholarly work at least, to a large extent.

Third, there were crucial and profound disagreements within the social sciences about methodological problems in general and value problems in particular. By the early thirties the debate was becoming increasingly sharp as lines were drawn and positions staked out. The problem was never strictly theoretical, since professional status, foundation grants, and the training of graduate students were all involved. Many scholars had

45

staked their careers on one or another approach. That heightening conflict thus set the stage for the late thirties when suddenly a professional debate over methodology became also a political and ideological debate over the most important moral and practical issues that the nation faced.

Throughout the interwar decades, one of the most striking features of social science was its implicit and often explicit ethical relativism; yet the social scientists who contributed to the spread of various forms of objectivism and naturalism were generally not moral relativists by personal preference. Rather they were led to varying kinds of ethical relativism through one or both of two nonrelativistic ideals—the intellectual ideal of creating an objective science of society, and the moral ideal of constructing a humane and truly democratic social order.

Perhaps their root difficulty lay in the ultimately antagonistic nature of those two ideals, though few social scientists at the time saw any basic contradiction. Their fascination with the ideal of a science of society may simply have pushed the moral ideal so far into the background that they temporarily lost sight of it. Or perhaps the difficulty was the result of the untheoretical nature of American thought in general, which unconsciously assumed the validity of certain values and could not imagine their rejection.

Until the crisis of the middle and late thirties, provoked by the combined rise of totalitarianism in Europe and a bitter rationalist and religious counterattack within the United States, most social scientists were able to maintain a placid conviction about the legitimacy and ultimate compatibility of both ideals. Those who emphasized the need for objectivity and moral neutrality in social science remained closely tied to traditional American ideals. They were prepared to claim a complete moral neutrality for their social science because they so confidently assumed the existence of an essentially moral and orderly universe. Some assumed that scientific objectivity would ultimately develop techniques of social "progress"; others merely accepted the specific values of their society as given. In either case, until the late thirties they continued to assume the complementary nature of their scientific and ethical ideals.

4

Non-Euclideanism:
Logic & Metaphor

Since Charles Sanders Peirce's seminal work on logic in the 1870s, American pragmatism had developed a powerful critique of metaphysical first principles. A priori rationality, Peirce maintained, did not mean "that which agrees with experience, but that which we find ourselves inclined to believe."[1] Metaphysics did not produce real knowledge, but merely put inchoate feelings into a seemingly logical form. Dewey carried the attack further, suggesting that metaphysical systems were originally the products of primitive fears in a world beyond human control and understanding, and that they were later adapted to serve as the ideological rationales of elite ruling groups.[2]

By the second decade of the twentieth century almost all American social scientists and a large number of philosophers shared that hostility toward metaphysics and a priori reasoning. It was one of the basic characteristics of the scientific naturalism that spread throughout American intellectual life. During the twenties and early thirties two complementary approaches, the referent linguistics of Charles Ogden and I. A. Richards, and the logical positivism of the Vienna Circle, further strengthened that antimetaphysical attitude.

In 1923 Ogden and Richards published The Meaning of Meaning, one of the most widely read and discussed books of the interwar years. Enjoying special prominence among many social scientists and legal theorists, The Meaning of Meaning offered a psychological-linguistic basis for particularist objectivism. Because of primitive beliefs in "words as natural containers of power" as well as mankind's tendency to employ philosophical abstractions carelessly, Ogden and Richards argued, men habitually acted as though words were in themselves real, substantive entities rather than merely convenient symbols capable of diverse uses.[3] Clarity in both language and thought would be impossible until men recognized that a word had meaning only insofar as it referred directly to some particular, identifiable object, its "referent."

The gradual spread of logical positivism into American intellectual life reinforced the arguments of Ogden and Richards. Stemming from the discussions of a group of Austrian and German intellectuals gathered at the University of Vienna after the war, logical positivism was an attempt to formulate a comprehensive philosophy of science that would take into account the revolutions in physics and mathematics that had occurred during the late nineteenth and early twentieth centuries. By the late twenties the Vienna Circle was publishing its own journal, *Erkenntnis*, and beginning to spread its ideas to a worldwide audience. Moritz Schlick, the central figure in the group, taught at Stanford University in 1929 and at Berkeley in 1931, and during the thirties such logical positivists as Rudolph Carnap, Karl Menger, Hans Reichenbach, Kurt Gödel, Carl G. Hempel, and Herbert Feigl took up permanent residence in the United States.[4] By the mid-thirties they were exerting a significant influence on American philosophy.

Accepting an extreme empiricism, the Vienna Circle maintained that all metaphysical, transcendental, and *a priori* concepts were strictly and literally meaningless. Only propositions that could be experimentally, observationally verified were in any sense true. Deduction, as in mathematics, was a legitimate form of reasoning only insofar as men recognized that it was wholly abstract and had no necessary connection with any empirical reality. Schlick himself carried positivism to an extreme physicalist position by maintaining that the only ultimately valid form of philosophy, the only way to clearly explain the meaning of a proposition, was to physically point to whatever concrete object or action the proposition referred to.

Ogden, Richards, and the logical positivists supported the position that any rational validation of ethical propositions was an impossibility, elaborating what came to be known as the emotivist theory of ethics. The use of the word "good" in a moral sense, Ogden and Richards argued, "is, we suggest, a purely emotive use." Since there was no scientific way to verify the ethical judgment of good or bad, the judgment itself could have no cognitive meaning. "When so used the word stands for nothing whatever." Empirically "it serves only as an emotive sign expressing our attitude to *this*."[5] Ethical propositions could thus be nothing more than manifestations of subjective likes and dislikes.

48

While generally not concerning themselves with the specialized problems of ethical theory, American social scientists agreed by the early thirties that the scientific method could offer no validation of ethical judgments. Though scientific investigation could clarify the conditions and consequences of various moral alternatives, it could not prove in any way that one decision was ethically superior to any other. A moral judgment was "in the final analysis deductive in character," asserted Stuart Rice. "*It must start from postulated or implicit objectives which are beyond the reach of scientific substantiation.*" [6] By denying the possibility of justifying value judgments empirically and making them necessarily deductive, Rice was in his own mind denying all possibility of rational validation.

While most American social scientists were rejecting the validity of prescriptive ethics because of their thoroughgoing empiricism, major developments in logical and mathematical theory were leading to the same conclusions from a different basis. During the nineteenth and early twentieth century logicians, mathematicians, and geometers severely restricted the scope of the deductive method, demonstrating that it was wholly formal and experientially void. Pragmatists and positivists had long scorned concepts of a priori self evidence and had tried to limit or even discredit the method of deduction in favor of inductive techniques. The new logico-mathematical theory, however, inspired in large part by the development of non-Euclidean geometries, seemed to demonstrate conclusively that deduction was by its very nature incapable of producing any authoritative system of ethics, and thus seemed to give final theoretical confirmation to the arguments of a line of philosophical empiricists that extended back through Hume. As scientific naturalism and particularist objectivism implied an unbridgeable gap between induction and ethical justification, non-Euclideanism proclaimed the identical gap between deduction and ethical justification. The two approaches together, closely related both theoretically and practically, meant that no method of human reasoning could deal meaningfully with the problem of validating any set of ethical beliefs.

For twenty-one hundred years the geometry Euclid had outlined in his *Elements* stood as a supreme mathematical and logical system. Based on five postulates and five axioms, Euclidean geometry deduced an elaborate system of propositions that seemed both to accurately describe physical reality and to compose a flawlessly logical system. Though innumer-

49

able geometers and mathematicians had tried to disprove or refine it, the system had withstood all challengers. Crucial to the development of modern philosophy was the assertion of Immanuel Kant that the example of Euclidean geometry proved that the human mind possessed synthetic a *priori* knowledge, a knowledge intuitively perceived as true concerning both the laws of the mind's operation and the structure of the external world.

Throughout the centuries much attention had focused on Euclid's fifth postulate, which held that parallel lines could never meet and that through any given point one and only one straight line could be drawn parallel to another given straight line. Euclid's original fifth postulate was more cumbersome and less obvious than his first four, and geometers tried to find some way of deducing it from the others in order to eliminate it as an independent postulate. Though none succeeded, they did come to realize that other postulates could be substituted that would allow the same deductions as Euclid's fifth.

By the beginning of the nineteenth century mathematicians began to understand that the fifth postulate could not be deduced because it was logically independent of the first four. In 1826 the Hungarian Farkas Bolyai and the Russian Nickolai Lobachevski separately published papers suggesting that if the fifth postulate were logically independent, then a postulate *contrary* to Euclid's could be substituted. Both suggested the same alteration: through a given point more than one straight line parallel to another given straight line could be drawn. Some thirty years later the German mathematician Georg Riemann produced yet another contrary postulate: through a given point no straight line could be drawn parallel to a given straight line. All three incorporated their contrary postulates into geometries that were fully developed and free from internal inconsistency, yet fundamentally different from Euclid's. "Out of nothing," tradition has Bolyai proclaiming, "I have created a strange new universe." [7]

The impact on mathematicians and geometers, who had always assumed that only one geometry was possible, was staggering. If Euclid's geometry was true, then the non-Euclidean geometries had in some way to be false. Yet no one was able to find any contradictions or inconsistencies within the systems of Bolyai, Lobachevski, or Riemann. Gradually during the latter half of the nineteenth century mathematicians and geometers came to understand that geometries were, in themselves, wholly formal systems with no necessary connection with any empirical reality.

Geometries were logical systems, based on arbitrary postulates, whose only necessary characteristic was self-consistency.

That discovery, although it implied a challenge to the belief in synthetic *a priori* knowledge, would perhaps not have had such a great impact had it not been for the work of a brilliant German physicist named Albert Einstein. In 1915, ten years after his original paper on the special theory of relativity, and aided by the mathematics of Henri Poincaré and Herman Minkowski, Einstein published *The General Theory of Relativity*. Among his monumental achievements, he demonstrated conclusively that Euclidean geometry did not completely describe the physical universe. When he dealt with gravitation and the deflection of light rays, he had successfully applied Riemann's geometry.[8]

Part of the genius of Einstein's theory lay in the fact that from an elaborate series of highly abstract mathematical calculations he had pointed to three observable, empirical phenomena that must obtain if the General Theory were correct. The first one, a discrepancy in the perihelion of the planet Mercury's orbit, was already widely known and had hitherto been inexplicable on Newtonian principles. Einstein's theory accounted for it exactly.[9] The second prediction dealt with the displacement of lines in the spectrum of the sun; for many years scientists were unable to evaluate this hypothesis, because they could not adequately measure the refraction. The third calculation predicted that the rays of light from a star would bend when passing the sun by an amount twice the size of that indicated by calculations based on Newtonian principles. That prediction could readily be tested under eclipse conditions, and as early as 1917 scientists began to anticipate the eclipse of 1919. As professor Arthur S. Eddington of the Royal Observatory declared in February, 1918, the coming eclipse "can be made a means of confirming or disproving Einstein's theory."[10]

The total solar eclipse of May 29, 1919, was probably the most important and exciting eclipse in scientific history. Two years of preliminary preparation had indicated that Sobral, Brazil, and the island of Principe off the west coast of Africa were the most favorable stations from which to observe the eclipse. In the early spring, two expeditions, one led by Eddington and the other by Dr. A. C. Crommelin, the Assistant Astronomer Royal of Great Britain, set out for those destinations. Enjoying good weather and obtaining generally successful photographs, the expeditions returned to Britain, where on November 6, 1919, at a joint meeting of the Royal Society and the Royal Astronomical Society, the investigators announced their conclusions to the world. "This is the most important result obtained in connection with the theory of gravitation since Newton's day," declared Sir J. J. Thompson, the president of the Royal Society. Einstein's reasoning seemed to be "one of the highest achievements of human thought."[11] The observed results were over twice the Newtonian prediction and exceedingly close to Einstein's. "After a careful study of the [photographic] plates," announced Sir Frank Dyson, the British Astronomer Royal, "I am prepared to say that there can be no doubt that they confirm Einstein's predictions."[12]

The impact of that confirmation was immediate, widespread and profound. Scientists, philosophers, and mathematicians all began to explore and debate the meaning and significance of the new theories. The dramatic setting of the eclipse and the sensational implications of the idea of "relativity" quickly made the subject a topic of popular discussion. For geometers and logicians, as well as for nonspecialist intellectuals, one thing was perfectly clear: at least one non-Euclidean geometry was not only internally consistent but in fact also accurately described certain aspects of the physical universe.

The popular discussion of non-Euclidean geometry was one of the broad results of the confirmation of the theory of relativity. Einstein himself, hailing Riemann's "depth of thought," repeatedly emphasized the importance of the new geometry.[13] Axioms and principles were "free creations of the human mind," Einstein insisted in 1922, and as such had necessarily "to be taken in a purely formal sense, i.e. as void of all content of intuition or experience."[14] All deductive systems were formal creations that might or might not connect with the world of physical reality. "One geometry cannot be more true than another," declared the great French mathematician Henri Poincaré in the first volume of the American Science and Education series; "it can only be more convenient."[15] Deduction could discover or prove nothing, and belief in synthetic a priori knowledge lacked any scientific, geometric, or logical basis. There was no reason to think that any allegedly self-evident truth was either self-evident or true. "The Kantians," summarized one scientist, "were most decidedly in the wrong when they assumed that the axioms of geometry constituted a priori synthetic judgments transcending reason and experience."[16]

The discovery, popularization, and scientific utility of non-Euclidean geometry helped create a widespread belief in the non-Euclidean possibilities of all lines of reasoning. The characteristics of geometry, many argued, were clearly the characteristics of all fields of deductive thought; it followed that social thought, political theory, and ethics could all produce non-Euclidean or nonconventional systems that would be as valid logically as the most traditional and thoroughly accepted theories. Though he himself later rejected the extensions of the idea of non-Euclideanism made during the twenties, the philosopher Morris R. Cohen pointed to the comprehensive implications of the new geometries as early as 1917. "The Kantians, however, are wrong in claiming absolute logical necessity for material principles such as those of Euclid's geometry, Newton's mechanics or Christian ethics."[17] Cohen's immediate recognition of the parallel between the material principles of Euclidean geometry and those of Christian ethics was crucial. Both were ordered systems of propositions that men had considered true. If non-Euclidean geometry proved that there were alternate but logically unassailable systems of geometry based on axioms fundamentally different from those of Euclid, then it appeared obvious that deductive reasoning, by assuming contradictory postulates, could produce systems of ethics radically different from that of traditional Christianity. If deduction were wholly formal, and its only criterion of validity was self-consistency, deduction could never prove the legitimacy of Christian ethics or any other system of moral propositions. Not only that, but deduction could also presumably create new ethical systems that would contradict traditional ideals and yet be logically valid. The concept of non-Euclideanism, generalized to include all types of deductive thought, robbed every rational system of any claim to be in any sense true, except insofar as it could be proved empirically to describe what actually existed.

Fitting in perfectly with the objectivism and naturalism of American social science, non-Euclideanism helped give theoretical confirmation to those attitudes. Though twenty-five years later mathematicians would become convinced that only the two non-Euclidean geometries were possible, and that Riemann's alone appeared applicable to the real world, intellectuals in the twenties and thirties envisioned the possibility of a continually expanding number of provocative new systems. Non-Euclideanism came, in fact, to stand not only for the presumably unchallengeable logico-mathematical proof of the inherent formalism of deductive reason, but also metaphorically for almost any new or radical hypothesis that might be put forward. It confirmed the pervasive dichotomies of words versus things and logic versus reality that underlay the work of most social scientists and philosophers. "Words" and "logic" were treacherous; "things" and "reality" were empirically confirmable and hence meaningful and scientific.

It was revealing, too, that in rejecting what they considered the earlier practice in social science of metaphorically applying concepts borrowed from the physical sciences, the intellectuals of the twenties and thirties accepted their own scientific metaphor. In focusing on science as method they raised the problem of the nature of human reasoning to a central theoretical position. Non-Euclideanism satisfactorily explained for them the nature of human reasoning and thereby became a meaningful scientific metaphor for a new generation of intellectuals.

Of greatest importance for social scientists, the concept of non-Euclideanism provided an underlying metaphor that gave theoretical significance to two major and related developments, the spread of the concept of plasticity and the popularization of anthropology. By the end of the twenties one of the most common assumptions in American social science was that of the nearly infinite plasticity of "human nature." Psychology and sociology both emphasized the determining power of the cultural environment in shaping human life along widely divergent paths. That assumption was the basis of stimulus-response behaviorism, and it suggested by analogy the innumerable non-Euclidean—i.e., not in the tradition of western civilization—possibilities for human societies. Anthropology demonstrated that many such "non-Euclidean" societies existed. One of the major reasons for its rapid rise during the twenties was that it served metaphorically as the science of non-Euclidean societies. As Einstein's application of Riemann had been to non-Euclidean geometry, anthropology's delineation of diverse cultures was to the idea of "non-Euclidean" ethical systems.

Awareness of non-Euclideanism did not penetrate the social sciences until the early twenties, but meanwhile it helped initiate the profound changes that had started by the mid-nineteenth century in the more directly related fields of logic and mathematics. Throughout the nineteenth century scholars in both fields had been seeking methods of greater generalization as well as insights into the theoretical foundations of their disciplines. Beginning with the innovations of the Englishman George Boole, who in the 1850s first developed a widely applicable symbolic algebra as a method of stating propositions, through the monumental work, *Principia Mathematica*, of Bertrand Russell and Alfred North Whitehead (1910–1913), logic and mathematics became closely intertwined and in some cases theoretically identical. "All pure mathematics deals exclusively with concepts definable in terms of a very small number of fundamental logical concepts," the *Principia* declared, and thus "all its propositions are deducible from a very small number of logical principles." [18] Morris Cohen stressed the same point when he addressed the American Philosophical Association. "The nature of the subject matter of logic may be better understood when it is seen to be identical with the subject matter of pure mathematics," he declared. "This identity of logic and pure mathematics is the discovery of the nineteenth century, and was not possible before the discovery of non-Euclidean geometry and of multiple algebra." [19]

Though most logical theory up through the middle nineteenth century had recognized the formal aspect of deduction, generally it had assumed one or more levels of connection between logic and reality. Mathematicians had usually assumed a direct empirical basis for their theory, regarding geometry as fully a part of the natural sciences. By the late nineteenth century, however, logicians and mathematicians had come to an almost unanimous agreement on the wholly formalistic and postulational nature of all deductive, logico-mathematical reasoning. When one set of mathematics proved to be inaccurate in empirical description "we must not say that our mathematics is wrong," explained Gilbert N. Lewis, a prominent scientist at the Massachusetts Institute of Technology, "but only that we have chosen the wrong mathematics!" [20]

Any system of mathematics or logic was thus based on certain axioms and postulates assumed at the start. There was no need to prove them since foundation postulates were necessary and unavoidable. There was no way to prove them, either, since initial postulates were wholly arbitrary. From those initial assumptions the mathematician or logician developed his system with no thought of its descriptive or empirical applicability. His only criterion was internal consistency. "In pure geometry what is demonstrated," declared the positivist philosopher Albert E. Blumberg, "is a theorem or more precisely the relation of analytic deducibility or tautological implication between postulate-set and theorem." All logico-mathematical reasoning was thus purely tautological, the elaboration of implications contained by definition in the foundation postulates. [21] In 1930 Kurt Gödel, one of the logical positivists who came to the United

55

States, produced his "incompleteness theorems," with which he demonstrated to the satisfaction of most of his colleagues that it was theoretically impossible to produce any final or ultimate solution to the problem of the foundations of mathematical logic.[22] All of the competing schools of mathematics, claimed E. R. Hedrick, the chairman of the mathematics section of the American Association for the Advancement of Science in 1932, accepted the full implications of non-Euclidean geometry and the formal nature of mathematical reasoning. "I may assume that no one of these schools would attempt to base its systems on a claim of reality."[23]

Assimilating many of those developments in mathematics, and inspired by the advances in non-Euclidean geometry and the new physics, philosophers began experimenting with the idea of new and different logical systems. Just as geometry had been dominated by the assumptions of Euclid, some argued, so philosophy had been dominated by the logical assumptions of the Aristotelian organon. Such philosophers as Whitehead, Clarence Irving Lewis, Oliver Reiser, F. S. C. Northrop, and Henry Bradford Smith all pointed to new logical possibilities that differed significantly from Aristotle's.[24] "Relativity (non-Newtonian) physics is moving toward a new system which requires a non-Aristotelian approach," declared Reiser. Aristotle's old subject-predicate logic had been destroyed, "never to return."[25]

The challenge to Aristotelian logic took a number of forms and provoked an intense and exciting debate among professional logicians. Many of the challengers zeroed in on the very foundations of Aristotelian and traditional western logic: the three so-called "laws of thought." Though questioned in the past, by both Hegel and Marx, for example, they still seemed to be absolutely necessary assumptions for all ordered thought. The first was the law of identity: everything is what it is, or A is A. The second was the law of noncontradiction: contradictory judgments cannot both be true, or not both A and not-A. The third was the law of the excluded middle: a thing is either true or false, or everything is either A or not-A. Perhaps those "laws" were merely assumptions, as Euclid's fifth postulate had proven to be. "Just as non-Euclidean geometries are not distinguished from the Euclidean on the basis of their applicability or lack of applicability to our perceptual or physical space," insisted the philosopher Paul Weiss, "the different systems of logic should be differentiated on some other ground than their possible application."[26]

Though he remained skeptical himself, Reiser pointed out that there were empirical reasons for questioning both the laws of identity and of noncontradiction. "In the main the doubt arises from unusual phenomena in physics."[27] He referred specifically to the principle of complementarity as it had recently been formulated by the Danish physicist Niels Bohr. Based on Werner Heisenberg's uncertainty principle, complementarity held that the energy quantum, the basic unit of reality according to the new physics, could be either wave-like or particle-like, depending on the particular experimental conditions.[28] Thus, Bohr held, quanta were not either wave-like or particle-like, as Aristotelian logic would demand, but rather were both wave-like and particle-like. Perhaps the principle of complementarity would do to Aristotle's laws of thought what the principle of relativity had done to Euclid's fifth postulate.

Of even wider impact on the philosophy of the twenties and thirties was the challenge to the law of the excluded middle implied in the successful elaboration of multivalued logics. Assuming that a thing need not be either A or not-A, the American philosopher Emil Post worked out in 1921 a logical method based on truth tables, which assumed that propositions could have any number of truth values. In the same year Ludwig Wittgenstein published his *Tractatus Logico-Philosophicus*, which employed a similar method of truth tables, thereby suggesting the possibility of multivalued logics.[29] Of greatest importance was the achievement of two Polish logicians, Alfred Tarski and Jan Lukasiewicz, who in 1930 published a careful description of a comprehensive three-valued logical system that was fully consistent. Until then most philosophers had assumed that only the traditional two-valued system could yield a complete and consistent deductive system. Tarski and Lukasiewicz destroyed that assumption and proved that the law of the excluded middle was not a necessary "law of thought."[30]

Clarence Irving Lewis, the Harvard pragmatist, soon emerged as the leading American advocate of non-Aristotelian, multivalued logics. A widely respected philosopher who had been largely responsible for popularizing symbolic logic in the United States during the twenties, Lewis seized on the work of Tarski and Lukasiewicz as proving that an indefinite number of logical systems was possible. "The law of the Excluded Middle is not writ in the heavens," he proclaimed in 1932: "it but reflects our rather stubborn adherence to the simplest of all possible modes of division."[31] In the same year, together with C. H. Langford of the University of Michigan, he developed a new five-valued logical system by further extending the method of Tarski and Lukasiewicz. The result, declared Sterling P. Lamprecht, a philosopher at Amherst College, "supports the supposition of a variety of non-Aristotelian logics akin to the variety of non-Euclidean geometries."[32]

The importance of Lewis's work lay not just in reemphasizing the tautological and formal nature of all logic, or even in producing a five-valued logical system, but rather in the fact that he placed the new multi-valued logics in a pragmatic framework. "There are no 'laws of logic' which can be attributed to the universe or to human reason in the traditional fashion," he argued. Rather all logical systems and "laws" were human conventions honored only for their utility. "The reasons why we use the particular implication-relation (or relations) which actually figure in our deductions," he emphasized, "are not exclusively considerations of logical truth and falsity: some further criterion, independent of truth and falsity, is required." Logical truth could not possibly serve as an ultimate criterion since the nature and form of that truth necessarily depended upon the prior choice of a particular logical system. And, Lewis pointed out, "the logical truths which are expressed by the laws of one system will not, in general, be expressible in terms of others." Before reasoning could even begin, then, a choice was necessary between systems. "In the nature of the case, the grounds of choice can only be pragmatic."[33]

Lewis thus gave the *coup de grace* to deductive reasoning as a method of validation. Not only did he maintain that it was wholly formal and unconnected with external reality, but he further argued that its use demanded a prior choice, not strictly logical, among different deductive systems. A pragmatic judgment was necessary to select one of the possible systems for use, and hence a pragmatic judgment was necessary to defend the choice of a deductive system rather than a deductive system being necessary to defend a pragmatic judgment. Lewis spent most of the rest of his professional life attempting to work out the guidelines of that ultimate pragmatic criterion. When he died in 1964 he left dozens of notebooks crammed with notes and fragments for his intended major work on the nature of moral judgments.[34]

Lewis's total rejection of the idea that men, through some deductive process, might develop a logically authoritative ethical system was intellectually much more effective than that of the earlier pragmatists had been. Dewey, for instance, rejected deduction fundamentally on a genetic basis. "Philosophy originated," he had declared, "not out of intellectual

58

material, but out of social and emotional material."[35] Deductive systems were thus bad because they were generated not by a concern for disinterested truth but by an interested elitist concern for preserving a hierarchical social order. Although perceptive in many ways, the genetic method was weak in that it did not strike at the essential nature of deduction, or of the particular deductive system itself. Lewis attempted just that. Not only were deductive systems based upon prior interests but they were dependent upon such prior interests in a necessary and unavoidable way. Previous social commitment was an intrinsic part of deduction, in that it determined the particular type of deductive system that was chosen.

While the work of such scholars as Lukasicwicz, Tarski, and Lewis was abstruse and highly technical, the confirmation and extension it gave to the dominant intellectual attitudes of the twenties and thirties guaranteed its broad dissemination. Lewis himself tried on occasion to explain the new developments in laymen's terms, though he much preferred the language of mathematical symbols. Numerous other interpreters, however, were willing to explain in everyday language the significance of the new logico-mathematics. Perhaps the two most prominent and widely read were the mathematicians Cassius J. Keyser and Eric Temple Bell.

In several brief and conversational books, Keyser, the Adrain Professor of Mathematics at Columbia University, focused on the formal and postulational nature of all deductive reasoning. Pointing to the importance of the non-Euclidean geometries, he insisted that "mathematical propositions assert that such-and-such propositional forms imply other such forms and they assert nothing else."[36] As the paradigm of deduction, mathematics started from certain unproven and unprovable postulates and proceeded to elaborate their definitional implications. That formal and postulational character was true of deduction "in all fields including those of moral and social sciences."[37]

Bell, a professor at the California Institute of Technology and former president of the Mathematical Association of America, was even more sharp and outspoken than Keyser. Mathematics was simply a tool created by the human mind, he maintained, and it had no connection with any metaphysical or theological absolutes. "Certainty has vanished, and there is no hope at present of its return in any form which we might recognize."[38] As practical tools, mathematics and logic could produce immense achievements, but they could never establish "truth" or any kind of absolute. "The philosophic theory of values is to the propagation of bunk," he charged, "what a damp, poorly lighted cellar is to that of mushrooms."[39]

In 1934 Bell published one of the most characteristic books of the period, *The Search for Truth*, in which he argued that the search was futile since there was no such thing as "Truth." The intellectual history of the human race had had four great landmarks, Bell maintained, the first being the initial crude discovery of measurement by the Egyptians around 4,000 B.C. and the second the Pythagorean concept of proof developed in the sixth century B.C. At that point in history Aristotle and Euclid appeared. In their respective fields both men produced absolute deductive systems that claimed to prescribe the laws of human thought and reveal the essential nature of reality. "To state the matter bluntly here," Bell asserted, "the supreme importance of the Greece of Aristotle, Plato, and Euclid for the history of abstract thinking is this: in that Golden Age were forged the chains with which human reason was bound for 2,300 years."[40] From that time until the early nineteenth century the "bigots of the Middle Ages" and their followers dominated most areas of human thought, imposing on man belief in the authority of deductive reason to produce absolute truths that should control all aspects of man's life.

The third and fourth great landmarks of human thought were the discovery of non-Euclidean geometry in 1826, which proved the postulational and arbitrary nature of deduction, and the demonstration of multivalued logical systems in 1930 by Tarski and Lukasiewicz, which extended the non-Euclidean insight into all areas of human thought. Lobachevski, "The Great Emancipator," destroyed the authority of Euclid; Tarski and Lukasiewicz destroyed the system of Aristotle, "this most obstinate of all superhuman Absolutes."[41] Thus human thought was "revolutionized" and finally freed from all the shackles of the past.

Widely read and respected by American social scientists and philosophers, Bell not only helped spread the ideas associated with non-Euclideanism, but he summarized and dramatized a view of intellectual history that most of his colleagues shared. American intellectuals were convinced that they were in the vanguard of the forces bringing human progress. Often expressing skepticism or disdain for mechanical or all-encompassing theories of progress, they nevertheless still believed in their own version—progress through intellectual and scientific advance. "I believe that only those things have human survival value," Bell concluded, "which enable human beings to think consistently and creatively."[42]

History since the time of Aristotle, Bell and most of his contemporaries believed, had been the record of an elitist, hierarchical imposition of absolute moral and social systems on the great majority of mankind, an imposition that caused both intellectual stagnation and social stratification. The idea of the middle ages, dominated by scholastic philosophy, an authoritarian church, and a hierarchical social order, emerged as the preeminent symbol of everything that was bad in human society. When Bell castigated "the credulous bigots of the Dark Ages," he articulated the emotional convictions of most American intellectuals.

Science, gaining strength since the seventeenth century, and finally able to discredit those "Dark Ages," was inextricably tied up in the minds of most intellectuals with everything that was best in human society. It represented not just intellectual and technological achievement, but political democracy, social equality, and complete human freedom. The scientific, antimetaphysical approach, Keyser maintained, "fosters scientific modesty, discourages dogmatism, favors tolerance, and makes for the maintenance and advancement of good will in the world."[43] Thus, like the social scientists who adopted particularist objectivism, mathematicians and philosophers who hailed the final rejection of deductive absolutism did so for the sake of intellectual achievement and social progress.

The concept of the wholly formal and postulational nature of deduction had an immediate impact on American social science. "The logico-mathematical instrument," Rudolph Carnap insisted, "is thus essential for every type of rational, planned activity."[44] Since it applied to all areas of human reasoning, many intellectuals assumed, then ethics, political theory, and all social thought had to be considered as capable of producing non-Euclidean systems. They equated traditional theory, whether classical economics or orthodox jurisprudence or customary prescriptive political theory, with the old Euclidean geometry. All, like Euclid's system, were essentially a priori, absolutistic, and deductive. Based on the new realization of the postulational nature of deduction, the non-Euclidean metaphor allowed intellectuals of the twenties and thirties to accomplish from a previously unexploited foundation three things dear to their hearts. It provided an ideal way to undercut all pretensions to a priori and absolute knowledge; it allowed contradictory and often striking new postulates to be put forward as the basis for various fields of social research; and it made empirical investigation the undisputed foundation of all knowledge and the validating criterion of all theory.

Suggesting that the balance concept of American government was not as adequate as many maintained, Charles Beard referred to it as a "Euclidean theory."[45] In his study of the theory of national sovereignty, Francis G. Wilson of the University of Washington urged political scientists to avoid embracing any one theory and recognize that under varied conditions any number of possible theories might be useful. Pragmatic and localized research must always determine theory validity, rather than vice versa.[46] Awareness of non-Euclidean possibilities, George Sabine of Cornell University argued, "tends to engender self-consciousness about the making of assumptions" and promised to help "open up new and promising lines of investigation."[47]

John M. Clark, one of the leading institutionalists, attempted to work out a tentative form of "non-Euclidean economics" in the early twenties. Accepting the essentially tautological nature of deduction, he pointed to the variety of theories that could be used to explain economic phenomena. "It appears that there are systems of economics with axioms as far removed from each other as the geometry of Euclid and the non-Euclideans."[48] Clark selected eight postulates of traditional economic theory, pointed to their weaknesses, and then offered alternatives for each one. With them, he argued, economists could construct a theory as internally consistent as older theories, and quite likely one that would have greater descriptive accuracy. "On these terms," Clark summarized, "inductive study may be allowed to range farther afield and gather materials for more fruitful generalizations on social economics than have yet been made."[49]

What Clark attempted in economics, Jerome Frank of the Yale Law School tried for legal theory. "The notion behind non-Euclidean geometry is not inherently mathematical," he declared, "but significantly affects thinking in any field."[50] Hoping to bring a greater empirical emphasis to legal study, Frank charged that traditional theory was "Euclidean" in both content and method. It proceeded deductively from a set of "self-evident truths" about the judicial process, holding that the "legal system can be worked out logically as the ancient geometers had worked out their system from self-evident geometrical axioms."[51] Drawing on the work of Russell, Whitehead, and Keyser, he maintained that a close empirical scrutiny would show many of the a priori assumptions of traditional theory to be largely inaccurate. As Clark had done, Frank suggested a large number of new postulates, which contradicted the established ones, as guides for legal research. Only concrete research, he insisted, could legitimize any theory of the legal process.

The proposed new science of semantics, one of the most characteristic developments of the thirties, grew out of the same attitudes that had actuated Frank and Clark. Drawing on a wide variety of sources, the new physics, the attacks on Aristotelian logic, the work of Ogden and Richards, and behavioral psychology, Count Alfred Korzybski, a Polish nobleman living in the United States, attempted to establish a new discipline called general semantics as a comprehensive, unifying system of knowledge. Though acknowledging recent challenges, he claimed that man's intellectual life was still in bondage to a world view stemming from Aristotle, Euclid, and Newton and marked by a belief in deduction, theoretical absolutes, and an elementalistic or oversimplified concept of human knowledge. His new approach was "non-aristotelian, non-euclidean, and non-newtonian" and was in line with the latest advances in scientific knowledge.[52] Basically he argued that most human problems were due to profound confusions in language that led men to assume, erroneously, that abstractions, absolutes, and identities were real things. Truth could only be attained by recognizing the physiological basis of human knowledge and relying solely on a strict experimental naturalism. The change from the old to the new system, from Aristotelianism to non-Aristotelianism, "will mark the difference between a period when the mystery of 'human knowledge' was not solved," he proclaimed, "and a period when it has been solved."[53]

Considering himself an intellectual prophet and a non-Aristotelian twentieth-century Aristotle, Korzybski published his magnum opus, Science and Sanity, in 1933. He promised that semantics would not only place human knowledge on a sound and realistic basis but also ensure the spread of personal sanity and world peace. Semantics would be a great help to "anyone who has any problems to solve,—be they personal difficulties with himself, his family, or his associates—the scientist, the teacher, or the professional person who wants to become more efficient in his own work."[54]

In spite of the tedious, turgid, and occasionally inane nature of Korzybski's work, semantics enjoyed a brief but enthusiastic vogue in the thirties. Gathering a small but devoted following, Korzybski founded the Institute of General Semantics and the International Non-Aristotelian Library, whose purposes were to develop and refine his insights and to spread the non-Aristotelian approach into all areas of human thought. Aided immeasurably by a number of popularizers who attempted to simplify and clarify Korzybski's position, semantics generated a spasm of interest because it summarized and integrated almost all of the ideas and assumptions associated with scientific naturalism and non-Euclideanism. Even such scholars as John Dewey and Charles A. Beard attempted to employ semantic insights in their discussion of the problems of reform, and many others seemed to follow Korzybski in his belief that semantics would become a social and political panacea.[55]

The most elaborate use of non-Euclideanism, as well as the most explicit statement of its implications for ethical theory, appeared in a book by the French philosopher Jacques Rueff of the *Ecole Polytechnique*. Keyser brought the book to the attention of American intellectuals as early as 1926, and in 1929 the Institute for the Study of Law at Johns Hopkins University arranged for its translation and American publication under the title *From the Physical to the Social Sciences*. Keyser, the economists Simon Kuznets and Philip G. Wright, and the legal scholars Herman Oliphant and Abram Hewitt all worked on the edition and heralded its appearance as a major contribution to the philosophy of science.

All science, Rueff argued, consisted of an empirical, experimental branch and a rational, deductive branch.[56] The first attempted to describe the external, physical world; the second attempted to develop a rational system of principles and laws that would relate and organize what the empirical branch had discovered. Any number of abstract rational systems were possible, as were any number of geometries. Whatever rational system most accurately and effectively summarized the empirical data in question was the best rational system at that moment.

Rueff insisted that ethics was every bit as much a science as physics or economics. "The truth of moral theories," he explained, "is deprived of all absolute value."[57] Instead, morals were simply the result of historical experience, which served to justify for men their personal preferences. Empirical study of human history and human mores would yield the ethical "laws" that men in fact proclaimed and in general followed. "Moral laws exist," Rueff maintained, referring to consistent behavior patterns, "and, from a scientific standpoint, that is all we are interested in."[58] Once scholars had ascertained what it was that men actually did and hence what they believed was morally good, then they could formulate ethical theory. "A moral or economic theory is good," he argued, "when it fully explains all the moral or economic facts known at the time under consideration." Moral theory became simply the enunciation of descriptive generalizations concerning the standards of right and wrong that any particular group of men held at any particular time in some particular place. Beyond that description, moral theory had no further significance. "To say that such an ethical theory is true," Rueff declared, "is an assertion devoid of meaning." [59]

Since Euclidean geometry best described the everyday physical world, Rueff called theories that generally encompassed traditional Judeo-Christian moral beliefs Euclidean ethics. It was possible, then, to create systems of non-Euclidean morals—systems based on logically consistent postulates that denied one or more of the central ideals of traditional morality. "Like the non-Euclidean geometries," Rueff pointed out, "they may become true some day when life has set up new empirical rules." [60] Since the purpose of ethical theory was to describe real behavior, those theories necessarily depended on empirical accuracy for their validity. Any non-Euclidean morality was potentially valid, and no moral theory had any experiential validity in itself.

Rueff thus made explicit and precise the implications of the non-Euclidean analogy when applied to ethical theory. "The book as a whole," commented George A. Lundberg, "is undoubtedly the completest statement of the philosophy of science in a brief compass which has yet appeared." [61] It clearly articulated assumptions that were widespread among American social scientists and philosophers. Questioning its discussion of ethics, George E. G. Catlin was both apt and fair when he characterized it as "indubitably a most important and significant book which shows the way thought is tending." [62]

Rueff's discussion of non-Euclidean ethical systems would likely have had little broader significance were it not for the rapid popularization of anthropology and the subsequent rise of Nazism. The former demonstrated quite convincingly that a large number of existing ethical systems were distinctly not Judeo-Christian, and thus gave empirical confirmation to what might have seemed merely the abstract possibility of non-Euclidean ethical systems. By the late thirties the rise of Nazism had made the whole concept of non-Euclidean ethics an immediate and frightening reality. *Mein Kampf* had outlined a crude but extremely dangerous system of non-Euclidean ethics.

Before the mid-thirties and the threat of Nazism, however, few intellectuals concerned themselves with ominous possibilities. Anthropology added a liberating and exciting element to intellectual life. The field itself blossomed in the twenties, and the knowledge of strange and diverse cultures was extremely useful to social scientists. Ethnological research seemed to disprove the existence of ethical universals, and it clearly indicated that only close empirical study could begin to delineate the variety of human societies. The concept of culture developed by the anthropologists seemed to many a most useful tool of social analysis and explanation. Finally, anthropological research demonstrated the biases of western civilization and western rationalistic social theories, thereby confirming the need for an objective and scientific study of human societies.

Throughout the twenties and early thirties social scientists in all disciplines emphasized the crucial role of anthropology in challenging the basic assumptions of western civilization. Such studies, summarized the editors of the *Encyclopaedia of the Social Sciences* in 1930, led scholars to view the assumptions of their own cultures "not as endowed with an unyielding and inherent place in the scheme of things, but as mutable and merely a variant."[63] Basing his treatment of human morality largely on the new anthropology, Horace M. Kallen concluded that it was impossible to discover, much less validate, any single, universal system of ethical beliefs. "So great is the diversity of patterns and principles of conduct that actually comes under the scope of morals," he insisted in 1933, "that it is impossible to analyze the subject matter scientifically on the basis of a single rule or formula."[64]

With the dominance of scientific naturalism and the formalistic conception of deduction, anthropology emerged by analogy as the science of non-Euclidean cultural systems. "All of us are born into a set of traditional institutions and social conventions that are accepted not only as natural but as the only conceivable response to social needs," declared Robert H. Lowie. Belief in those conventions was simply "purblind provincialism" that prevented men from recognizing the novel possibilities of social life. "Acquaintance with adjustments in one society after another that rest on wholly different foundations from those with which we are familiar," he maintained, "enlarges our notion of social potentialities as the conception of *n*-dimensional space enlarges the vision of the non-Euclidean geometrician."[65]

The American school of historical anthropology that was inspired

66

by the towering figure of Franz Boas began largely as a reaction against the linear universalism of the evolutionists who had dominated the field during the last thirty years of the nineteenth century. In a seminal essay published in 1896, Boas attacked the evolutionists both for their rigid schematizations and their prejudiced "Anglo-Saxon" orientation. "The comparative method, notwithstanding all that has been said and written in its praise, has been remarkably barren of definite results," he declared, "and I believe it will not become fruitful until we renounce the vain endeavor to construct a uniform systematic history of the evolution of culture." [66] By concentrating on the specific development of individual societies, Boas insisted, scholars could place their field on a solid, empirical basis and at the same time lay the only legitimate foundation for possible future generalization. Minute and careful historical description offered anthropology its most promising method of investigation. Following his own injunction, Boas produced a vast library of descriptive materials on various primitive societies, publishing over 5,000 pages on the Kwakiutl Indians alone. [67]

In contrast to the dominant methodological assumptions of the other social sciences, Boas's approach down-played the importance of discovering scientific laws and emphasized an historical approach. Still, however, it shared two central assumptions of the period. First, and most important, it implied a nominalism that clearly linked it with the characteristic empiricism of the interwar years. In anthropology, as in all of the social sciences, Boas declared, "the center of investigation must be the individual case." [68] By the thirties that nominalism had helped lead him to deny the possibility of discovering laws of human society. "On account of the uniqueness of cultural phenomena and their complexity," he argued, "nothing will ever be found that deserves the name of a law excepting those psychological, biologically determined characteristics which are common to all cultures and appear in a multitude of forms according to the particular culture in which they manifest themselves." [69] Even specific "biologically determined characteristics" were not wholly equivalent, but rather appeared in a "multitude of forms," which the student had to consider separately for accurate analysis. Cultural phenomena were indeed "unique." The second similarity with the general social thought of the period was the desire for complete objectivity and moral neutrality in the scholar. "The scientific study of generalized social forms requires, therefore, that the investigator free himself from all valuations based on our culture," Boas insisted. "An objective, strictly scientific inquiry can be made only if we succeed in entering into each culture on its own basis." [70]

Boas helped drive racism and Anglo-Saxonism out of anthropology and installed in its place a deep sympathy for all the societies the scholar studied. Rejecting western ideas of "progress," he insisted on equality of treatment for even the most "primitive" or "savage" society.[71] As with many of his contemporaries, moral neutrality camouflaged only slightly his personal convictions about the equality of man and the dangerously egocentric nature of western social thought. As with them, too, his idea of neutral scholarship was intended to serve not only the cause of scientific objectivity but also the moral cause of human equality.

Though various disagreements developed among Boas's numerous students, they remained loyal to a high degree to those two basic methodological assumptions. Any discussion of value, Lowie declared, was "extraneous to our science except as an observational datum."[72] The anthropologist discovered his facts and followed them wherever they led. "The kind of synthesis he gives must depend on the nature of his facts," Lowie explained, assuming the particular nature of facts and their independence from any overarching interpretive theory. His *Primitive Society* reflected well its guiding principles, proposing no major interpretations and emphasizing instead the striking diversity of primitive social groups.[73] Lowie, Albert L. Kroeber, Alexander Goldenweiser, Paul Radin, and many others continued the particularist and value-free orientations throughout the twenties and thirties.[74]

That particularist attitude led a number of American anthropologists to move from the study of individual social groups to the study of specific human beings, the ultimate reduction of ethnological particularism. Investigators should become "interested in the question of the way in which the individual reacts to his whole social environment," Boas urged, "and to the differences of opinion and of mode of action that occur in primitive society."[75] Radin argued that all generalized concepts of men and women should be severely restricted. Social scientists should recognize, for example, that it was not "a Crow Indian who has made such and such a statement, uttered such and such a prayer, but a particular Crow Indian."[76] Radin carried the position to practical fulfillment in 1926 when he wrote the biography of a single Winnebago Indian.[77] "It is this particularity," he insisted, "that is the essence of all history."[78]

The assumptions of moral objectivity and historical particularism reinforced one another, with the concentration on specific facts providing the method that assured a value-free description. Such objectivity led to the assumption of the equality of all cultures and ensured that different cultures would be treated as independent and self-fulfilling wholes. Particularism led directly to an emphasis on the cultural differences between various societies and hence on the variety of organizational and ethical possibilities. "There is no more reason to infer cultural or psychological universals from Trobriand culture than from our own," Kroeber pointed out. "That is the first and by now quite elementary lesson of anthropology."[79]

Anthropology seemed to prove the validity of four assumptions that were common among American intellectuals. First, it strengthened the naturalistic assumption of the social origin of all values by elaborating the concept of culture, the sum total of the values and assumptions a society imposed upon its young. "Rules of etiquette, religious dogma, political convictions, and to a great extent the specialized outlook of a social or professional class," Goldenweiser explained, "become fixed in the mind of the individual before he is quite aware of what is taking place."[80] By discussing various specific cultures and showing how the process actually worked, they provided a detailed, naturalistic account of the origin and transmission of values.

Second, anthropology confirmed the widespread disbelief in absolutes of any kind by elaborating the structures and assumptions of many diverse societies. "The conception of our civilization as one of the many forms of human social life," declared Boas, was "brought home forcibly by a presentation of the general data of anthropology."[81] From his extensive work on American Indian culture Clark Wissler developed the concept of "culture areas," the idea that the world was divided into rough and uneven areas each of which had developed its own distinct and divergent culture. "What all anthropologists seem to be agreed upon is that culture in the concrete is found in patches instead of scattered at random throughout the world's population," he declared in 1927.[82] The concept of the culture area allowed for the organization and comparison of anthropological data, while at the same time preserving the idea of cultural differences as a central reality. Though it was criticized on many grounds, no one disputed its emphasis on variety.

Third, the new research gave convincing proof to the dominant belief in the nearly complete plasticity of so-called "human nature." A major assumption of all behaviorists and most other intellectuals, plasticity was obvious from the infinite diversity of cultural forms that the ethnologists popularized. "Anthropology . . . has made it clear," summarized John Dewey, "that the varieties of cultural and institutional forms which have existed are not to be traced to anything which can be called original unmodified human nature but are the products of interaction with the social environment."[83] Margaret Mead, one of Boas's later students, popularized the idea of plasticity in a series of books intended for both lay and scholarly audiences. "We are forced to conclude that human nature is almost unbelievably malleable," she insisted.[84]

Finally, anthropology seemed to demonstrate that no basis existed for evaluating cultures that was not itself culture-bound. Though impossible to avoid completely, Wissler pointed out, cultural values "are chiefly matters of group prejudice."[85] A general knowledge of cultural processes, Lowie concluded, clearly showed that values "can be graded only on subjective grounds and must scientifically be treated as incommensurable." There was no way to escape "the impossibility of grading cultures."[86] The idea that all human value judgments were necessarily culture-bound paralleled C. I. Lewis's claim that every selection of a system of deduction was necessarily pragmatically based. Cultural standards, like logical postulates, were theoretically arbitrary assumptions that could never serve as criteria for any objective or universal value judgment.

The problem of evaluating divergent cultures immediately suggested the application of the non-Euclidean metaphor to ethnological discoveries. "No sooner is this issue broached," Goldenweiser explained, "than it becomes at once apparent that no conclusion can be reached here without postulating some standards of reference." And, as with any theoretical postulate, its opposite was quite conceivable. If western man, or anyone else, were allowed to postulate cultural criteria, "then others must be granted the right to proceed similarly."[87] Since any number of contradictory ethical postulates were possible, such rational processes could end only in bitter and unresolvable disagreement. There was no resolution to the problem of finding authoritative rational or cultural criteria for the evaluation of ethical beliefs.

The non-Euclidean possibilities of anthropology received their most elaborate and popular statement in Ruth Benedict's *Patterns of Culture*, which appeared in 1934, became a best seller, and went through several printings before World War II. A broad interpretive study of the nature of culture, the book illustrated its message by examining three primitive tribes, chosen to demonstrate the diversity of cultural forms and the organic unity of individual cultures. Such elemental acts as murder and suicide, she pointed out, were judged very differently in different cultures and "relate to no absolute standard."[88] Again, homosexuality, generally considered an evil practice in western civilization, was an integral part of other societies, including that of ancient Greece. The homosexual, she explained, held an important and respected role among many tribes of American plains Indians.[89] Cultures were consistent, integrated wholes that could conceivably be developed on any number of possible assumptions. "The diversity of the possible combinations is endless," she concluded, "and adequate social orders can be built indiscriminately upon a great variety of these foundations."[90]

As organic growths, of course, cultures were not like logically constructed geometries; yet, though the metaphor lacked precise elaboration, the comparison of human behavior patterns with geometric systems exerted a subtle appeal to American intellectuals in the twenties and early thirties. It implicitly and perhaps subconsciously suggested that, as geometries could be consciously created on certain chosen postulates, human societies could be scientifically constructed—or reconstructed—on new and better value premises.

Though they seemed to discredit many traditional ethical beliefs, anthropologists throughout the interwar years saw their work as not only scientific, but also didactic and moral. Almost unanimously they were arguing for a broader tolerance toward all racial and ethnic minorities, both in the primitive societies they studied and in the United States itself. After the turn of the century anthropology was one of the strongest and earliest forces in attacking racism in all its forms. Boas's work had attempted to demonstrate the equality of all mankind by tracing specific differences to cultural, not racial, variation. His students had followed the same course. "With great confidence we can say that since the same race at different times or in different subdivisions at the same time represents vastly different cultural stages," Lowie maintained, "there is obviously no direct *proportional* relation between culture and race."[91] They hoped that recognition of cultural relativity and diversity would produce a greater respect on the part of all men toward one another. "To contribute to this larger tolerance and balance of mind," Kroeber declared, "is one of the functions of anthropology."[92]

So too the common assumption of plasticity was seen as contributing to a definite moral goal. If human nature was malleable, then striking social reforms were possible, and the hopes of many for a more humane and democratic social order were potentially realizable. "The knowledge that the personalities of the two sexes are socially produced," Mead explained in 1935, "is congenial to every programme that looks forward towards a planned order of society."[93]

In the context of the intellectual optimism that marked the twenties and early thirties, ideas such as the relativity of values and the plasticity of human nature seemed morally hopeful and useful. It was not until the middle thirties that that optimism began to dissipate. Though she viewed the idea of plasticity as the basis for a more cooperative and democratic society, Mead felt constrained by 1935 to add an ominous warning. Plasticity was actually "a two-edged sword that can be used to hew a more flexible, more varied society than the human race has ever built," she pointed out, "or merely to cut a narrow path down which one sex or both sexes will be forced to march, regimented, looking neither to the right nor to the left."[94]

By 1935, however, when doubts began to proliferate, the elements of non-Euclideanism were fully formed. First, the idea of synthetic *a priori* knowledge was discredited, and internal analysis of the deductive method had demonstrated its wholly formal and experientially void nature. The method could never prove or justify anything about human behavior or empirical reality. It was postulational and therefore arbitrary in its essence. That discovery meant that no deductive ethical system could ever claim prescriptive authority over human affairs, and that any number of logically consistent—and therefore rationally valid—ethical theories were imaginable. Second, confirming the existence of those theoretical possibilities, anthropology demonstrated the fascinating variety of human moral codes and the almost infinite plasticity of human nature. Had a rationally authoritative ethical system by which to judge empirical diversity been possible, then social theorists could have dismissed the variations as aberrations. The powerful non-Euclidean critique of deduction, however, destroyed that possibility. Social scientists were thus forced to accept the moral precepts of all cultures as nondebatable postulates. The implications of non-Euclidean geometry and the elaboration of cultural diversity crystallized into a fundamental metaphor. A culture, many began to assume, was analogous to a geometry. Both were built on a few postulates chosen from an indefinite number of possibilities; both were inter-

72

nally consistent, interrelated wholes; and neither could be proven or dis-proven in any ultimate sense or by any criteria beyond its own chosen postulates. As scientific naturalism had denied the possibility of validating ethical judgments by inductive methods, non-Euclideanism denied it to deductive ones. At the same time non-Euclideanism established cultural mores as beyond rational criticism and suggested the possibility of any number of new and different ethical systems that would be logically valid. By the early thirties the most fundamental epistemological assumptions of American intellectuals rejected the idea that any prescriptive ethical theory could possess rationally compelling authority.

5

The Rise of Legal Realism

The interest in non-Euclideanism manifested by such legal scholars as Jerome Frank and Herman Oliphant was part of a broad and dynamic attempt during the twenties and thirties to alter significantly the assumptions of American jurisprudence. As a field traditionally associated with the rigorous use of deductive logic, the law was an obvious and inviting target for those who shared scientific naturalist and non-Euclidean assumptions. Although those attitudes had spread rapidly after the turn of the century, they managed to penetrate legal thinking only slowly and haltingly. The law, with its basis in centuries old custom, its traditionalist orientation, and its comparative intellectual isolation, proved a much less receptive field than did philosophy and the newer social sciences.

By the early twenties, however, scientific naturalism and non-Euclideanism had made definite inroads into American jurisprudence. They provided the catalytic force that produced one of the bitterest and most sustained intellectual debates in the nation's history. A new generation of legal scholars, inspired by Justice Oliver Wendell Holmes, Jr., and attempting a scientific study of law, had developed the outlines of a sweeping critique of traditional legal thought that went far beyond the criticisms of such sociological jurists as Roscoe Pound and Benjamin N. Cardozo. By the early thirties their vigorous attack on established legal conceptions began to alarm traditional-minded jurists and within a few years raised distressing questions from the standpoint of democratic theory about the nature and basis of law.

Although the eighteenth-century concept of natural law and rigid theories of common law precedent had been eclipsed in the early decades of the nineteenth century, both had returned to a central position in American legal thinking by the 1880s. Together with a formalistic, deductive concept of legal reasoning, a vague belief in natural law and a rigid theory of precedent became the pervasive assumptions behind American jurisprudence. That predominant legal theory claimed that reasoning proceeded syllogistically from rules and precedents that had been clearly defined historically and logically, through the particular facts of a case, to a clear decision. The function of the judge was to discover analytically the proper rules and precedents involved and to apply them to the case as first premises. Once he had done that, the judge could decide the case with certainty and uniformity.[1]

"The rules of law are founded upon principles of right and justice that never change," declared the authors of one legal study published in 1924. The judge surveyed precedents, customs, and statutes to discover the correct preexisting principle that should control the case, they maintained. "He then declares the rule of law which governs."[2] The establishment of the facts of the case became the minor premise, and from the general principle and the particular facts a logical decision automatically followed. "Every judicial act resulting in a judgment," summarized another legal scholar, "consists of a pure deduction."[3]

That logical orientation had been strengthened by the case method of legal study, widely adopted in the United States by World War I. Introduced originally into American legal education in 1871 by Christopher C. Langdell, the dean of the Harvard Law School, the case method rested on the assumption that a close study of past judicial decisions would reveal the basic principles and rules of the law that had led to the various decisions. Langdell himself thought all the materials necessary for a sound knowledge of the law existed in those decisions and that the case method provided the means of making legal study scientific.[4] Focusing on the logical analysis of judicial opinions and emphasizing the desirability of doctrinal consistency, the case method reinforced a rationalist and deductive theory of judicial decision.

In spite of its continued predominance, however, that orthodox theory had already come under forceful attack before the twenties. As early as 1881 Justice Holmes, then a young lawyer in Boston, had published his famous study of the common law, which he placed in an evolutionary Darwinian framework. Holmes argued that practical expedients, necessitated by the needs and conflicts of human society, were more central to the development of law than were any logical propositions. "The felt necessities of the time, the prevalent moral and political theories, intuitions of public policy, avowed or unconscious, even the prejudices which judges share with their fellow men," he declared, "have had a good deal more to do than the syllogism in determining the rules by

75

which men should be governed."[5] *The Common Law* was, to use a Holmesian metaphor, the first cannon shot in his fifty-year battle against the armies of legalistic formalism.

By 1897 the basic outline of his skeptical, empirical attack was clear. Law was not an abstract problem of logic, but a practical question of social management. Judges did not in fact settle cases by deductive reasoning; rather they necessarily decided, consciously or unconsciously, what was socially desirable according to their personal and class beliefs. Those beliefs, like all moral values, were wholly relative and determined by one's particular environment. The power of deductive logic and the ethical and social absolutes that it claimed to establish were simply illusions that masked the actual working of the legal process. By the law, Holmes declared, he meant no metaphysical truths or grand moral principles such as a rationally knowable "natural law," but only "the incidence of the public force through the instrumentality of the courts." The lawyer's sole duty was to predict how the courts would use that force, and hence to advise his clients most effectively. "Nothing but confusion of thought can result from assuming that the rights of man in a moral sense are equally rights in the sense of the Constitution and the law." Thus defining the law in empirical, behavioral terms, Holmes urged his colleagues to study "the operations of the law" rather than its logical consistency or moral connotations.[6]

By the first decade of the twentieth century other scholars were beginning to follow Holmes's lead and to apply the insights of his skeptical, functional approach. John Chipman Gray, a professor of law at Harvard University, stressed the preeminent role of the individual judge as opposed to the logic of the law itself in deciding particular cases. In spite of all the theories about preexistent law, Gray declared, the courts in fact created new law when they decided cases.[7] Louis D. Brandeis, a prominent Boston lawyer, argued that judges must consciously consider the probable social results of their decisions. Scientific studies of social needs and problems, rather than syllogistic reasoning, should be the determining factor. To guide the judges in their assessment of those social results, he began in 1908 to employ briefs loaded with a maximum of sociological evidence and relatively little logical argumentation. The brief Brandeis submitted in *Muller v. Oregon* (1908) contained two pages of legal argumentation and well over a hundred of sociological statistics and analysis.[8]

Much of the theoretical justification for the "Brandeis brief" came from Pound's early work, which insisted on the need for and relevance of a new sociological jurisprudence. "The sociological movement in jurisprudence," he explained, "is a movement for pragmatism as a philosophy of law." Fundamental to the new approach, Pound argued, was "the adjustment of principles and doctrines to the human conditions they are to govern rather than to assumed first principles."[9] Criticizing the older "mechanical" jurisprudence, he called for an empirical study of the way the legal process functioned in practice. Rather than examine the internal logic of legal arguments, he maintained, "it is much more important to study their social operation and the effects which they produce."[10] By 1921 the widely respected legal scholar Benjamin N. Cardozo, a New York State Supreme Court Justice, argued that the "sociological method" should be one of the principal tools of judicial practice.[11]

Agreeing with Holmes that legal scholars must study the way laws operate in practice, Pound insisted that the overemphasis on logical uniformity and theoretical certainty that characterized much of the older approach often frustrated the just settlement of particular cases. Only by studying the social impact of legal principles and rules could men know whether the law in fact brought about the administration of real justice. Holmes and Pound agreed on many points, especially on the mechanical and abstract nature of the older legal theory, but Pound's greater emphasis on the ideal of justice conflicted with Holmes's more cynical view of moral values in the law. Ultimately that difference would be one of the central reasons for Pound's rejection of Holmes's disciples, who were to some extent also his own, in the 1930s.

It was thus in a rigid and formalistic profession that nevertheless had produced a Holmes and a Pound, and in a broader intellectual environment that recognized science as the only method of reaching truth, that the so-called "legal realists" came of age. Of a sample of twenty-three of the most important new critics, only six had been born before 1880, whereas eight were born during the 1880s and nine after 1890. By 1930, when their collective efforts were first termed "legal realism," their average age was still only forty-two.[12] The realists thus formed a younger generation of scholars who had grown up with the triumph of scientific naturalism and the rapid proliferation of the social sciences. Suspicious of what they regarded as the rigid ways of the past, they were much more willing than their predecessors to accept new ideas and methods.

With few exceptions the realists were full-time law school teachers, a

77

profession that had not existed in 1870 and that only became widely established at the turn of the century. As social scientists had become professionalized between 1880 and 1910, so too had the law school teachers. No longer a retired practitioner or one who lectured part-time from old notes, the new teacher stood by the first decade of the twentieth century as a full-time, nonpracticing specialist who was expected to devote himself to the dispassionate study of the law and to the improved training of his students. In 1900 the teachers founded their own organization, the Association of American Law Schools, and in 1914 they felt confident enough to break away from the American Bar Association and schedule their annual meeting separately.

The beginnings of sociological jurisprudence had been rooted not just in the spread of scientific naturalism but also in the concurrent emergence of that new profession. Acknowledged success in producing better lawyers established a strong and expanding institutional basis that allowed the profession to flourish. The very idea of a professional teacher of law suggested the role of a specialized expert capable of objectively evaluating the social consequences of legal institutions. The general problem of professional identity, acute for lawyers newly separated from practice, made self-definition in terms of the scientific method an obvious recourse. Functional differentiation and diverging professional values created inevitable friction with the practicing bar, which helped breed critical attitudes toward the actual operation of the legal system. Finally, the formative years of professional growth paralleled the surge of prewar reform. A number of law school teachers, already striving to develop broader social views, joined the drive toward domestic reform; and at the same time young lawyers who shared reform attitudes enthusiastically chose teaching careers as an alternative to a narrowing private practice.[13]

The realists, then, represented both a development of and a reaction against the new professionalism. On the one hand they fully accepted the institutional role of objective students as well as the goal of an empirical science of law. They insisted, however, that the profession cast off its antiquated and unsophisticated concepts and keep up with the latest advances in empirical theory and research. If they were to be professional scientists, they argued, then they must be truly scientific. In the twenties that injunction pointed in just one direction—cooperation with the confident new social sciences. On the other hand, the realists bridled at the abstract treatment of legal problems, which they believed had grown unwittingly out of the law teachers' functional separation from practice. As the tide of reform ebbed and the Association of American Law Schools reconciled itself with the A. B. A., the conservative political stance of the whole profession and the continued formalism of both scholarly writing and judicial opinions loomed ever larger. The realists urged their fellow teachers to abandon the ivory tower focus on doctrinal logic and return to the actual legal process, not as practitioners but as true scientists.

The state of American law invited and even necessitated the devastating attacks of the realists. The inconsistencies between the practices of a rapidly changing industrial nation and the claims of a mechanical juristic system had grown so acute by the 1920s that, in the minds of many, the orthodox jurisprudence could no longer justify and explain contemporary practice. It had become clear, Judge Cardozo declared in 1932, that "the agitations and the promptings of a changing civilization" demanded more flexible legal forms and demanded equally "a jurisprudence and philosophy adequate to justify the change." [14]

At the same time even many of the strict proponents of the older jurisprudence had to admit that widespread confusion and uncertainty threatened the American legal system. Such a stalwart of orthodoxy as Elihu Root acknowledged that "the confusion, the uncertainty was growing worse from year to year" and that as a result "the law was becoming guesswork." [15] Root, like many other lawyers, found the cause of confusion primarily in the massive growth of case law during the previous decades. The whole case law system had, in fact, become unwieldy since the 1870s when the National Reporter system was inaugurated. At that time the West Publishing Company had begun printing all federal court opinions throughout the United States, in addition to all higher and some lower state court decisions. By the beginning of the twentieth century the National Reporter system had turned the inevitably increasing number of cases into an avalanche of reported precedents that made it impossible for judges and lawyers to stay properly informed. [16] "At the present rate of accumulation," commented Harlan F. Stone, the dean of the Columbia University Law School, "no library ever designed or built by the hand of man could in a few generations house the books of a complete working law library." [17] To their great chagrin and bewilderment, members of the legal profession began uncovering contradictory and conflicting decisions with ever-increasing frequency.

That plight was so widely recognized that in 1923 Root and a number

79

of his orthodox colleagues helped establish the American Law Institute to abolish confusion by a clear and updated "restatement" of the law. The organization's first report emphasized, in addition to the flood of precedents, a number of other contributing causes of legal uncertainty, including a lack of precision in the use of legal terms and a lack of agreement on basic common law principles.[18] For many of the new critics the widely acknowledged confusion was clear evidence that the syllogistic certainty of the law was a hollow claim and that the actual role of the individual judge was wider and more crucial than the orthodox jurisprudence allowed.

The very fact that the new American Law Institute was attempting a "restatement" of the law was an additional factor provoking the new critique. Since the Institute would be forced to choose among conflicting decisions and precedents, Herman Oliphant maintained, it would in fact be making new law. "There can be no mere restatement of the law."[19] The idea of such a restatement assumed that the law preexisted in some whole form that could be discovered by logical analysis and that the job of the American Law Institute was merely to discover it and to write it down. Most of the members of the Institute still believed in the validity of the older juristic method and thought that a more rigorous application would resolve their difficulties. Convinced that law was a human product related to changing social and cultural conditions, the new critics rejected the idea of an official restatement as an impossible goal.

By the end of the twenties Yale, Columbia, and Johns Hopkins universities had become the centers of the new legal criticism. Charles E. Clark, who succeeded Robert M. Hutchins as dean of the Yale Law School in 1929, presided over such aggressive scholars as Frank, Walter Nelles, William O. Douglas, Thurman Arnold, and Edward S. Robinson. In cooperation with Johns Hopkins, three of the most scientific-minded lawyers, Oliphant, Walter Wheeler Cook, and Hessel E. Yntema, founded the research-oriented Institute of Law in 1929. At Columbia Karl N. Llewellyn, often regarded as the most important of the new critics, joined with Edwin W. Patterson, Underhill Moore, and others in publishing sharp essays that challenged the abstractions of traditional jurisprudence. Dean Leon Green of Northwestern University, Felix S. Cohen of the New School for Social Research, Max Radin of the University of California, Thomas Reed Powell of Harvard University, and Judge Joseph C. Hutcheson of the United States District Court in Texas were among those whose work placed them in the forefront of the new movement.

Though much of the new criticism had been elaborated during the twenties, the debate over legal realism as a collective movement began in 1930 when Karl Llewellyn and Jerome Frank published separate essays that struck the legal profession in rapid succession. Llewellyn used the phrase "Realistic Jurisprudence" to describe his suggested approach, and Frank spoke specifically of the new legal realism. Soon the term "legal realism" came to stand for the general attitude of all the new critics. Most of the so-called realists disliked the label, but their enemies seized upon it as an epithet to brand what they considered an unsound and often dangerous attitude.

Typical of the empiricism of the twenties and thirties, Llewellyn's article on "Realistic Jurisprudence" centered on the distinction between abstract legal verbalisms and concrete behavioral facts. "The traditional approach is in terms of words; it centers on words," he explained, adding pointedly, "it has the utmost difficulty in getting beyond words."[20] Legal phrases and concepts were devices to make the world more manageable, but the history of American law showed that those necessary abstractions "tend to take on an appearance of solidarity, reality and inherent value which has no foundation in experience."[21] Hence they led to a rigidity that forced new facts and situations to conform to outmoded concepts or else ignored the new altogether. Much of the law was an exercise in painful definition and strained syllogism that bore little resemblance to the real world it was supposed to govern.

Such an important concept as that of the legal rule was a perfect example of the danger and ambiguity inherent in rigid abstractions, Llewellyn declared. While such authoritative rules were supposed to lead judges to proper decisions, they were in fact often so vague and confused as to be no help at all. When a lawyer talked of a legal rule, no one knew whether it was the lawyer's rule or the court's; whether it represented what the courts should do, or what they had done in fact; whether courts actually followed it, or merely used it to justify a decision reached on other grounds. Such fuzzy conceptions of legal rules led to large-scale uncertainty and contradiction in actual decisions and caused massive and often absurd twisting of terms in legal argumentation. Fundamental conceptual imprecision, Llewellyn insisted, could only mean "confusion, profuse and inevitable."[22]

Not only were legal rules vague and misleading as tools of analysis, but their mere existence as "rules" led to additional confusion. Since men knew them as supposedly authoritative guides, they tended to accept them without examining the reality of the legal structure. In fact, Llewellyn insisted, there was almost always a gap between the so-called rules of a case and its practical settlement. Admitting that legal rules had some uncertain influence on judges, he resolutely maintained that a realistic study of the law demanded an examination of the extent to which the rules actually controlled or influenced the case. "You cannot generalize on this, *without investigation.*" If men were ever to understand the legal system, they would have to study individual cases empirically. "The significance of the particular rule," he stressed, "will appear only *after* the investigation of the vital, focal phenomenon: the behavior." [23]

Llewellyn's empirical approach concentrated on behavior as the proper subject of study for the legal scholar. Behavior was real, whereas most legal argumentation was simply verbal game playing. Following Holmes's lead, Llewellyn defined law in terms of the coercive actions taken by government officials. Regardless of syllogisms and definitions, the actual law was what the public force would support. "*What these officials do about disputes,*" Llewellyn wrote in a sentence that returned to haunt him, "*is, to my mind, the law itself.*" [24] Given such a definition, the whole legal process was clearly susceptible to empirical study. Again following Holmes, Llewellyn declared that concepts of justice and ethical right had to be ignored when the actual operations of the law were analyzed. Such concepts merely confused the investigator by mixing considerations of "ought" where only the realities of "is" were relevant. "The most fruitful thinking about law," he remarked, "has run steadily toward regarding law as an engine (a heterogeneous multitude of engines) having purposes, not values in itself." [25] Happily acknowledging his intellectual debt, Llewellyn proclaimed that "Holmes has provided every man possessing eyes with vision." [26]

Accepting most of Llewellyn's ideas, Frank went far beyond them in earning his reputation as one of the most extreme realists. Whereas Llewellyn believed that rules and precedents were relevant and of some importance, Frank did not even consider them a meaningful part of the law. "The rules are incidental, the decisions are the thing." [27] To him law meant a particular judicial determination upon a particular and singular set of facts. Reducing law to what he considered an unequivocal empirical minimum, Frank equated it solely with the specific individual judicial decision. "Until a court has passed on these facts," he insisted, "no law on that subject is yet in existence."[28] The characteristic particularism of the twenties and thirties had received its full legal statement.

Rules and precedents were not part of the law because they had little if any effect on actual judicial decisions. No one could reason out a decision by syllogism, Frank declared. Instead judges had "hunches" about how cases should be decided and then looked up the proper rules to support their "hunches." "Judicial judgments, like other judgments," he maintained, "doubtless in most cases, are worked out backward from conclusions tentatively formulated."[29] A judicial opinion was actually only the judge's rationalization, not the real explanation for his decision. Judges manipulated precedents in the same way: after making a decision, they sought favorable precedents or reinterpreted unfavorable ones to support it. "What the courts in fact do," Frank charged, "is to manipulate the language of former decisions."[30] As it had in Llewellyn's work, the word-thing dichotomy centrally informed the approach of *Law and the Modern Mind*.

In addition to personal prejudices, Frank argued, judicial objectivity was further deflected by the necessity of relying on secondhand evidence concerning the facts, relayed by lawyers, parties to the case, and witnesses who distorted the facts through prejudice, misunderstanding, ignorance, or simple falsification. The facts of any case were thus necessarily elusive and essentially subjective. Not legal rules or precedents, but the judge's concept of justice and his social and political prejudices decided cases. Not concrete, objective facts, but what one or twelve biased and fallible observers took to be the facts determined the outcome of any trial. "The coefficient of legal uncertainty is unquestionably large," Frank concluded. Not even empirical study of actual decisions could make it wholly clear and certain. "To predict the decisions of the courts on many a point is impossible."[31]

In spite of the practical uncertainty and subjectivity, he continued, most lawyers and judges still insisted that the law was essentially rational and certain. The explanation for that contradiction, Frank suggested, lay in what he called the "legal absolutist" mind. The father-child pattern, bred deeply during every individual's childhood, drove most men continually to seek some powerful authority figure which would act as a substitute for the "Father-as-Infallible-Judge."[32] Because the law served as a natural authority figure, it subconsciously stimulated the latent childish emotions of those who studied it. "We would seem to be justified in surmising that the subject-matter of the law is one which evokes, almost irresistibly, regressive emotions."[33] That subconscious drive prevented most lawyers and judges from recognizing the true nature of the legal system.

The manipulation of abstract concepts provided the method by which lawyers and judges constructed a facade of certainty and absolute rationality over the confused legal process. Referring to such manipulation as "platonism" and "Scholasticism," Frank charged that the absolutists used "magical phrases" to convince themselves that all was well and to rationalize awkward facts. Such abstractions were merely escapes and delusions. "Virtually empty concepts," he remarked, "seem to give to the metaphysician the stable world he requires."[34] Because the concepts were empirically empty—they bore no definite or constant relation to any concrete reality—they were liable to almost any imaginable interpretation. In such a way lawyers were able to reconcile completely contradictory judicial decisions as "logical" under the same principle or precedent.

Although he declared that the great majority of men believed in the certainty of law, Frank was primarily interested in, and hostile toward, traditional legal theories and their contemporary advocates who controlled the bench and bar. Using a technique reminiscent of that of Veblen, Frank on several occasions remarked in footnotes or appendices that his psychoanalytic approach provided only a partial explanation for the legal quest for certainty. But after making that qualification in obscure places, he continued in the text to write as if that approach were the only explanation. Indeed, while consistently proclaiming lawyers and judges highly intelligent and learned men, he described them throughout as immature, childish, and irrational.

The solution to the problems that plagued American jurisprudence, Frank argued, was quite simply for men to grow up. When they recognized that the law was an unconscious substitute for the just and absolute father, they would be able to throw off their irrational demands for a logical and certain legal system. Their thinking would then be fully adult, accepting change readily, welcoming doubt as healthy, and enjoying challenges to old conventions and beliefs. Those attitudes were the exact opposite of the ones associated with the traditional legal mind. "They are the attitudes of the so-called scientific mind," Frank pointed out,

". . . which we may now translate as the emotionally adult or mature mind."[35] It was indeed fitting that he ended his book with an extended tribute to the influence, insight, and maturity of Mr. Justice Holmes, "The Completely Adult Jurist."

The two works by Frank and Llewellyn had an immediate impact. Pound, then dean of the Harvard Law School and the most renowned legal scholar in America, responded early in 1931, ironically in an issue of the *Harvard Law Review* dedicated to Justice Holmes on his ninetieth birthday. Although Pound had earlier espoused many of the views associated with realism, by 1931 he had become wary of some of the more radical implications of pragmatism and skepticism in the law. He was perhaps additionally moved to reply by the fact that both Llewellyn and Frank had specifically attacked his work on juristic theory. Undoubtedly having Frank most clearly in mind, Pound accused an unnamed group of "realists" of allowing their naive faith in empiricism to lead them into a philosophical nominalism that denied the existence of legal rules, doctrines, principles, and concepts. They overemphasized irregularities and contradictions and ignored the uniformity and reasonableness of the law. By focusing on subjective motives and the behavior of judges, Pound asserted, the realists were leading legal science into a dead end.[36]

Considering his attack unfair, Llewellyn and Frank replied jointly and asserted that Pound's criticisms were almost wholly unwarranted. The importance of the reply was that Llewellyn and Frank gathered together and defended twenty of the better-known critics who, they explained, could be taken as a fair sample of the new approach to the law. While emphasizing that the twenty represented no "school" and were by no means in complete agreement in their own attitudes, Llewellyn and Frank admitted that their criticisms of existing legal theory sprang from similar attitudes. By the end of 1931 the new critics had been attacked and defended, and, most important, they had been personally identified and categorized.[37]

Frank alone had attempted a sweeping psychoanalytic interpretation, but he and Llewellyn had agreed on several key points. They assumed that human knowledge could never be certain and uniformly logical and that law was a constantly changing phenomenon. They denounced abstract verbal formulas and absolutes as the bane of clear thinking, legal or otherwise. They agreed that the "is" and the "ought" should be temporarily separated for the purpose of precise study. Finally Llewellyn and Frank were united in calling for careful empirical studies of the way the law actually operated in society, sharply questioning the practical impact of legal rules and suggesting that judicial logic was in large part rationalization.

Because of their concern with the practical operation of the legal process, the realists looked to their colleagues in the social sciences for useful methods and hypotheses. As the law school most closely allied with realism, Yale developed the most elaborate program for a reformed legal education. The law library added a large amount of social science material to its holdings, and the school encouraged younger faculty members to study the social sciences at New Haven or elsewhere. Additionally the law school added several social scientists to its regular faculty, including Walter J. Dodd, an expert on state government, the institutional economist Walton Hamilton, and the psychologists Donald Slesinger and Edward S. Robinson. In 1928 the law school joined with the medical school, the Institute of Psychology, and the social science departments to form the Yale Institute of Human Relations. For the Yale realists the new Institute seemed an ideal way to start converting the law into a full-fledged social science.[38]

Economics, statistics, and psychology elicited the greatest interest from the legal critics. "When one approaches the law, not with the idea of formulating its rules into a system, but with an eye to discovering how much it does or can effect . . . ," Llewellyn acknowledged, "economic theory offers in many respects amazing light."[39] He called special attention to John R. Commons's institutionalist study, *Legal Foundations of Capitalism*, as an example of how much economics and law could learn from one another. When in 1932 Adolph A. Berle, Jr., and Gardiner C. Means published *The Modern Corporation and Private Property*, a study of the interrelated legal and economic methods of corporate control, they brought to brilliant fruition many of the pleas for such interdisciplinary research.[40]

The realist enthusiasm for adopting social science techniques in legal study led to a comparable interest in the new statistical methodology. Yntema maintained that a "system of judicial statistics" was one of the major prerequisites for a scientific study of the law and pointed to some of the preliminary steps that were being taken to establish such a system.[41] "There is reason to believe," declared Leon C. Marshall, a member of the Johns Hopkins Institute, "that the time is ripe for a definite advance in securing a flow of reliable comparable data in the judicial field."[42] In arguing for the subjectivity of judicial decisions, Frank pointed gleefully to a statistical study of judges in the New York City Magistrate's Court, which he asserted had been discontinued because it revealed the great divergence between judges in dealing with comparable offenses. "The bench and bar," Frank exclaimed, "did not want to have called to their attention the extent to which judging is affected by the temperament, training, biases and predilections of the respective judges."[43] Statistical studies would clearly prove such subjectivity, he argued, and hence prove much of the realists' case.

Because of their focus on the problems of judicial motivation, psychology held a special interest for the new critics. A large literature on legal psychology grew during the twenties, with behaviorism, Freudianism, and abnormal psychology all playing a role.[44] The nature of the law was such, declared Edward S. Robinson, that "all of the more basic principles involved must be psychological."[45] Underhill Moore made the most elaborate attempt to work out a behavioral system for studying and predicting judicial decisions, while other realists attempted to apply the insights of modern psychology to such problems as the rules of evidence.[46] "It will be helpful," suggested Donald Slesinger, "to start with the hypotheses of legal students and develop a set of rigidly defined behavior units that can be reliably observed."[47]

The realists were especially sympathetic to the new social science because they shared many of its assumptions. They were wholly naturalistic in their approach to the problems of knowledge, and they continually emphasized the empirical basis of all human knowledge. "We are to re define the concepts of abstract thought," Felix Cohen declared, "as constructs, or functions, or complexes, or patterns, or arrangements, of things that we do actually see or do."[48] Though some, like Frank, were skeptical about attaining any completely objective knowledge, they hoped to make the study of the law as objective as possible. The separation between the "is" and the "ought" for research purposes proclaimed that desire. If the process of judicial decision proved in fact to be subjective, ignoring the fact would accomplish nothing.

Sharp hostility toward abstractions and generalizations tied them closely to the characteristic particularism of the period. "Realism," Radin declared, "is the sworn foe of conceptualism as a legal ideal."[49] Abstract and mystic concepts were the major obstacle to any attempt at realistic analysis. "Naturally we have come to feel that our materials in the social sciences are illusive," Oliphant commented. "Just so would the botanist if, through his pages, wood-nymphs and satyrs still paraded."[50] The legal confusion that helped call forth the American Law Institute was not to be remedied by larger and more comprehensive generalizations, Oliphant insisted. It was rather the proliferation of such "obscurant abstractions" that had caused the confusion in the first place. The only satisfactory solution lay in the return to a rigorous emphasis on sharp, specific precedents marked by "an ever greater and greater particularity."[51] As with many of their social science colleagues, the realists had use only for ideas directly referable to something concrete and specific.

Although the realists were firm believers in democratic government, the empirical naturalism they embraced and attempted to apply to legal theory raised both practical and theoretical questions about the nature of democratic government. The most important practical point of their argument was questioning and in many cases rejecting the idea of a government of laws rather than of men. Most democratic legal theories—and many state constitutions—held that established and known laws alone should be binding on free citizens; the realists maintained that such laws were nonexistent and impossible to attain. Frank had argued that law was uncertain in administration and depended largely on the subjective motivations of the individual judge who heard the case. "It is fantastic, then," he had declared, "to say that usually men can warrantably act in reliance upon 'established law.' "[52]

Judge Joseph C. Hutcheson asserted that all judges reached their decisions by "hunches" based on an "intuitive flash of understanding" that revealed the proper decision in a case. He was referring, Hutcheson pointed out, not to the rationalization or the "logomachy" that the judge used to explain his opinion, but to the actual way in which he decided a case. "The vital, motivating impulse for the decision," he remarked, "is an intuitive sense of what is right or wrong for that case."[53] Pointing to the number of conflicting rules that could apply to any case, Radin argued that personal motivation was an unavoidable part of judicial judgments. "Since a choice implies motives," he explained, "it is obvious that, somewhere, somehow, a judge is impelled to make his selection—not quite freely, as we have seen, but within generous limits as a rule—by those psychical elements which make him the kind of person that he is." Regardless of the undesirable implications, that interpretation was empiri-

88

cally true. "That this is pure subjectivism and therefore an unfortunate situation is beside the point."[54]

Though admitting that the judge was not free to be wholly arbitrary, largely because he necessarily shared the value standards of at least an important part of the community, the realists maintained that the personal element was paramount. "Of the many things which have been said as to the mystery of the judicial process," Yntema argued, "the most salient is that decision is reached after an emotive experience in which principles and logic play a secondary part." The very fact that a case was contested meant that there were rules, principles, and precedents purporting to support both sides. The private motives and values of the judge, not the existence of rules, or even constitutions, provided the key to understanding the law. "The ideal of a government of laws and not of men," Yntema concluded, "is a dream."[55]

The rejection of the orthodox theory of judicial decision was the central point of the realist critique, and it relied heavily on non-Euclidean assumptions. Walter Wheeler Cook, one of the founders of the Johns Hopkins Institute of Law, helped to introduce his colleagues to the new advances in logic and geometry. Having received his early training as a physicist, Cook looked to the established physical sciences for much of his methodological inspiration. "The development of these new types of geometry, each one of which has developed by deduction from its set of postulates," he explained in 1927, "has played an important part in bringing about a revolution in our ideas as to the scope of mathematics and of the function of deductive logic in the search for scientific truth." Citing Cassius J. Keyser, Gilbert Lewis, and other non-Euclidean popularizers, Cook emphasized the strictly formal and, to him, rather trivial nature of deductive logic. The logician, he remarked, could state that "All gostaks are doshes, All doshes are galloons." Then, quite properly and flawlessly, the logician could deduce that "All gostaks are galloons." Although the statement was logically unassailable, Cook commented, it proved nothing. Whether all doshes were in fact galloons was certainly questionable; whether there were actually any gostaks in reality was also unknown. Men could know reality only by concrete investigation and experiment. Relying only on logic, "we do not know what we are talking about."[56]

Frank, Oliphant, Yntema, Felix Cohen, and others shared that non-Euclidean assumption and elaborated it as a crucial part of their theory of judicial decision. Assuming the geometric analogy, Felix Cohen equated the allegedly clear rules of the older jurisprudence with "theorems in an independent system." Since they were neither descriptions of concrete reality nor conscious statements of ethical ideals, they could be nothing but definitions in "an autonomous system," that is, in a kind of geometry.[57] As such, orthodox jurisprudence might have been self-consistent, but it had no necessary relevance to the actual process of judicial decision. In fact, the realists insisted, practical applicability was precisely what it lacked.

Judicial judgment was logically indeterminable, not just because of the nature of human psychology, but because of the nature of logic itself. First, since deduction could neither produce nor validate any substantive principle, no legal rule could possess any intrinsic or necessary logical validity. "Recent studies, both in logic and in ethics," declared Felix S. Cohen, the most knowledgeable logician among the realists, "have made it clear that any claim that 'logic supports' any legal rule (or any other judgment about human conduct) must be false."[58] Second, because a judicial decision was a practical matter and not one of tautological implication, it could be the result of no logically necessary reasoning. "To say that a given judgment is required by logic," Felix Cohen explained, "is to affirm that no other judgment could have been given by any man possessed of reason."[59] It was to affirm, in other words, that the judgment was one of tautological implication. Accepting the non-Euclidean dichotomy between tautological, self-consistent deduction on the one hand and experimental, empirical induction on the other, the realists readily concluded that logic could have no determining influence on a case. Non-Euclideanism led them to equate a logical reason with a logically necessary reason, and, failing to discover the necessity, they rejected logic as a determinant altogether. Third, since deduction necessarily proceeded from arbitrarily selected postulates, then every judge had to select his first premise, or rule of the case, in a way that was logically wholly indeterminate and therefore arbitrary. "We now can see that the choice between the legal principles competing to control the new human situations involved in the cases we pass upon," Oliphant summarized, "is not dictated by logic."[60] Judicial decisions, then, had to be the result of some unacknowledged inductive process, which could only mean the subjective way that the judge evaluated the probable social results of his decision.

Morris R. Cohen, a philosopher at the City College of New York, and an often sympathetic and occasionally harsh critic of realism, pointed to what he considered the antidemocratic implication of such a judicial theory. "To be ruled by a judge," he declared, "is, to the extent that he is not bound by law, tyranny or despotism."[61] When the realists said that every judge's decisions were necessarily subjective, and that those decisions were the only law, Cohen charged, they were justifying judicial despotism and political authoritarianism.

At that point, the theoretical force of the realist critique became clear, for it rejected any concept of a higher law that could provide judges with objective, rational guidance to assure a just operative law. A pervasive scientific naturalism that seemed to undermine any rationally determinable or absolute moral standard underlay the realist assumptions. Llewellyn, Frank, and the others had all assailed deductive rationalism and scorned all absolutes. Their determination to make concrete empirical facts the touchstone for all analytical concepts seemed necessarily to exclude ideas of "ought" in favor of facts about "is." If what men ought to do was not identical with what they did in fact, then there was no basis in the realist approach for discussing moral concepts except as mere psychological data. It would, in any case, be impossible to establish the objective validity of any such ethical values.

Some of the realists explicitly avowed a sweeping relativism. Cook maintained that human knowledge had "reached the era of relativity." By relativity, he explained, he meant "a point of view, which, whatever may happen to specific doctrines, seems destined to remain as a permanent achievement in human thought."[62] Neither legal nor moral theory could escape that era. Moore similarly rejected the idea of absolutes. "Ultimates are phantoms drifting upon the stream of day dreams." Arguing for a pragmatic standard of judgment, he insisted that "human experience discloses no ultimates."[63]

Walter Nelles, a young professor at Yale, carried the rejection to its extreme. "I deny ethical *right* and *ought* without qualification," he declared in 1933. Not restricting his denial to systems of absolute or transcendental ethics, Nelles denied just as forcefully the possibility of a scientific ethical system. Any attempt to leap from an "is" to an "ought" was both logically and empirically a complete "non-sequitur." Fortunately, he explained, the moral assumptions of the past that demanded a belief in some kind of ethical standard were fast disappearing. "In the twentieth century," Nelles declared, "popular feeling of the wickedness of

91

denying ethical *right* and *ought* can no longer command the unconscious deference of an important mind." [64]

The pragmatism and apparent ethical relativism of men like Cook, Moore, and Nelles shocked much of the legal profession. Although the counterattack did not reach its bitterest phase until after 1935, it had clearly begun by the early thirties. John Dickinson, a professor of law at the University of Pennsylvania and one of Pound's most prominent disciples, criticized the realists for dismissing the importance of legal rules in the judicial process. Hermann Kantorowicz, a professor at the New School for Social Research, pointed to philosophical and epistemological inconsistencies in the realist approach. Basically they agreed that the realists had made a contribution to juristic analysis, but maintained that they had gone too far in focusing on the uncertainty and subjectivity of the law and had overemphasized the place of behavioral research. [65]

Morris Cohen and Mortimer Adler criticized the realists from the viewpoint of philosophy, insisting on the need for objective standards of judgment beyond mere empirical facts. The realists, Cohen argued, "do away altogether with the normative point of view in law." [66] He insisted that legal science had the obligation to be normative, and that the realists had overlooked that fundamental difference between legal and physical science. Adler charged that the new critics were ignorant of the values of deductive logic and argued that there was a rational "law in discourse," which men could know with certainty and use as a standard to judge the practical "law as official action." Frank drew his special condemnation as "a splendid illustration" of the weaknesses of American jurisprudence. [67]

Though most of the criticism directed at legal realism before 1935 was discriminating and often technical, such scholars as Pound, Adler, and Morris Cohen pointed to the challenge the new movement posed for traditional democratic ideas. By excluding ethical considerations and reverting to a philosophical nominalism, some suggested, the realists were necessarily destroying the ethical basis of democracy and making force the only meaningful arbiter of human affairs. Explaining the source and character of natural law, the Reverend Charles C. Miltner of Notre Dame claimed that its principles could determine the intrinsic ethical quality of all human actions. "This basis of moral judgment is objective," he declared, "and therefore free from the inevitable variations and inconsistencies of purely subjective standards." [68] Such an objective norm was necessary, he suggested, to provide the moral foundation and justification for democratic government.

To harm the cause of democratic government was the last thing the realists wished to do. In attacking traditional abstractions and nonempirical concepts of justice, they were usually assailing what they considered the practical injustices of American society. Abstraction in economics and politics, as in the law, they believed, had been one of the biggest obstacles to the attainment of a truly democratic society. Frank, Oliphant, Clark, Arnold, Douglas, and Felix Cohen all became ardent New Dealers, sharing a strong hostility to the method of juristic reasoning that struck down social welfare laws and wrought what they considered great human injustices. Most of the other realists expressed equally strong disapproval of the social and economic situation in the thirties, and they viewed themselves as fighting to extend democratic social values. The new criticism was thus not intentionally hostile toward the idea of democratic government. As early as 1931 Frank defended the realists against charges that they excluded ethical considerations from the law. "The point is," he retorted, "that the rational and ethical factors are thwarted in their operations by the conventional tendency to ignore the non-rational and non-ethical factors." [69] The problem was not whether there was something abstract called justice, but rather how human relations could be made more just in practice. Though the theoretical problems the realists raised left them open to bitter and telling attack, the obtuse formalism of American constitutional interpretation throughout the first third of the twentieth century helped drive them to their extreme positions. The manifest human needs created by the depression further convinced them of the necessity for a more realistic and flexible legal theory.

Like most of the philosophers and social scientists who shared the same basic assumptions, the realists were driven by the twin motives of intellectual discovery and social improvement. They hoped to understand the legal process in a new and more useful manner, and they hoped to see both political and legal reform flow from their discoveries.[70] They readily recognized the fundamental importance of moral ideals and values in human society and consciously hoped to see them reach greater practical fulfillment. "It is no evidence that a student of law is deficient in moral sense," Oliphant declared, "if he merely observes and records the uniformities of social behavior with which the law is concerned." [71]

93

As with their colleagues in philosophy and the social sciences, however, the realists' motives could not explain away the intellectual problems they generated. Intentionally or not, their theoretical position raised two basic questions about traditional democratic theory. First, how could the idea of the subjectivity of judicial decision be squared with the doctrine that free men should be subject only to known and established law, one of the hallmarks of republican as opposed to despotic government? Second, if the acts of government officials were the only real law, on what basis could anyone evaluate or criticize those acts? What, in other words, was the moral basis of the legal system in particular and of democratic government in general? Most revealingly, Felix Cohen, who alone among the realists attempted an elaborate analysis of ethical theory, admitted that his conclusions remained "in the shadow" of doubt and bordered on failure.[72] That was an unsatisfactory solution to almost everyone after the middle thirties.

6

The New Study of Politics

While new movements in law were challenging the orthodox interpretation of the legal process, students of American politics were simultane-
ously undermining other pillars of democratic theory. Sharing the general
intellectual assumptions that characterized the legal realists and most
social scientists, political analysts turned toward a scientific study of the
governmental process. In addition to raising the same theoretical problem
about the ethical justification of democracy, their new approaches directly
challenged two central assumptions of traditional theory, the rationality
of human nature and the practical possibility of a government of or by
the people.

Under the leadership of such scholars as Charles E. Merriam, Harold D. Lasswell, and George E. G. Catlin, political scientists increasingly
emphasized the need to achieve a true science of politics by close empirical
studies of political behavior. While the debate raged over methodology
and orientation, by the middle twenties those advocating a more rigor-
ously empirical approach dominated the field. "The great need of the
hour," declared Arnold Bennett Hall, the chairman of the National Conference on the Science of Politics, "is the development of a scientific
technique and methodology for political science."[1] The complexity of
political affairs made them difficult and cumbersome to study, acknowledged another political scientist. "But the scientific as distinguished from
the a priori method of approach," he concluded, "becomes the more essential because of these very difficulties."[2] That approach, most political
scientists agreed, was objective and morally neutral. "Nothing is more
liable to lead astray," declared A. Gordon Dewey of Columbia University,
"than the injection of moral considerations into an essentially non-moral,
factual investigation."[3]

Political science, declared Merriam, "must be founded upon a study
of the political process out of which institutions are made, as well as a
description of their external features or their operation."[4] Since philo-

sophical problems concerning moral ideals were not susceptible to scientific treatment, the functional approach led directly to a special interest in the idea of power. In 1934 Merriam published his *Political Power*, a major study which assumed that the central reality of society was the ability of small groups to dominate and control the majority of the population. "In political power situations," he explained, "there appears a type of force through which masses of human beings are manipulated as if by some magnetic attraction or aversion."[5] The proper subject for a true science of politics was the actual exercise and use of that compelling force.

Lasswell took the same approach. His work, "restricted to political analysis, declares no preferences," he insisted. "It states conditions." Since natural science strove to state the objective realities of physical cause-effect relationships, political science could only probe the objective realities of analogous human cause-effect relationships, which meant the exercise by some of determinant power over others. "The study of politics," he declared, "is the study of influence and the influential."[6] Lasswell appropriately entitled his book *Politics: Who Gets What, When, How*. "The political element in human life," summarized another scholar, "is necessarily one of human relations and deals primarily with those relations as affected by power—control exercised by some over others whether it be purely governmental control or not."[7] Catlin stated it even more directly. "Ultimately politics resolves itself into a question of power."[8]

Focusing on process and power, political scientists increasingly studied the tactics and influence of organized pressure groups. Close, firsthand observation of pressure group behavior, explained Leonard D. White, would produce a political science that was "realistic, objective, and impartial."[9] Such groups, predominantly though not exclusively economic, provided obvious, empirical units for analysis and allowed scholars to explain American politics as the result of a balancing of power relations. "Public policy," E. E. Schattschneider maintained, "is the result of 'effective demands' upon the government."[10] There was almost a vector metaphor underlying the pressure group approach.

The desire for a truly scientific methodology created the same enthusiasms in political science that it had in other fields. "Unquestionably," Merriam declared, "the new politics will involve wider use than ever before of statistics and of psychology."[11] Recent conferences among political scientists, Hall pointed out, clearly suggested a general agreement "that scientific progress in politics can be greatly facilitated by more intimate knowledge of the contributions of psychology and statistics to scientific method." [12] Those with a strong behavioral emphasis in their work, such as Catlin, Floyd H. Allport, and Stuart Rice, emphasized the methodological unity between the two approaches. "A socio-political-psychology, quantitative in method," Rice insisted, "is the goal with respect to which orientation is sought." [13]

Harold F. Gosnell, a colleague of Merriam's at Chicago, was one of the first to employ statistical tools as the basis of political studies, and throughout the twenties and thirties he urged others to follow his lead. [14] Because of its objective appeal, its quantitative nature, and its institutional importance, voting behavior became an early concern of the political statisticians. Rice and Herman C. Beyle developed indices to discover the relative cohesion between identifiable groups within legislatures. [15] L. L. Thurstone, one of the leading innovators in the field of attitude measurement, refined techniques of multiple factor analysis for the more precise and specific identification of various types of voting blocs. [16] Gordon Allport, F. Stuart Chapin, and E. V. Huntington were among those who attempted to expand further the application of statistics to other kinds of political problems. [17] Such methodological advances, most agreed, were the most promising road to scientific objectivity. "The care exercised," proclaimed one political statistician in 1933, "has eliminated any question regarding either the author's preconceptions or possible errors in judgment." [18]

As great as was the interest in statistics, it did not match the enthusiasm for the new psychology. While it would not quickly solve all the problems of political science, Merriam proclaimed, it nevertheless offered "golden possibilities to the student of the social sciences." [19] Perhaps Merriam's greatest single influence was in generating the enthusiasm for psychology that spread through American political science during the twenties and thirties. He continually proclaimed his confidence "in the possibilities of the rising science of political psychology." [20] In his position as chairman of the Chicago department, he encouraged his colleagues, especially Gosnell and Lasswell, to examine the relationship between political institutions and psychological discoveries.

Merriam was not alone in his enthusiasm for psychology. John A. Fairlie, a professor at the University of Illinois and managing editor of the *American Political Science Review*, told his colleagues that the study of politics demanded a wide knowledge of the latest developments in the new field. Charles E. Gehlke of Western Reserve University examined the relationship between social psychology and political theory, while Horace M. Kallen, a political philosopher lecturing at the New School for Social Research, declared simply that "living political science never was anything but psychology."[21] In both 1924 and 1925 roundtable discussions held by the Association seemed to agree, and the newly established Committee on Psychology and Political Science recommended joint meetings with the American Psychological Association.[22] By the late twenties the importance of psychology was widely acknowledged and enjoyed a greater acceptance in political science than in any of the other social sciences.

While many political scientists rushed to embrace the allied discipline, however, a sharp and ominous debate was raging among psychologists themselves. During the First World War the army had given intelligence tests to more than 1,700,000 enlisted men. The results startled many people, for they apparently showed that 60 to 70 per cent of the soldiers had a shockingly low level of intelligence. The results were especially upsetting because the army had dismissed everyone identified as feebleminded before giving the tests, so that the group that took the tests supposedly represented an above-average sample of the population.

As soon as the results were made public a vigorous debate broke out over the reliability of the tests and the implications of the scores. One group, led by the psychologists Lewis M. Terman, Edwin G. Boring, and William S. McDougall, maintained that the tests were valid and that the results proved the low intelligence of the majority of Americans. McDougall, a respected psychologist at Harvard, was most insistent in arguing that the tests proved that democracy was a dangerous and debilitating form of government. Combining the test scores with a strident Nordic racism, he declared that the United States was "speeding gaily, with invincible optimism, down the road to destruction."[23] Civilizations were built upon a definite racial stock, and when that stock degenerated, the civilization would collapse. Negroes and non-Teutonic immigrants were changing the composition of the American people and bringing the country to the point of decay. "If nature has made men of unequal value, the cruelty is hers, not ours," he noted. "We do no wrong in ascertaining and recording the facts."[24]

The widespread movement after World War I to crossbreed the insights of psychology and political science came at a time inauspicious for democratic theory. The dominant movements in psychology since the turn of the century rejected the idea of the rational man, one of the central postulates of democracy. Americans were becoming more and more familiar with such European thinkers as Sigmund Freud, Carl G. Jung, Jean Piaget, and Pierre Janet who emphasized the idea of the unconscious and man's irrationality. By the twenties their ideas had become common currency among educated Americans. Additionally the physiological psychology of Edward L. Thorndike and John Watson's behaviorism seemed to many to debase the human mind by robbing it of any intellectual freedom and making it merely a mechanical function of the body. By emphasizing the stimulus-response mechanism behaviorism closed the gap between human and animal nature and suggested that man's mind exercised little or no independent reason.

A large number of writers, both scholars and popularizers, increasingly emphasized the predominance of irrational motivation in the years after World War I. In the normal person the "conscious mind usually does little more," explained one writer, "than supply him with reasonable explanations for unreasonable actions and opinions which his unconscious mind has dictated."[25] Pushed by such scholars as Charles A. Ellwood, H. E. Cunningham, William Fielding Ogburn, Carleton H. Parker, and many others, Freudian ideas spread into the social sciences.[26] The historian James Harvey Robinson asserted that human actions were determined by subconscious prejudices and that "most of our so-called reasoning consists in finding arguments for going on believing as we already do."[27] By 1930 the concept of the irrational was informing much of American social thought. "The shift in emphasis from rational to irrational motivation is a contribution of the first order to our understanding," explained Beardsley Ruml, "and it is affecting profoundly the social sciences."[28]

Furthermore, while psychology was emphasizing the irrational or nonrational, social theorists in Europe had been examining the implications of nonrational ideas for political society and drawing conclusions that questioned the possibility of democratic government. In the 1890s two French thinkers, Gabriel Tarde and Gustave Le Bon, had argued that human political behavior stemmed from irrational motivations of mass suggestibility and unconscious emotional drives. Democracy, Le Bon pointed out, stimulated crowd behavior, mass emotionalism, and demogogic political leaders. During the first decade of the twentieth century the widely read English political theorist Graham Wallas demonstrated the importance of human psychology for understanding political behavior. Because of the inability of most men to act reasonably and wisely in making public decisions, he concluded that popular government was difficult and dangerous. When Walter Lippmann followed many of Wallas's suggestions and attempted to apply Freud to political theory in *A Preface to Politics* (1912), he argued that the best human society would be one in which a few intelligent leaders directed the majority into wise and satisfying channels of action.

After the war those intellectual forces combined with a virulent nationalism and a rekindled nativism in the United States to cause an upsurge in open and purposeful antidemocratic and racist thought. Men such as Madison Grant, Lothrop Stoddard, Alleyne Ireland, and Charles W. Gould popularized the idea of Nordic racial superiority and warned against the imminent dangers of race corruption. "In a democracy like ours the character of the government depends chiefly on the character of the people," Ireland wrote. "The character of the people is determined chiefly through the operation of biological laws."[29] Those laws, he pointed out, condemned democracy as an inefficient and undesirable form of government. Although many scientists, among them Franz Boas and Edwin Grant Conklin, defended democracy on anthropological and biological grounds, the idea of racial inequality enjoyed a renewed scientific vogue in the twenties and appealed to a large number of scholars and pseudoscholars.

In addition to attracting such popularizers as Harry Fuller Atwood, H. L. Mencken, Ralph Adams Cram, Irving Babbitt, and Everett D. Martin, racist and antidemocratic ideas spread among social scientists. Such widely respected psychologists as Robert M. Yerkes and Carl C. Brigham, both of whom had helped prepare the army tests, finally succumbed after having initially rejected the racial interpretation. Drawing upon the work of Grant and Gould, Yerkes, a past president of the American Psychological Association, began to see the results of his testing research as definite empirical support for the idea of racial inequality. Brigham, too, turned to the idea of race when he wrote *A Study of American Intelligence*. "The intellectual superiority of our Nordic group over the Alpine, Mediterranean and negro groups," he concluded, "has been demonstrated."[30]

Harry Elmer Barnes, a professor of sociology at Smith College, maintained that "differential psychology has proved the intellectual inferiority of the masses." Empirical study of actual political behavior revealed dangerous weaknesses in popular government, he declared, for "social psychology has further demonstrated the difficulty of securing rational behavior in political life."[31] Two years earlier Barnes had carried those attitudes to their logical conclusion. Psychology and the social sciences had "given scientific confirmation," he claimed, "to the old Aristotelian dogma that some men are born to rule and others to serve."[32] When Gosnell examined the practical applications of psychology to government, he suggested the possibility of tests to distinguish "good citizens" from bad, to serve as a scientific basis for limited disenfranchisement. Psychologists could prepare the tests, he commented, after political scientists had determined the standards of good citizenship.[33] Even Merriam, though convinced that there was yet no scientific basis for a condemnation of democracy, admitted that students of government would have to be aware of the possibility.[34]

Although most social scientists soon rejected the racial doctrines, psychological analysis and empirical research continued relentlessly to challenge the ideal of popular government throughout the twenties and early thirties. As the concepts of the irrational and subconscious became more widely known in America, psychologists and students of government applied them to the processes of political behavior with greater confidence and certainty. When they combined the psychological approach with empirical observations of the way American government actually operated, they developed a powerful and deadly critique of the democratic ideal.

Elton Mayo, an Australian who came to the United States after the First World War, helped develop the growing discipline of social and industrial psychology, first at the Wharton School of Finance and Commerce, and after 1925 at Harvard. The studies of neurosis and shell shock made during the war heightened his interest in psychological analysis and led him to examine what he considered the irrational causes of social conflict. Familiar with the latest theory in the field, especially that of Freud and Janet, Mayo saw the irrational and subconscious behind most of the problems of modern society. "Whenever groups of men and women are gathered together," he declared, "it will be found that this partially concealed irrationality, more than any other mental factor, is determining their group attitude and behavior."[35]

101

Mayo distinguished between what he called the "night-mind" and the "day-mind." The former described the attitude of impatience and terror in the human being confronted with a world he saw as ominous and uncontrollable. Fear and ignorance led to the formulation of magic and witchcraft, which gave men the illusion of control and security. Dominating the nether region of the subconscious, the "night-mind" still controlled many areas of modern society. "Even people of education, in the ordinary sense," he remarked, "are still far more dominated by magic and the night-mind than by clear thinking." As a result, social affairs were often controlled by the irrational. "The night-mind plays a very large part in our social, political and industrial affairs."[36] Democratic politics merely exacerbated that basic problem, hindering the chance for real solutions to problems as well as prospects for peaceful government. "The plain fact is that class obsessions are continually cultivated in the name of democratic self-government, and these recurrent disorders are their product."[37]

Lasswell elaborated Mayo's approach when he began his study of propaganda techniques used during the war. Recognizing that propaganda had become a major subject of study, he maintained that such interest testified to the collapse of a naive faith in democratic government throughout the world. "Familiarity with the ruling public," he remarked in 1927, "had bred contempt." Discussions of democracy since the war generally concluded that the old democratic ideal was a delusion. As a result, democratic politicians tried to preserve the fiction in theory, while in practice they would "inform, cajole, bamboozle and seduce in the name of the public good."[38]

Lasswell went beyond Mayo's emphasis on the irrational and attempted to apply the data of psychoanalysis directly to the political process. Arguing that the fundamental ingredient of politics was human behavior, Lasswell believed that the insights of psychoanalysis could reveal the hidden sources of political action. Encouraged in this endeavor by Merriam, he did special work with Mayo at Harvard while preparing his research.

Basing his hypotheses on the case histories of a number of political agitators and administrators who had received psychoanalytic treatment, Lasswell argued that deep psychological motivations lay behind the careers, ideologies, and tactics of men engaged in political action. In order to help control or give vent to their deep hatreds and drives, these men tended to transfer them from the initial family object or personal desire out of which they had developed to objects and symbols of a public nature. By such a transfer men were able to indulge their psychological drives and release their emotional feelings in a way that they could not have done with the original objects. Thus, he explained, hatred of the father easily became hatred of the state or of some other authority figure. To admit that one hated his father would cause disturbing guilt feelings, but no such censure was attached to the hatred of some symbol of public authority. Lasswell's key point was that attitudes toward questions of public policy were largely the result of a subconscious emotional drive stemming from purely personal and private experiences. Once they had made the transfer, men rationalized their psychological motivations by the use of some commonly accepted political argument. "Political movements, then, derive their vitality from the displacement of private affects upon public objects," he concluded, "and political crises are complicated by the concurrent reactivation of specific primitive motives." [39]

Democrats had consistently argued that men were the best judges of their own interests; Lasswell maintained that such a faith was obviously unfounded. In the mistaken hope of satisfying their rationalized hatreds and fears, men were often led into symbolic acts that could only bring them practical harm. "The findings of personality research," he declared, "show that the individual is a poor judge of his own interest." [40] Lasswell charged that the traditional commitment to free and open discussion usually obfuscated political problems rather than bringing them closer to satisfactory solutions. Democratic politics tended to excite psychopatho logical motivations and encouraged useless and harmful symbolic acts.

Lasswell and Mayo, as well as a large number of their colleagues, recognized the clear conflict between traditional democratic ideas and the implications of the new emphasis on irrationality. Instead of directly rejecting democracy, however, they suggested that an administrative and scientific elite would be able to "direct" popular government along rational and objective lines. "The world over," Mayo declared, "we are greatly in need of an administrative elite." [41] For over a century, and especially since the beginning of the twentieth century, many had argued that experts in government were needed to cope with the increased complexities of industrial society. By developing the concept of the irrational, however, many social scientists made the use of experts a matter of necessity rather than of convenience or wisdom.

103

The emphasis on irrationality, with its implicit skepticism about the possibilities of popular government, had a special appeal to many social scientists in the twenties and thirties. Heralding their new objective understanding of social processes, they were often anxious to distinguish themselves from the majority of people who lacked their special knowledge. Psychological theories that emphasized irrationality did just that. Many social scientists readily accepted the concept of the subconscious with its political implications because their belief in and professional commitment to an objective science of society had already implicitly challenged the idea of popular government. "Our problem," Lasswell declared, "is to be ruled by the truth about the conditions of harmonious human relations." That truth was obviously not an intuitive truth, but one which only the trained social scientist could come to know. "The discovery of the truth is an object of specialized research," he pointed out; "it is no monopoly of people as people, or of the ruler as ruler."[42] While Lasswell and most of his colleagues explicitly denied that their findings supported an authoritarian form of government, their faith in objective social science raised crucial questions. How were social scientists to disseminate their knowledge? Who would control the new knowledge? What of the inevitable conflicts between expert "knowledge" and popular "opinion"? Few before the late thirties saw any major conflict, for they assumed that popular opinion would easily accept, on its own or by manipulation, the knowledge of the scientists. "The social psychologist and educationist," Mayo declared, "cannot be allowed to escape from the burden of responsibility which is rightly theirs."[43]

At the same time that the new emphasis on political psychology rejected the idea of the rational man and hence questioned one of the pillars of democratic theory, new discoveries about the actual operation of American politics seemed to disprove the idea that popular government was even possible. Mayo and Lasswell began with psychological theories and applied them to politics; others started with empirical observations on American politics and were then led to psychological explanations for the gross aberrations they discovered. Walter Lippmann, who had left the New Republic in 1920 to become an editorial writer for the New York World, was one of the first to examine critically the nature and role of popular opinion. His disillusionment with the politics of the Wilson administration combined with his consistent political elitism to lead him toward a complete repudiation of the traditional belief in the effective and dominant role of popular opinion in the decisions of a democratic government. A study of the actual operation of public opinion, Lippmann argued, showed that democracy was a hollow ideal. As traditionally conceived, it simply did not exist.

Since modern times, Lippmann maintained in *Public Opinion* (1922), nations and communities throughout the world had become closely interrelated. Almost every problem that faced the citizen dealt with realities that he could neither directly see nor easily understand. He had to rely on such inadequate sources of information as newspapers, rumors, and political propaganda. "The only feeling that anyone can have about an event he does not experience," Lippmann declared, "is the feeling aroused by his mental image of that event."[44] Past experiences, personal values, individual prejudices and fears, in addition to a meager amount of factual information, combined to form the images on which men relied to interpret the course of events. In all instances, he continued, there was "the insertion between man and his environment of a pseudo-environment." The pseudo-environment was the individual's interpretation of what was happening in terms of his store of mental images. "These fictions determine a very great part of men's political behavior."[45]

Because of the difficulty of obtaining reliable information, Lippmann insisted, it was extremely difficult to keep one's mental images accurate and flexible. Instead of even trying, most men tended to rely on certain culturally and psychologically predetermined patterns of images. "In the great blooming, buzzing confusion of the outer world we pick out what our culture has already defined for us," he declared, "and we tend to perceive that which we have picked out in the form stereotyped for us by our culture."[46] Thus certain stereotyped attitudes dominated human thought, and even the bits of accurate information that one came across had to filter through a narrowed and partially unseeing mind before they could register meaningfully.

Even more important, the stereotypes were terms of judgment and valuation. "The stereotypes are loaded with preference, suffused with affection or dislike, attached to fears, lusts, strong wishes, pride, hope," he explained. "Whatever invokes the stereotype is judged with the appropriate sentiment." Thus, men did not see different people and new things, but rather they saw symbols and signs that immediately called up stereotyped images. In making judgments—as most people in fact consistently made them—there was little concern for hard data, for the judgment was made almost automatically without investigation. "Neither justice, nor mercy, nor truth, enter into such a judgment," Lippmann insisted, "for the judgment has preceded the evidence."[47]

Although it was possible for men to develop a critical, scientific attitude, few were able to do it. Unfortunately for the ideal of democratic government, the vast majority of men remained dependent on their stereotypes. That fact was clear from observing the actual methods politicians used to create a favorable public opinion. The stereotyped symbol had become the crucial element in democratic politics. "The symbol in itself signifies literally no one thing in particular," Lippmann claimed, "but it can be associated with almost anything." Because it was a generalized emotional stimulus, shrewd politicians could cleverly link it to any event or policy. Because it commanded a common response among all citizens or among certain large groups of citizens, it served as a bond to unite them behind political movements. "A leader or an interest that can make itself master of current symbols," he warned, "is master of the current situation." Empirical observation confirmed the sad truth that "nowhere is the idyllic theory of democracy realized."[48]

In *Public Opinion* Lippmann had retained some hope for a chastened, elite-controlled democracy, but he abandoned even that during the next three years. *The Phantom Public*, which he published in 1925, revealed an almost complete despair about the possibility of democratic government. His last hope was that people could be taught simply not to meddle in public affairs. If that were possible, private interests could somehow make the governmental process work. The public did not and could not govern. Modern man lived at a time when events happened too quickly and problems were too complicated for him to understand. "He lives in a world which he cannot see, does not understand and is unable to direct."[49]

The actual control of any society, he argued, lay in the hands of a relatively small number of men who made private arrangements concerning the specific situations in which they were directly involved. The really important private arrangements that constituted government seldom came to the public's attention and were altogether too complex and obscure for its members to understand.[50] Except in the most spectacular cases, the insiders were accountable only to other insiders—wealthy men, high office-holders, and powerful interests directly concerned. The most the majority ever did was throw its support to one particular group of insiders and against another in an uninformed and fundamentally un-intelligent manner. "When public opinion attempts to govern directly," he concluded, "it is either a failure or a tyranny."[51]

Lippmann's work was received quite favorably. Even those who re-fused to abandon the democratic ideal admitted the power of his critique and the challenge it presented. Although Lippmann's attack grew out of his own experiences and preferences, it shared many of the assumptions of the new social science. His psychological orientation both developed from and contributed to the greatly increased interest in the irrational, in propagandist manipulation, and in the emotive power of public symbols. His focus on the fictive nature of abstractions and generalizations drew on widespread particularist and objectivist assumptions that rejected non-empirical concepts. The strong elitist strain, a consistent mark of Lipp-mann's thought, complemented his general belief in the possibility of an accurate, if not fully scientific, knowledge of society as contrasted with the irrationality that dominated the actual thinking of most people. Lipp-mann's work, John Dewey ruefully acknowledged, "is perhaps the most effective indictment of democracy as currently conceived ever penned."[52]

During the twenties a number of political scientists attempted quan-titative, behavioral studies of the process of American government and came to conclusions that seemed to support the hypotheses of such schol-ars as Lippmann, Mayo, and Lasswell. Stuart Rice purposely set out to test Lippmann's concept of stereotypes by a controlled empirical study of human judgments. "The existence of common stereotypes concerning the appearance of various classes of persons (senators, bootleggers, etc.) is clearly indicated," he concluded. "These led to numerous errors of judgment."[53] Rice's study gave empirical confirmation to Lippmann's theory and also suggested that most people would never be able to correct their prejudices.

In a study of attitude formation Floyd H. Allport and D. A. Hartman of Syracuse University noted a significant "tendency toward emotional bias." Their preliminary research suggested the existence of a personality characteristic they termed "atypicality." Some persons, usually marked by especially strong and intense convictions, exhibited atypical attitudes that were probably the result of "covert emotional conflict."[54] In addition to confirming the belief in the irrational basis of many political attitudes, their study also demonstrated the way in which most "value-free" ob-jectivists in fact uncritically accepted common community values. "Atypicality" itself became proof of irrational motivation, rather than evidence of the need for a critical evaluation of both typical and atypical attitudes.

Another study of voting motivation concluded that "the successful campaign was the one which dealt least with rational motives and most with simple appeals directed toward the arousal of specific instinctive, emotional, and habit pattern-responses." Political parties purposely attempted to manipulate voters through symbols and irrational appeals, and by and large they succeeded. On most substantive issues the voters had "few reasoned conclusions" and could "easily be confused." As many of his colleagues were doing, the author pointed directly to the theoretical implications. The nature of public opinion and voting motivation laid "open to question anew the fundamental assumption of democracy"—that men would act rationally on reliable factual information.[55]

In their massive study of voting in Chicago elections, Merriam and Gosnell emphasized their desire to use empirical techniques to "get behind some of the current notions as to the way in which democratic government is working." They concluded that only half of the electorate bothered to vote and suggested that the party experts possessed a shrewd understanding of individual motivation that enabled them to manipulate political behavior.[56] In The Phantom Public Lippmann had drawn extensively on their research. Studying the Chicago primary of 1926, one of Merriam's students concluded that the whole campaign was based on the selfish struggle between groups of insiders who usually assumed that the populace was "ignorant and irrational." Their appeals were successful. "Voting was indiscriminate and unintelligent, and the primary practically meaningless as an expression of public opinion."[57]

By the end of the twenties many students of government had come to reject what they considered the romantic idea that all men should actively engage in governing the country, assuming the irrationality of most men and the practical impossibility of actual popular control. John Dickinson, a prominent legal scholar and opponent of realism, declared that one of the principal difficulties was with the idea of popular government itself. It was romantic and stereotyped, Dickinson explained, and men had turned it into a form of "democratic theology." Only confusion and disruption resulted when they took it seriously and tried to put it into practice.[58] Walter J. Shepard, president of the American Political Science Association in 1934, proposed a substantial reorganization of American government, including a rejection of the "dogma" of universal suffrage.

"The ignorant, the uninformed, and the anti-social" should be excluded from the franchise, and government controlled by "an aristocracy of intellect and character."[59] W. F. Willoughby, who had preceded Shepard as president of the A.P.S.A., suggested that the most important research topic facing political scientists was "Popular Government: A Reexamination of Its Philosophy and Its Practical Operation in the United States."[60]

American government, declared Benjamin F. Wright of the University of Texas, was in fact drifting away from democratic practice. Popular government was neither an historical nor a moral absolute, he suggested, but rather the product of a specific historical period. During the preceding hundred years conditions had changed drastically, and the theory of democracy no longer seemed either intellectually compelling or descriptively accurate. "I have doubted," he summarized, "whether such theories are still true generalizations from the facts of our time." The only good form of government was one that suited the total culture of its people, and the old idea of democracy was losing its practical legitimacy. "At the present time we do not support it as it requires because it is no longer one of our really primary interests," Wright declared, "and because it is infinitely more difficult to support than was the case fifty or a hundred years ago."[61]

Neither the wholly skeptical attitude toward democracy nor the objectivist approach won unanimous support among American political scientists. Indeed, some who were quite skeptical about democratic hopes rejected objectivism, and some objectivists never lost faith in the ideal of popular government. By and large, however, the new objectivism and skepticism concerning democracy went together. The new empirical, statistical techniques appeared to confirm the arguments of those who claimed popular government did not and could not work.

Some students of government explicitly defended the validity of the old theory, at least as a social ideal.[62] Others sharply criticized the assumptions behind the new objective political science. "Any concrete political situation, however seemingly transparent, cannot be dealt with by reason alone," declared Alpheus T. Mason of Princeton University; "it can only be grasped by a process similar to artistic perception."[63] The same methodological debate that characterized law and the other social sciences furnished much of the inner dynamism that generated the methodological developments in political science.[64]

Two of the most prominent critics of both the antidemocratic and the objectivist approaches were Edward S. Corwin of Cornell and William Y. Elliott of Harvard. Though Corwin, like most defenders of the democratic ideal, admitted the effectiveness of much of the new critique, he insisted that popular government was still both morally desirable and practically attainable. Many Americans failed to vote and otherwise engage in politics, not because they were incompetent, but because they were basically satisfied with the American system. Thus there was a fundamental rationality in their behavior. Rejecting the possibility of establishing a true science of politics, Corwin maintained that the field of political science grew out of the democratic revolutions of the eighteenth century and was obliged to retain that ethical orientation. "That the primary task of political science is today one of popular education," he maintained, "and that therefore it must still retain its character as a 'normative,' a 'telic,' science, is, then, my thesis." The objectivist approach was essentially antidemocratic, he suggested, for it "repudiates, if not with scorn and contumely, at any rate with scientific finality, the most fundamental assumption of the democratic dogma, the assumption that man is primarily a rational creature." [65] Those who embraced behaviorist objectivism had thus prejudged the case for popular government rather than disproved it.

Elliott, a specialist in political theory, agreed with Corwin's position but fashioned his attack even more broadly. Anticipating what would become a common and widely used argument in the late thirties, he insisted that such approaches as behaviorism, objectivism, and pragmatism were not only essentially antidemocratic but were also directly related to authoritarian and fascist political systems. Throughout the twenties he repeatedly insisted that "the gospel of pragmatism" lay behind the growing "rejection of Liberalism, parliamentarianism, and the whole democratic machinery of representative government." [66] The strict emphasis on power and factuality in the study of politics led to a condition in which "respect for law is gone and a period of feudalistic strife among the interests ensues, with the cycles of degenerative force set up in full swing." [67] Because of its dismissal of religious and moral principles and its emphasis on practical expediency, Elliott charged in 1928, the attitudes associated with pragmatism resulted in "an apology for the Fascist ideal" and in the end could only be "suicidal." [68]

While Elliott was the most insistent opponent of the new objectivism in political science, his attack convinced few of his colleagues during the twenties and early thirties. Most respected his scholarship but rejected his conclusions. The intellectual climate harbored too much enthusiasm for the new methodology and too much optimism about its utility to allow acceptance of his plea for a return to a more normative and philosophical political science.

In responding to Elliott's critique, however, Catlin foreshadowed the response that most objectivists would make in the late thirties. Rather than the new political science being necessarily antidemocratic, Catlin argued, it in fact provided an essential support for political freedom. The scientific, objective approach challenged all absolutist moral theories, which traditionally lay behind authoritarian governments. Speaking for most of his colleagues in the social sciences, Catlin emphasized the belief that science was necessarily connected to political and social freedom. "The most remarkable thing about Mussolini," he charged, ". . . is his Platonism—moral regulation, inquisition, myths, socialism organized in a functional hierarchy, and all."[69] Instead of pragmatism or objectivism leading to fascism, he maintained, it was the absolutistic or nonempirical approach of philosophers such as Elliott that inevitably supported political and social authoritarianism.

The arguments of Catlin and Elliott provoked little interest in the twenties, but they would shortly become the standard positions of the objectivist and pragmatic social scientists on the one hand and of their bitter critics on the other. The debate of the late thirties was already implicit in the twenties, but few yet considered it significant or crucial. The Elliott-Catlin exchange, however, not only previewed much of the later conflict, but also demonstrated the futile nature of a debate based on those rigid polar categories. As long as American intellectuals divided themselves into relativists and absolutists, they would never be able to resolve the theoretical problem of the moral basis of democratic government. Each approach could claim a logic that possessed at least enough persuasive power to keep its adherents satisfied, but not enough to convert an opponent. Only the crisis of the late thirties and early forties, together with the intellectual developments of the postwar period, would create a theoretical unity strong enough to lay the philosophical problem of moral justification to rest—at least temporarily.

In 1935, when the most intense phase of the conflict was beginning, Thurman Arnold, a professor at the Yale Law School, brought many of the intellectual trends of the previous twenty years to a culmination in

The Symbols of Government. Lippmann had earlier maintained that only by ignoring the split between noble ideal and harsh reality could men preserve "the pristine image of democracy"; Arnold developed that disjunction into a general theory of political behavior. Every nation had to have both a set of theories and symbols that proved the moral superiority of its government and at the same time an effective, efficient governing process. The former was necessary for reasons of conviction and morale and the latter for reasons of practical administration, but the two were in fact totally opposed. "To actually govern," Arnold declared, administrators "must constantly violate those principles in hidden and covert ways."[70]

Relying on a hard realism that revealed a humorous but bitter disillusionment with both abstract thinking and political idealism, he turned on the stock of American political ideas with a satirical fury. His purpose, he declared, was to examine the "symbols of government," by which he meant "both the ceremonies and the theories of social institutions." Normally men had studied those theories not as symbols, "but as the fundamental principles of the separate sciences of law, economics, political theory, ethics, and theology." Rather than accept them as the absolute principles of right, however, Arnold proposed to examine their functional roles in society. He would consider them not as principles of truth, "but as symbolic thinking and conduct which condition the behavior of men in groups."[71]

Rather than deal candidly with reality, men preferred to create ideal concepts that would explain the world in terms that pleased them. Social and political theories were thus manifestations of romantic human desires. "Almost all human conduct is symbolic," he declared broadly. "Almost all institutional habits are symbolic."[72] They existed, along with their human expounders, Arnold maintained, "because of an emotional need for the dramatization of conflicting ideals to which all of us respond." Because men had many conflicting ideals to represent, "the symbols are everywhere inconsistent."[73] Rational and moral principles were useless as explanations of the truth and had only emotional significance.

Although *The Symbols of Government* was an entertaining book whose purpose was clearly to support New Deal reforms, it was realistic to the point of total cynicism. Arnold slashed at the symbols of jurisprudence, economics, and political theory, but he harbored no belief that he could destroy them. Indeed, he maintained, the emotional need for symbols was so deep that they were necessary for any efficient, happy society. The best social organization, therefore, was "one where theories and ideals protect its institutions from criticism and permit them to function with confidence without either guiding them or interfering with them."[74] More than that, if the symbols were to be really effective, they had to uphold ideals that were the exact opposite of actual practice. "If an economic theory is to perform this function it must be false."[75]

In order to reform society men had to work through the symbols rather than against them. Changes that disrupted traditional symbols were bound to fail, for men would inevitably revert to the old ways. Reformers had to use the current symbols for their own purposes and establish reforms under their sanction. Arnold's seeming disregard for the intelligence of the majority of people led him to a wholly manipulative solution. "A symbol which is a fundamental philosophy, as religion, or an eternal truth in the mind of one man, may be a very useful tool in the hands of another, who wishes to exercise social control."[76] Though Arnold expressed some hope that changes were coming, he seemed to have little faith in democratic government in the traditional sense. "The fanatical alignments between opposing political principles may disappear," he wrote, "and a competent, practical, opportunistic governing class may rise to power."[77] The key word was, of course, "class." Even in his moment of optimism, Arnold relied only on the possibility of a distinct group of technical experts who might control the government. The most the people could do, he believed, was to become sufficiently aware of their emotional needs and practical incapacity to turn the government over to the appropriate governing class.

Lippmann had revealed many of the inconsistencies and weaknesses in traditional democratic theory; Arnold went beyond him and made those contradictions the very bone and marrow of the political structure. Democratic theory was not simply inconsistent and therefore false, but it was necessarily inconsistent and false. Lippmann distinguished between necessary, rational abstraction and unconscious, irrational fictions, but Arnold lumped them together in one class as emotional symbols having no connection with reality.

Arnold thus exemplified the full challenge to traditional democratic theory that had emerged by the early thirties. Emphasizing the irrational, he discarded the idea that most men could participate realistically in an effective popular government. Accepting the need for a dominant elite, he proclaimed the necessity of a social order based on the manipulation of the many by the few; democracy as traditionally conceived was an impossible and unrealistic form of government.

Theoretically, Arnold's approach abandoned completely any possibility of ethical justification. By making all principles and theories necessarily false and symbolic, he left no intellectual basis on which to justify any moral position. Though he himself urged a broad humanitarianism, he was left with no rational means of defending or justifying that humanitarianism. At one point he equated the "practical" attitude with the humanitarian, but that was merely begging the question.[78] The international politics of the late thirties would make it very clear that many people could consider policies far from humanitarian to be quite practical.

Thinkers from Plato to Mencken had challenged democratic ideas without tarnishing them for the majority of Americans. When such scholars as Mayo, Lasswell, Lippmann, and Arnold criticized democracy, however, the situation was different. They raised especially disturbing and perplexing questions because they represented the new scientific approach to the social process. Their work had been based on observations of the actual operations of American government, and their theories were among the most sophisticated of the new social sciences. Their whole purpose, they had declared, was to reach an objective, realistic, and scientific understanding of the political system. "That is in fact," Mayo had announced, "the method for which I stand."[79]

III

The Crisis of Democratic Theory

7

America & the Rise
of European Dictatorships

The disappointment with Woodrow Wilson's idealism after the First World War and the parallel resurgence of nativism and elitism had combined with such new doctrines as the irrational nature of man and the impracticability of government by the "common man" to spur a forceful reaction against democratic ideas in the United States. Although most Americans undoubtedly continued to cherish their form of government—however they interpreted it—the twenties and early thirties produced more doubts and despair about democracy than had any other period since the early nineteenth century. Democracy led to "mobocracy" and its attitude toward property was "communistic," declared an official United States Army *Training Manual* in 1928. Widely used by the War Department, the manual concluded that democracy resulted "in demogogism, license, agitation, discontent, anarchy."[1] Popular novels, magazine articles, scholarly monographs, and even official publications of the United States government pointed out the weaknesses and excesses of democracy.

One more factor informed the changed attitude toward popular government in the years after World War I. A growing number of dictatorships abroad and a shrinking number of democracies led to disturbing and pressing questions: as the nineteenth century had seen the triumph of democracy, would the twentieth see the triumph of dictatorship? Had democracy failed and was dictatorship alone capable of meeting the problems of advanced industrial society?

The bolshevik revolution of November, 1917, inaugurated the new wave. Initially the war situation completely colored America's reaction. Although many were instinctively repelled by communism, most of those who opposed the revolution did so because they feared that the bolsheviks would take Russia out of the war. Those who supported the revolution, except for the extreme antiwar socialists, thought the bolsheviks would help the allied war effort.[2] Without the taint of czarism, many Americans reasoned, the allies were truly a democratic coalition. Arthur Bullard, a pro-war socialist who had dealings with many allied officials during the war, said that he had never heard the bolsheviks condemned for anything but their possible harmful effect on the war effort.[3]

When the bolsheviks signed the treaty of Brest-Litovsk in January, 1918, removing Russia from the war, however, few Americans were prepared to defend them. People of all political persuasions bitterly denounced the bolsheviks for treason to the cause of freedom.[4] Some accused the bolsheviks of being tools of Germany whose sole purpose was to aid the German war effort. In the fall of 1918 Edgar Sisson, a member of the Committee of Public Information serving in Russia, came into possession of a series of documents that allegedly proved bolshevik complicity in German policy. Clayton R. Lusk, an early communist hunter from New York, continued even after the war to claim that many radicals and socialists throughout the world were "paid agents of the Junker class in Germany," helping in "their program of industrial and world conquest."[5]

The internal strife that convulsed Russia in the first year or two after the revolution, together with the earlier American image of the bomb-throwing radical, helped to fasten an anarchist label on the bolsheviks. The original impression of many Americans was thus far from that of an oppressive dictatorship. "There is slight distinction between the anarchists and the Communists," wrote Arthur W. Dunn, a free-lance journalist, "but it is a distinction without any particular difference."[6]

Americans hoped for a restoration of order in Russia, and some hailed Lenin's gradual assumption of power as necessary and good. But as order returned to the Soviet Union, it became apparent that it was not to be a democratic order. The bolsheviks had their strong defenders, but few of them liked the political dictatorship that was established in the years after 1918. Opponents abounded. Abandoning the initial charge of anarchism, most critics began calling the new Russian government a tyranny and a despotism. Some compared the rule of the bolsheviks to the Reign of Terror during the French Revolution. The bolshevik idea "of maintaining internal peace," declared an editorial in *Outlook*, one of the magazines most hostile to the communists, "is not far different from that of the Jacobin committees in France in the first days of the Guillotine."[7]

Although the infamous "red scare" of 1919 and 1920 brought criticism and vilification of the Soviet Union to new peaks, Americans continued to attack the bolsheviks throughout the twenties, emphasizing their manipulative propaganda, political coercion, and continually expanding control of Russian society. Sensitive to the newly discovered power of propaganda, many critics pointed to the massive indoctrination the bolsheviks used to maintain their power. Lenin, declared one writer, "is the master phraseocrat of the world."[8] Bolshevik control over religion and education drew continued fire from critics, *Catholic World* maintaining that under communism "the state owns the child."[9] The bolsheviks, others pointed out, were attempting to dominate every area of Russian life in order to ensure their complete political control. "The only two departments that function with efficiency," charged another bitter critic, "are the Tcheka (the secret service) and the army." They had to operate efficiently, he argued, for "it is upon them that the government's solidarity rests."[10]

Most critics continued to describe bolshevism as a traditional type of dictatorship, but a number of intellectuals were struck by the drive toward total domination over all aspects of Russian society. Though no clear theory emerged during the twenties, they were groping toward the idea of totalitarianism that was to crystallize in the middle and late thirties. W. Stephen Sanders, a Protestant clergyman, argued that the bolshevik rule was unlike earlier dictatorships, and was "something quite different —the Servile State."[11] Franklin H. Giddings, a prominent sociologist and editor of the *Independent*, referred to "absolutist communism," which was based on adherence to "creeds as dogmatic as Calvin's Institutes of Theology."[12] He pointed to an element that American intellectuals would come to see as a crucial common characteristic between communism and the forms of fascism that would later emerge: the existence of a ruling party that claimed monopoly on an absolute truth, which it used as a rationale for total political control.

In spite of the pervasive criticism, the bolsheviks were not without their supporters. A number of Americans saw the communist government as an exciting attempt to build a new, humanitarian society. The Russian example exerted its greatest appeal on those intellectuals who were dissatisfied with domestic conditions in the United States and desperately needed some kind of practical anchor for their hopes amid what they regarded as the reactionary political currents of the twenties. Social workers, labor leaders, social scientists, and philosophers visited the Soviet Union during the twenties, and many of them returned with highly favorable opinions of the reconstruction that the communists were attempting. "The achievement of the last two or three years in the field of public health and preventive measures," declared the social worker Lillian D. Wald after a visit in 1924, was indeed "extraordinary." [13] Often ignoring and usually down-playing the harsher aspects of Soviet life, those travelers and other sympathizers provided during the twenties and early thirties a significant counterweight to the widespread condemnations of the bolshevik government.

Perhaps more than anything, the Russian example appealed to sympathizers as a great social experiment. Both sympathetic and critical observers often commented on the pragmatic technological attitude that Soviet leaders adopted. Several thousand American engineers, especially in the late twenties, worked in Russia, and many of them reported favorable impressions of the broad engineering attempts to reconstruct Soviet industry and transportation. A striking community of outlook, based on a shared technological approach, united for a time the generally anti-bolshevik American engineers with their Soviet employers.[14] The belief that Russia represented a great social experiment was especially important in shaping the attitudes of many American social scientists who accepted an instrumentalist approach. Referring to the new Russia as a great experiment, John Dewey proclaimed in 1928 that it was "a release of human powers on such an unprecedented scale that it is of incalculable significance not only for that country, but for the world." [15] Such social scientists as Rexford Tugwell and Paul Douglas joined in Dewey's praise, viewing the communist government as an attempt at pragmatic, scientific social engineering. One of the most significant intellectual changes between the early and late thirties would be the reinterpretation of communism that American pragmatists developed. Most of them came to see the bolsheviks not as social experimentalists, but as dogmatic absolutists. The change was a part of the major intellectual reorientation that would mark the late thirties.

Until the appearance of other new dictatorships that spread across Europe during the twenties, most Americans, whether sympathetic or critical, regarded the authoritarian aspects of bolshevism as manifestations of traditional Russian despotism. It was indigenous to the country, regardless of the governing group. "Its methods cannot be approved," declared the *New Republic* of the bolshevik rule, "but can only be condoned as no worse than the methods that would be applied by the counter revolution if it came into power."[16] Bolshevist rule, explained the journalist William Hard, was merely an extension of czarist tyranny.[17]

Just as the revolutionary turmoil in Russia was abating, another new dictatorship appeared. In their much publicized "march on Rome" the Italian fascists caused a governmental crisis that led the king to call upon their leader, Benito Mussolini, to form a new ministry. The bolsheviks had found more opponents than supporters in the United States, but the Italian fascists received widespread acceptance and even praise, largely because of the militant anticommunism that marked their program. Even so astute a political observer as Walter Lippmann asserted that fascism should be judged on the basis of its success in preventing a communist takeover in Italy.[18] Although Lippmann questioned whether or not the fascists had really saved Italy, he thought such an accomplishment would justify the means that they had used. "In no small measure," declared another writer, "dictatorship is the people's answer to Bolshevism."[19]

Many thought that the fascists represented the weak Italian middle class, which was being crushed between large industrialists on the one side and the rising proletariat on the other; the fascists were thus carrying on a struggle with which many Americans were in complete sympathy. Again, since fascism, unlike bolshevism, was originally a nationalistic movement that did not call for the overthrow of other governments, Americans felt more at ease in dealing with it. A large Italo-American population, which tended to look sympathetically on Mussolini's call for national greatness, also helped guarantee fascism a favorable hearing. Mussolini's authoritarianism seemed to many the inevitable result of the long line of weak and inefficient governments that had tried to rule Italy since the end of the nineteenth century, and it seemed also to have the support of a majority of the people. Additionally, the slogans the fascists adopted—efficiency and honesty in government, respect for capitalism and private property—further appealed to many Americans and seemed to prove that fascism was conservative and responsible.[20]

Finally, Mussolini worked consciously to promote a sympathetic personal image in America. He went out of his way to impress and accommodate visiting newsmen, tried to control all the news that left Italy, and in 1927 organized a special press service in the United States to ensure that his position would receive full publicity. Picturing himself as a self-

121

made man of action, he appealed to some of the most basic values of American culture. The social conditions that made the twenties a period of hero worship helped make Mussolini one of its heroes.[21]

Before the march on Rome the American press gave the fascists a large amount of publicity, often criticizing their violence but usually defending their goals. The *Independent* called them a "sort of Ku Klux Klan," but maintained that "there is little doubt that the Fascisti have rendered priceless service to the state."[22] Only a few magazines, such as the *Nation*, held to a consistently critical line. By the end of 1922, after the fascist takeover, even the more critical journals tempered their attacks. The proper solution for Italy's problems, declared the *New Republic*, might lie with "these politically youthful aspirants to glory."[23] The fascists were, many Americans initially believed, a natural solution for a particularly Italian problem.

Praise for Mussolini and the fascists was widespread in the United States, and at times lavish. Many foreign correspondents pictured Mussolini as a strong and courageous leader who bordered on being a superman. The *Wall Street Journal* expressed the attitude in verse:

> On formula and etiquette
> He seems a trifle shy;
> But when it comes to "go and get,"
> He's some two-fisted guy.[24]

Mussolini had transformed Italy into a strong and efficient nation and made it a first-class power. When judged by results, *Commonweal* declared, his government "would have to receive almost universal commendation."[25] Alvin Owsley, the national commander of the American Legion, held the fascists in such high regard that he equated them with his own organization. "Do not forget," he declared, "that the Fascisti are to Italy what the American Legion is to the United States."[26] Like many commentators, the *Christian Century* disliked authoritarianism but admired its accomplishments. "The hope of democracy will revive," an editorial stated, "when it learns how to do the things that need to be done as efficiently as autocracy does them."[27]

The initial ambiguity of fascism, its lack of any coherent and established program, helped to appeal to diverse groups in the United States. It drew its strongest support from Italo-Americans, businessmen, Catholics, and confirmed anticommunists, but it provoked some interest even among pragmatic liberals. Herbert W. Schneider, Charles Beard, Horace M. Kallen, and Herbert Croly all for a short time thought that fascism might provide some solutions to the problems of modern industrial society. Though only a small number of such reform-minded intellectuals considered fascism a serious hope, they were moved by many of the same attitudes that led larger numbers to turn toward the Soviet Union. In the business-dominated atmosphere of the twenties they were searching for real possibilities of social change. The general pessimism about the practicability of democracy perhaps made them more willing to consider the possibilities that Mussolini's economic plans might suggest. As in the response of some pragmatists to bolshevism, the experimental nature of fascism struck them as most hopeful. "The fascist revolution is not unlike the Communist revolution," Kallen commented in 1927. Each represented an attempt to reconstruct society along consciously planned lines. "Each should have the freest opportunity once it has made a start, of demonstrating whether it be an exploitation of men by a special interest or a fruitful endeavor after the good life."[28] Though their "flirtation" was neither widespread nor long lasting, it indicated the desperation of some intellectuals and the ambiguous nature of Italian fascism in its early period.

Newspapers and magazines continued to present a generally favorable picture of Mussolini into the thirties, but opposition began to grow during the middle twenties. Members of the Italo-American labor movement, with the support of the small but vigorous Italian-language socialist press, formed the Anti-Fascist Alliance of North America in 1923. Though meeting powerful opposition within the Italo-American community as well as from the American government and public opinion at large, the A F A N A served as a constant source of anti-fascist agitation and propaganda.[29] A number of intellectuals, led by the economist Frank Taussig, Oswald Garrison Villard, and Rabbi Stephen S. Wise, formed the "American Friends of Italian Freedom" to investigate and expose the spread of fascist propaganda in the United States.[30] The Nation, perhaps the best known anti-fascist journal in the country, kept up a steady fire at Mussolini, calling him such things as "a drunken cowboy," an "impudent swashbuckler," a "self-appointed thug," and the "mad dog of Europe"— all by 1926. Fascism, the Nation continually insisted, was simply an arbitrary and authoritarian regime.[31]

Although it was not until after 1935, with the Italian invasion of

Ethiopia, that Mussolini's popularity began its sharp decline, a series of events from the mid-twenties began to strengthen the anti-fascist cause. The murder of the Socialist Deputy Giacomo Mateotti in 1925, implicating high Italian officials, caused a considerable reaction.[32] The discovery of Mussolini's attempt to organize fascist groups in the United States and to demand continued national loyalty from Italo-Americans set off a hostile reaction in part of the American press and led to Congressional and State Department inquiries.[33] The increasing international belligerence of the fascists after the middle twenties caused the most widespread concern. As Mussolini consolidated his power, strengthened his armed forces, and gained in personal stature, his attitude became more aggressive and his posture more threatening. Frederick Palmer, an experienced foreign correspondent, reported in late 1926 that Mussolini was putting the country on a war footing by building heavy armament industries, expanding the army, and intensifying his war propaganda. "The prospect, to one who studies precedents," Palmer wrote, "is not pacific." He called fascism the greatest threat to European peace and charged that Italy had strong colonial ambitions. "War is the logical outcome of such a regime as that at present existing in Italy."[34]

Although fascism was the sworn enemy of communism and represented a very different set of theoretical values, a number of Americans pointed to basic similarities between the two systems. "Whatever the ends of Fascism may be," the political scientist William Y. Elliott pointed out in 1926, "there is general agreement that its methods are precisely those of Bolshevism."[35] The New Republic, which was generally sympathetic to the Soviet Union and for a time neutral toward fascism, had noticed the fundamental similarity three years earlier. "Politically there is a close parallel between the course of events in the Italian and the Russian revolutions," the journal declared. It pointed to the elitist nature of both movements and to their successes in overthrowing weak constitutional governments through methods of violence. "Mussolini and Lenin are in perfect accord as to the superiority of force to traditional rights."[36] Most Americans disliked the violence and authoritarianism of both fascism and bolshevism, and began referring to their political similarities. "Moscow and Rome, enemies in a word," explained one writer, "are exactly the same thing under a different name."[37] Until the middle thirties the differences between the two seemed more significant to most Americans, but still they were aware of certain important similarities. By the late thirties they would begin to see those similarities as essential and the differences as merely peripheral.

Political developments in Europe during the twenties began to strengthen the belief that bolshevism and fascism had more in common than their ideologies would admit, and suggested at the same time that their dictatorships were due not so much to intrinsically national problems as to worldwide conditions that affected all nations. "Not since modern democracy made its appearance on the stage of politics," declared one writer in 1926, "have there been so many dictators in Europe at one time as now."[38] Listing the countries that had turned to dictators since the war, he pointed to a fact that attracted the attention of most thinking Americans. "Within the space of three years Portugal, Spain, Italy, Greece, Turkey, Russia, Poland, Czecho-Slovakia, Belgium have endured, even where they have not welcomed, dictators." The spread of dictatorships to nine countries in three years made the issue clear. "No one who surveys the political situation of the world today but must admit that modern democracy seems to be facing the greatest trial of its brief career."[39] The American press devoted a large amount of space to the rise and triumph of the dictatorships, emphasizing the breakdown of representative government throughout much of Europe. By November, 1933, the *Congressional Digest* could add four more countries—Austria, Germany, Hungary, and Yugoslavia—to the list in its review of the "Principal Foreign Dictatorships."[40] Other writers pointed to Japan and various countries in South America as additional proof of a worldwide trend.

Throughout the twenties Americans followed the spread of dictatorship with growing concern. "Within the last few years, more than half the population of the continent," commented one writer, "has seen the government under which they were living changed from a more or less genuine brand of democracy to a more or less despotic type of dictatorship."[41] By the end of the decade the recognition of the clear, if not yet desperate, opposition between two hostile forms of government had become commonplace. "Today," summarized another writer, "governments may be defined as Democracies or Dictatorships."[42] The spread of dictatorships held no immediate threat to the United States, but their spread did serve to weaken the cause of democracy everywhere. "Democracy is once more, and more perilously than ever in its history, on trial before the world," declared a journalist in 1928.[43]

Turmoil and confusion in both France and England during the

twenties increased the growing pessimism about democracy's future. The situation was indeed perilous, if even the two oldest and strongest European democracies were in grave trouble. Charles Maurras, editor of *L'Action Français*, the journal of the French fascist movement, wrote in *Outlook* of the supposed disgust with which ever increasing numbers of Frenchmen were looking upon representative government. "Who can wonder that we have had enough of it?" he asked his American audience.[44] An American political scientist confirmed that view. "There can be little if any doubt that the parliamentary system is today in discredit in France."[45] A number of foreign correspondents reported on the serious troubles that the English government was having in trying to deal with the problems of postwar reconstruction. England was under great stress, one commented, and the establishment of a dictatorship was a possible solution.[46] Democracy demanded both an informed public opinion and a concern for the common good, wrote another American political scientist. "As regards England I feel certain that neither condition is yet fulfilled."[47]

The travail of European parliamentarianism impressed and worried many Americans, whose sympathies were almost entirely on the side of representative government. In addition, however, the rise of dictatorships strengthened the arguments of the critics of democracy in the United States and seemed to demonstrate their contention that popular government was inferior and would prove itself unworkable. The one ability of democratic politicians, asserted one critic, was the ability to court public favor in order to win elections. "They are helpless now that they face the real problems of a modern government."[48] The philosopher Will Durant charged that democracy disqualified men of ability and learning from public office. Unless the situation changed, he declared, "assuredly democracy is a failure."[49] Even the stalwartly libertarian *Nation* pointed to the same problem. "Unless we can find through democracy a way to efficiency, justice, and liberty, we shall get dictatorship—and we shall deserve it."[50]

The Great Depression intensified those fears. It was a potentially fatal challenge to representative government, and one that called for the strongest leadership and firmest action. "The times are rich in talk of the passing of democracy, which is adjudged ill indeed," reported *Commonweal* in the summer of 1932.[51] Nicholas Murray Butler, the president of Columbia University, charged that democracy had put midgets in the seats of the mighty, and Frank A. Vanderlip, a prominent banker, maintained that universal suffrage was a "grotesque theory."[52] The appeal of both communism and fascism to many groups of Americans increased in the early thirties as the depression grew in severity and as Italy and the Soviet Union both seemed to show greater economic stability and a firmer control over their social problems.[53]

As the crisis of the depression deepened, some Americans called openly for the reorganization of the government, even to the point of giving dictatorial powers to the president or to some special board. Delivering the commencement address at the University of Notre Dame in 1932, Owen D. Young, a well-known international banker, urged that the system of checks and balances in the Constitution be partially nullified and the president given greater power.[54] Henry Hazlitt, a political commentator, suggested that both houses of Congress be abolished and replaced by a board of twelve men with special powers to handle the crisis. Democracy, he maintained, was unintelligent and inefficient.[55] There were numerous stories that prominent people were considering the possibility of establishing a dictatorship. One writer reported secret meetings in Chicago and New York, evidently of bankers and industrialists, at which men discussed the idea of a dictatorship but agreed only on the need for a "coalition super-Cabinet of bankers and industrialists."[56] A few people, such as Senator David A. Reed of Pennsylvania, Bernarr Macfadden, and the editors of *Vanity Fair*, openly called for a strong man to take control of the country and solve its problems.[57] Democracy was quite possibly passing out of existence, declared the historian James Truslow Adams, and the United States "looks toward Rome."[58]

The depression added a crucial ingredient to the debate over the merits of democracy and dictatorship. The twenties had already laid the intellectual foundation for the condemnation of representative government. The spread of dictatorships throughout much of Europe had demonstrated the weaknesses of democracy and given substance to the claim that dictatorship was the "wave of the future." Finally, the depression created the economic chaos in the United States that could have prepared the way for a dictator. By the early thirties there were dozens of small fascist organizations operating in the country. Sinclair Lewis's heavy irony was clear when he published his novel about the rise of an American fascist movement entitled *It Can't Happen Here*.

There was, of course, no fascist revolution in the United States during the thirties, nor in retrospect was the country ever close to one. Yet many Americans thought it was a possibility, and a few thought it quite likely. Many of the conditions were present, and the example of Europe haunted the memory. Instead of turning against popular government, however, Americans embraced it more firmly. Conditions that made a dictator seem possible helped rekindle the belief of most Americans in the worth of popular government. As the depression shattered the complacent confidence of conservatives and the New Deal overcame the political helplessness of liberals, they began to cling to democracy with a new conviction.

That conviction became desperate because the depression was not the only challenge that the thirties presented. There was a new cloud on America's horizon, a cloud that was soon to make Mussolini seem almost an amateur and within ten years to make the Soviet Union a strong ally. The great crash of 1929 had brought large-scale domestic misery to the United States and to much of the rest of the world, but it also helped to bring a new force into world politics. In the fourth year of the Great Depression, Adolph Hitler became chancellor of Germany.

"At the present moment," wrote one journalist in 1929, "nobody with whom I talked could name a possible German Mussolini."[59] Before September 14, 1930, the Nazis were still a minor party little known outside of Germany. In the national elections held on that day, they made spectacular gains, drawing six and a half million votes and raising their membership in the Reichstag from twelve to one hundred and seven—second only to the Social Democrats. From that day on Hitler and the National Socialists were the dynamic force in German politics.

Though the election of 1930 received considerable attention in the United States, most writers expressed little anxiety over the Nazi gains. Until 1932 Americans regarded the problem of war debts and the crumbling German economy as much more important than the rise of a new fascist movement. Heinrich Bruening, the German chancellor from 1930 to 1932, who ruled on the basis of President Paul von Hindenburg's emergency powers, commanded much respect and convinced most commentators that he could pull the country out of its crisis. In any case, some argued, Hitler's extremism was moderating as he came closer to power. If the National Socialists "should come into a position of responsibility," wrote the historian Sidney B. Fay, "they would probably become more moderate, as has always been the case with radicals who attain responsible office."[60] Others, convinced of Moscow's designs for world domination, insisted that the German communists posed the real threat to the rest of the world. "Of the two stormy factions," declared *Commonweal*, "at present the Communists are apparently the most to be dreaded." The anticommunism of the Nazis had some justification, for the communist attack on religion in Germany, as elsewhere, was "the central front of their world invasion."[61]

Into 1932 most continued to believe that Hitler would be a quickly passing phenomenon. Some thought that he was bound to fail and be cast aside even if he did become chancellor. Since Hitler could bring no new resource to the government, he would be unable to fulfill his promises and incapable of solving Germany's crisis. "Inescapably," declared Frank H. Simonds, a frequent writer on German affairs, "Hitler must be the victim of the same circumstances which destroyed the monarchy after defeat on the battlefields and the republics following economic and financial collapse."[62] Like most writers of the time, Simonds was unable to understand the incredible nature of the National Socialist movement. Even after the summer elections of 1932 when the Nazis won two hundred and thirty seats in the Reichstag and became the largest single party in Germany, some Americans retained their calm attitude. "There is as yet definitely no alarm as a result of the political readjustment," *Business Week* informed its readers in December, 1932.[63]

Not all Americans were so sanguine. As early as October, 1930, the *Nation*, recalling the spread of dictatorship throughout Europe, had predicted that Germany would follow the trend in an attempt to solve its economic difficulties. "An actual dictatorship, then, severe or lenient as circumstances may suggest, temporary or indeterminate as time may show, appears to be in store for Germany." The editors thought that Germany's defection from parliamentary government would have a crucial impact on the future of democracy. Because of its size and importance, "the repercussions of its surrender will be world-wide."[64]

After the huge Nazi gains in the summer election of 1932, no German politician was able to form a stable government even with the backing of President von Hindenburg. Finally, on January 30, 1933, von Hindenburg appointed Hitler chancellor of the republic. Using his official powers, Hitler dissolved the Reichstag and called for new elections. Bully tactics against the opposition parties, monopoly control of the radio, suppression of hostile newspapers, and finally the suspension of constitutional guarantees of free speech enabled the Nazis and their Nationalist Party allies to win a slim majority in the Reichstag election of March 5, 1933.

When the newly elected delegates assembled, they voted Hitler dictatorial powers for four years and then adjourned indefinitely. German democracy had committed a kind of forced suicide.

As Americans watched the National Socialist government operate during its first few months, their uneasiness and general dislike transformed itself into an open and vigorous hostility. "Out of their own mouths and by their own acts the Nazis may be judged," declared the *Nation*. "They incarnate tyranny without parallel in our time."[65] The *Christian Century* attacked the National Socialists and strongly criticized the churches of Germany for failing to oppose their excesses.[66] "The Brown Terror is, both for the number of the victims and for the inhumanity of the methods used, one of the most frightful atrocities of modern times," declared an editorial in *Living Age*, adding, "and in no way comparable with the Red Terror of revolutionary Russia or France."[67] The world had witnessed oppression before, explained George N. Shuster, a member of the editorial staff of *Commonweal*, but Hitler's terror continued to grow "until it would seem to the outside world an endless, monstrous nightmare."[68]

Under the auspices of the American Jewish Congress, thousands packed Madison Square Garden on the evening of March 7, 1934, in one of the most dramatic early demonstrations against the Hitler government. Such diverse figures as Bainbridge Colby, secretary of state under Wilson, Abraham Cahan, novelist and editor of the *Jewish Daily Forward*, Harry Woodburn Chase, chancellor of New York University, Matthew Woll, vice-president of the American Federation of Labor, Senator Millard E. Tydings of Maryland, the historian Mary Beard, Alfred E. Smith, the Democratic presidential candidate in 1928, and Fiorello H. La Guardia, the Republican mayor of New York, all denounced Nazism and its works. "I hate Hitler and Hitlerism," declared Raymond Moley, former special assistant to President Roosevelt. "I hate this thing because it is the enemy of my country, of my faith and of my right to be free." After a series of bitter attacks, the group adopted a resolution condemning the anti-Semitism, coercion, and repression that marked Nazi rule. "The German government," they declared, "stands convicted by its own acts of a crime against civilization."[69] As Nazi persecution of the Jews increased in barbarity during the late thirties, large numbers of Americans throughout the nation expressed their outrage and demanded that the government attempt to dissuade the Nazis and aid their victims. Americans, however, were more united in their verbal attacks than in their commitment to such practical action as enlarging Jewish immigration into the United States.[70]

In addition to the horror expressed over Nazi domestic policies, many Americans saw another European war as a very real threat. If the National Socialists continued their course for very long, H. L. Mencken wrote in late 1933, then the rest of the world would have to put them down with force. In such a situation "we are probably in for another World War."[71] Sigmund Neumann, a professor of government at Wesleyan University, argued that the very nature of Nazi rule necessitated the development of a war mentality and the constant threat of actual war. Only in such a crisis atmosphere could Nazism justify itself and constantly increase its power and internal control.[72] Frederick L. Schuman, a political scientist with strong sympathies toward the Soviet Union, was one of the most persistent writers to insist that Hitler would start another war. The Nazis, he argued, "believe that everything is possible with sufficient determination and fanaticism."[73] He emphasized the determined war propaganda that the Nazis were spreading through Germany in preparing their countrymen for the future. The resulting psychological preparedness would make the new Germany a much greater threat than Imperial Germany had been in 1914. "War is highly probable within a decade," he warned, ". . . as soon as Nazi diplomacy has behind it a fighting force that seems likely to succeed in a clash of arms."[74]

Coincident with the fear of war came the fear of Nazi propaganda and the possibility of internal subversion. As early as the fall of 1933 Nazi activities had aroused so much concern and opposition that Congressman Samuel Dickstein of New York pushed a measure through the House calling for a thorough investigation. By 1934 the House had established a committee under the chairmanship of John McCormack of Massachusetts. The subsequent investigation revealed that the Nazis were sponsoring several anti-Semitic and pro-German organizations in the United States. A number of people, including representatives of two prominent public relations firms, had accepted German money for purposes ranging from relatively innocent publicity work to purposeful political indoctrination.[75] "Nazi propaganda," declared a writer in Catholic World, "is at work throughout the world."[76]

Some continued to cherish the hope that either the German people or some conservative group would defeat Hitler domestically and thus end the threat. A few writers saw a popular uprising as likely, and others hoped for an inter-party coup that would replace Hitler.[77] The *World Tomorrow* declared simply that Hitler was the tool of responsible business interests who merely wanted a stable government. "The conservatives who are using him want neither inflation nor any anti-Semitic nonsense." Those who believed in Hitler's anti-Semitism would find that they had been duped. "It was only election propaganda."[78] In early 1935 the *Christian Century* maintained that the steady influence of Dr. Hjalmar Schacht, who controlled the German economy, and the growing power of the Reichswehr after the S.A. purge of 1934 indicated that the Nazi revolution was reverting to a form of traditional Prussian dictatorship that would be quite conservative and normal. The "professional army caste" would dominate the state, the magazine predicted, and "big business" would determine foreign and economic policy.[79]

In spite of the determined optimism that a handful of writers continued to nourish, by 1935 most had come to believe that Hitler's power was secure and that Nazi Germany presented a frightening challenge to Europe and possibly even to the United States. The Nazi takeover gave further proof that dictatorship was becoming the characteristic form of social and political organization in the twentieth century. "A review of the political world at the present time," said one journalist, "gives unmistakable evidence that our generation has rejected the dominant political idea of the last century."[80] Another emphasized the debilitating effect that the spread of dictatorships had on democrats throughout the world. "Mentally the world crisis has everywhere undermined faith in democratic institutions and left belief in these, even in the countries where they survive, like a creed the rites of which are still celebrated amid much skeptical indifference." It was possible, he noted, that "the political institutions associated with democracy have outlived their present usefulness."[81]

Events seemed to confirm those fears. In March, 1935, Hitler proclaimed that Germany would rearm. In less than a year he renounced the Treaty of Versailles and the Locarno Pact and sent troops into the previously demilitarized Rhineland. In October, 1935, Italy invaded Ethiopia and conquered the country the next year in spite of the protests and sanctions of the League of Nations. In October, 1936, Germany and Italy reached the formal agreement that established the Rome-Berlin axis. Supporting the semi-fascist rebellion of General Francisco Franco in the same year, they helped push Spain into a bloody three-year civil war. At the same time Japan, which had invaded Manchuria in 1931 in total disregard of the League, withdrew from the three-power naval treaty with the United States and England, and thereby inaugurated a new naval arms race in the Pacific. On November 25, 1936, Japan signed a treaty with Germany that extended the Rome-Berlin axis to Tokyo. By the end of 1936 the League of Nations was in shambles, and the Spanish Civil War was entering its most bitter phase. Hitler continued his aggressive actions, occupying Austria in early 1938 and winning at the Munich conference later the same year a large section of democratic Czechoslovakia. A poll conducted in November, 1938, revealed that 92 per cent of those interviewed believed that Hitler's ambitions were still unsatisfied and that he would continue to seek further territorial expansion.[82]

Though Americans disagreed on the practical measures necessary to deal with Nazism, they were nearly unanimous in their hostility toward it. The Nazi threat was a major cause not only in ultimately changing the direction of American foreign policy, but also in leading most Americans by the late thirties to equate communism, fascism, and Nazism as nearly identical forms of modern authoritarianism. The actions of Nazi Germany, many began to argue, were merely the logical extensions of the arbitrary, one-party rule of fascist Italy and Soviet Russia. Though many still saw significant ideological differences, most came to believe that their authoritarian political methods made their similarities more important than their differences. The example of Nazism increased the sensitivity of many Americans to the evils of political authoritarianism, and the subsequent course of events between 1935 and 1939 seemed to confirm the practical identity of the three even in the minds of most earlier supporters of fascism or communism.

Until 1935 Mussolini's popularity had remained high in the United States. The pragmatists who had for a short time been attracted to his supposed "experimentalism" had moved into complete opposition by 1930, but only with the Italian invasion of Ethiopia in 1935 did fascist sympathies decline among almost all groups in the United States.[83] A rapid succession of events completed the general disillusion: Italian aid to Franco in the Spanish Civil War, the alliance with Germany and Japan, the establishment of anti-Semitic laws similar to those in Germany, and finally the Italian "back door" invasion of France in 1940. Beginning in the mid-thirties a prominent group of Italian refugee intellectuals— Max Ascoli, Gaetano Selvemini, Giuseppe Borgese, Enrico Fermi—received academic appointments in the United States and used their positions effectively to denounce the tyrannical nature of the fascist government. More and more intellectuals, including David Starr Jordan, Edward A. Ross, William Y. Elliott, Underhill Moore, Felix Frankfurter, Paul Douglas, and Father John A. Ryan, rallied to the cause of active anti-fascism. By 1939 the identification of fascism with Nazism was largely complete.[84]

Contrasted with the steady swing against fascism in the years between 1935 and 1939, American attitudes toward the Soviet Union were somewhat more complex and ambiguous. Large numbers of Americans had long disliked the communists, but during the middle and late thirties there was an increasing sympathy toward them. The severe depression years created a strong sympathy for Marxist theory and the Soviet attempt at collective planning. When the Soviet Union took the lead in establishing a "popular front" against fascism in 1935 it won even broader support in the United States. Other events, however, increased suspicion of the communists at the same time that their anti-fascist leadership was winning considerable sympathy. The Moscow Trials, which lasted intermittently from 1935 to 1938, though defended initially by many friendly Americans, indicated to others the arbitrary and ruthless nature of the communist government. The first trial in 1935, which convicted Kamenev and Zinoviev, two of the most important leaders of the bolshevik revolution, came as a great shock. As the purges continued and grew in severity a number of Americans who had previously supported the communist experiment began to denounce the Stalin government.

The tension between the approval many Americans gave to Soviet anti-fascism and the growing distrust of the trials ended abruptly in August, 1939, when Russia to the surprise of most signed a non-aggression pact with Nazi Germany. The following month both countries invaded Poland, and Russia attacked Finland. By early 1940 Communist Party membership in the United States had dropped drastically, and most of those who had supported the Soviet Union felt a bitter sense of disillusion and anger.[85] Though a few defended the Russian action and some still considered the Soviet Union a necessary enemy of Nazism, the general impression was unavoidable that the communists, the Nazis, and the fascists were all on the same side. In early 1940 President Roosevelt expressed this general feeling. Pointing to his earlier admiration for many of the goals the communists had set, he affirmed his complete rejection of the course that Russia had more recently taken. "The Soviet Union, as a matter of practical fact, as everybody knows, who has got the courage to face the fact," he declared, ". . . is run by a dictatorship, a dictatorship as absolute as any other dictatorship in the world." [86]

In the half dozen years before the Nazi-Soviet non-aggression pact, there had been much debate about differences and similarities between Soviet communism on the one hand and Italian and German fascism on the other. Many writers insisted that the differences in ideology, class basis, and acknowledged goals were essential, but American intellectuals came increasingly to see the regimes as fundamentally the same. The three major dictatorships, explained one, "whether Fascist or Communist in character, are as alike as peas in a pod so far as the essentials of political form and method are concerned." [87] One-party rule, political terrorism, complete government control of all sources of information, and the subjection of the individual to the state characterized the practice of all three. "Good heavens," exclaimed Oswald Garrison Villard, "how can one differentiate morally between the slaughtering of the bolshevists, between Mussolini's atrocious blood-letting in the early days of his regime, and these foul crimes of Hitler." [88]

As Americans concentrated more attention on the three and came to consider them immediate threats to peace, democracy, and civilization, a new term entered the language of politics. "Daily the press brings new tidings of the progress of the Hitler government toward gaining its goal— a totalitarian state," declared the *Christian Century*.[89] National Socialism represented something new in human history, declared one German exile to his American audience, and "the word 'totalitarian state' is its great contribution to the civilization of the world." [90] The Nazis themselves proclaimed *der totale staat* as their goal, and gradually Americans picked the term up and began applying it ever more frequently to Russia and Italy, in addition to Germany. Although the Italian fascists had earlier spoken of the totalitarian state, reported Sidney B. Fay, the Nazis were making it a living and brutal reality. "This means that the Nazi revolution must go uncompromisingly forward," he maintained, "until it embraces the totality of the German people in every phase of activity." [91]

The term became common after 1935, and its increasingly frequent use was significant. It provided a convenient term, especially after 1939, under which to join communism, fascism, and Nazism. It suggested that such modern regimes were somehow different from traditional dictatorships. "We have never seen anything like this before," Villard declared in 1938.[92] By means of technological innovations developed in the twentieth century, modern governments were able to exert a degree of control over their people that would have been impossible in an earlier day. In that sense, totalitarianism was a uniquely twentieth century product. "Since the advent of the Hitler regime in Germany," declared one political scientist, "it would appear that almost every phase of collective and individual activity has been 'coordinated' with the political ideals and social objectives of the party program."[93] By emphasizing the total control of the state over the person, the word quickly became an emotional symbol that stood for everything that Americans had traditionally hated. While its evocative power was not as powerful before World War II as it would later become, it had taken on strong emotional coloring by the late thirties. Dictatorship was viewed as good or bad, depending on the circumstances, but totalitarianism was wholly evil.

Calvin B. Hoover, an economist at Duke University, was one of the first Americans to develop the new concept. In 1925 he had published a study on *The Economic Life of Soviet Russia*, and eight years later he wrote an analysis of the German economy under the Nazis. Thoroughly familiar with both systems, he was struck by their similarity both economically and politically. By 1934 he was working toward a combined analysis of communism and Nazism. "I began to understand that there was developing in both Germany and Russia a new form of social organization, which differed in important respects as it manifested itself in one country after another," he wrote, "but which had as its core the principle of totalitarianism."[94] Admitting that communism and fascism were theoretically different, Hoover insisted on their similarity in practice. His insight led him to suggest the possibility of a Nazi-Soviet *"modus vivendi"* over two years before the actual pact, and at a time when many other Americans would have considered it impossible. "No unbridgeable gulf any longer separates the National Socialists and Soviet ideologies."[95]

Hoover recited the familiar charges against both governments. The nation or group was superior to the individual, whose only purpose was to serve the state. Violence and propaganda were the pillars of society. No human dignity was left the individual. The single-party structure was the basis of administration and power. Modern conditions gave immense power to the rulers, and that awesome power distinguished the totalitarian state from the dictatorships of the past. "The completeness with which the economic, political, and social structure can be controlled by Stalin, Hitler, or Mussolini could hardly have been paralleled by the power of any Caesar." [96] At a time when the concept of totalitarianism was still relatively new, Hoover was shrewd enough to point out that there was no absolute totalitarian type—a point some of his successors evidently overlooked.[97] Totalitarianism was useful as a concept to distinguish a certain type of modern state, he argued, but it did not define an exact form of government. If a totalitarian government arose in any other country, it would surely be somewhat different from the three that already existed.

By 1937 talk of the "totalitarian menace" and the equation of communism, fascism, and Nazism were common. The similarities between the three were "manifest," declared George H. Sabine of Cornell University. "Every value, economic, moral, cultural, is a national value, and the state overlaps and regulates them all; in this sense the state is 'ethical' or totalitarian to the end that it may be strong." [98] Hamilton Fish Armstrong argued throughout the late thirties that democracy, like it or not, was engaged in a death struggle with all the totalitarian nations. "Between the two doctrines there is no compromise," he warned. "Our society or theirs. We or they." [99] In early 1939 a large group of intellectuals, including Dewey, Arthur Bentley, Percy W. Bridgman, Sidney Hook, Robert Lowie, Wesley C. Mitchell, and Horace M. Kallen joined in declaring the essential identity of fascism, Nazism, and communism. "Under varying labels and colors but with an unvarying hatred for the free mind," they proclaimed, "the totalitarian idea is already enthroned in Germany, Italy, Russia, Japan, and Spain." [100]

Many Americans did not accept the contention that the United States would be unavoidably drawn into a new European war. Deep and profound differences separated them on the question of the proper foreign policy for the United States from the middle thirties until Pearl Harbor. Most, however, agreed on the identification of communism, fascism, and Nazism as evil totalitarian movements, and equally agreed by 1936 or 1937 that a new European war was a clear and immediate possibility. Crisis, fear, desperation, and even panic marked those half dozen years after 1935. Americans had to face a whole series of issues stemming from the revolution in European politics. Should the country accept neutrality legislation or ship vast amounts of armaments to England and France? What attitude should the country take toward the Spanish Civil War?

Should America's defense perimeter be the Rhine, the English Channel, or the Atlantic Ocean? Could the United States survive if England and France fell? Could England win without American aid? Was a war likely between the axis powers and the United States? Did the clear ideological split between democracy and totalitarianism make a fight to the finish inevitable?

Owing to the complexity of those questions, Americans looked inward with greater certainty than they looked outward across the Atlantic. The threat of "alien" totalitarian ideologies, together with the country's strong moralistic and democratic outlook, led to a passionate reaffirmation of traditional political principles. Those principles, most firmly believed, were morally right and good. Nazism, unlike either fascism or communism before 1933, had forged a unity among all groups in the United States. Hitler provided the dynamic example that created a profound fear of modern authoritarianism, a conviction that any one-party rule was fatally dangerous. The concept of totalitarianism became a polar opposite for the concept of democracy, uniting fascism and communism into evils at least nearly equal. Dividing the world into two implacably hostile camps, Americans came to see more and more the virtues of their society and its unquestionable superiority over any form of totalitarianism.

In the half dozen years before the United States entered the Second World War the call for an understanding and popularization of democratic "principles"—though variously defined—echoed across the country, growing louder and more insistent. In order to survive, many Americans maintained, the country had to become convinced of the superiority and desirability of its form of government. The challenge of totalitarianism brought Americans face to face with the central theoretical question: was it possible to justify democracy on a rational, ethical basis? Much of the work that had been done in the twenties and early thirties implied and even explicitly maintained that it was not. Democratic theory had reached its crisis point, for rational justification was urgently needed at the very time when it seemed impossible to accomplish. The question was theoretical, but it was no longer academic. Action was imminent, and conviction was necessary. While their scientific predispositions had led many intellectuals in one direction, their moral beliefs and political attitudes pulled them strongly in another. Totalitarianism was an intellectual and emotional challenge to their entire world view. Thus democratic theory was not alone at its crisis point. American intellectuals were also at theirs.

8

Counterattack

In November, 1929 the University of Chicago inaugurated a new president. Robert Maynard Hutchins, boyish-looking at only thirty, became the fifth president of the most dynamic university in the United States. Coming from the deanship of the Yale Law School, the center of legal realism, Hutchins seemed a perfect choice to lead Chicago's prestigious and science-oriented faculty. One of the new president's first duties was to dedicate the recently completed but already famous social science building, which represented the early achievements and the boundless hopes of the scientific naturalists. "If this building does not promote a better understanding of our society, we shall know that there is something wrong with the social sciences or something wrong with us," he proudly announced at the ceremony; "for here for the first time everything that can serve the social investigator is ready to his hand."[1] His address was confident and expansive, yet the careful listener could perhaps detect a hint of doubt.

Born in Brooklyn, New York, on January 17, 1899, Hutchins had entered a family devoted to education. His father, William J. Hutchins, a Presbyterian minister and teacher, moved his family shortly after Robert's birth to Oberlin, Ohio, where he began teaching at the college. Later the elder Hutchins became president of Berea College in Kentucky, and after his retirement was succeeded by his son, Francis, known for his extensive educational work in China. Hutchins later recalled that while at Oberlin the family's day revolved around the school. The college dominated the town, and the family regularly ate at the faculty boarding house, with the timing of meals determined by the hours of chapel and his father's classes.[2] When he was ten, Robert watched his grandfather, also a minister, conduct Memorial Day services. As a dramatic appeal, the elderly man got down on his knees in front of the congregation to show backsliders how Abraham Lincoln had supposedly prayed. The scene greatly upset the boy. Years later the coldly intellectual Hutchins recalled that he had gagged at the sight and had ever since intensely disliked all forms of emotionalism.[3]

In 1915 Hutchins entered Oberlin and two years later transferred to Yale. His initial stay in New Haven was brief, for later the same year he went abroad with an ambulance corps and subsequently fought in the Italian theatre. After the war he returned to Yale, worked his way through school, and received his bachelor's degree in 1921. Celebrating his graduation in traditional American style, he immediately married, and then spent a year teaching English and history in a Lake Placid, New York, high school. Hutchins returned to Yale the following year, enrolled in the law school, and upon graduation in 1925 was asked to remain as a member of the faculty. Quickly gaining a widespread respect both for his intellectual powers and his administrative abilities, he accepted two years later the appointment as dean of the Yale Law School.

Coming of age intellectually in the early twenties, Hutchins was swept up in the currents of legal realism that swirled through the Yale Law School and by the mid-twenties dominated the thinking of the faculty. Though the traditional logical approach was still powerful in the profession as a whole, Hutchins recalled, "I personally was brought up believing that law was what the courts would do."[4] As dean of the law school he became a strong advocate of realism and worked to increase the empirical and social science emphasis in the curriculum. " 'The law' as something which may be discovered, seized upon, and learned; something concrete, fixed, and immutable," he declared in 1928, "has retarded the progress of legal education in more ways than one." Rather than an unchanging, self-evident reality, the law was what the courts in fact enforced. Hence, "the main duty of a lawyer is to predict intelligently what governmental officers are likely to do in a certain situation."[5]

As the law was what the courts would do, and the lawyer's job the prediction of that action, the source of all judicial decisions was the judge's expectation of probable social results. "The court must consciously or unconsciously reach its conclusion according to the results which may be expected to flow from its enunciation of the law."[6] All the best law schools recognized that fact, he declared, and the real problem was to develop a reliable method of predicting the social results of various possible judicial decisions. In the past judges had tried introspection, logic, and even crude induction to establish the principles of judicial decision. "After searching our hearts for centuries we have utterly failed in the

140

hunt," Hutchins claimed: "its result has been a mass of conflicting rules, of metaphysical doctrines, of methods of concealing the truth now sanctioned in our courts."[7] The only recourse from such confusion and failure was the application of scientific methods to the study of legal problems. "The scientific approach to the law through the painstaking collection of facts as to its practical results seems possible, desirable, and inevitable."[8]

As with most of the realists, Hutchins found the key to the situation in the emerging social sciences. A judge could try to guess the effects of his decisions, he argued, but "unless he is in touch with modern developments in the social sciences he can hardly make an intelligent guess."[9] Hutchins himself, while still teaching, began a study of the relationship between certain aspects of the law of evidence and developments in contemporary psychology. In conjunction with Mortimer J. Adler and Jerome Michael of Columbia University and Donald Slesinger, one of the psychologists working at the Yale Law School, Hutchins published a series of monographs arguing that psychological discoveries had undermined the validity of many legal assumptions concerning "memory, mind, and mental processes."[10] Having nothing better to rely on than speculation or crude empiricism, judges accepted rules that were often artificial and sometimes completely unsound. Contemporary scientific psychologists, however, offered legal scholars a great opportunity. "By careful use of their proved results in these and other fields, we may yet build a law of evidence more closely related to the facts of human behavior."[11]

Throughout his tenure at Yale, Hutchins remained a legal empiricist. His journey from New Haven to Chicago in 1929 was matched in the early thirties, however, by an intellectual hegira of even greater significance. During the next several years Hutchins abandoned the realist approach with its attendant assumptions and embraced a neo-Aristotelianism that put him in the forefront of the attack on scientific naturalism that exploded in the thirties. His move toward Aristotelian metaphysics was a personal answer to the intellectual problems he faced, yet the general problems confronted all thinking people in those years. For the events of the thirties—the depression and the threat of totalitarianism—strained the resources of American thought and challenged the best minds in the nation.

As with most men's intellectual growth, there was no clear and sudden break. During his last year at Yale, Hutchins had already begun to

feel a vague uneasiness about the sufficiency of the realist approach. Together with Charles E. Clark he had started a large-scale empirical study
of legal procedure in Connecticut, assuming that speed in the disposition
of cases was good and delay bad. After collecting much of the material,
however, Hutchins began to wonder about the validity of their assumed
criteria as well as their methodological basis for analyzing such a collection
of cases. Though he did not reject realism, a nagging doubt about its assumptions began to bother him.[12]

The move itself helped accentuate that doubt. Though Chicago was
as much a hotbed of empiricism as the Yale Law School, Hutchins's realism gradually faded under the pressure of new circumstances. He had left
behind the friends and associates of his earlier years, and he was no longer
deeply involved with the Yale realists in their attempt to pioneer new approaches to legal education and analysis. His new position removed him
from the immediate concerns of research and gave him what he came to
regard as a broader perspective from which to judge the achievements of
contemporary scholarship. While his new position tied him down in some
ways, it freed him intellectually to become an academic generalist and a
wide-ranging commentator on American education. Finally, as president
of a large and prominent university, Hutchins began to come into conflict
with a powerful faculty over such questions as curriculum changes, de-
partmental reorganization, and academic requirements. The opposition
his proposed educational reforms generated further convinced him of the
narrow-mindedness of the scientific orientation. Administrative friction
intensified the intellectual differences that would shortly emerge. By the
middle thirties there was a sharp hostility between the new president and
a large part of his faculty.

The slow change in his thinking was difficult to chart because it took
place within the framework of consistent beliefs and interests. From the
beginning of his career Hutchins had insisted that the goal of education
was a thorough understanding of human activities in all their ramifica-
tions. That belief supported his conviction that law should be studied in
its social operation, that the mere knowledge of precedents and principles
had little value. Law schools had no obligation to turn out mere technicians, he had said in 1928, but rather should strive to bring the students to
a more complete awareness of the full meaning of the law. When he later
claimed that the higher learning should be totally intellectual and con-
centrate on principles, he was operating on the same basic assumption; it

was his particular concept of the nature of understanding that had changed. Again, he was always concerned with the need for educational reform and was constantly trying to establish a better system for helping students to the understanding he so valued. He carried on the work at Yale with enthusiasm and conviction, and when he left he took with him the same strong desire to improve American education generally. As he continued to make suggestions and offer reforms, slowly working toward a neo-Aristotelian position, he was in his own mind only furthering the work he had earlier started. Finally, Hutchins's belief in democratic government marked his thought throughout the interwar years. Although his critics later charged him with elitism and authoritarianism, Hutchins retained his belief in human equality and free government. His later position was "elitist" only in a very restricted sense, and one that had not been uncommon among other democratic theorists. Throughout his career, Hutchins remained committed to the values of democratic society and as president of Chicago emerged as one of the most outspoken defenders of free speech and academic freedom in the United States.

Within that consistent intellectual framework, the first clear hint that Hutchins was working toward a new synthesis came in an article he wrote in March, 1931, entitled "The University of Utopia." His interest in using the university to help solve practical problems and his concern with interdepartmental social research still dominated, but a new strain appeared. Hutchins was clearly disappointed with the progress made in American education. The depression had revealed a glaring inability to control social and economic forces. "If the aim of education is to train intelligence and to substitute it at last for stupidity and prejudice," he exclaimed, "we must concede that it has signally failed so far."[13] His ideas, however, were still inchoate. Undoubtedly influenced by the broad and continuing efforts at curriculum and administrative reorganization that had begun at Chicago in 1925, he did call for a restructuring of the university that would abolish strict lines between various disciplines.[14] He advocated the reduction of external quantitative requirements such as credit hours and semesters in favor of judging students according to their performance on general examinations administered whenever they thought they were ready. He suggested nothing startlingly new in 1931, nor did he appear ready to reject the basic content of contemporary university training as he would do within a few years. His disillusionment at the apparent inability of trained intelligence to deal with the depression, however, was

143

acute. That disillusionment, combined with his conviction that salvation could come only through more education and "the development of intellectual leadership," pointed in the direction of fundamental reforms in university education.

The depression challenged him in another way. As a university president he was responsible for securing the money to support Chicago's educational program. By 1932 the depression was beginning to cramp such fund-raising severely. In response to the financial difficulties he argued that the schools, whose main purpose was the advancement of knowledge, could save needed revenue by streamlining their curricula and abandoning the "nursing function" they had developed.[15] He suggested pruning practical and vocational training from the university and leaving only the strictly "intellectual" subjects such as the humanities and "pure" science. The difficulty of soliciting funds led Hutchins in another more important direction. If the universities were to get the money they needed, he decided, they must have a clearer idea of their purpose and a rational defense for their activities. The average person did not even understand what a college or university was, Hutchins declared in December, 1932, "and we can make only the feeblest efforts to illuminate him because we are somewhat confused ourselves."[16] The next year he made the point in even stronger language. "We as educators cannot demand these things on behalf of education," he told the National Educational Association, "unless we have a system that can be understood and defended." The solution to the problems posed for education by the depression was to be found in a deeper understanding and reorganization of education itself. Hutchins interpreted the depression-born crisis in terms of his own long-standing beliefs in the efficacy of intellectual leadership and the desirability of educational reform. He combined them with a new ingredient—the necessity for developing a rationally ordered educational structure. "If we can present to the country an intelligible program we can get the money to support it," he continued. "If we shrink from the task of clarification we may find taken away from us even that which we have."[17]

By 1933 Hutchins was not only acutely dissatisfied with the educational structure, but he was actively searching for some intellectual method of reordering it. In thinking about these problems and observing the impact of the depression, he was struck by the reality of change as he had never been while at Yale. Many things had changed since he had come to Chicago. American society had been dynamic before 1929, but change had seemed to be under conscious control and humanly benevolent. Since then changes came by themselves, against the wishes of individuals; and they were definitely not benevolent. Uncontrolled change and chaos seemed to be dismantling American society. As others had done in past times of rapid, confusing and harmful change, he slowly began groping both for an explanation and for some more permanent reality in which to place his confidence.

In the fall of 1930 Hutchins had called Mortimer J. Adler to a position in the law school at Chicago. He had known Adler since the middle twenties when they had collaborated on a study of psychology and the law. From his work at Columbia, Adler brought a keen interest in the study of "great books," which Hutchins in his intellectual curiosity had come to share. Together they taught an undergraduate honors course based on the great books. From his growing acquaintance with the classics, and especially with Plato, Aristotle, and Aquinas, Hutchins began drawing on a new source of knowledge. "That was the first education I ever had," he later commented.[18] As he began to question his old pragmatic ideas under the pressure of events, the Aristotelian-Thomistic synthesis came to seem the answer to many of his intellectual problems.

Looking back to the legal training he had sponsored at Yale, Hutchins by 1933 had serious doubts about its validity. They were due partially to the extreme lengths to which some of the legal realists carried their approach during the early thirties, but the main cause was Hutchins's own intellectual development. "Could it be that in presenting our students with fact-situations of the present or immediate past," he asked, "we were actually handicapping them in their battle with fact-situations of the future?" If lawyers—or any educated person—knew only concrete facts, understood only familiar techniques, what would happen to them in a new and different environment? "Mastery of all the facts about the Sherman Act painstakingly acquired in the course in trade regulation," he pessimistically suggested, "might be a positive disservice under the N.R.A."[19]

While Hutchins was struggling with such problems, he was also becoming more and more disenchanted with the whole idea of legal realism. By December, 1933 he was ready to openly reject it. In spite of some peripheral relevance, he remarked, psychologists had never touched on the really important problems of the law of evidence. Nor could the psychologists even suggest ways to study them scientifically. As far as legal education and scholarship were concerned, "the social scientists added little or nothing."[20] In addition, the search for facts to discover how the law operated had failed in its purpose, for without some basic ideas of the true nature of law, legal researchers did not know what facts to look for nor what to do with them once they found them. The resulting research "did not help us to understand the law, the social order, or the relation between the two."[21] The whole concept of the "fact situation," Hutchins concluded, threatened the legal profession "with a *reductio ad absurdum*." For if the best training for the law was practical experience in numerous fact situations, then law schools were in reality superfluous. "We could not successfully imitate experience in the classroom."[22] The only necessary and useful legal training would be day-to-day work in a law office.

An additional problem that he noticed, and one that would gradually become more important in his thinking, was the confused relationship between scientific naturalism and the role of value judgments. Though Hutchins had accepted the realist approach, he had never accepted the idea of moral relativism. As his philosophical outlook changed, he came to see more clearly the ethical implications of scientific naturalism and reacted sharply against them. "There were no such things as principles in our definition of our science," he explained of his days at Yale. Instead the realists relied on pragmatism and tried to judge rules of law according to their success in practice. Many of them, for example, had favored the opinions of Justice Brandeis in public utility law over those of Justice Butler. Looking back, Hutchins claimed that he was not sure whether that choice was due to a preference for "liberals" or for the lower rates which they thought Brandeis's rule would bring. In retrospect, however, the motives of his colleagues were not of importance. What was crucial was the fact that they had been forced to surreptitiously bring in their own personal value judgments in order to make the pragmatic criteria viable. "In attempting to decide which rule worked better," he pointed out, "we had to assume a social order and the aims thereof."[23] He did not amplify the difficulty of reconciling pragmatism and value judgments at the time, but he was growing increasingly aware of the problem. As he developed and clarified his views in the later thirties, he came to focus on it as the central and fundamental weakness of scientific naturalism.

Legal realism, Hutchins decided, led only to a series of dilemmas. If students had to learn to predict what the courts would do, what happened to the law as an intellectual discipline? Lawyers would need only to become technicians, and in doing that would have no time to become truly educated. If the law office would provide more effective training than the law school, what was the purpose of the latter? If researchers did not know what to do with the facts they discovered, what good was it to collect them? And finally, if law was only what the courts would do, what happened to the ideal of law as the embodiment of justice?

By 1935 Hutchins had found his answers to those questions and was ready to announce and defend them. "These dilemmas," he declared, "are the inevitable consequences of our notion of law and our conception of science." Those notions were not totally wrong, but "they are not complete and not fruitful for the study of the law."[24] The necessary reformation had to start with a new definition. "I suggest that the law is a body of principles and rules developed in the light of the rational sciences of ethics and politics." Decisions of the courts should be judged by their conformity to the rational principles of law, which in turn should conform to the ultimate principles of ethics and politics. "The duty of the legal scholar, therefore, is to develop the principles and rules which constitute the law," Hutchins explained. "It is, in short, to formulate legal — theory."[25] He asserted the reality of absolute truths, existing independent of man, which conferred an ethical sanction on human actions. Rational science, the reflective consideration of human experience, could discover those ultimate principles and formulate them into rules of conduct. As such they ordered society and provided the basis for human morality. Hutchins's intellectual sojourn was complete.

In 1936 Hutchins published a long essay, The Higher Learning in America, in which he elaborated his new position. University education in the United States, he maintained, was beset with fundamental confusions. A crass love of money that characterized the universities and society had helped distort the true role of the higher learning. Universities had become mere vocational schools whose aim was to teach the "tricks of the trade," so that students could make more money when they graduated. A perverted ideal of democracy had caused content to be watered down and education reduced to the fulfillment of intellectually sterile requirements, such as hours of credit and years of residence. Specialization had led to the isolation of one academic field from another, to the extent that supposedly educated men could no longer converse meaningfully with one another. The cult of science had led to an overemphasis on fact-finding for its own sake, with no concern for integrating the mass of data into any theoretical whole. As a result, American universities were fragmented and chaotic, devoted to narrow professionalism and success-oriented vocationalism. They had abandoned the intellect. "Thus the modern temper produces that strangest of modern phenomena," Hutchins declared, "an anti-intellectual university."[26]

The underlying cause of all the confusion was the skepticism of scientific naturalism. Hostile to philosophy and reason, it had led to blind and unthinking empiricism. A relativism that allowed no final conclusions had combined with an anarchistic concept of freedom to reject any universal truths or intellectual authority. Chaos followed from such an attitude because "there is no ordering principle in it."[27] Lacking established rational guidelines, American universities had easily been distracted from their proper intellectual goals and had turned into thoughtless and routine "trade schools."

Rejecting the apparent aimlessness of American education and fearing the depression-born turmoil that engulfed the whole society, Hutchins called loudly for a new philosophical and moral unity. "Real unity can be achieved only by a hierarchy of truths which shows us which are fundamental and which subsidiary, which significant and which not." The medieval university had such an ordering principle, Hutchins asserted. It was theology. Yet he was not so sanguine as to believe that theology could unify the modern university. "These are other times," he acknowledged. "We are a faithless generation and take no stock in revelation." Americans were thus far removed from the middle ages and closer to the ancient Greeks for whom "metaphysics, rather than theology, was the ordering and proportioning principle."[28] A proper metaphysics could serve that role in the twentieth century.

"Metaphysics deals with the highest principles and causes," Hutchins declared. "Therefore metaphysics is the highest wisdom." The universally valid principles of metaphysics could bring order to American education by establishing the priority of first truths and clarifying the foundations of all knowledge. "The natural sciences," he explained, in reality "derive their principles from the philosophy of nature, which in turn depends on metaphysics." In the same way all other subjects, such as ethics, politics, and economics, derived their theoretical principles from metaphysical assumptions. A proper metaphysics was therefore the foundation of all knowledge and could provide a systematic philosophy necessary to unify all academic disciplines. "It is the highest science, the first science, and

148

as first, universal."[29] Empirical data were useful in aiding men to understand and clarify those first principles, which in turn ordered the data and gave them meaning.

Hutchins did not elaborate his metaphysical principles in great detail, nor did he explain how in practice they would unify the universities. It was not clear how a "faithless generation" could be expected to give its assent to his Aristotelian-Thomistic system. Hutchins simply argued that metaphysics was a universal science, and therefore by its nature valid for all men at all times. "Knowledge is truth," he declared, and "the truth is everywhere the same." He believed that the process of rational demonstration could convince all reasonable men, and hence presumably alter the general assumptions of American intellectuals over a period of time. His references to Plato, Aristotle, and Aquinas supported that view. "Truth or rectitude is the same for all," Hutchins maintained, quoting Aquinas, "and is equally known by all."[30]

During the middle and late thirties Hutchins vigorously pursued his attack on the structure of American education as well as on the confusions he saw in scientific naturalism. He used his nationally prominent position to focus attention on his ideas, writing for and speaking to a wide variety of audiences. In the presence of student groups he debated such respected educators as Dean Ernest O. Melby of Northwestern and Chancellor Oliver C. Carmichael of Vanderbilt. Because of his position, his personal prestige, and his power as a public speaker, Hutchins commanded a hearing among intellectuals throughout the country.

His charges quickly drew rebuttals. Such scholars as Benjamin F. Wright, Thomas Vernor Smith, Talcott Parsons, Donald Slesinger, and Mark Van Doren criticized Hutchins's approach. William Allen Nielson, president of Smith College, Glenn Frank, president of the University of Wisconsin, and Hutchins's old colleague Charles E. Clark, who had succeeded him as dean of the Yale Law School, joined the chorus of academic critics. Harry D. Gideonse, an economist at Chicago and later president of Brooklyn College, devoted an entire book to the refutation of Hutchins's Aristotelian-Thomistic educational theory, and in April, 1937, the International Journal of Ethics published six different essays discussing the controversy.

Three times Hutchins tried to change the curriculum at Chicago to conform more closely with his ideas, and three times the faculty voted him down. "To follow the reactionary course of accepting one particular system of ancient or medieval metaphysics and dialectic, and to force our whole educational program to conform thereto," announced a faculty manifesto, "would spell disaster."[31] T. V. Smith, a philosopher at Chicago, suggested that Hutchins was only engaging in "dialectical self-exhibitionism." If one wanted to understand clear and distinct first principles, he charged, "he need only narrow his sympathies so as not to see the points of view of others."[32] Anton J. Carlson, one of Hutchins's most forceful opponents at Chicago, even attacked him in his address as president of the American Association of University Professors in December, 1937. Referring to "the neophyte administrators who are ever attempting by diverse means to make over the university into their own image," Carlson scarcely veiled his assault on Chicago's president. "The University is, or should be, so great, its duties to society are, or should be, so diverse," he pointedly told his audience, "that there is no man big enough to serve as the exclusive model."[33]

Since Hutchins's subject matter was education and a rationalist metaphysics underlay his position, it was natural that he quickly attracted the eye and aroused the combative instinct of John Dewey. Although Dewey was seventy-eight years old in 1937, his mind was as sharp and his interest as keen as those of Chicago's young president, who was not yet half that age. "President Hutchins' book, *The Higher Learning in America,* seems to me to be a work of great significance," Dewey declared. It was significant not just because it raised questions that Dewey considered fundamental and pressing but, more important, because it set the stage for what Dewey hoped would become a great debate covering many of the questions that he had been concerned with for almost forty years. "As far as I can see," he charged, "President Hutchins has completely evaded the problem of who is to determine the definite truths that constitute the hierarchy."[34] Hutchins's position, like all philosophical absolutisms, implied a political authoritarianism, Dewey maintained, for it demanded some elite group that could interpret the hierarchy and hence impose its decisions on others.

As the rebuttal spread, Hutchins's supporters rushed to his defense. Adler, Stringfellow Barr, John U. Nef, and Scott Buchanan, all of whom Hutchins had brought to Chicago, supported him firmly and reiterated his accusations. After Hutchins had accepted the board chairmanship of St. Johns College in Annapolis, Maryland, in 1936, Buchanan and Barr moved there in an attempt to establish a working model of the new university. The group succeeded in focusing attention, Adler insisted, upon "the crucial issue of our day: *whether science is enough, theoretically or practically.*"[35] Support was not confined to Chicago. "If a sound modern humanism must be developed through education, no one is better qualified than Mr. Hutchins to become its standard bearer," declared Allen Valentine, president of the University of Rochester.[36] "President Hutchins stands out indeed in a wilderness of fact-gathering scientists and metaphysics-shy philosophers," maintained another supporter, "as one of the hopes of American educational life."[37]

The diverse and widespread reactions to Hutchins revealed both the importance of the problems he discussed and the deep split among intellectuals in the thirties. While he addressed himself primarily to educational problems, the debate quickly and unavoidably expanded from that subject to the broader intellectual issues that lay behind it. Hutchins helped to define the philosophical battle lines of the thirties, and he took a strong stand in favor of one set of answers. His candor and forthrightness acted as an immediate challenge to those who did not share his assumptions. It was not simply the content of his attack that stirred the academic world, but rather its timeliness. "The idealists and the pragmatists," noted one commentator, "have 'squared off' for a fight to the finish."[38]

The opposition, and especially the charge that his philosophy implied a political authoritarianism, cut Hutchins deeply and pushed him to an ever more vigorous defense. Most intellectuals had rejected the Aristotelian-Thomistic synthesis, he argued, because they were victims of four dominant intellectual "cults." The cult of skepticism held that all beliefs, with the possible exception of scientific discoveries, were simply matters of opinion with no possible rational validity. The cult of presentism maintained that only the present was meaningful, and that all ideas from the past were merely functions of a particular time and place with no broader legitimacy. Scientism, not to be confused with true science, assumed that empirical knowledge was the answer to all human problems and that anything not scientific was antiquated and irrelevant. Anti-intellectualism, the final modern cult, downgraded the intellect and raised the human will to a position of primacy. It rejected any and all restraints on human desires. Those who accepted the four cults—the majority of American intellectuals—could not distinguish good from bad, and they gradually became willing to establish as true whatever personal values they happened to have. "And here," Hutchins argued, returning Dewey's charge, "the journey from the man of good will to Hitler is complete."[39] Scientific naturalism led to totalitarianism.

Throughout the late thirties Hutchins was the storm center of American academic life. The breadth of his attacks, the fact that he himself was an apostate realist, and his acceptance of a medieval philosophy—the prime historical symbol of ignorance and oppression to most American intellectuals—all helped spur the intense rebuttal. In spite of the opposition, however, Chicago's president exerted a considerable influence on educational thought. Hutchins gave strength to the campaign for a renewed emphasis on the liberal arts in American universities and served as the focus for a resurgent neo-Aristotelianism in the United States. He brought his great personal prestige, and together with his numerous followers, the prestige of a significant part of American academic life, into a rationalist assault on the major intellectual currents of the past fifty years. "One cannot but feel that we have won an ally," declared one Jesuit publication.[40] Perhaps of greatest significance, Hutchins served as a living example of a prominent intellectual discovering fatal weaknesses in his earlier optimistic pragmatism and abandoning it in favor of some form of philosophy or theology. His enthusiastic advocacy of legal realism in the twenties gave all the more weight to his total rejection of naturalism in the thirties. In that repudiation Hutchins exemplified the reversal a number of intellectuals made, which seemed to indicate, as the result of the depression and the rise of totalitarianism, the possibility of a fundamental reorientation in American thought.

Walter Lippmann and Reinhold Niebuhr were among those who followed from the late twenties to the late thirties paths that seemed at the time roughly parallel to the one Hutchins had trod. Lippmann, who had begun his long career as an outspoken pragmatist, remained firmly in the naturalist camp through the end of the twenties. In his best-selling book, A Preface to Morals, published in 1929, Lippmann accepted a starkly naturalistic world view, picturing man as alone in a cold and unfeeling universe. "Until and unless he feels the vast indifference of the universe to his own fate, and has placed himself in the perspective of cold and illimitable space," he remarked, "he has not looked maturely at the heavens."[41] Though he held out the hope that men could develop a naturalistic ethical system based on humanism and the common moral teachings of the great world religions, his conclusions seemed pale and lifeless. Lippmann himself soon abandoned them. His growing concern with the

problem of the rational basis of human morality together with an awareness of the unsatisfying implications of his own attempt at developing an
ethical theory led him to doubt the validity and desirability of the naturalistic world view. The depression, the rise of Nazism, and his growing
conviction that the New Deal represented a collectivist tendency that
could only end in totalitarianism provided the historical impetus that
transformed his dissatisfaction with naturalism into an open acceptance
of a largely laissez-faire economic theory and the concept of a natural
moral law.

Drawing on a belief that had marked his work at least since *Public
Opinion*, Lippmann maintained in 1937 that the total environment was
too complex and the human mind far too limited for men to understand
the scope and operation of their social activities. "It is, therefore, illusion
to imagine that there is a credible meaning in the idea that human evolution can be brought under conscious control."[42] Any form of "collectivism," therefore, whether democratic, communist, or fascist could
end only in practical failure that would lead to an ever hardening totalitarianism. Economic regulation inevitably led to an authoritarian political
system, for only an absolute government could control the whole economy
and cover up the unavoidable mistakes and hardships that resulted from
its inability to plan successfully. "That is equivalent to saying that a democratic people cannot have a planned economy," he declared, "and that in
so far as they desire a planned economy they must suspend responsible
government."[43] The only solution lay in a return to the true principles of
laissez-faire economics and the concept of a free market.

While the industrial changes of the past century had generated the
move toward collectivism, further essential support for totalitarianism
came from the "aimless and turbulent moral relativity" that characterized
the twentieth century. "The denial of the human soul was the perfect
preparation for these revivals of tyranny," Lippmann charged.[44] Because
of that denial the ideals of liberalism were lost. Ideas of absolute state
power developed in their place. Mass support for various forms of collectivism confirmed Lippmann's acute distrust of popular government
and convinced him of the necessity of some higher restraint on the popular will. Unable to justify his classical liberalism by reliance upon popular
sovereignty, but unable to reject it completely without weakening his
argument against totalitarianism, he sought recourse in the ancient concept of the "higher law."

He had moved far from the pragmatism that had marked his earlier thought, but Lippmann's "higher law" still retained traces of his naturalistic outlook. The law was no metaphysical creation, nor was it the result of a system of rational deductions from immutable principles. It was basically a historical, cultural phenomenon. "To those who ask where this higher law is to be found," he remarked, "the answer is that it is a progressive discovery of men striving to civilize themselves."[45] Although its content was not specific, all civilized communities recognized its existence and authority. "The denial that men may be arbitrary in human transactions is the higher law."[46] Unlike Hutchins, Lippmann avoided metaphysics and rejected abstract ethical theories. He based his concept of the "higher law" instead on what he regarded as a fundamental human intuition. "If there is no higher law, then there is no ground on which anyone can challenge the power of the strong to exploit the weak."[47] Whatever its logical faults, Lippmann's intuitive, progressively developing "higher law" represented another resolution to the moral problems that confronted American intellectuals. Together with his acceptance of classical economic theory, it indicated that Lippmann, like Hutchins, had found his earlier pragmatic naturalism unsatisfactory.

Niebuhr's transformation was more complex and subtle, and in some ways less complete, than that of either Hutchins or Lippmann. Still it represented a similar move away from an intellectual optimism with its faith in the benevolent possibilities of the social sciences. Niebuhr had slowly gained a reputation as a dedicated social gospel minister at Detroit's Bethel Evangelical Church, where he served as minister from 1915 until 1928. Even in the twenties Niebuhr prided himself on his skepticism about liberal Protestantism and his realistic view of politics, but he continued to share a confidence in the benevolent potential of human science. "There doesn't seem to be very much malice in the world," he wrote in 1923. "There is simply not enough intelligence to conduct the intricate affairs of a complex civilization." Though he pointed to the tragic and complex nature of human affairs, he believed that intelligent social analysis could overcome ignorance and help reform the evils he saw in American society. "It is necessary, therefore, that we approach the facts of life experimentally and scientifically, rather than traditionally."[48]

The alteration in Niebuhr's attitudes between the late twenties and late thirties proceeded in two stages. The first began shortly after he left his pastorate and accepted a professorship at Union Theological Seminary in 1928. The increased opportunity for reading and reflection coincided with the onset of the Great Depression, and together they led Niebuhr to a new interest in Marx and a deeper conviction about the impersonal, structural evils in American capitalism.[49] In *Moral Man and Immoral Society*, published in 1932, Niebuhr totally rejected what he regarded as the bland and mistaken faith in progress that marked both liberal Protestantism and the social sciences. Drawing on his earlier belief in the incommensurability between individual and group morality, and accepting a large part of the Marxian theories of ideology and class conflict, he argued that religious liberals and optimistic social scientists alike failed to realize that societies were dominated by necessarily selfish groups. Neither scientific knowledge nor popular education nor universal Christian love could end social oppression or group conflict. "What is lacking among all these moralists, whether religious or rational," he charged, "is an understanding of the brutal character of the behavior of all human collectives, and the power of self-interest and collective egoism in all inter-group relations." Contemporary social scientists assumed a rational, benevolent universe, and those assumptions were fundamentally wrong. The world was dominated by power, selfishness, and passion. "Complete rational objectivity in a social situation is impossible," he maintained.[50] Scientific knowledge would necessarily become the tool of the dominant social groups and not a method, by itself, for any kind of humane social reformation.

Rejecting the theoretical assumptions of liberal Protestantism and contemporary naturalism, Niebuhr then developed what he called "a more classical interpretation of religion," which by the late thirties was widely if somewhat inaccurately termed "neo-orthodoxy." Reading deeply in Augustine for the first time, and delving into the "crisis theology" of such European thinkers as Karl Barth, Niebuhr began to emphasize the sinfulness of man and the transcendence of God. "No society and no individual can ever escape the vicious circle of the sin which aggravates human insecurity by seeking to overcome it," he remarked in 1937. "All societies and individuals therefore remain under the judgment and the doom of God."[51] The rise of Nazism had confirmed Niebuhr in his new convictions, and throughout the late thirties he continued to insist that belief in human progress and scientific achievement represented the height of sinful pride and led unavoidably to disastrous failure. It was the paradox of the human situation that the greatest intelligence and the noblest ideals inevitably led men to set themselves above the teaching of God and ultimately resulted in broader and more violent conflict between human groups. Though the tragedy of the human situation could never be overcome and the manifestations of sin never abolished, acceptance of a profound Christian humility before a transcendent God could help alleviate much social oppression. Failure to acknowledge the finiteness of man and the partiality of his vision could lead only to greater and greater oppression, chaos, and war.

As Hutchins and Lippmann had done, Niebuhr linked the intellectual tendencies he rejected with the growing European totalitarianism and pictured his own beliefs as the only road by which modern man could escape its grasp. Unlike the other two, Niebuhr retained a strong pragmatic strain in his thought which he transformed into his theological sense of paradox and irony. His pragmatism, deriving from William James rather than John Dewey, was often overlooked in the heat of the late thirties, however, and Niebuhrian neo-orthodoxy was seen by most as a complete repudiation of pragmatism and scientific naturalism. Together with Hutchins and Lippmann, he symbolized a profound shift in American thought from confidence and optimism in social scientific rationalism to some form of philosophical or religious transcendentalism.

As the storm of war broke over Europe, Hutchins confronted the central problem of justifying democratic government in a carefully prepared convocation address at the University of Chicago. Before a hushed audience that included many of his most determined intellectual opponents, the no longer boyish president posed the fundamental intellectual question he saw facing his country. "Is democracy a good form of government? Is it worth dying for?" he asked. "If we are to prepare to defend democracy we must be able to answer these questions." [52]

Hutchins's belief was firm. "Now democracy is not merely a good form of government; it is the best." Democracy, he explained, was the only form of government that could combine three essential principles: law, equality, and justice. Since a totalitarian state could achieve none of those, it was the worst of all governmental forms. [53] The rational, ethical basis of those principles, he argued, consisted of five logically related ideas in which men "must believe" if they were to justify democracy: that man acted not from instinct alone but through the power of reason; that non-empirical truth existed; that an objective ethical standard existed; that

156

the proper end of man was the fulfillment of his moral and intellectual powers; and that the preceding truths could all be known explicitly through the process of right reason. Men should test all political organizations by their conformity to those ideas. "If we do not believe in this basis or this end," he concluded, "we do not believe in democracy."[54] Hutchins defined the scientific naturalists out of the democratic camp.

The problem with his argument, however, which many of his critics immediately seized upon, was that he anchored the ethical justification of democracy to a series of beliefs. He claimed that men must "believe" certain things; and that if they did, they would as a result believe in democracy. But certainly there was no proof in his argument, for democracy was implicit in the beliefs that he demanded people hold. Once grant his ethical assumptions, and democracy would follow. He was actually arguing that people must hold the beliefs logically necessary to justify free government; if they did, they would have a logical defense for their political belief. It was, and remained, a belief, and Hutchins evidently realized that, for he continually used the words "believe" and "assumption" as the underlying basis for his argument.

He was also implying that those beliefs were in fact necessary for a democracy to exist. He may have been right, but he did not prove the connection. In itself such a statement was only an empirical hypothesis: if a democracy is to exist, a certain set of beliefs must be present. Whether, in practice, democracy did manifest such assumptions and whether those assumptions were connected to the democratic structure in a causal relationship remained subject to empirical test. It was at that point that the naturalists were later to strike.

Hutchins's inability to "prove" the ethical goodness of democracy was not in itself signal, for that was a task that seemed, according to the developments of scientific naturalism and modern logic, an impossibility. Its significance lay in the attitude of mind it revealed, for Hutchins continued in his address to castigate the forces of scientific naturalism that he had come to oppose. Americans were not prepared to defend those five principles, nor presumably democracy itself, he argued, since for "forty years and more our intellectual leaders have been telling us they are not true." Those leaders claimed that there was "no difference between good and bad," that everything depended on expediency. Since there could be no right or truth, only force was important. "There is little to choose between the doctrine I learned in an American law school," he exclaimed, "and that which Hitler proclaims."[55] Hutchins thus attacked the scientific naturalists as relativists and nihilists at the same time that he himself announced "belief" as the foundation of his ethical justification. True, the philosophical realities in which he believed differed from the beliefs of the naturalists, yet according to his own admission they were ultimately beliefs. Why, then, was his system better than the others? The only answer he gave was essentially pragmatic—that his ideas necessarily led to democracy. Why, indeed, was democracy itself desirable? That was the question Hutchins had attempted to answer, but instead he used the apparent ethical goodness of democracy as a justification for his philosophical assumptions. It was a circular argument that never resolved the central difficulty.

Still, Hutchins virulently condemned the naturalists and thought that he had proposed a rationally convincing solution. By the late thirties the intellectual debate in the United States had progressed in bitterness and extremity to a point where calm theoretical analysis was nearly impossible. Charges and counter-charges flew. The terrifying rise of Nazism frightened American intellectuals, and they tended more and more to cling to their beliefs with desperation. Hitler was a relativist because he transgressed every doctrine of human morality that had traditionally been honored in western civilization, many came to believe. Any form of relativism was therefore evil and potentially totalitarian.

While critics and skeptics had persisted, Americans had confidently assumed the moral superiority of democracy during most of their history. The crises of the thirties, however, forced many, in spite of their personal beliefs and emotional commitments, to ask for an intellectually convincing demonstration. Acute domestic failures severely tarnished the image of democracy, and shocking totalitarian ideas challenged its moral worth. Neither of those events could have produced the intense soul-searching that racked the late thirties, however, if thoughtful Americans had shared a common set of intellectual attitudes to match their political and moral ones. Instead, however, they were bitterly divided. Such normally abstract questions as the nature of reality, the meaning of truth, and the scope of human knowledge suddenly became urgently relevant, and men dragged them from their academic pedestals into the thick of national debate.

9

Crisis in Jurisprudence

When Robert M. Hutchins returned to Yale for a lecture appearance after several years absence, he met Thurman Arnold, an old acquaintance from his New Haven days. "Hello, Cardinal," Arnold greeted his former dean. Philosophically few men could have been farther apart. When Arnold's work was hailed as unique, Hutchins replied sharply. "Yes, Thurman Arnold is unique. So is a rattlesnake unique." [1]

The early critiques directed against Arnold and the other legal realists tended to be mild and often discriminating, but by 1936 they were becoming almost wholly denunciatory. The tone of the attack grew in bitterness in proportion to the spread of fear and uncertainty created by the success of the totalitarian governments of Europe. As Americans became more acutely aware of the despotic and repressive practices in Russia, in Italy, and most especially in Germany, the great majority condemned them in clear and forceful terms. As the possibility of another war drew nearer, they clung more tightly to the ideal of democracy as the best and morally ideal form of government. In their rejection of the rationalist theory of judicial decision and in their broad naturalist approach the legal realists had raised, unintentionally, fundamental questions about the possibility and validity of democratic government at a time when the country needed reassurance and conviction.

Inevitably the law became a center of the intellectual crisis. It was a field of the greatest social importance, and at the same time one that had always dealt with broad philosophical questions. More than any other practical profession, the law was specially concerned with problems of ethics and of values. Into that traditional field a scientific naturalism had entered, first as sociological jurisprudence and then as legal realism. The forerunners—scholars such as Holmes, Pound, and John Chipman Gray —had always had their critics, but they had seemed to represent an ever-strengthening force in an old and slowly changing discipline. The preceding forty years had set the stage with a built-in conflict between scientific naturalism and the moral foundations of traditional legal theory. The development of totalitarian law, especially in Hitler's Germany, pressured that conflict into an angry eruption. By the late thirties criticism turned into a direct frontal assault on realism as a form of skepticism, nihilism, and moral relativism that was helping to destroy American civilization.

Against the background of the ominous totalitarian threat, a new extremism in the realist movement itself was working to invite the bitter counterattack. In December, 1934, Frederick K. Beutel of Tulane University outlined an "experimental jurisprudence" which would study the operations of various legal systems and attempt to formulate "jurisprudential laws" relating different juridical institutions to their observed social results. "The ultimate good need not be known," he remarked, for the sole criterion of evaluation would be the efficiency of each legal system in relation to its own expressed goal. "It may be a hedonistic one of the greatest good for the greatest number...," he pointed out. "Again it may be one of race power, national aggrandizement, or spiritual or intellectual advancement." Beutel's objectivist recognition of "race power" and "national aggrandizement" as possible legal goals seemed to mark the total abandonment of any idea of fundamental moral foundations in the law. "The ethical problem of what is the ultimate good, although it may eventually become one of the problems of jurisprudence," Beutel himself declared, "is today too far removed to require consideration."[2]

In 1935 Arnold and Edward S. Robinson, who jointly conducted seminars at the Yale Law School on psychology and the law, published major studies that assumed a sweeping ethical relativism. The Symbols of Government, Arnold's first book, argued that ethical and legal ideals were rationally meaningless slogans which men necessarily violated in practice. Robinson, who revealed a marked antipathy toward traditional legal thought, maintained in Law and the Lawyers that the whole judicial system should be reformed in line with the discoveries of modern scientific psychology. Committed to a thorough-going empiricism, he charged that "there is not now and never has been a deductive science of ethics."[3] Moral values developed, instead, out of concrete situations and were intelligible only in that context.

Shortly after those contributions appeared, at a time when men could see the rampant brutality of Nazism in action, the vigorous counterattack began its harshest phase. In February, 1936, Rufus C. Harris, dean of the Tulane Law School, published a scathing denunciation of realism, which he said replaced rationalism with irrationalism and led to a completely subjectivist theory of morality.[4] Later the same year Philip Mecham, a professor of law at the University of Iowa, charged that the realists repudiated the concept of value altogether and branded their approach a "Jurisprudence of Despair."[5] Morris Cohen continued his critique, insisting that the realist approach "naturally leads to the assumption that what is, is right."[6] Karl Llewellyn's statement that "*What these officials do about disputes is, to my mind, the law itself*" came in for special condemnation. At least a dozen different scholars, including John Dickinson, A. B. Goodhart, Herman Kantorowicz, and Roscoe Pound, used it as specific evidence of the amorality of legal realism.[7]

Fundamental to the attack on realism was the belief that it did, or at least could, lead to totalitarianism. Jerome Hall of Louisiana State University confronted the realists on their home grounds in the *Yale Law Journal* and warned against the "sweeping inroads of Positivism upon liberal governments generally."[8] Positivism, he charged, could lead to Nazism when applied to the law, for it denied any rational moral standard and tended to identify all government and judicial actions by definition with legality. Edgar Bodenheimer, an attorney in the Department of Labor, accepted a similar interpretation in his important work on jurisprudence. "There is a certain danger that the skepticism of realistic jurisprudence may, perhaps very much against the intents and wishes of its representatives, prepare the intellectual ground for a tendency toward totalitarianism."[9] Even the milder sociological jurisprudence, Bodenheimer suggested, was equally unable to resolve fundamental ethical questions, since it too was closely tied to positivism.

The growing condemnation of realism reached a climax in 1940 when two of the most prominent and respected legal scholars in the country, Roscoe Pound and Lon L. Fuller of Duke University, published lectures assailing the new movement. While Pound had been one of the original critics of legal realism, his comments had retained a certain balance since he had been at one time or another in agreement with almost all of the general attitudes associated with realism. During the late thirties, however, he grew increasingly hostile. In 1937 he charged that the realists identified law completely with the actions of government officials, an accusation meant to imply that the realist view left no basis from which to criticize the legal acts of the Nazi government. That view, Pound continued, overthrew the whole classical tradition and ultimately "rejects the conception of a government ruling according to law." [10]

By 1940, when he published his lectures, Contemporary Juristic Theories, Pound called realism a "give-it-up-philosophy." Western civilization was in danger from a widespread revival of political absolutism, one of the most significant developments in recent history. "One might use a fashionable phrase of the time and call it a brute fact," he declared harshly, "since to the self-styled realist of today brutality seems to be a measure of actuality." [11] Philosophical relativism and positivism, by encouraging skepticism about the ability of normal legal processes to administer justice, was a principal cause behind that trend. "The political and juristic preaching of today," he exclaimed, "leads logically to [political] absolutism." [12] Though he refused to distinguish among the various realists or to advance his own theory beyond the suggestion of a vague natural law hypothesis, Pound's blanket condemnation carried the great weight of his professional reputation and added immeasurably to the anti-realist cause.

Fuller, like Pound, had shared some of the attitudes associated with legal realism in the late twenties and early thirties, though his work had been quite moderate. By 1934 he had grown more critical of realism, and during the next few years became increasingly hostile. A series of book reviews in 1939 signaled his complete repudiation of "legal positivism." Describing the new movement as "pointless," "fatuous," and ultimately "self-destructive," Fuller charged that it was wholly derivative and sterile as an approach to legal theory. "When the search for the Pure Fact of Law is finally abandoned," he predicted hopefully, "the problem of right law and a right juristic method will necessarily come to the fore." [13]

Fuller's sporadic attacks on realism reached their fully developed form in his 1940 lectures entitled The Law in Quest of Itself. "Specifically the problem is that of choosing between two competing directions of legal thought which may be labeled natural law and legal positivism." [14] The latter approach insisted on separating the law that existed from the law that ought to be in order to purge legal science of all personal and subjective elements. "Generally—though not invariably—the positivistic attitude is associated with a degree of ethical skepticism." Convinced that men could know nothing that was objectively true about moral values, positivists limited the study of law to what they could know empirically. [15] "Natural law, on the other hand," Fuller continued, "is the view which

162

denies the possibility of a rigid separation of the *is* and the *ought.*"[16] Neither what law was nor what it ought to be was ever perfectly clear; in practice the two merged imperceptibly into one another in the constant process of becoming. "Value and being," he remarked, "are not two different things, but two aspects of an integral reality."[17] The choice the legal scholar faced was not between studying a concrete, existing law or speculating about an unattainable ideal. Rather it was between two different theoretical modes—one that tried to isolate a nonexistent "law that is," and another that tried to understand the full scope and nature of law in process, a nature that necessarily included both an is and an ought.

The fundamental theoretical weakness of legal realism, then, was that it attempted the impossible. Based on a misconception, realism had led to triviality and confusion. "A specious objectivity has been bought at the cost of significant, if intangible, realities." In addition to compiling useless statistics, the realists had missed the central problem of all jurisprudence. "The facts most relevant to legal study," he declared, "will generally be found to be what may be called moral facts."[18] Concern with judicial motivation led the realists into a morass of conflicting psychological theories and away from useful legal analysis. Focus on the behavior of officials left them without any meaningful criteria to distinguish the legal from the nonlegal. "Even within the framework of its own premises," Fuller charged, "it remains formal and sterile."[19]

Moving to the broader social problems of the day, Fuller linked realism to the worldwide crisis of the late thirties. Since positivists held that reason could formulate no meaningful and valid conception of justice, they logically left physical force as the only arbiter of human affairs. Accepting democracy only because the majority could normally enforce its decisions, they were following a dangerous and, in the world of 1940, a "suicidal" line of reasoning. "The negative conception of democracy played an important part, I am convinced," Fuller argued, "in bringing Germany and Spain to the disasters which engulfed those countries."[20] Although he did not equate relativism with totalitarianism as many critics did, he called it the necessary first step toward the disintegration of society and the ultimate rule of brute force. Faith in reason and its power to discern the ethically good were the necessary prerequisites of democracy. Realism, he declared, denied both.[21]

When he turned to the strengths of the corresponding natural law approach, Fuller lapsed into a vagueness that weakened the impact of his

163

argument. Basically, he seemed to think that the idea of natural law served to liberate the human mind and give it the confidence needed to establish the rule of reason in society. Positivism inhibited the mind by placing restraints on its ability to settle the important question of valid ethical standards, whereas the natural law approach enabled it to settle such problems and gave it firm support for its decisions.[22] Fuller, like Pound, refused to accept any complete or formal system of natural law, nor did he adopt any kind of a *priori* absolutism. His whole discussion of natural law was, in fact, vague and imprecise. He was much more certain of the weaknesses of realism than he was of the foundations of a system of natural law. He sensed the direction toward which the weaknesses pointed, but he failed to develop any philosophical position that would resolve them. In that difficulty he was typical of a large number of American intellectuals who responded to the theoretical crisis of the late thirties. The intellectual problem was relatively clear, but its resolution defied equally clear formulation.

Fuller's acceptance of the idea of natural law, in spite of his vagueness, met with the approval of many critics of legal realism. "As world events of cataclysmic force make it imperative for American scholars to take a firm stand towards the basic problems of political and social life," Edgar Bodenheimer declared, "the issue of natural law versus positivism moves to the forefront in the realm of legal science."[23] Brendan Brown, a professor of law at the Catholic University of America, was even more outspoken. "It is most encouraging and gratifying to the foes of legal realism in its pseudo-sense," he exclaimed, "to realize that the full prestige of Professor Fuller's scholarship and universally recognized competence in the domain of jurisprudence is being thrown into the battle on their side."[24]

In his acute sense of conflict, Brown was speaking for most, if not all, of the Catholic legal scholars in the country. The most severe and extreme attacks on legal realism and all forms of philosophical naturalism came from a large number of Catholic Thomists who during the thirties helped generate a resurgent neo-scholastic legal movement in the United States. "The non-Euclidean school of legal thinking is unacceptable," declared one, "to those who look for justice, liberty and the democratic way of life, under law."[25] Dean Clarence Manion of the Notre Dame Law School charged that American intellectuals refused to "shoot dictatorship in the heart" by attacking it on theological grounds. He suggested that the realists were part of a widespread intellectual conspiracy to suffocate religion and replace it with some form of moral relativism, and hinted that they were also communists, working to bring about a class war in the United States "in the approved Marxian manner." By ignoring the theological foundations of the law, Manion charged, the realists and their sympathizers were betraying the American citizen and "preparing to sell him into slavery."[26]

While many of the Catholics were extreme, others were more balanced. Although he defended the orthodox teaching on natural law, Brendan Brown recognized that the realists had their own conceptions of justice and morality which did not intentionally equate ethical good with positive law and which admitted the desirability of some extralegal moral criterion by which to judge the law.[27] Walter B. Kennedy, a professor of law at Fordham University and perhaps the most widely respected Catholic legal scholar in the country, recognized the contributions of realism even though he had been in opposition since the mid-twenties. Like the previous theorists whom they had rejected, Kennedy maintained, the realists were themselves guilty of imprecision and vagueness in both conception and analysis. They had given naive and uncritical acceptance to a number of dubious social science concepts, and were unable to arrange their insights into any kind of coherent and organized legal theory.[28]

Much of the impetus for the neo-scholastic jurisprudence grew out of the work of the American Catholic Philosophical Association, which began a roundtable on philosophy and law at its annual meeting in 1933 and shortly thereafter established the Committee on the Philosophy of Law and Government as a permanent body. In addition to the preparation of papers for the roundtables, the committee encouraged the publication of studies developing Thomistic legal theory and attempted to organize a unified jurisprudence among professors at all Christian church-related law schools in the country.[29] The new jurisprudence, explained one of the original supporters, should be "consistent with the premises of an immutable oughtness, a personal Deity, a free will, and a discernible, fixed idea of human conduct."[30] Although relatively few non-Catholics expressed interest, the suggestion drew a vigorous response from Catholics. They were convinced that a return to scholastic jurisprudence was a necessity in the face of the totalitarian menace. The Committee on the

Philosophy of Law and Government, declared one of its founders, "inaugurated a movement which may some day be recognized as one of the most important of this twentieth century."[31]

The Catholic law schools responded promptly. The legal journals of such universities as Notre Dame, Fordham, Georgetown, Detroit, and St. John's published innumerable critiques of legal realism and expositions of Thomistic legal principles. In 1939 the *Notre Dame Lawyer* held a symposium on natural law and subsequently published a number of the papers, not all of which were strictly Thomistic. "At the present time when the commonly accepted restraints of law and morality have been thrown into the discard by men who have substituted force in their stead," explained the editors, "it seems prudent to resort to basic concepts to avert the chaos which is otherwise inevitable."[32] James Thomas Conner, dean of the Loyola University School of Law in New Orleans, called on his colleagues to "develop a distinctly Catholic law school." While non-Catholic scholars were in most cases sincere and intelligent men, they simply did not have the proper foundation with which to understand the moral nature of the law. "Truly," he exclaimed, "there is a challenge worthy of an Aquinas!"[33] William F. Clarke, dean of the De Paul University College of Law, echoed that call, urging Catholic law schools to permeate their courses with the "unchanging fundamentals" upon which right law should be universally based.[34] Of great importance for the schools, Father Francis P. Le Buffe, S.J., completed in 1938 the third edition of his *Jurisprudence*, a textbook intended for use in instructing students in the principles of the natural law. "Against this totalitarian, absolutist philosophy of law," Le Buffe declared, "this present book stands in flat contradiction." The principles applied were "wholly within the domain of reason," he explained. "One not a Catholic may accept it, as many, among them our Founding Fathers, have accepted it."[35]

Responding to the challenge of totalitarianism and the relativism in modern thought, as well as to the broad change in the intellectual tone of the late thirties, the Catholics advanced their doctrines with a renewed aggressiveness. "The chaotic stage through which the whole world seems to be passing," declared Brendan Brown, was to a large extent "a result of rejecting natural law philosophy in international relations."[36] Believing that totalitarianism was a direct result of such relativism, the Catholics launched a bitter attack on all the trends that characterized twentieth century thought, especially pragmatism, legal realism, and behaviorism. While men who adhered to those doctrines might have professed an interest in truth, declared Dietrich von Hildebrand, a professor of philosophy at Fordham University, their work actually developed an attitude of indifference to, and finally disrespect for, real truth. That disrespect was the cornerstone upon which the edifice of totalitarianism had been built, and modern "relativists" were directly responsible for its successes. Such charges exceeded those of most other critics, for many of the Catholics refused to qualify them in any way. They saw such a direct and definite causal connection between ethical relativism and totalitarianism that they seemed to believe in what has been called the autonomy of ideas. Disregarding such factors as economic structures and political institutions, they argued that the ideas associated with legal realism and ethical relativism, by themselves, would lead naturally and inevitably away from traditional democracy to a ruthless totalitarianism. "The responsibility of all subjectivists and relativists in reference to the dethronement of truth," Hildebrand insisted, "must be fully acknowledged."[37]

Not hesitant in naming names, the Catholics castigated such scholars as Holmes, Pound, Cardozo, Brandeis, Frankfurter, Arnold, and any number of others. "The lack of a complete natural law," charged one, "is the all-vitiating deficiency in Pound's jurisprudence and disqualifies it as a guiding science for rulers."[38] Thus not even Pound, himself a dedicated foe of realism, was sufficiently Thomistic to satisfy many of the Catholics.

Of all the subverters, however, the most insidious by far was Holmes. While he came in for increasing condemnation throughout the late thirties, the almost libelous vilification did not begin until 1941, abetted by an accident of publishing. In that year Holmes's private letters to Sir Frederick Pollock, a prominent British jurist and one of Holmes's oldest friends, were published. The correspondence with Pollock, filling two volumes, revealed clearly many of Holmes's personal attitudes which had not been quite so apparent, or at least so baldly stated, in his previously published writings. Though Holmes had enjoyed a reputation as a great liberal and even humanitarian because of his judicial decisions, the letters demonstrated that he was not properly classified as either. They documented his rather callous attitude toward human life, his belief in a harsh conception of "the survival of the fittest," a complete disregard for absolute truths and formal logic, and an overriding skepticism about the intellectual validity of all ethical and moral values. In the context of the triumphant totalitarianism of 1941, the correspondence provided a rich storehouse from which to draw the most damaging quotations.

Father Francis E. Lucey, S.J., a regent of the Georgetown University School of Law, was one of the first to exploit the new source. "The functional approach, with the pragmatic test of what works, as the sole criterion of what makes right," Lucey charged, "sounds very much like what must have been the theme song of the Nazi storm troopers." Pragmatism led directly to the doctrine that "might makes right," and it was Justice Holmes who was largely responsible for the spread of judicial pragmatism.[39] He had denied all absolute truths and universal oughts, and in so doing had helped prepare for the brutality of the twentieth century. "One cannot help admiring Holmes's brutal frankness, even though one detests his theory." The inevitable result of Holmesian jurisprudence "is a rather disagreeable (ugly) conclusion; one which is causing a Second World War." The issue in his mind was clear. "Democracy versus the Absolute State means Natural Law versus Realism."[40]

Lucey's charges did not surpass those of a number of Catholic scholars in the early forties. Holmes's theories were "not very different from the widely abhorred theories of force which have been the controlling principle in Europe," echoed one scholar. The "ultimate result" of Holmes's approach was political absolutism, and his denial of "self-evident" truths was simply "sterile skepticism."[41] Joining the chorus, Father Paul L. Gregg, S.J., a professor of jurisprudence at Creighton University, declared that totalitarianism could flourish under a Holmesian legal doctrine. "If totalitarianism ever becomes the form of American government," he suggested, "its leaders, no doubt, will canonize as one of the patron saints Mr. Justice Holmes."[42] By 1944 Father John C. Ford, a professor of moral theology at Weston College, who wrote a series of articles denouncing Holmes, declared that his "ultimate philosophy of law and life was a crude form of totalitarianism."[43]

If legal realism and ethical relativism led to totalitarianism, Thomistic rationalism led to democracy. By logically demonstrating the existence of God as the creator and supreme law-giver, the Catholics proclaimed, Thomism provided an absolute justification for the natural law along with its consequent doctrine of natural rights. "The first and most fundamental truth then upon which our American conception of government rests," explained Father Charles Miltner of Notre Dame, "is

168

the Fatherhood of God." Without that truth, all concepts of natural or inalienable rights, or any other ethical standard, would be "unmitigated bunk."[44] With the immutable principles that Thomism discovered and demonstrated, however, men could easily understand the moral justification for democracy and prove its ethical worth to any man who was open-minded and rational.

In spite of their confidence and aggressiveness, however, the resolution that the Catholics provided for the crisis of democratic theory was highly questionable. The almost inextricable intertwining of their rational philosophy with their particular theology raised doubts as to where the one began and the other left off. It was certainly religious faith, as any of them would have admitted, that made them so purposeful in their adherence to Thomism and their rejection of realism. At the same time, however, they claimed that Thomism could stand by itself on strictly rational grounds. Mortimer Adler and Father Walter Farrell, O.P., for example, attempted an elaborate logical demonstration of the moral validity of democracy, going beyond traditional canons of Thomism to claim its superiority even over other "just" forms of government. Their work, they maintained, would prove conclusive to any reasonable person.[45] Their arguments, however, were simply not convincing to most American intellectuals.

Basically the Catholics never faced the crisis of democratic theory in the same way that other American intellectuals did. Because of the close union between their religious faith and their philosophical training, they had a ready justification for democracy, just as they had a ready justification for an entire system of morality, based on theology, philosophy, and simple religious faith. The problem of justification was, then, no problem to them. While they addressed themselves to the question of the moral basis of democratic government, they did not feel and struggle with the full emotional and intellectual difficulty that marked the work of most non-Catholics. They were much closer in their intellectual and emotional response to the great majority of Americans who simply accepted democracy as an ethical good on grounds of tradition, faith, habit, and necessity.

Behind the attacks of most of the Catholics there were additional complex social motives. The intellectual attitudes they associated with legal realism denied their deepest articles of religious faith and emotional conviction. The Catholic faith in its fundamentals was indissolubly linked with a hierarchical institution that claimed ability to interpret an absolutely true moral law, based on the truths of revelation and reason. Realism and scientific naturalism rejected those foundations, and the Catholics began their assault in defense, not just of their conception of democracy, but of their faith and their church. Although the Catholics expressed great certainty in the power of reason to discover ultimate principles, their attacks revealed a defensive attitude that at times reached extreme proportions. In spite of their fervent convictions, they realized that they were fighting against the intellectual trends that for the past three hundred years had continually grown in strength and influence. Thomistic rationalism, at least in the minds of most intellectuals, simply could not stand against the combined forces of pragmatism, scientific naturalism, and modern critical philosophy. The vitriolic tone and extreme accusations made against such movements as legal realism showed clearly the sense of intellectual frustration and institutional anxiety that underlay Catholic thought in the thirties. The identification of realism and naturalism with totalitarianism was the ground on which the Catholics hoped to make their belated victorious stand against the dominant intellectual forces of the twentieth century.

Additionally, having long been regarded by many as not completely "American," Catholic scholars seized upon the crisis of the late thirties as a perfect opportunity to identify their beliefs with the basic and traditional ideas of American democracy. Father Patrick J. Roche, an educational philosopher, explained that in analyzing the Declaration of Independence "it can be readily shown that its ancestry was Catholic and its principles ultimately derived from the Schoolmen." It made no difference that some of the Founding Fathers might have been deists, agnostics, or atheists, for when they selected the principles "to be enshrined in American life" they instinctively fell back on those traditional ideas that came from the "Christian and scholastic current of thought."[46]

For his support Roche drew on the work of such Catholic historians as Father Moorehouse F. X. Millar who had written a series of essays arguing that "sound" democratic ideas, including those of the American Revolution, stemmed from Catholic Thomistic thought.[47] Because of that historical source, declared Father Wilfred Parsons, S.J., a professor of political science at the Catholic University, Roman Catholics were becoming the true defenders of American democracy. "By a sort of natural affinity," he explained, "the modern intelligent Catholic finds himself drawing ever more closely to American cultural origins at the same time that his fellow non-Catholic Americans are disavowing those origins with almost indecent haste." Early American culture was not without its flaw, since "it had cut itself off from the living source of truth" by remaining Protestant and separate from Rome. "It was this, of course," Parsons pointed out, "that was ultimately to disintegrate its very philosophy and to prove to its own adherents that its external worship had no meaning." In spite of that fatal weakness which ultimately caused the intellectual confusion of the twentieth century, American culture still retained many of the fundamental truths of the Catholic faith. It was for that reason, Parsons insisted, "that the modern secularized American hates and fears the original American culture, and that the modern Catholic finds himself in sympathy with it."[48]

It was crucial for all Americans to realize that historical connection, declared William Franklin Sands in Commonweal, for the "positive and definite American philosophy of life" was "drawn directly from the Catholic philosophy of life." If Americans studied their institutions and traditional ideas, they would see the true sources of their government. "I am integrally part of America," Sands affirmed. "America is integrally part of me!"[49] Catholics, more than any other group, they implied, were the true descendants of the American Revolution and the true defenders of American democracy. Catholicism in a social and psychological sense was thus as important as intellectual Catholicism in breeding their attacks.

In addition to the special attitudes of the Catholics, ulterior motives helped spur other groups in their common assault on realism. Some critics, for example, were representatives of the wealthy groups that had violently opposed the New Deal since 1934 and who correctly understood the devastating relevance of realism to their strained method of constitutional interpretation. One of the most determined condemnations came from a New York lawyer, Raoul E. Desvernine, who had been chairman of the Lawyers' Committee of the American Liberty League. "It seems to me that our civilization cannot stand up against the impact of this sociological jurisprudence," he declared. "Its corrosive force is disintegrating our institutions." When he charged in 1941 that realism was "radically subversive of the American way of life," few could have doubted that he had specifically in mind the realist argument for a more permissive constitutional attitude toward New Deal legislation.[50] For those who already regarded the New Deal as protototalitarian there was no real distinction between attacking the Roosevelt administration and condemning legal realism as undemocratic. Rather, the accepted fact of New Deal regimentation gave evidence to the charge against the legal attitude that defended and justified such regimentation.

In spite of the social motives that added strength to the antirealist forces, however, they did not fully account for the rejection of realism itself. There were too many non-Catholics and New Dealers—Fuller, Hutchins, Dickinson and Morris Cohen, for example—who feared the intellectual implications of the new movement. There was, instead, a growing conviction by the late thirties that any legal theory that did not focus on the moral foundations and aims of the law was an incomplete theory and, even more, a dangerous theory.

In the context of the late thirties the logical implications of realism, morally and politically, seemed too apparent and too frightening. Much of its work had slighted the importance of ethical theory. Its philosophical assumptions had undermined the concept of a rationally knowable moral standard. Its apparent ethical relativism seemed to mean that no Nazi barbarity could be justly branded as evil, while its identification of law with the actions of government officials gave even the most offensive Nazi edict the sanction of true law. Juxtaposing that logic to the actions of the totalitarian states, the critics painted realism in the most ominous and shocking colors.

The damning charges forced the realists to assert their innocence. "I hope," declared Max Radin, "I have never said that ideas like wrong and right, or any ideas, are worthless or meaningless terms."[51] An empiricism that tried to predict actual decisions was "an *incomplete* way to see law," Llewellyn admitted in 1940, for "the heart and core of Jurisprudence" was the problem of ethical purpose in the law. "I for one," Llewellyn exclaimed, "am ready to do open penance for any part I may have played in giving occasion for the feeling that modern jurisprudes or any of them had ever lost sight of this."[52] Jerome Frank, Hessel Yntema, Edwin Patterson, and Felix Cohen all explicitly defended the realists against their critics, arguing that they had never denied an ethical goal in the law. The realists, Patterson insisted in 1941, "are also concerned with what the law ought to be, with the theory of justice."[53] That defense was only partially relevant, however, since the fundamental question was whether the basic philosophical and methodological assumptions that characterized realism left any rational basis for affirming the legitimacy of an ethical goal.

Facing a barrage of criticism for his extreme views, Frank ultimately drew closer to the natural law school than any of the other realists. While as late as 1938 he was still emphasizing the cultural limitations and irrational motivations behind moral attitudes, he began to emphasize democracy as an ethical ideal more and more after 1940. Frank had always been committed to that ideal, and during the early forties he looked increasingly for its moral justification and seemed to find it in the Thomistic concept of natural law. By 1945 he was maintaining that most Americans refused to accept the natural law concept because of a confusion in terminology that gave them a wrong idea of its true meaning. "Most intelligent Americans, if the 'basic principles' of scholastic natural law are described to them," he argued, "will find them completely acceptable."[54] Although he rejected certain particularly "Catholic Views" on natural law, such as the prohibition on artificial birth control, he accepted the general idea enthusiastically. Three years later he made his position clear and unequivocal. "I do not understand how any decent man today can refuse to adopt, as the basis of modern civilization, the fundamental principles of Natural Law, relative to human conduct, as stated by Thomas Aquinas."[55] Although Frank still called for empirical analysis of the legal system and insisted on the uncertainty and confusion in the application of moral principles, he had come a long way from the philosophical implications of *Law and the Modern Mind*.

Llewellyn, too, moved in the direction of natural law, though he stopped short of Frank's enthusiastic acceptance. He acknowledged a recent "debt" to Aquinas for the Schoolman's work on the philosophy of law, but he embraced neither Thomism nor any specific rational theory.[56] He accepted instead the general idea of a natural law, but translated it into a less precise and more intuitive concept. Natural law, he believed, was the name given to a universal human "urge" or "drive" for "right, or decency, or justice." Rather than being the opposite of legal empiricism as many had charged, Llewellyn declared, natural law was "an interesting and highly useful complement."[57] Scientific study was still necessary to frame workable measures and techniques and at the same time to act as a constant check on practice to ensure that the "legal" continued to approximate the "just." There was absolutely no relationship between empirical research, he maintained, and a tendency to disregard ethical ideals.

While Llewellyn added a general concept of natural law to his legal theory and emphasized the importance of proper ethical ends in law, he

173

retained a firm skepticism concerning the powers of deductive logic to produce philosophical absolutes. "When it comes to ultimate substance of the Good," he wrote in early 1942, "I repeat that I can find no clarity, or any conviction of reason, or of deduction as to specific matters, from the broad ultimates others have found clear." He still believed that deduction from general principles, meaning the demonstration of a logically necessary connection, could in no way command a practical specific. "I do not find them *dictating* even such major ways and means as form of government." If pressed for an ultimate justification for democracy, or for any values, he admitted, "I have no answer."[58]

In spite of their early leadership, neither Llewellyn nor Frank was typical of the other realists in the move toward natural law. Radin and Walter Wheeler Cook perhaps best represented the others. Acknowledging that realism must place an added weight on ethical considerations, Radin declared that "the lawyer's task is ultimately concerned with justice" and emphasized that "any legal teaching that ignored justice had missed most of its point."[59] But even with the modification in his outlook, Radin remained a convinced empiricist with no use for abstract formulations. "We need not ask ourselves whether justice is eternal or unchanging," he remarked. Such questions were unanswerable and unnecessary. The important and meaningful reality was the specific tradition out of which modern western man had developed. "As far as we are concerned, we are the inheritors of a social tradition that regards as just the type of human conduct which does not materially infringe the security of life, liberty, property or family relationships," he explained, "and as unjust, conduct which does infringe this security."[60] Justice did not demand an absolute guarantee of that security, but it did demand that such security exist generally throughout a society. Justice or any other idea, he declared in 1940, "has no objective existence." Hence it existed only in the minds of men and was, therefore, only meaningful to the extent that actual men subscribed to it. In that case the concept held by judicial officials was the source of a community's operative concept of justice. "In the last analysis," Radin argued, "justice must be a common denominator of what a specific group—the judges themselves—think is just."[61]

Instead of acknowledging the problem of ethical justification, as Frank and Llewellyn had done, Radin kept his approach wholly empirical and factual. He insisted that justice must be the guiding force of the law and acknowledged in that sense the importance of moral and religious values as partial determinants.[62] He equally insisted, however, that justice was not an abstract or an absolute, either as an ethical ideal or a social reality. The only legitimate concept of justice was to be found in the actual, concrete idea that the great majority of a community shared. "Objectified" justice was real, fundamental, and essential; but it was necessarily a changing concept, wholly relative to the moral beliefs of the community in general and the judges in particular.

Agreeing with Radin that justice was no absolute reality, Cook rejected his assertion that communal valuation was the only standard of morality. "Absolutists" and "apriorists" had struggled over the problem of values for centuries, he declared, and had "obviously failed completely."[63] The only solution left was to turn to a scientific, pragmatic theory of ethics. "The key to Dewey's empirical theory of the evaluation of values," Cook explained, "may be found in his emphasis on the fact that we do not really understand our 'ends' until we have considered the probable consequences of carrying them out in practice."[64] Abstract ideas of "goodness" were almost universally agreed upon, and the only meaningful problem was the particular resolution of specific, concrete issues. Thus the pragmatic method could clarify the meaning of different "ends" and in so doing demonstrate which ones were in fact good under what social conditions. Summarizing Dewey's position, Cook insisted that it and it alone could provide an intelligent and rationally legitimate ethical theory.

The realists agreed in conceding the importance of moral ideals in any society, though they disagreed on its foundations, whether natural law, community standards, the scientific method, or simple humanitarian sentiment. Even Thurman Arnold, who had gone the farthest in scorning the possibility of developing any rational ethical system, fully accepted the last. Although Frank finally accepted the Thomistic concept of natural law, the other realists remained firm in their adherence to a philosophical naturalism which denied the existence of self-evident principles and rejected the claims of a priori deduction. Even Frank continued to emphasize that the natural law gave little or no help in solving particular problems, believing that it merely furnished the basic ethical imperative to do good and to avoid evil.

Thus, while the realists modified their tone and protested their innocence, they did not, with the exception of Frank, give in to their critics on any fundamental point. They agreed that deduction was sterile in the field of values and claimed that their critics were as unable as they were to demonstrate conclusively the ultimate validity of any ethical ideals. Most would have agreed with Cook, who compared the advocates of deductive ethical systems to the infants in John Watson's experiments who exhibited "fear reaction" when they lost their sense of physical support. "They fear the loss of support of fixed principles which can be used automatically in cases of doubt," Cook charged. Hence, they struck out wildly at those who pointed to the limits of human reason and suggested the true relativity to be found in reality.[65]

As most of the realists lost little of their confidence in science, so too they lost little of their desire to retaliate. Pound's condemnation of realism in light of his own earlier work, Yntema charged, "bears a tragic aspect of schizologic abberation."[66] Fuller's legal theory, Patterson pointed out, was marred throughout by a pervasive ambiguity. "Surely the clarification of basic confusions does not hamper the exercise of the creative reason," he commented dryly.[67] Myres S. McDougal, a young professor at Yale University, accused Fuller of "preaching pseudo-inspirational sermons." The day would come, McDougal hoped, when lawyers could be trained as scientific scholars "and not as priests in outworn and meaningless faiths whether of 'law' or of 'ethics.'"[68] Fred Rodell, another of the younger realists, charged that all those legal thinkers who spoke in sacred terms of some abstract "Law" had been "taught in mental goose-step."[69] It was only appropriate to the spirit of much of the debate that Walter B. Kennedy of Fordham returned the same charge in 1941 by calling realism a "goose-step philosophy."[70]

By 1941 when America entered World War II, the bitter debate within the legal profession had reached its most intense phase, and it revealed a number of important facts about American thought in general and legal theory in particular. Most important, the debate demonstrated the depth of a basic split that divided two groups of American intellectuals who, for want of better terms, might be called scientific naturalists and rational absolutists. The realists, inspired by the successes of modern science, believed that truth was wholly dependent on empirically established facts; the absolutists, such as Hutchins, Adler, and the Catholics, believed that human reason could discover certain universal principles of justice by a philosophical analysis of the nature of reality. Those two fundamentally irreconcilable attitudes were in large part responsible for the intensity and extremism in the debate. Since both sides started from widely divergent assumptions, each was often unable to understand, let alone sympathize with, his enemy's position. The realists saw rational absolutism as pointless and often subjected it to ridicule and scorn. Felix Cohen referred to it as "Transcendental Nonsense," while Arnold and Frank compared it to superstitious incantations chanted by witch doctors and faith healers. The rational absolutists returned the scorn in full, charging realism with everything from atheism to communism to nihilism. As the realists were often unable to understand how anyone could accept some of the canons of rational absolutism in light of the discoveries of modern science and philosophy, their critics were equally unable to see how any man could fail to accept that which was self-evident and necessary to give support to a universally valid ethical system. With each side committed to its own obvious truths and faced with an implacable opponent, vilification and the questioning of motives became an almost automatic response. Those who would not see must have some hidden and unworthy purpose.

That deep division was also evident in the awkward positions taken by Pound, Fuller, Morris Cohen, and a number of other critics of realism. Such scholars knew the severe limitations of deductive logic and were committed to some form of legal empiricism. At the same time, however, they saw the theoretical problems realism created, and they agreed, when faced with the challenge of totalitarian ideology and practice, that some supralegal moral standard was necessary as the basis for moral judgments. Torn between two conflicting attitudes, they tried desperately to reconcile them or to develop a coherent ethical position that would withstand the criticisms from both sides. Fuller's concept of natural law, for example, placed him distinctly outside the realist movement, but failed to bring him into any real philosophical agreement with the Thomists. It was too abstract and murky for the one side and too intuitive and positivistic for the other. And Pound, though rejecting the non-Euclidean interpretation of logic and insisting on the practical clarity of legal ideals, admitted that the problem of the moral foundations of the law had to rest on pragmatic approximations. "No doubt," he acknowledged in 1941, "we cannot answer it absolutely."[71]

The long debate clearly revealed the plight of ethical theory in the middle of the twentieth century. The incisive criticisms of modern philosophy and the dramatic impact of experimental science had made rational absolutism untenable in the minds of most educated Americans. Many were ready to conclude that moral justification in any ultimate sense was an impossible and meaningless concept. "Having surrendered the quest for certainty," Cook insisted, quoting Dewey, "we can offer no guarantees."[72] Though difficult for most to deny intellectually, that conclusion was profoundly dissatisfying at the time when Nazism was perpetrating its outrages on both Germany and the rest of Europe.

10

Crisis in Social Science

Although the lines of combat were not as clearly drawn in the social sciences as in law, the multicornered debate reached similar peaks of bitterness and hostility. The rise of totalitarianism forced social scientists, as it had legal scholars, to clarify their central assumptions and to confront the problem of the ethical basis of democracy. Working under great external pressure and already in the middle of an unresolved debate over the theoretical foundations of their disciplines, many social scientists felt an immense strain at the necessity of trying to integrate their philosophical assumptions with their practical and immediate moral judgments.

While Catholic social scientists did not assert themselves as broadly or as often as their coreligionists in the law had done, they nevertheless emerged as major spokesmen in the renewed attack on naturalism. Reiterating the familiar charge that "the totalitarian powers, after all, have learned their lessons from our scholars and scientists," Catholic philosophers and social scientists emphasized that a rational ethical system and a belief in God were essential for the preservation of democratic society.[1] In 1939 Notre Dame University began publishing the Review of Politics, which served as a national forum for Catholic political philosophy. The new journal devoted itself almost exclusively to elaborating the Catholic interpretation of contemporary political and intellectual events. "Now the Church realized the threat sooner than any other group and signaled the danger," declared the philosopher Goetz Briefs, referring to the inseparable evils of positivistic social science and totalitarianism.[2] World salvation, peace, and political liberty all depended upon man's recognizing his true place in the universe and returning to the natural moral law and the law of God. "It is plain to all but the willfully blind," declared one writer in 1941, "that the universe in which we live is an ordered universe, not a chaos." Above all others, the Catholic church understood the nature and demands of that order.[3]

Appropriately, the editors of the Review of Politics chose an essay by the French Thomist Jacques Maritain as the keynote article in their first issue. As perhaps the most widely respected and sophisticated Catholic philosopher in the world, Maritain was an obvious and impressive choice. Since the early thirties he had devoted himself to attacking Nazism, rejecting the positivism of the twentieth century, and developing Thomistic principles into a broad defense of democratic society. To a large extent "the firm and total vision of a Maritain" became to Catholics the criterion by which all others were measured, and their political theorists and social scientists drew on the Frenchman's work freely and confidently.[4]

As the Catholic legal philosophers had singled Holmes out for special condemnation, the social scientists did the same for John Dewey. While Thomists had been criticizing Dewey for many years, the charges grew in intensity during the late thirties. Largely through Dewey's efforts pragmatism had spread through American thought, insisted Leonard J. Eslick of St. John's College, and "the effect of this is inevitably moral skepticism, and from this to *realpolitik* and totalitarianism the distance is not very far." Pragmatism and the other false doctrines of modern thought must share "in responsibility for the error of totalitarianism."[5] It was of course revealing that he chose to term totalitarianism an "error." Father Stephen F. McNamee, S.J., a professor of ethics at Georgetown and president of the Jesuit Philosophical Association of the Eastern States, maintained that "American non-Catholic university professors have, for the most part, been sappers instead of architects and builders of democracy." Dewey, of course, was their intellectual leader. "The utter irony of the situation," McNamee exclaimed, "is that the American philosopher who most radically applied the ax to the principles upon which this democratic government, as we know it in these United States, is erected, is openly hailed as *the* philosopher of democracy." McNamee charged Dewey with denying God—"his most insidious error"—denying man's God-given rights, and denying the true purpose of government as the protection of those rights. Dewey made the state absolutely supreme, he declared, and man completely subordinate. "The plain truth is that John Dewey, more than any other single American writer, has undermined the principles on which American democracy rests."[6]

While the Catholics as a group generated the most organized attack on naturalism, an increasing number of social scientists and philosophers began in the years after 1935 to express similar skepticism about the naturalistic world view. With attitudes ranging from haunting doubt to virulent hostility, they subjected the naturalistic viewpoint, and especially the objectivist variety, to a sharp and probing reevaluation. "We need," announced Max Ascoli of the New School for Social Research, "a few elementary certainties based on clear reason and on unequivocal moral decisions."[7] By the late thirties the primary demand in the minds of many social scientists was no longer for an objective science of society, but rather for a direct moral commitment.

More and more scholars, some with naturalistic orientations themselves, came to suspect or even believe that there was indeed some kind of connection between the intellectual changes of the preceding decades and the rise of totalitarianism. "There can be little doubt," wrote Arnold Brecht in the American Political Science Review, "that totalitarianism has greatly profited from that value-emptiness which has been the result of positivism and relativism in the social sciences."[8] In spite of the diversity of American social science, the complexity of its methodological problems, and the number of theoretical issues involved, a number of scholars began to speak in terms of a monolithic "relativism" as the intellectual evil which had brought the twentieth century to the brink of destruction. "Democracy not based on, careless of, or indifferent to, fundamental moral values," argued Herbert Martin of the State University of Iowa, "can neither carry on, long endure, or even be."[9] As the ideological hostility to totalitarianism sharpened and the debate among American social scientists intensified, a small but growing number of scholars seemed to accept the contention that ideas by themselves were major social determinants and that a pervasive naturalism had largely caused the political crises of the thirties.

As the naturalists had developed a theory of historical progress based on the emancipation of men by science from superstition and a priori rationality, those who rejected that naturalism began their own reinterpretation of world history. During the nineteenth and early twentieth centuries, declared Oscar Jaszi of Oberlin College, positivism generally triumphed throughout western civilization. "Those who tried to introduce values, the conception of right and wrong in their social and political speculation, were regarded as antiquated preachers or obscurantists." The result was a general crisis and breakdown of moral values and political democracy. World War I had revealed that "fatal collapse," but because of the pervasive naturalistic orientation of American scholars "no satisfactory analysis was given to those fundamental structural and moral

181

changes in society which alone could explain an event of such universal magnitude." Instead of generating historical progress in any meaningful sense, naturalism was leading western civilization toward chaos and suicide. Though acknowledging that his interpretation was "crudely simplified," Jaszi insisted that those major intellectual changes had "undermined the liberal democratic idea before the World War."[10]

Turning to methodological specifics, the critics focused on the value-free orientation of many social scientists and what they considered their excessive empiricism. "The social sciences must admit that they cannot always be, and perhaps fundamentally can never be, 'scientific' in the sense that the physical sciences are," declared the economist John Donaldson. "Further, they must always take 'value' into account—a difficult responsibility."[11] The alleged value-free orientation had two fatal weaknesses. First, it failed to recognize the crucial importance of values and hence ignored an element essential for an understanding of human society. "If civilization is largely a matter of values and civilization represents the product of society's on-goings to date, and if sociology is the scientific study of this society," charged the sociologist Howard Odum of the University of North Carolina, "the omissions of social values assumes a larger significance than the errors of a pre-Copernican astronomy which assigned to the earth its wrong place in the scheme of things."[12] Ignore human values, a political scientist argued, and then, in fact, "men in societies cannot be described at all."[13] The second weakness they pointed to was the obvious fact that scientific investigation of any kind had to be based on some values or preferences to begin with, and hence in its very nature was value-oriented. Complete freedom from values in social science was thus an impossibility, and the objectivist naturalists were simply deluding themselves. It was essential that social scientists become aware that objectivity was an illusion, Albert Salomon of the New School maintained, for if the scholar did not recognize and supply his own values, then some outside force would ultimately do it for him. "A decision must be made, and the more urgently," Salomon declared in 1939, "since it involves the moral responsibility of intellectuals for the preservation of freedom and democracy."[14]

Along with their increased concern over the centrality of values in social science, the critics insisted that both science and philosophy were fundamentally rationalistic in their structure. While naturalistic technique had made significant contributions to sociology, Charles A. Ellwood explained, it became an impediment to scientific understanding "when it is backed up by a metaphysical monism, which asserts that only the physical has 'existential reality.' "[15] Facts were important, but only in the context of broad interpretive theories, which were necessarily rationalistic structures. "I would, however, especially emphasize as the great need of today," Ellwood declared, "sane and rational interpretation of social facts."[16] Empiricism by itself was meaningless and pointless. Economics was "not based on or derived (abstracted) from experience," argued the economist Ludwig von Mises. "It is a deductive system, starting from the insight into the principles of human reason and conduct."[17] In a meaningful social science, declared the economist A. B. Wolfe, deductive theory "will lead the way which empirical statistical analysis will have to follow."[18] While empirical techniques were quite useful, they agreed, they were clearly subsidiary to deductive theorizing and intuitive insight. "The imagination," proclaimed one sociologist, "is the medium for understanding the socio-psychological facts of the social sciences."[19]

In reemphasizing the importance of deductive theory, the critics were not only rejecting what they considered extreme empiricism but also preparing the methodological basis for returning value theory to the social sciences. Once deductive analysis was restored to a position of centrality, then normative ethical theory could be reintroduced. "In the end, so the Aristotelian position would imply, a social natural science cannot be constructed," argued Albert Balz of the University of Virginia, "unless a rational science of what ought to be is an integral portion of our enterprise."[20] A social science based on deductive analysis could include a logical role for normative ethical theory, and hence overcome the problems of both the value free orientation and excessive empiricism. It could also presumably meet the theoretical challenge to democratic government posed by European totalitarianism. "The ethics of hard facts, if pursued to its ultimate consequences," declared Paul Kecskemeti of the New School, "is the ethics of dictatorship."[21] The ethics of normative deduction, then, while essential to the success of social science, was also the ethics of democracy.

Kecskemeti and his colleagues on the graduate faculty of the New School for Social Research, many of them refugee intellectuals from Germany, were among the leaders in the attack on objectivist naturalism. Especially sensitive for personal reasons to the totalitarian threat and deriving from a less empirical and more theoretically oriented social science

183

tradition, they were sharply critical of what they regarded as the anti-rational and even anti-intellectual tone of many of their American counterparts. As a young student in Germany, Emil Lederer commented, he remembered Max Weber and Werner Sombart defending the proposition that science was necessarily neutral in relation to value judgments. While their argument had seemed convincing twenty years earlier, he noted, recent history had made it clear that the interpretation of science as morally neutral was inadequate and dangerous. Even though some valuations might be beyond the realm of scientific method, a more complete philosophical approach would substantiate certain ethical values and provide useful guidelines to social scientists in a time of crisis. "It does not follow that we ought to forfeit our right of judgment about all values," Lederer insisted, "or that there are not certain values which we are not only justified in denying but are even obliged to deny." [22]

Strengthening the reinvigorated defense of deductive ethical theory, Kecskemeti and Max Wertheimer, another German exile at the New School, rejected the possibility of an indefinite number of logically valid non-Euclidean ethical systems. Though acknowledging the postulational nature of logic, Kecskemeti argued that in practice no elitist ethical theory could really be self-consistent. He implied, though without demonstration, that a consistent normative theory would necessarily be humane and democratic. [23] Wertheimer maintained that the logical basis for the idea of non-Euclidean ethical systems was simply "not true." Identities existed in all societies and in all men, and those identities were the basis for a universally valid and logical system of ethical propositions. [24] As Kecskemeti had done, however, Wertheimer rested his case on certain general assertions and failed to produce or demonstrate his universal ethical system.

Morris Cohen and Ernest Nagel joined in rejecting the idea of non-Euclidean logics, defending the validity and necessity of the Aristotelian laws of thought. In their widely used textbook *An Introduction to Logic and Scientific Method*, Cohen and Nagel admitted that logic was formal but insisted that it still dealt with the external world and was essential to all human thought. "We do not believe that there is any non-Aristotelian logic in the sense in which there is a non-Euclidean geometry," they declared. [25] Though they did not attempt to defend logic as a method of establishing ethical propositions, their vigorous defense of the

Aristotelian laws of thought and of the critical necessity for logical analysis gave added weight to the revived emphasis on deductive theory in the social sciences.

Perhaps the two most prominent critics of naturalistic social science were the political scientist William Y. Elliott and the sociologist Pitirim A. Sorokin. Looking back on his early critique of pragmatism in the twenties when he had stood almost alone, Elliott maintained that his work "had the merit and the good fortune to point in the right direction." It had insisted on "the legitimate, even the necessary effort of evaluating politics in the light of the moral norms," and hence had helped to redirect the work of political scientists and eventually alter some of their naturalistic assumptions. The events of the thirties, Elliott declared, had demonstrated the fatal flaw in the various forms of pragmatism, for as long as totalitarianism was successful it could never be criticized or condemned on practical grounds. "And until the day of catastrophe, no criterion of Mr. Dewey's Instrumentalism may say the leader-principle nay."[26] Political science and political theory, he suggested, had to be based on some type of natural moral law.

Sorokin, who had begun to criticize the behavioral emphasis in sociology during the late twenties, grew increasingly hostile during the thirties toward the "insane ambition" of the social sciences to become "pseudo-mechanics, pseudo-physics, or pseudo-biology." Excessive empiricism had reached a dead end. "This truth of senses must be replaced by a more adequate *integral system of truth*," he insisted, "*consisting of the organic synthesis of the truth of senses, truth of reason, and truth of intuition, each mutually checking and supplementing the others.*"[27]

Striving for the organic synthesis he advocated, Sorokin published in 1937 the first three volumes of his ponderous and amazing *Social and Cultural Dynamics*. Consciously conceived as a treatise in the "great" tradition of world sociology, *Social and Cultural Dynamics* offered a sweeping interpretation of the nature of social change based on a massive quantitative and interpretive study of western civilization from approximately 600 B.C. to the 1930s. In fact, it was the most thorough formulation of the antinaturalist interpretation of history produced during the whole period. Western civilization, Sorokin charged, had been in decline since roughly the rise of nineteenth-century positivism. With conscious irony he made elaborate and wide-ranging use of statistical tabulations and quantitative correlations in order to prove that contemporary society, characterized by "overripe" naturalism, was at the threshold of a profound and inevitable disintegration.

Not only did he employ massive statistical correlations, but he also borrowed the non-Euclidean analogy. "Euclid's and Lobachevski's systems of geometry are both logically unimpeachable; both follow the canons of the same mathematical logic in the most perfect way," he pointed out; "yet their theorems and deductions differ." [28] Cultures, he suggested, were like geometries, in that they might be built on different first premises. Hence, varying cultures could be completely logical within their own system of assumptions and yet differ fundamentally in any number of ways. *"The canon of logical norms remains the same in the study of all the different cultures,"* he declared, *"but the logicality or nonlogicality of each is judged always from the standpoint of its major premises (if it has any)."* [29]

As Sorokin used statistics to demonstrate the decline of empiricism, however, he used the non-Euclidean analogy to overcome what he regarded as rampant relativism and nihilism. Whereas earlier writers who had accepted the non-Euclidean analogy assumed that it revealed the incommensurability of cultures, Sorokin argued that from a broader perspective it revealed the outlines of a comprehensive theory of social dynamics and at the same time demonstrated the wisdom of his attempted "organic synthesis." Based on the pattern of historical changes that he discerned in western art, epistemology, ethical philosophy, and legal theory, he concluded that social change could best be explained as a series of fluctuations between two polar types of wholly integrated cultural forms, the sensate and the ideational. Each represented a complete and comprehensive logical unity, just as did the systems of Euclid and Lobachevski, and each was the total opposite of the other. "The sensate mentality views reality as only that which is presented to the sense organs," he explained. "It does not seek or believe in any supersensory reality." [30] Sensate culture emphasized change and flux; its needs and goals were physical; its ethics were utilitarian and hedonistic; its methods were directed toward exploiting the external world for individual satisfaction. In ideational culture, "reality is perceived as nonsensate and nonmaterial, everlasting Being." [31] It focused on permanence; its needs and goals were primarily spiritual; its ethics were absolute and supernaturally oriented; its methods were directed toward elimination of physical needs and the perfection of

186

the inner self. "When one of these forms becomes dominant, various traits logically belonging to it begin in fact to infiltrate into the art and manifest themselves in all fields," he concluded. "These characteristics are at once logical elements of each of these forms and symptomatic of its presence." [32]

While according to their inner logic each was consistent and beyond criticism, a comprehensive view of the dynamics of cultural change—the fact that constant oscillations between the two polar forms was "without doubt"—demonstrated that each form was based on an important but partial perception of the truth about man and the universe. Since "the whole truth is infinite in its aspects and unfathomable in its depth," no cultural form was able to comprehend it completely. Thus cultures moved toward one of the poles, reached a point of near complete integration, and then carried the assumptions to the extreme of either asceticism or hedonism which ultimately provoked a reaction back toward the opposite polar form. "According to the principles of limit and immanent self-regulation of the sociocultural processes, when, in our eagerness, we go too far beyond the legitimate limit of a given theory," Sorokin maintained, "a reaction sets in and leads to its decline." [33]

Viewed in the broad terms of world cultural dynamics, then, each of the cultural forms was subject to meaningful and scientific criticism. The truly wise man could approach the deepest possible insight by drawing on the most profound perceptions that each offered. "In these eternal oscillations there is a great value, a great fascination, and a great optimism," he declared. "They mean that we are almost always in close touch with the ultimate reality, in spite of our inability to grasp it fully." [34] Among the variety of mixed, transitional forms, there was in fact one type, the idealistic, which struck that profound and judicious balance. "This is the only form of the Mixed class which is—or at least appears to be—logically integrated." [35] Claiming the balanced, idealistic viewpoint as his own, Sorokin made his position clear by identifying the most complete historical example of idealistic culture as "the *idealistically rationalistic system of truth of the medieval Scholastics* of the twelfth to the fourteenth centuries." [36]

The upshot was simply that Sorokin could claim to have transcended the logical limitations of the non-Euclidean analogy, to be able to demonstrate the futility of the extreme naturalists, and to predict their approaching downfall and the dawn of an age based on either the ideational or idealistic form. The sensate culture of the twentieth century was "dying" because of its own excesses and was entering a process of unavoidable disintegration. "This is something quite different," he noted, "from skepticism or its allies."[37] Indeed it was. In spite of the mass of scholarly detail and the considerable emphasis on the scientific nature of his study, Sorokin concluded along most familiar lines. The laws of *Social and Cultural Dynamics* demonstrated that the first third of the twentieth century was an age of relativism and materialism in which force naturally became the only ethical reality. "Such a rise of force to the position of the supreme moral arbiter is but an immanent result of the excessive development of the hedonistic and utilitarian moral mentality of our days." Sorokin made the connection explicit. Sensate culture readily led to the "use of force by every state that feels it can use it safely, be it Japan, Italy, Germany, Russia, or any other country."[38] Sensate culture had led to totalitarianism, and return to an ideational or idealistic culture was the only road toward salvation. Also, in spite of what anyone might say, it was inevitable.

Four years later, in 1941, Sorokin condensed and sharpened his broad argument in a book entitled *The Crisis of Our Age*. In the briefer and more direct form, Sorokin's ideas gained a somewhat wider acceptance, especially among nonprofessionals. The Methodist Student Movement proclaimed it "the best book on the subject of the present crisis" and arranged for Professor Paul E. Johnson of the Boston University School of Theology to prepare an even briefer condensation that could serve as a widely usable discussion guide. Sorokin gave wholehearted approval to the plan and wrote a special preface for the edition. "So far," he told the Methodist students, "the crisis of our age has been unfolding according to the diagnosis and predictions of my *Social and Cultural Dynamics*."[39]

Just as the existence of the totalitarian threat and the concerted attack of their opponents had forced the legal realists to modify their positions, so the assault of such scholars as Elliott and Sorokin forced many social scientists to qualify or reverse their earlier attitudes. The relativist historian Carl Becker discovered his "Generalities That Still Glitter," and declared that the values of democracy "have a life of their own apart from any particular social system or type of civilization."[40] Disregarding his earlier focus on the wholly formal nature of mathematics, Eric Temple Bell proclaimed that "mathematics has gained something more substantial, a faith in itself and in its ability to create human values."[41] Alexander Goldenweiser, Margaret Mead, and Bronislaw Malinowski all began to reemphasize the virtues of democracy and the great need to defend its moral achievements.[42] Sharply rejecting operationalism and extreme behaviorism, Howard Becker declared that "the slogan, 'No value-judgments in sociology,' has been misused by its adherents (and here I make no exception of myself)." While still maintaining a belief in the objectivity of truly scientific formulations, Becker insisted that the idea of a value-neutral scientist was "arrant nonsense."[43] Even Harry Elmer Barnes, one of the staunchest proponents of the new social science, was induced to speak kindly toward—of all things—Charles Ellwood's attempt to apply the gospel of Jesus to social problems.[44]

In political science the change in tone was equally marked. Referring to democracy as the government of justice through majority rule, Harold Lasswell declared that "it is timely to affirm the dignity of man and the commonwealth of mutual respect."[45] "All is not relative," George E. G. Catlin concluded from his study of the history of political theories. Rather, he discovered "a rational Grand Tradition of Culture" which demonstrated to his satisfaction "a certain agreement among rational men upon the objective good, upon the means of its expression in social life."[46] Charles Merriam concurred with his two colleagues. "Democracy," he declared in 1941, "is the best form of government yet devised by the brain of man—the ideal form of political association."[47] Although he did not examine the philosophical problem of justification, Merriam insisted that the ethical goodness of democracy was clear and demonstrable. "We know this by reason; we know it by observation and experiment."[48] The basic assumptions of democracy, he summarized, were the innate moral dignity of all men, the possibility and desirability of improving the material conditions of all men, and the propriety of making all political decisions through the processes of free discussions and elections. "For the proof of some of them we should look primarily to rational and perhaps to ethical analysis," he explained, "and for others to the body of observations, analyses, and conclusions accumulated by modern science."[49] The significant point about Merriam's statement was that it indicated that such rational and ethical proofs were available and clearly conclusive at a time when no American intellectual had been able to produce them. Merriam himself based his contentions not on any convincing ethical analysis but merely on a series of affirmations.

As part of that new mood of affirmation, the earlier skeptical view of the practical workings of democratic government began to receive careful reinterpretation. "Democracy must restore, revive, or win anew faith in its purpose and its destiny," Peter H. Odegard of Amherst College insisted; "for if such faith is lacking we face inevitable defeat."[50] Though motivated by a desire to understand American politics and to improve its performance, commented Francis O. Wilcox of the University of Louisville, "we may have been *too* critical of our democratic institutions."[51] At the annual meeting of the American Political Science Association in December, 1940, one of the roundtable discussions unanimously passed a resolution reaffirming the association's adherence to the principles of democracy and calling upon all political scientists to consciously spread its moral ideals. "We rededicate ourselves to the continuing task of promoting an understanding of democracy, and generating confidence in its institutions."[52]

Before the United States finally entered the Second World War, the practical refurbishment of the democratic ideal was far advanced. Of special interest was the problem of human irrationality which political scientists had utilized so widely in the previous decades. "It is my contention," declared Carl J. Friedrich of Harvard, "that we can restate the belief in the common man in such a way as to allow for what is sound in these antirationalist doctrines and yet retain what is essential for democracy."[53] In a book devoted specifically to that purpose, Friedrich maintained that "the common man" was, after all, entirely capable of carrying the load of meaningful democratic government. "Despite threats and occasional set-backs," declared another political scientist, "we move toward an increasingly rational public opinion in the modern world."[54] In 1940 Pendleton Herring of Harvard published *The Politics of Democracy*, a comprehensive study of American government and politics, which had a major impact in revising the political scientist's working image of democracy. "The politics of democracy, with all its weaknesses, hesitations, and irrationalities, is realistically based upon human nature," he argued; "hence it has a resiliency that competing forms of governance lack."[55] Parties, conventions, bureaucracies, political machines, and almost every other aspect of American politics emerged from Herring's work as basically rational, useful, and beneficent. Indeed, as E. E. Schattschneider exclaimed in his review, "confronted with the prospect of losing our institutions, we look at them with new eyes."[56]

Even though political scientists thus began to sharply alter their treatment of American government, the broader attitude change of many social scientists toward the problem of values was ambiguous and somewhat misleading. In spite of the fact that many came to question behavioral objectivism and to reject the idea of complete value neutrality, the majority of American social scientists remained committed to one or another form of philosophical naturalism. A few moved toward some variety of rational absolutism, such as neo-Aristotelianism, but most were still convinced that such a philosophical stand was intellectually dubious and practically dangerous. The change that marked the work of most social scientists was essentially a change in tone, emphasis, and concern, but not, in most cases, a fundamental philosophical change.

The crisis in social science theory was evident not only in the attacks of the Aristotelians, but also in the debate and confusion among those who remained, in one way or another, philosophical naturalists. While such critics as Sorokin, Elliott, and the Catholics drew a rigid line separating naturalism, ethical relativism, and totalitarianism on one side from rationalism, ethical absolutism, and democracy on the other, that simple division did not satisfy the majority of social scientists. No problem could be resolved "by retreating from an industrial economy and returning to the days of handicraft and self-sufficient agriculture," charged the sociologist Maurice R. Davie, "nor by taking flight from reality through preoccupation with Aristotle and St. Thomas Aquinas."[57] It was, after all, quite possible to accept the criticisms made against the goal of a completely objective, behavioristic social science, and still remain committed to a naturalistic theory of knowledge. It was also quite possible to emphasize the importance of human and democratic values while at the same time rejecting the idea that such values had any absolute or supernatural basis. Though in the heat of the debate a number of social scientists spoke of the absolute moral basis of democracy, most refused to accept any philosophical or religious system that traditionally supported such a claim. While most acknowledged a greater need for rational theory and a stronger emphasis on an irreducible human element, the majority still accepted the assumptions of a naturalistic world view.

In broad and necessarily rough terms the social scientists who accepted a basically naturalistic theory of ethics fell into three divergent groups. The first, including such scholars as Charles Beard, Robert M. MacIver, George H. Sabine, and Frank Knight, wholly rejected the claims of the behavioral objectivists. Positivist philosophers, Knight declared, "at bottom are simply bad metaphysicians."[58] Insisting that value judgments were unavoidable and essential to any meaningful social science, they agreed at the same time that there was no clear or certain way to establish the validity of any particular set of ethical judgments. "If we have different notions about honor or duty or shame or the rights of man," MacIver commented, "there is no decisive appeal." [59] Beard, who had long scorned both absolutism and the concept of value neutrality, stuck most of the time to his contention that no values could be demonstrated. "Our democracy rests upon the assumption that all human beings have a moral worth in themselves and cannot be used for ends alien to humanity," he argued. "This is an assumption and cannot be proved." [60] Thus, while joining critics of objectivist naturalism in proclaiming the central and unavoidable role of values, they consistently admitted that there was no way to prove the values for which they stood. In the context of the late thirties that appeared a most anomalous position. All vigorously defended democracy—MacIver argued for its "genius"—but all equally acknowledged that their beliefs had no conclusive rational basis.

Sabine's skepticism was perhaps the most striking of all. When he published A History of Political Theories in 1937, he established himself as one of the foremost authorities in the world. From that comprehensive study he concluded that all political theories were examples of "social relativism" and were determined by historical situations and not by reason. "It cannot be supposed," he declared, "that any political philosophy of the present time, more than those of the past, can step out of the relationships in which it stands to the problems, the valuations, the habits, or even the prejudices of its own time." To justify political ideals in any intellectually compelling way was beyond human power. "It is impossible by any logical operation to excogitate the truth of any allegation of fact, and neither logic nor fact implies a value." [61] Rejecting equally objectivist naturalism, Thomistic absolutism, and pragmatic ethics, Sabine affirmed both the relativity and unavoidability of human value judgments. Though he traced his attitudes to Hume rather than to Riemann, he maintained a strict non-Euclidean attitude toward all forms of deductive rationalism. "There is no logical reason," he insisted in 1939, "why a social philosopher should not postulate any value he chooses, provided only that he avows what he is doing and does not pretend to prove what he is merely taking for granted." [62]

The second group equally rejected behavioral objectivism. "To regard nature as mechanical and everywhere mensurable in terms of operational units," declared Ellsworth Faris, the chairman of Chicago's sociology department, "is indeed to rule man out." [63] Such scholars as Faris, Merriam, Lasswell, Robert S. Lynd, Rexford G. Tugwell, and Peter H. Odegard, argued for a pragmatic social science oriented toward human problem-solving. In his widely read book *Knowledge for What?*, published in 1940, Lynd argued for a social science directed toward the construction of a vastly improved society and the preservation of human values. [64] The claim of objectivity, he charged, tended too easily to become a tool for defending the status quo. Social scientists had the obligation to consciously criticize the controlling assumptions of their society and work for progressive change. To strengthen and help fulfill the ideals of democracy, Lynd suggested, seemed the most desirable general guideline upon which to develop efficient social techniques.

By and large, the second group differed from the first in two ways. First, they exhibited, mainly in tone, a greater confidence in the development of a meaningful social science. "To some of us it appears that the promise of sociology is encouraging," Faris explained. "We assume that the laws of human nature can be known." [65] If science were defined as the careful correlation of means to ends, commented Peter Odegard, going somewhat beyond many of the pragmatists, "there is no reason why political science may not be as truly scientific as chemistry or physics." [66] While social laws would be neither wholly mechanical nor absolute, most in the second group agreed, general principles of human and institutional behavior could be discovered which would give man a reliable control over his society. The second and more important difference was that most of those scholars believed, either confidently or only hesitantly, that scientific techniques could substantiate in some meaningful way human value judgments. "I affirm the validation of democratic assumptions," Merriam announced, "by a comprehensive program vigorously directed toward the attainment of democratic principles." [67] Successful democratic consequences, achieved through pragmatic social planning, Merriam believed, would demonstrate the moral propriety of democratic assumptions. Lynd, although refusing to clarify his idea of the theoretical relationship between science and ethics, strongly suggested that the discerning social scientist could wisely judge human wants and needs. "The science of human behavior in culture, as a science charged with appraising man's optional futures in the light of himself and of present favoring and limiting conditions," he maintained, "can no more escape dealing with man's deep values and the potential futures they suggest than it can avoid dealing with the expressions, overlayings, and distortions of man's cravings which appear in the institutions of a particular culture."[68] Neither Lynd nor any of the other pragmatically oriented social scientists extensively analyzed the philosophical question of the justification of values, but they generally thought that between such widely accepted ideals as "the common welfare" and the techniques of an instrumentalist social science they could practically settle any moral problem.

Indicative of the partial move away from the complete objectivist position, E. L. Thorndike and Read Bain, two of the most enthusiastic behavioral quantifiers of the twenties, began in the late thirties to speak of the great need for a scientific ethical theory. Rejecting any kind of transcendent moral system, Thorndike accepted a pragmatic theory based on the belief that "judgments of value are simply one sort of judgments of fact." His new interest was due to the fact that "the topic is important for workers in all sciences, and is especially important now."[69] Bain, remaining close to his previous orientation, attempted to develop an approach to ethics based on psychoanalysis and the concept of functional social integration. Accepting the legitimacy of a kind of normative social science, he still had to admit that his new position was "not wholly satisfactory."[70]

The third major group, from which Thorndike and Bain were edging away, was made up of those who retained the objectivist and behaviorist viewpoints, insisted on the moral neutrality of science, and denied completely the possibility of rationally justified ethical judgments. The major lesson of the past centuries, one scholar reaffirmed, was "the importance for political science of its long struggle to put 'is' in place of 'ought to be.' "[71] Wesley Mitchell, J. R. Kantor, Stuart Rice, Arthur F. Bentley, Luther L. Bernard, Earle E. Eubank, and L. L. Thurstone were among those who continued to emphasize the objective nature of social science and its complete separation from value judgments. Such phenomena as instincts, wills, and inherent rational processes, charged Kantor, were simply "imaginary processes."[72] Though he clearly felt a strong pressure, and by 1940 began referring to the necessity of recognizing "feelings" in scientific work, Mitchell still insisted that "science itself does not pronounce practical or esthetic or moral judgments."[73] Of course few, if any, of the objectivists had ever believed that human feelings and values played no part at all in scientific research. Rather they had argued that training and especially empirical techniques could eliminate them and produce thereby an objective and morally neutral knowledge. Mitchell still held to that belief. "It is not the business of the social sciences to say what is good and what bad," he reiterated; "all they can do is to trace functional relationships among social processes, and so elucidate the most effective means of attaining whatever ends men set themselves."[74]

In the middle of the intense methodological and theoretical debate George A. Lundberg and Stuart C. Dodd, the two most ardent advocates of operationalism in sociology, cooperated in giving the extreme objectivist approach its fullest systematic statement. In 1939 Lundberg produced his *Foundations of Sociology*, an extensive theoretical discussion that tried to outline a fully operationalist sociology. Three years later Dodd completed his *Dimensions of Society*, which developed an elaborate mathematical-statistical method of analyzing and classifying a wide range of sociological phenomena. "The only answer which a scientist needs to give to the question as to how 'spiritual' data are to be handled within the scientific framework," Lundberg announced, "is to point out that all the *observable behavior* covered by this category is readily and fully provided for in the scientific framework."[75] Though the Lundberg-Dodd approach did not gain widespread acceptance, owing to the changed climate of opinion as well as to its practical narrowness and aridity, objectivist naturalism continued to exert a considerable influence on the social sciences.

While those who retained their objectivist orientations responded to the crisis of the late thirties and early forties with their own strong affirmations of democratic government, most of them remained convinced that their declarations had no convincing rational basis. Stuart Rice unequivocally rejected the appeals of totalitarianism, but doubted the rational legitimacy of his judgment. "I must admit that my objections are based largely on emotion and prejudice," he confessed.[76] Percy W. Bridgman merely noted that most educated people seemed to think that democracy was a preferable system of government. "Never," he declared, "has any institution been justified in terms that anyone capable of close thinking could accept without stultification."[77] Charging that many of his colleagues had turned democracy into a "master dogma," Lundberg scorned the idea that any political or moral ideal could be justified or proven good. "The mere fact that I, personally, happen to like the democratic way of life with all its absurdities, that I probably would find some current alternatives quite intolerable, and that I may even find it worthwhile to die in defense of democracy," he proclaimed, "are matters of little or no importance as touching the scientific question at issue." Lundberg remained the most irreconcilable objectivist of the day. "My attachment to democracy may, in fact, be of *scientific significance* chiefly as indicating my unfitness to live in a changing world."[78]

Indicative of the attitude of the late thirties, a group of scholars under the leadership of Moses J. Aronson of the College of the City of New York established in 1935 the *Journal of Social Philosophy*, appropriately subtitled *A Quarterly Devoted to a Philosophic Synthesis of the Social Sciences*. Lamenting the fact that social scientists had become "estranged from everything faintly reminiscent of philosophy," the editors saw themselves responding "to a need for critical analysis and integration experienced by an ever-growing number of scholars in the social disciplines."[79] The lineup of contributors consisted of most of the major figures in American intellectual life. All seemed to accept the great need for theoretical integration as well as a broader philosophical orientation, but beyond that general agreement their essays continued to be marked by both a striking diversity and a continued commitment to a basic naturalism. Indeed, Aronson himself, who had strongly called for a more comprehensive theoretical synthesis, made it clear that his goal was "the ultimate formulation of an empirically grounded social philosophy."[80] Philosophical rationalists and neo-Aristotelians contributed essays to be sure, but they merely added additional unconvincing and often shrill voices. Rather than resolving any fundamental methodological or theoretical difficulties, the *Journal of Social Philosophy* simply mirrored the very divisions that had helped bring it into existence. In 1942, after seven years of publication, it went out of existence.

By the time the United States entered World War II, American social scientists had reached a complete impasse. Theoretical disagreement was rife and hostility intensifying. The sharpest conflict centered around the critical issue of the nature and basis of human value judgments, and on that problem there seemed little chance for any broadly acceptable, convincing resolution. Indeed, many social scientists strongly believed that there was no intellectually legitimate way to demonstrate the truth of a moral judgment and that the question itself was meaningless. All agreed that democracy was preferable to totalitarianism, and almost everyone expressed a willingness to help defend it in whatever way he could. But beyond that, neither methodologically nor theoretically, was there any positive consensus on the nature of ethical judgments.

11

Toward a Relativist Theory
of Democracy

"The pressure of events these days," acknowledged one scholar in early 1942, "is continuously turning criticism against social scientists because of the position they take toward values."[1] While the late thirties and early forties were surely a rhetorical harvest time for philosophical and religious absolutists, they were unable to force the majority of American intellectuals to abandon the naturalistic orientation that they had begun to embrace some fifty years before. If America were to avoid a regression "into the distant past of forest and jungle," declared one political scientist, intellectuals had to achieve "the necessary reconciliation of science, including modern psychology, with the ethical basis of the democratic way."[2] A theoretical resolution to the crisis of democratic theory was essential, most agreed, but it had to be accomplished within generally naturalistic assumptions.

The most highly visible fireworks usually exploded in exchanges between the absolutists and their "relativist" foes, but there was an equally sharp and eventually more important debate burgeoning among the naturalists themselves. Assaults on social science theory came not just from religious spokesmen and a priori rationalists but equally from innumerable philosophical naturalists who severely criticized one another. The division among the naturalists was evident in the diverse reaction they accorded Thurman Arnold's The Folklore of Capitalism, which appeared in 1937. Focusing on the inconsistent, emotional "principles" that served as the folklore of groups and nations, Arnold maintained that all "social creeds, law, economics, and so on have no meaning whatever apart from the organizations to which they are attached."[3] When analysts learned to ignore the slogans as principles of truth and began to view society objectively in terms of organizational conflict, they could finally begin to achieve practical understanding and control. Essentially Arnold was defending the

New Deal and arguing for large-scale national planning along admittedly "humanitarian" lines. The folklore that most attracted his attention was that of the Republican party and American business.

A number of intellectuals, especially those with strong New Deal sympathies, greeted the book with great enthusiasm. "I go the whole hog for 'The Folklore of Capitalism,' " declared Fred Rodell of Yale University. "Bluntly, I think it's a great book."[4] Delighted with the book's incisive mockery of the principles and ideals used to attack the Roosevelt administration, they regarded it as one of the finest examples of realistic, group-conflict political analysis. "Professor Arnold has left little room for disagreement with his exposures of the trumpery through which we have supported our political and economic institutions," commented Leon Green, former dean of the Northwestern Law School and a fellow legal realist.[5]

Substantial criticism, however, came from many scholars who were themselves committed both to a philosophical naturalism and to some form of economic change.[6] The most searching and comprehensive commentary came from Sidney Hook, a professor of philosophy at New York University. Accusing Arnold of wholesale confusion and inconsistency, Hook focused on the central weakness: "there is no place for a theory of the good in Arnold's analysis." Any social theory which lacked rigorous ethical criteria, Hook argued, sounding in that respect very much like the Thomists, was incomplete and dangerous. "After all, the most successful political organizations of our time are those headed by Hitler, Mussolini, and Stalin." Acknowledging that Arnold's ideals were humanitarian and his purpose a defense of the New Deal, Hook concluded that the confusions merely indicated that "his thinking is in the pre-reflective pupa stage."[7]

Arnold answered by deriding Hook as an "inspirational philosopher" who simply did not understand the political process. Defending his work as an objective account of the way political groups struggled for power and influence, Arnold insisted that any kind of moral theory merely handicapped the scientific observer. "It is, I think, this habit of the philosophical mind of first determining what they want to look for, before they actually look," he argued, "which makes them inept in actual organization." Arnold admitted that he made certain value assumptions, but insisted that discussing or analyzing them was both useless and obstructive.

"My own observation," he reiterated, "leads me to believe that philosophies have no meaning apart from organizations."[8]

Enraged by Arnold's "debonair irrelevance," Hook charged that the reply "fails to join the issue with me on any of the basic points I have raised." By ignoring the nature of values, their causes and consequences, Arnold was denying men the power to discriminate among ethical possibilities and separate the better from the worse. "If Mr. Arnold maintains that such knowledge can be achieved without analysis," Hook charged, "he is literally committed to an inspirational theory of value." Their fundamental disagreement was "whether politics as a science and art can dispense with normative judgments." His answer, Hook emphasized, was definitely not. Arnold's answer was unclear. "What Mr. Arnold really believes is his own secret, but the *objective* effect of his verbal confusion is to support the position that whatever is, is right."[9]

The exchange between Hook and Arnold indicated clearly the split among those who shared a general scientific naturalist orientation. Hook was by no means an "inspirational" philosopher, at least in the *a priori* sense. He was every bit as committed to an empirical, pragmatic naturalism as was the author of *The Folklore of Capitalism*. Both rejected absolute principles, *a priori* metaphysics, and self-evident moral universals. They disagreed on the possibility of an analysis of the nature of ethical judgments.

Hook and Arnold never resolved the theoretical issues that separated them, as indeed social scientists, philosophers, and legal theorists in general failed to reach clear agreement on any number of intellectual problems that confronted them. Most especially the questions of the validity and justification of value judgments remained moot, and no philosophy, neither pragmatism nor any other, commanded broad allegiance in its specific value theory. While a number of scholars in the late thirties tried to resolve the problem of justification, particularly the problem of the moral basis of democracy, their attempts seemed to attract little attention and exert even less influence.[10] No rational ethical system, most American intellectuals seemed to think, could ever really prove the legitimacy of a moral proposition. Wherever the philosopher started and whatever his approach, at some point, they believed, he must beg the question and hence logically fail. "The truth seems to be that in politics and ethics one can postulate what values one chooses," George H. Sabine commented; "consistency will then determine what follows, but it cannot either rule out or substantiate the postulate." [11]

While intellectuals reached no general agreement on a philosophy of values, they did begin in the late thirties to develop the clear outlines of a broadly naturalistic and relativistic theory of democracy. Abandoning the idea of logically demonstrating the validity of democratic government, they moved toward a pragmatic interpretation of the social consequences of absolutist versus relativist political theories. The Thomists had attacked them on what were actually pragmatic grounds: ethical relativism in practice led to totalitarianism. Assuming as most of them did the historical connection between absolutist philosophy and the authoritarianism of medieval society on the one hand and between science and the democratization of western civilization on the other, they were well prepared to refute the contentions of their critics and to return the charge with equal vigor.

John Dewey had in fact been arguing that philosophical absolutism implied political authoritarianism for over three decades. The complete fusion of the two lay in the central metaphor of Dewey's *Reconstruction in Philosophy*. "Classic thought," he argued, referring to the Platonic-Aristotelian tradition, "accepted a feudally arranged order of classes or kinds, each 'holding' from a superior and in turn giving the rule of conduct and service to an inferior." Attempting to describe the nature of absolutist philosophies, Dewey seized upon the feudal metaphor to argue that such systems in their very structure necessarily implied an elite ruling class. Absolute philosophy was logically analogous to a feudal society as well as historically its intellectual manifestation. Any such philosophical structure was necessarily general and vague and could not therefore automatically apply to specific human problems. As long as people believed that some such system of social and moral truths existed, then, there had to be an authoritative group or institution which could interpret and apply it. The classic tradition in philosophy gave man no actual truths but instead merely justified "power over other men in the interest of some class or sect or person." The metaphor culminated when Dewey described the change that the experimental attitude had wrought. "The net result may be termed, I think, without any great forcing, the substitution of a democracy of individual facts equal in rank for the feudal system of an ordered gradation of general classes of unequal rank." [12] As long as all facts could be critically and publicly examined in light of their social consequences, all men could freely make up their own minds about the nature of truth. No authoritative ruling group was required or needed. Dewey, whose philosophical method insisted on banishing all epistemological dualisms, left American social theory with one controlling dichotomy: absolutism and authoritarianism versus experimentalism and democracy. The heat of the late thirties helped forge that dualism into one of the central *political* assumptions of most American intellectuals.

Since the early twenties Dewey had tried to interpret political events in the light of that controlling dichotomy. Significantly, however, until the middle thirties he was not completely sure what actual governments belonged in which category. In 1921, while the meaning of events in Russia was still unclear and many people ridiculed the bolsheviks as anarchists or absurd idealists, Dewey explained them as theoretical absolutists. "At the present time there is one militantly active form of this philosophy of one movement in history and one law in society entrenched in Russia." Because of distracting and false reports people had "failed to grasp the situation in its simplicity." [13] Later, however, along with certain other pragmatists, Dewey began to see the Soviet Union as a social experiment and hence as belonging in the nonabsolutist category. At another time he lumped the communists together with the fascists and American capitalists as all being absolutists. "The disciples of Lenin and Mussolini vie with the captains of capitalist society," he declared, "in endeavoring to bring about a formation of disposition and ideas which will conduce to a preconceived goal." The absolutism of all three groups brought the same consequences. "Whatever form it assumes it results in strengthening the reign of dogma." [14] Thus while Dewey's theoretical categories were established, their concrete specification was uncertain and changing during the twenties.

It was not until the middle thirties, with the advent of Nazism, that Dewey decided on the final application of his theoretical categories. Communism, fascism, and Nazism were totalitarian and absolutist; American society, even with a restrictive capitalism, was nonabsolutist and relatively free. The more clearly the concept of totalitarianism emerged, the more firmly Dewey insisted on its philosophically absolutist foundations. The sharper the split grew between the polar terms totalitarianism and democracy, the less absolutistic and more experimental the United States appeared. "Conditions in totalitarian countries have brought home the fact, not sufficiently realized by critics, myself included," he acknowledged in 1939, "that the forms which still exist [in the United States] encourage freedom of discussion, criticism and voluntary associations, and thereby set a gulf between a country having suffrage and popular representation and a country having dictatorships, whether of the right or left." [15] That attitude represented one of the major changes of the thirties, as American intellectuals accepted Dewey's absolutist-relativist dichotomy as fundamental and, even more important, applied it to the political situation in the same way.

Dewey's equation of philosophical absolutism with political authoritarianism proved the linchpin of the developing relativist theory of democracy because it provided the one basis on which most American intellectuals could unite. It was grounded on a thorough naturalism; it required the acceptance of no specific ethical theory or philosophical system; and, best of all, it claimed that rational and religious absolutism was the real enemy of democracy. In short the absolutist-authoritarian equation appealed to all of the intellectual and emotional convictions of a great number of American scholars and at the same time allowed them to defend both naturalism and democracy by aligning their absolutist critics with European totalitarianism.

The crisis of the late thirties led a majority of intellectuals to fully transfer the issue of philosophical absolutism out of the area of epistemology and into the realm of politics. Nazism seemed the complete institutionalization of nonempirical, ideological absolutism, and hence the perfect example of what a number of anti-absolutists had been suggesting for many years. By the early forties philosophical naturalists, regardless of their other disagreements, were almost unanimous in maintaining that theoretical absolutism of any kind was the logical concomitant of totalitarianism. Allow an absolutism into social or political theory, argued the political scientist John D. Lewis in 1940, and any *Führer* or *Duce* had a perfect rationale for action. "It invites the dangerous conclusion that since *one* right course exists, since there is an absolute common good," he maintained, "an elite group, however small, which is able to rise above petty and partial interests to a vision of the *true* national interest is the best guardian of the welfare of the state." [16]

Though European totalitarianism was the shocking catalyst, naturalists vigorously applied the equation to their domestic critics. Jerome Frank attacked individuals like Mortimer Adler who were "confident that they alone are the true prophets of the Lord." Democracy, he claimed, was in danger from "Adlerian authoritarianism."[17] Max Lerner, a professor of political science at Williams College, termed both Adler and Hutchins "authoritarians," and maintained that the ideas Walter Lippmann expressed in *The Good Society* would lead to domestic fascism.[18] Assailing the "medievalism" of the *a priori* absolutists, another scholar equated them with dogmatists and obscurantists, emphasizing the "less deep-lying but equally significant indications of the medievalist tendency of both Fascist and Communist."[19]

Their anti-absolutism together with a growing anger over the attacks of the Thomists led a number of naturalists to bitterly condemn the Catholic church both as a *de facto* ally of fascism and an intrinsically authoritarian institution. The Catholic church, declared Malcolm Sharp, a professor of law at the University of Chicago, "has probably the best claim to the invention of 'fascism' because it gave Mussolini all his ideas and made and protected Franco."[20] Howard Mumford Jones of Harvard denounced "Catholic authoritarianism," while Frank Knight charged that the Inquisition and other forms of political coercion were the inevitable result of the application of Catholic principles.[21] Writing in the *Partisan Review*, Sidney Hook called the church "the oldest and greatest totalitarian movement in history." Like fascism, Stalinism, and Nazism, he continued, the church used dogmas, rituals, and the promise of human salvation "to order a society in behalf of the interests of a bureaucratic minority." Going beyond the theoretical equation of absolutist philosophy with political authoritarianism, Hook charged that the church was an ambitious, self-seeking organization that used men and ideas with no regard for anything but its own power and prestige. The political programs of Catholicism had no necessary connection with its practically pliable dogma, but rather were "to be explained by the concrete interests of the Church as an historic Organization in time."[22]

The counterattack against the church spread. The *New Republic* published a series of articles examining the influence of the church on American politics. "No one can fail to note," the author declared, "the increasing attacks of the Catholic hierarchy on the right of free speech for those who oppose or criticize its doctrines." While the Constitution protected the church's independence, the church tried to deprive its opponents of an equal protection. "Its tactics have been to paint all liberalism Red and to brand as Communist all who strive to uphold that individual freedom disparaged by the Church."[23] Writing in the *Nation*, another journalist argued that many Catholic periodicals, including *America* and the *Sign*, were clearly fascist in orientation. The Catholic press had almost unanimously supported Franco in the Spanish Civil War, and the church itself was more interested in its own organizational interests than in any kind of political freedom. "On international issues," he concluded, "the Catholic press has always advocated whatever political cause would further Church power."[24]

Growing increasingly alarmed over the world crisis, the wholesale assault of Catholic intellectuals, and the gathering strength behind the move to return "fundamental values" to American education, naturalist intellectuals organized a series of conferences during the early forties to rally their supporters. Such scholars as Dewey, Hook, Harry D. Gideonse, Bruce Bliven, Floyd H. Allport, Anton J. Carlson, Charles W. Morris, Herbert W. Schneider, Henry Margenau, and Horace M. Kallen joined in warning of the dangers of accepting any nonempirical, absolutist philosophy as a solution to the problems of the twentieth century. "World War II had, as might be expected, opened many doors leading to reaction and to claims of authority," declared Eduard C. Lindeman of Columbia University. "Indeed, a new authoritarian movement, almost a coalition although not consciously organized, had arisen in our midst."[25] The Catholics were the most powerful and therefore the most dangerous. "In principle and in practice," Kallen argued, "their intent is a spiritual fascism, a moral and intellectual totalitarianism, which has its peers in those of the Nazis and their ilk."[26] The second conference, held in early 1945, focused on "The Authoritarian Attempt to Capture Education" and urged all Americans who valued democracy to join in defending their intellectual freedom. There was, Dewey proclaimed, an "organized attack now being made against science and against technology" which could lead only to social regression and intellectual obscurantism.[27] The arguments of the Thomists and neo-Aristotelians were clearly having an effect, and during the middle and late forties the naturalists often found themselves having to mount their own counterattack.

In spite of the apparent inroads the absolutists were making in public debate and especially in educational philosophy, a number of thinkers began elaborating a naturalistic theory of democracy which won the support of a majority of American scholars and helped preserve the intellectual dominance of naturalism into the postwar period. Basing their approach on the powerful naturalist anti-absolutism, they assumed first

204

of all the de facto connection between theoretical absolutism and practical authoritarianism. Second, they developed the logical corollary: only social theories that recognized all truths, including ethical truths, as tentative, changing, and uncertain could support and justify democratic government. Finally, they argued that ethical theories by themselves were not in fact crucial to democracy, that they were important only to the extent that they were actually reflected in a society's cultural forms.

Though logically distinguishable, all three were parts of the same general attitude. Democracy, the naturalists assumed, was a social organization which celebrated diversity in all forms and on all levels. Its true meaning lay in its acceptance of disagreement, variety, novelty, change, and, ultimately, compromise based on reasoned discussion. An absolutist philosophy could not accept such a society. Only an intellectual conviction that all ideas were tentative and subject to constant criticism could prize a free and flexible social order. That conviction was crucial to the creation and preservation of democracy, not as an abstract theory, but as a broad social attitude that pervaded the thinking of citizens and found strength in a consequent wide range of independent and competing cultural institutions.

An absolute philosophy by its very nature constantly posed the threat of authoritarianism. Were its assumptions to spread widely throughout a society that threat would become immediately dangerous. A relativist philosophy could never pose such a challenge. Instead, it constantly embraced new and different ideas, insisting only that none of them ever be taken as absolute and considered unchangeable. If there were no absolutes, no one would ever have the theoretical justification for imposing his views on anyone else. Democratic governments could fight to preserve their fluidity and their intellectual and institutional pluralism, but never to impose any particular creed or principle. Democracy was therefore justified, not because anyone could prove or demonstrate certain ethical propositions, but because the idea of an absolute moral demonstration was itself a rational impossibility. "Now it follows that if there are no political ideas towards which the attitude of dogmatism can be justified," summarized one scholar, "then certainly absolutistic and autocratic political methods also cannot be justified."[28] Hence democracy alone was based on a rational and scientific attitude toward human understanding and political morality. Scientific naturalism necessarily implied an open, diverse, democratic social order.

That naturalistic justification of democracy developed along two lines, both of which were necessary for its general acceptance. The first one stemmed directly from Dewey's pragmatism and argued that the scientific method in a positive sense justified and proved the reasonableness of democratic government. The second, deriving largely from the inspiration of Justice Oliver Wendell Holmes, Jr., emphasized the impossibility of proving any value judgments and suggested that only a complete negation of the idea of universal moral principles could justify a free society. It was indicative of the unbridgeable chasm between the Thomists and many American intellectuals that the man who had been judged "the Totalitarian Mr. Justice Holmes" could provide for others the most persuasive defense of democratic principles available.

Reiterating his basic beliefs throughout the late thirties, Dewey insisted that science in two ways provided intellectual justification for democratic government. First, by revealing the experiential, human source of all valuations, scientific analysis indicated that expected social consequences were in fact the criteria that peoeple used to discriminate between values. A scientific value theory could then demonstrate that a democratic social order brought about the human consequences which were actually deemed most desirable by the greatest number of people, and hence that democracy was pragmatically the most reasonable and satisfying type of social organization. Second, since science was clearly the most reliable method of developing human knowledge, the social organization which most closely approximated the scientific method in its governing process was the most rational and desirable form of government. "Freedom of inquiry, toleration of diverse views, freedom of communication, the distribution of what is found out to every individual as the ultimate intellectual consumer," Dewey declared, "are involved in the democratic as in the scientific method." [29] The two were in fact analogous, and it followed that if the scientific method was the best method of intellectual advance then the democratic process was the best approach to social advance. Science, Dewey suggested, could only prosper in a democracy; and democracy could only succeed in its tasks if it employed scientific means. The two were different manifestations of the same attitudes.

A number of scholars elaborated Dewey's approach. "Our analysis of science and democracy to show their equivalence has been largely logical," declared the philosopher Horace S. Fries of the University of Wisconsin;

"that is, we have attempted to show an identity of structure in the method of each."[30] Sidney Hook insisted that democracy was the social system that allowed the greatest critical freedom to scientific method and hence was the most intelligent form of political organization. Since all attempts at value justification ultimately rested on a series of predictions about the future consequences of various lines of action, the scientific method could readily provide democracy with the most reliable ethical foundation possible.[31] Jerome Nathanson, another ardent Deweyite, identified the two logically and emotionally. "In the last analysis, the faith in intelligence is nothing but the faith in a democratic society."[32]

Nathanson's emphasis on faith was not unusual among naturalists at the end of the thirties. Recognizing the depth of the threat that totalitarianism posed they came to believe in the primary need for a determined moral commitment. They did not suggest a faith that abandoned critical intelligence, but a faith in the potential of human understanding and of democratic goals. "It is quite true," Dewey declared in 1939, "that science cannot affect moral values, ends, rules, principles as these were once thought of and believed in, namely, prior to the rise of science." Men had to give up their absolutes and instead place their faith in the power of the scientific method to delineate and then create a better world. "A culture which permits science to destroy traditional values but which distrusts its power to create new ones," he cautioned, "is a culture which is destroying itself."[33] At some ultimate point, men simply had to have faith.

In spite of Dewey's enormous prestige, many naturalists could not accept his value theory or his contention that the scientific method logically supported a moral theory of democracy. To those who were skeptical of the legitimacy of any positive value theory, the figure of Justice Holmes seemed especially meaningful. "Freedom is what we are fighting for—and Holmes was in a deep sense a democrat," declared Max Lerner in 1943. "Today more than ever we stand in need of Holmes the good soldier, Holmes the partisan of civil liberties, Holmes who was skeptical of the omniscience of any elite."[34] In moral theory a complete relativist and in judicial practice a renowned civil libertarian, Holmes served as a striking example of the democratic implications of intellectual skepticism. "I suspect that the tough-minded liberal faith that Holmes defended—a liberalism that is honest because it is based upon a faith in democracy—," wrote Felix Cohen, "will probably survive the pontifical curses of Mr. Lippmann."[35]

Although Holmes had died in 1935, his memory was still very much alive, not only in the law but throughout American intellectual life. Perhaps more than any other man, Thomas Vernor Smith was responsible for drawing on his inspiration to clearly formulate the negative justification of democracy. A professor of philosophy at the University of Chicago, Smith had grown increasingly skeptical about the possibility of justifying ethical values. By 1934 he was arguing that the human conscience, as the ultimate source of all absolute values, represented mainly "a push for power." Men habitually wrapped their desires and ambitions in the folds of conscience and thereby justified aggression and repression. "Men of action have had the most robust consciences of history," he argued, and the best examples in modern times were men "like Mussolini, Lenin, Hitler." [36] As long as men considered conscience an absolute moral guide —as long as they allowed any moral absolutes—the inevitable result was conflict and war. Even theoretical absolutes that claimed to justify personal freedom were intellectually suspect. "Conscience becomes the final denier of what it affirms: there can be no equality while one usurps the pontifical role of arbiter for either the judgments or the actions of all." The only road to a peaceful, decent, and libertarian society, then, lay in the direction of intellectual relativism and moral skepticism. "Civilization, consequently, lies somewhere beyond conscience." [37]

Throughout his life Smith was fascinated with American politics which, to him, meant the politics of incessant compromise. The success of America's political institutions, he maintained, was due to a genius for horse-trading and a refusal to deal with practical issues in terms of moral absolutes. His dedication to politics, as well as his practical shrewdness and effective public manner, won him two terms in the Illinois State Senate and one in the United States House of Representatives from 1939 to 1941. His legislative career strengthened his belief that an emphasis on morality only hindered those practical adjustments among various interests that made democracy work. Relishing his political role, Smith continually emphasized that an unbending moral attitude brought only confusion and disruption. People should treat the whole world, he implied, as a huge legislature. [38]

While he was sharpening his attack on moral absolutism and embarking on his political career, Smith drew closer and closer to Holmes as his intellectual guide. In the same year that he published *Beyond Conscience*, Smith began his extended discussion of "how Holmes doubted his way to democracy."[39] From his early conviction that all absolutes and all certainties were merely delusions, Holmes was directly led to a broad social toleration. Since nothing was certain and since men always disagreed, Smith explained, Holmes concluded that the only humanly wise and intellectually justifiable course was to allow men as much freedom as possible while at the same time preserving a necessary minimum of social order. Unlike the Nazis and the neo-Thomists who sought to escape from doubt, Holmes embraced it and made it the basis for a theory of the open society. He defended the right of the majority to alter social institutions, but he also defended the right of the individual to think and speak freely. Skepticism could legitimately only breed tolerance and a hatred for any kind of oppressive absolute. As long as the democratic form of government existed, Smith declared, "Holmes is one of its immortals." He had, in fact, "the mind in our generation most like the great minds of our Founding Fathers."[40]

Combining Holmesian skepticism and his practical experience with the philosophical eclecticism that marked his work, Smith pushed the relativist argument to its logical conclusion. In 1942, when the cry for national unity on fundamental values was nearing its peak, Smith declared that "democracy does not require, or permit, agreement on fundamentals."[41] He added, implicitly and explicitly, his one relativist caveat: democrats must agree not to insist on the public acceptance of their private moral beliefs. The profound insight that democracy did not permit agreement on fundamentals was the legacy of the great Justice. "In our time no man has done more, I think, than Oliver Wendell Holmes, Jr., to safeguard democracy's future."[42]

By the middle forties the equation between intellectual relativism and democracy had been widely articulated and accepted. "This 'relativism' has been for centuries the only effective weapon in the struggle against any brand of totalitarianism," declared Philipp Frank, a philosopher at Harvard University.[43] The two major lines of argument, one stemming from Holmes and the other from Dewey, were quite similar and based on many of the same assumptions. Those who followed Dewey placed a greater weight on the logical analogy between science and democracy, and often argued that a rational, scientific justification of human values was possible. Those who leaned toward Holmes tended to doubt the persuasiveness of pragmatic value theory and found sufficient intellectual justification in the negative argument against the legitimacy of any absolutist, and therefore nondemocratic, society. In spite of numerous variations, most naturalists accepted one or the other form of the relativist theory. "Democracy then becomes identified with this principle of relativity, as contrasted with the absolutism of dictatorships," Boyd M. Bode of Ohio State maintained. "There is no middle ground." [44] Together the two major variations provided a basis for most naturalists to join in affirming the rational propriety of democratic government and the authoritarian danger of any theoretical absolute, whether fascist, communist, or Thomist.

Thomas Vernor Smith's conclusion that democracy could not permit agreement on fundamentals suggested the kind of cultural focus that was the third major characteristic of the relativist theory of democracy. The relativistic-democratic equation was not just a logical theory: it was also an empirical prediction. It was not only an ethical justification of democratic society, but it was also a description of the kind of cultural foundation that a democracy demanded. There was thus a kind of ambiguity in the relativist theory of democracy, for the idea of the relativist basis of democracy meant two distinctly different things: the logical argument that attempted to justify democracy in theory and the empirical social structure that was the *sine qua non* of democracy in fact. That ambiguity helped bring about a subtle shift in the thought of many naturalists from the logical problem of justification through the relativist solution to a growing concern with the nature of a specifically democratic type of culture. The problem of justification thus led to an emphasis on the cultural bases of various political forms and later, in the postwar years, to the idea that a functioning democratic culture—and especially, American culture —was itself a normative phenomenon.

A focus on culture was not a logical necessity for the theoretical justification of democracy. The naturalists, however, habitually thought in terms of social structure, institutions, and culture. The absolutist-relativist dichotomy was itself founded on the idea of social consequences. The Thomist contentions were attacked not just on the basis of logic but, more important, on the grounds that the practical implementation of an absolutist ethical system would lead to political authoritarianism. Ideas were crucial, the naturalists believed, not abstractly in themselves, but only when they were embodied in cultural institutions. Accepting the lessons of the new anthropology, they believed in general that culture in its broadest sense was the dominant factor in explaining human behavior. Thus, they came to assume that there must be a specifically democratic culture that underlay democratic political forms and equated that type of culture with an institutionalized relativism—a culture that denied absolute truths, remained intellectually flexible and critical, valued diversity, and drew strength from innumerable competing subgroups. From that assumption it was not difficult to jump to the conclusion that American society represented that specifically democratic type of culture and that it was in fact the norm for understanding the operative basis of democracy. Developed in defense of their country when it was locked in a death-struggle with European totalitarianism, the naturalist idea of a relativistic and democratic culture came understandably to bear a close resemblance to the actual society that existed in the United States.

The move from the logical to the cultural level additionally provided the solution for a practical problem relativistic theory raised. If democratic societies were actually characterized by such widespread disagreement and diversity, what held them together and prevented continuous civil wars? A common culture was the obvious answer. With its widely and often unconsciously accepted patterns of behavior and perception, a common cultural framework could cement together individuals and groups who disagreed on any number of specific issues. Cultural homogeneity was the practical balance to intellectual diversity.

Finally, subtle doubts about the legitimacy or the final persuasiveness of the relativist justification of democracy helped induce many naturalists to move from the logical to the cultural level. As Dewey had suggested, once the absolutist attitude was abandoned it was impossible to provide an absolute justification. Admitting the difficulty of producing a completely convincing rational argument and acknowledging a considerable opposition to his pragmatic value theory, Dewey seized on the idea of culture as a way around the theoretical problem. Whatever one thought about the foundations of morality, he reasoned, strong individual and communal values in fact existed. Modern anthropology demonstrated that such values arose out of a general cultural matrix which characterized every society. The crucial practical problem confronting democracy, then, was the discovery of what kind of culture produced democratic institutions. "The problem of freedom and of democratic institutions," he argued, "is tied up with the question of what kind of culture exists; with the necessity of free culture for free political institutions." Cultural habits and attitudes were the foundation of all successful governmental forms: "political institutions are an effect, not a cause."[45]

Though the jump from justification to culture was logically a non sequitur, Dewey made the connection in terms of the relativist-absolutist dichotomy. "Shrewd observers have said that one factor in the relatively easy victory of totalitarianism in Germany was the void left by decay of former theological beliefs." While the acceptance of a particular religion had disappeared, the cultural habit of relying on authoritative pronouncements had remained. "Those who had lost one external authority upon which they had depended were ready to turn to another one which was closer and more tangible." Thus absolutism as a cultural form underlay totalitarianism. "The problem," Dewey then pointed out, "is to know what kind of culture is so free in itself that it conceives and begets political freedom as its accompaniment and consequence." The answer was clearly science, but not just science as an intellectual force. Science instead was and could become a motivating cultural force. "In some persons and to some degree science has already created a new morale—which is equivalent to the creation of new desires and new ends."[46] Thus the dichotomy between absolutism and relativism characterized cultures as well as philosophies, and explained in social terms why some countries were more susceptible to totalitarianism than others. Though Dewey continued to defend democracy on logical grounds, he was led by the tendencies of his own assumptions to embody his absolutist-relativist antinomy in cultural forms and thereby help shift the focus of American intellectuals from the relativistic justification of democracy to its cultural analysis.

Dewey's contribution in *Freedom and Culture*, declared Charles Merriam, "is one of the most penetrating and stimulating contributions yet made to modern political science." The cultural orientation seemed especially useful for an analysis of the problem of American government. Though Dewey's attempt failed to achieve a completely satisfactory synthesis between political theory and cultural analysis, it pointed in the most fruitful direction. "The design of lifting the problem of democracy above economic determination, above emotional violence, above outdated psychology, tribal or industrial, and of elevating the discussion to a scientific-moral, cultural basis," Merriam concluded, "is a noble and challenging one."[47] The phrase "scientific-moral, cultural basis" revealed with striking clarity the naturalist mentality at the end of the thirties. It joined together three logically quite distinct ideas and assumed that they were, or at least could be, integrated into a theoretical whole.

Indicative of the extent to which the explicit relativist democratic theory grew out of the common assumptions of American naturalists, the historian Jacques Barzun produced in the same year that *Freedom and Culture* was published an almost identical formulation. Claiming that the absolutist-relativist dichotomy was the central reality of twentieth century thought, he equated absolutism with intellectual failure and political defeat. "Whatever the dogmatist may feel about it," he argued, "this relativist, instrumentalist philosophy is the philosophy of free democracy par excellence."[48] Though he expressed his indebtedness to James rather than to Dewey, Barzun moved toward the cultural level in much the same way Dewey had done. "If democracy is not an institution or a set of institutions, what is it?" he asked. "It is an atmosphere and an attitude; in a word —a culture." Equally, he agreed that culture was the dominant political determinant and that a democratic culture was necessarily a kind of institutionalized relativism. "Democracy is thus originally the result and not the cause of our deep-seated desire for diversity, freedom, and tolerance," he maintained. "It follows—and this is the twofold thesis of this book— that culture must be free if men's bodies are to be free; and culture perishes if we think and act like absolutists."[49] A ringing defense of both democracy and relativism, Barzun's work represented the logical reformulation of American naturalism when confronted with European totalitarianism on the one side and philosophical and religious absolutism on the other.

While a number of intellectuals were clearly and explicitly formulating the relativist theory of democracy, political scientists began to interpret the processes of government along the same lines. Condemnations of the authoritarian implications of moral absolutism abounded, and most looked upon the Aristotelian revival as suspect at best.[50] But beyond that, the emerging relativist theory of democracy became the instrument for a marked reevaluation of the theory of American politics. Perhaps two of the most significant early revisionists were colleagues in the department of government at Harvard University, Carl J. Friedrich and Pendleton Herring.

As late as 1937 Friedrich had emphasized the traditional idea, put in classic form by the former British Prime Minister Sir Arthur Balfour, that a democracy was only possible when its citizens shared a common agree-

213

ment on fundamental values.[51] By 1939, however, he had changed his
view. "It seems highly questionable whether fundamental agreement, or
the absence of dissent in matters of basic significance," he remarked, "is
really a necessary or even a desirable condition for a constitutional democracy." Responding to the increasingly high-pitched pleas for a unity on
"fundamentals" in order to meet the totalitarian crisis, Friedrich pointed
out that the most successful and resilient democracies, such as the United
States and Switzerland, were in fact nations that comprised widely divergent racial, ethnic, and religious elements. "May it not be that modern
constitutional democracy is the endeavor precisely to organize government in such a way that agreement on fundamentals need not be secured?" he asked. American government, he argued, surely did not work
because of any agreement on religious or ethical systems, but rather by a
process of pragmatic compromise. Assuming the absolutist-relativist dichotomy, Friedrich drew the line sharply. "Since certainly dictatorship of
the modern totalitarian variety, and perhaps a good many other forms of
government require such agreement on fundamentals, constitutional democracy is possibly the only form of government which does not require
such agreement." Appropriately, he invoked the memory of Justice
Holmes in defending his view.[52]

To anchor his new conviction that democracy uniquely did not demand agreement on fundamentals, Friedrich transferred his focus from
the theoretical to the cultural level. "I think it is in the light of these
undeniable facts," he declared, "that we can fully appreciate the importance, from a realistic standpoint, of realizing that these 'freedoms' or
'liberties' are essentially patterns of behavior." Theoretical principles or
ethical ideals were generally so vague as to be practically meaningless;
when they were brought down to specific issues, they usually caused only
bitter disagreement. What in fact held societies together and overcame
ideological disputes was a largely unconscious, common cultural tradition.
As long as men acted according to shared cultural behavior patterns and
focused on practical tasks, they could work out mutually satisfying com-
promises. "Here let us emphasize again that what binds a free people together is not an agreement on fundamentals," Friedrich explained, "but
a common way of acting in spite of disagreement on fundamentals."[53]
The fact was that men in general acted according to a belief that such
things as murder, theft, and brutality were bad, regardless of the different
reasons they might adduce. Thus working out the assumptions of relativist

214

democratic theory, he substituted cultural givens for conscious agreement as the basis of free government. Democracy required a kind of unity to endure, but it was a pragmatic, relativistic, cultural unity and not a theoretical, ethical, or absolute unity.

While Friedrich worked on a broad comparative scale, his colleague Pendleton Herring dealt with the specific, practical processes of American government. Discarding theoretical principles as dogmas, Herring insisted that absolutes had no place in the politics of democracy. "The unvarying truth or falsity of the democratic dogma is not of determinant importance," he explained, but a general attitude of tolerance, flexibility, and compromise was. "The significant thing is that the ideology of democracy permits the peaceful resolution of interest conflicts through accepted institutions." Popular government was a practical process that assumed widespread diversity and constant change. Indeed, he maintained, "democracy's first duty is the preservation of the conditions that permit this toleration of disagreement." Quoting Friedrich favorably and referring to Holmes as one of the great spokesmen for the "values of American life," Herring firmly placed American politics within the relativist framework. "Democratic government is not a set of principles which must be consistently followed," he reiterated.[54] Instead it was essentially a set of procedures for compromising diverse interests, none of which could be taken as absolute without endangering the whole system.

Herring, too, emphasized the necessity of a common cultural basis to preserve democracy's working unity amid political and ideological conflict. "For its successful functioning democracy assumes a society naturally integrated," he pointed out. "There must be a pattern of community life with meaning to its people."[55] As the determinant political factor, the idea of cultural consensus enabled social scientists to ignore the problem of democracy's rational moral basis. The actual appeal of the democratic ideal, Herring claimed, could, in fact, best be discussed as a myth—a set of attitudes and values which primarily had emotional strength. "The word 'myth' is used here not in a derogatory sense but rather to underscore the assertion that in speaking of democracy we are not dealing with final values or even with a systematic philosophy," he maintained. "We are faced rather with an attitude, a tradition, a set of ideas that have proved significant to a large number of men during a brief historical period." Above all, it was important to remember that "the strength of a myth does not rest primarily in logical consistency."[56] An understanding of the na-

215

ture and meaning of democracy lay in the area of cultural, not logical, analysis.

Not only was it unnecessary for citizens to agree on theoretical fundamentals, Herring continued, but their outright indifference to them was a crucial factor in the actual success of popular government. Suggesting the direction many political scientists would later take, he accepted such facts as massive nonvoting, general lack of active political participation, and the apparent fickleness of public opinion—facts earlier scholars had used to argue the incompetence of the average citizen—and erected them into significant supports of the democratic process. Rather than being a drag on democracy, nonvoters, by their very indifference, provided popular government with a pluralism which prevented the whole society from being divided into sharply opposed coalitions. Those who merely voted, but participated in no other way, helped equally to preserve democracy by ensuring that no impassioned commitment would mobilize large numbers in a sustained confrontation. Even much-maligned public opinion, to a large extent because it was changeable and unpredictable, was a crucial force in guaranteeing democracy's success. "Thus the concept, by referring to the 'people' for the ultimate sanction of authority, retains flexibility and even uncertainty as to the focus of authority within our society." Fickle public opinion meant that "power can never be crystallized in a final determinate human will."[57] Answering both the theoretical absolutists and the earlier critics of democracy, Herring argued that indifference to fundamental values and political principles was not harmful but beneficial. It allowed American politics to function peacefully and tolerantly, while preserving a maximum degree of freedom. A broad concern with fundamental values would be a serious danger.

Responding to the crisis of democratic theory that American naturalists faced, Friedrich and Herring gave the assumptions behind relativist theory the form of concrete analysis. Together with such scholars as Dewey, Smith, and Barzun, they helped to reformulate the common assumptions of most American intellectuals into an explicit and coherent justification of democratic society. Continuing to reject the appeals of philosophic rationalism, they retained their naturalist orientations and turned the charges of their domestic critics back against them. If an absolute demonstration of democracy's moral foundation were impossible, that only meant that any absolute moral-political demonstration was impossible. And that, they reasoned, meant that logically no individual or group could justify asserting any set of values over others. By continuing to insist that the issues be treated in terms of social consequences and cultural realities, they avoided the theoretical problem of justification as it had traditionally been posed. The clear reformulation thus proved convincing to most naturalists because it remained within their set of fundamental assumptions and at the same time provided both a logical and empirical resolution to the theoretical crisis they faced. The barbarities of Nazism demanded a commitment to democracy. The assaults of the Thomists demanded a defense of naturalism. The relativist theory of democracy provided a rational basis for both.

12

Theoretical Principles & Foreign Policy

In September, 1940, over five hundred American intellectuals gathered in New York City for a special conference on science, philosophy, and religion. A huge tent was erected in the central quadrangle of the Jewish Theological Seminary to accommodate the meetings, and representatives from all over the nation attended. The object was to bring together scholars from all fields and with all points of view in order to formulate the basic principles that underlay the democratic ideal.

On the first day of the conference Mortimer Adler addressed the assembled scholars. "With a few notable exceptions, the members of this conference represent the American academic mind," he declared. "It is that fact itself which makes it unnecessary, as well as unwise, for me to make any effort in the way of reasoning." Charging American academics with embracing a skeptical positivism that corroded all ideals, he accused them of being largely responsible for the political crisis that had culminated in World War II. "For all of these reasons," he repeated emphatically, "I say we have more to fear from our professors than from Hitler." In fact, he concluded, Hitler might even be an instrument of God for the purification of modern culture, just as the Babylonians and the Assyrians had been instruments for chastening the Jews. "A civilization," Adler proclaimed, "may sometimes reach a rottenness which only fire can expunge and cleanse."[1]

Amidst a turmoil of shock and indignation, Sidney Hook proceeded to the platform. "The progress of scientific knowledge flies full in the face of every one of his assumptions about the nature of knowledge," Hook charged, and such philosophical absolutism could lead only to oppression and authoritarianism. "Whether Mr. Adler is aware of it or not—and I sometimes think he has not yet learned to read his own words—this constitutes a justification of religious intolerance." Those implications were "confirmed by what he has to say of the cultural beauties of medieval culture, of which the liquidation of religious heresy and the Inquisition were integral parts." As distinct from Adler, Hook continued, "I do not believe that there is any such thing as a philosophical fifth-column." Given such an opportunity, however, he was unable to resist. "But if there were anything that could possibly be regarded as such," Hook declared, "then I believe that it could be demonstrated that it would be not positivism but the views of Mr. Adler."[2]

While the conference contributed little to either American unity or democratic theory, it contributed a great deal to general animosity. Hook had been intemperate in his reply, most seemed to agree, but he had certainly been justified. The *New Republic* gleefully reprinted Hook's address and gave it wide publicity. The *Christian Century*, which thought Adler and Hutchins had a "good case" on philosophical grounds, criticized the former's insulting and dogmatic manner. "It is doubtful," the magazine commented, "if a more indecent spectacle has ever been staged in the long tradition of American culture and scholarship."[3]

After September 1, 1939, the internal debate between the advocates of scientific naturalism and their critics took place in the context of a new and terrifying world war. During the first two weeks of September the German army seized most of western Poland, and on the seventeenth the Russian army invaded from the east. Before the month was over, Poland had surrendered. A new Russian-German treaty established respective zones of control. While Russia strengthened her western borders by occupying Lithuania, Latvia, and Estonia and by invading Finland, the Germans conquered Norway and Denmark. Then in the spring of 1940 the Nazi blitzkrieg struck the Netherlands, Belgium, and Luxemburg. As the French armies moved north to support the Belgian front, the major German attack drove below them into central France. In less than a month Belgium had surrendered; the British had been forced to evacuate the continent; and the Nazi armies were poised on the Seine. On June 10 Mussolini invaded France from the south, destroying the last French hope of reinforcing the northern and eastern fronts. The Germans entered Paris on June 14, and by the end of the month dominated all of western and much of eastern Europe.

Hitler's successes, and especially their shocking suddenness, transformed the earlier discussion of totalitarianism and foreign policy into a national debate that reached frenzied proportions. As the Roosevelt administration moved slowly but steadily toward throwing the strength of the United States against Germany, Americans divided bitterly over its actions. A very small but slowly increasing number advocated immediate American entry into the war on the side of the British. A larger number, probably a majority, agreed that the United States should give some aid to England, but divided over the question of exactly how much. Some of those clearly hoped to move the nation step by step into the actual war, while most just as firmly hoped that limited aid would be sufficient to save England and thereby guarantee that America would not become directly involved. Public opinion, while generally supporting aid to England, remained opposed to direct involvement. Finally, another large group, decreasing in size but increasing in vigor, sought to prevent the United States at all costs from being drawn into the conflict. They vehemently opposed Roosevelt's foreign policy, and argued that the United States should confine its interests to the western hemisphere.[4]

While debating foreign policy and such issues as neutrality legislation and lend-lease, Americans generally saw the crisis as confirming whatever beliefs they had held all along. Businessmen urged that Nazism demonstrated the essential need for free enterprise and maintained that the threat of war made the considerations of industry supreme. Social reformers maintained that Nazism and the threat of war necessitated a greater economic equality in order to make democracy a living reality that men would willingly defend. Churchmen declared that the crisis proved the need for a greater attention to religious beliefs which could strengthen people in such frightening days. Addressing Congress on January 4, 1939, President Roosevelt declared that religion was the "source" of democracy. "Religion, by teaching man his relationship to God," the president explained, "gives an individual a sense of his own dignity and teaches him to respect himself by respecting his neighbors."[5]

While not all intellectuals accepted Roosevelt's interpretation, spokesmen for almost all points of view agreed that the crisis required a firm and unshakable belief in democracy itself. "Let us repudiate the defeatists," cried Henry M. Wriston, the president of Brown University. "More fundamental than guns, more fundamental than butter, is the reawakening of faith in the validity of our ideals, a resurgence of faith in the democratic process."[6] Comparing the appeal of various forms of government to religions, Alex A. Daspit, a professor of government at Louisiana State University, concluded that "ultimately communism, fascism, and democracy must be considered on the level of faiths."[7] Individuals as far apart as Hutchins and Dewey agreed with that. Above all, they insisted, Americans had to believe in democratic ideals and share a democratic faith, if the nation were to weather the crisis.

The widespread agreement on the need for faith and commitment, though shared by scientific naturalists, encouraged the attack on pragmatism and relativism. More and more, politicians, literary critics, businessmen, artists, and journalists accepted the apparent *prima facie* logic that philosophical relativism led to moral relativism, which led to cynicism and nihilism. Relativism was "debilitating." It destroyed all values and left its adherents helpless. The western democracies had fallen, and America was endangered, the argument ran, because debilitating relativism had spread widely and robbed people of their convictions and their will to fight.

Allen Tate, the distinguished literary critic at Princeton University, called positivism "the temper of our age" and argued that it was responsible for a "deep illness of the modern mind." By disrupting the continuity between the physical and the spiritual, and teaching that reason was unimportant, Tate charged, "Deweyism" created intellectual disorder and acted as "a powerful aid to the coming of the slave society."[8] The courage and conviction of American intellectuals, suggested a columnist in the *American Mercury*, had been undermined by "a mind dissolving empiricism" that "has made them hollow."[9] Archibald MacLeish, poet, social critic, and curator of the Library of Congress, maintained that fascism was largely the result of "a condition of men's minds."[10] Rejecting their common cultural tradition, intellectuals had sought objectivity and forgotten their responsibility for the moral life. The instrumentalist mind, declared the novelist Waldo Frank, "is dark and decadent" and was "rotten ere it was half ripe."[11]

Lewis Mumford, who became a determined interventionist in foreign policy, maintained that "pragmatic liberalism" was as dangerous an enemy as rampant fascism. "A thousand years separate 1940 from 1930," he remarked, for by 1940 the full threat of "pragmatic liberalism" had become clear in the light of the European debacle. When confronted by the challenge of Hitler and Stalin, such liberalism had shown itself helpless. It had acquiesced in tyrannies and sacrificed its most fundamental values. In every country which had suffered from the fascist onslaught, Mumford charged, the pragmatic liberal "has shown either that he does not possess stable convictions, or that he lacks the courage and the insight to defend them." [12]

In 1940 Mumford joined a group of interventionist intellectuals who issued "A Declaration on World Democracy," which tied scientific naturalism to the spread of fascism and condemned both. Hans Kohn, Herbert Agar, Van Wyck Brooks, Ada L. Comstock, William Y. Elliott, Dorothy Canfield Fisher, Alvin Johnson, and Reinhold Niebuhr were among those who were convinced that there could be no compromise with "the totalitarian mind." "The major choice is no longer ours," they declared. "War, declared or undeclared, actual or virtual, has chosen us." Preparedness would be most difficult, for America and much of the world had been the victim of "an education adrift in a relativity that doubted all values, and a degraded science that shirked the spiritual issues." Intellectuals were thus largely responsible for the desperate situation of the world. "This recognition of guilt must pave the way, not to maudlin regrets," they declared, "but to immediate atonement." [13]

The ideas of guilt and atonement appeared frequently in the writings of interventionist intellectuals, some of whom had earlier sympathized with or upheld the ideas associated with scientific naturalism. They now saw totalitarianism, according to the historian Hans Kohn, as the logical culmination of "the denial of universal values and truth, their relativization and 'nationalization.' " [14] Scientific naturalism was one of the sources of totalitarianism; it was ill-conceived and destructive. As the attacks of Lippmann, Hutchins, and Niebuhr had an extra force because of their earlier optimistic attitude toward science, so the passionate sense of atonement gave the charges of many interventionists a special persuasiveness.

The sweep and certainty of the interventionist attack gave it a great rhetorical force, and interventionists often found themselves reiterating many of the same charges that the rationalist and religious foes of scientific naturalism had used. Although such interventionists as Waldo Frank, Mumford, and MacLeish accepted no religious or philosophical absolutism, they agreed with the accusations against relativism made by fellow interventionists who had already rejected scientific naturalism, men like Lippmann, Elliott, and Niebuhr. How, the interventionists asked, could any decent and honest man refuse to acknowledge the need to oppose Hitler by force of arms? Moral relativism seemed a satisfactory answer. The argument was based, not on any close analysis of how men who held different philosophies actually behaved, but rather on a prior hostility to a particular philosophical or political position, which was then accused of exemplifying a "debilitating relativism."

The condemnation of relativism implied three general charges: that relativists were unable and unwilling to defend democracy, that they refused to condemn totalitarianism, and that they failed to actively oppose Nazism, especially in the crucial period between September, 1939 and December, 1941. Since the United States produced no native totalitarian movement of any significance, the charges related to American attitudes toward affairs in Europe. Without entering into the vast problem of the origins and causes of totalitarianism, which was itself a central part of the absolutist-relativist debate, it is clear that in the United States during the late thirties there was little difference between the ways that relativists and absolutists reacted, as groups, to the practical issues of foreign policy.

The first charge, that relativists were unable and unwilling to defend the democratic ideal, was simply wrong. Virtually everyone in the United States supported the democratic ideal. Among social scientists, lawyers, theologians, philosophers, and almost every other group in the country, affirmations of the moral validity of democracy overwhelmed the presses and the air waves. Those who had earlier criticized democracy ignored or altered their earlier attitudes and maintained that, whatever its deficiencies, democracy was the best possible form of human government. Regardless of what may or may not have happened in Europe, American intellectuals criticized their political system only when it was secure and firmly established. When the international crisis of the late thirties arose, they defended it with the greatest dedication. Even the objectivists rallied to the defense of American democracy, though they often continued to reject the idea of ethical justification. "If talk and writing about democracy will save it," commented one political scientist, "salvation for it is sure." [15] On the level of democratic affirmation, there was little difference between relativists and absolutists.

Though Thomists and other critics found relativism morally insufficient for democratic theory, most scientific naturalists rejected their logic. Accepting the assumptions behind the relativist theory of democracy and often its explicit formulation, they believed that naturalism was not only capable of justifying democratic government but also that it was, in its relativistic and pluralistic form, the most persuasive defense of democracy

223

possible. Sharing a profound faith in both democracy and scientific naturalism, they joined them together in a tight synthesis. In defending one they were defending the other, and they confidently upheld both.

The argument that relativists failed to condemn totalitarianism, the second charge, was equally unfounded and misleading. Though American responses to totalitarianism were complex and varied, relativism itself produced no unique infirmities. As the ideal of democracy drew unanimous affirmation, totalitarianism called forth nearly universal condemnation. Beyond the level of mere words, there were considerable disagreements over the nature of actual governments, especially those of Mussolini and Stalin. Some relativists and pragmatists defended Mussolini for a time, but so did representatives of every other group in the United States, including philosophical absolutists and religious spokesmen. Conversely, other relativists and pragmatists opposed Mussolini, as did some representatives of all the other groups. Comparatively, in fact, pragmatists tended to oppose Mussolini earlier and more strongly than did many other groups in the United States.

Mussolini had much broader support in the United States than did Stalin, but Russia exerted a greater appeal among intellectuals. Was that support due to their relativism? Some, Catholics for example, claimed that the allegiance was due to a lack of faith in absolute principles; others, pragmatists, for example, rejected Marxism as itself an absolute philosophy. The obvious fact was that the support of many intellectuals for the Soviet Union was not based on any philosophical relativism. Those who remained sympathetic to Russia throughout the thirties did so because of their firm conviction in the truth of Marxism and of the destined, progressive role of the Soviet Union. They may have been quite wrong, but they were hardly examples of ethical nihilism or valueless moral relativism.[16]

American attitudes toward Nazism were the most unanimous of the three—Nazism was almost universally condemned. And Nazism was, in fact, the precipitator of both the intellectual debate and the international political crisis. Perhaps it was largely because Americans so completely repudiated Nazism that they came to focus on the philosophical bases behind their various condemnations. Additionally, if some intellectuals were suspect for their long commitment to the Soviet Union, a number of Catholic spokesmen could be considered equally suspect for insisting until the late thirties that communist Russia represented a greater threat to western civilization than did Nazi Germany. "The term fascism itself," one Catholic writer equivocated as late as 1938, "is only in process of definition and covers too broad a field, at least in popular concept, to be singled out for final analysis."[17] Whatever threat Russia posed, it was clearly neither as immediate nor as desperate as that which Nazism presented.

By the late thirties all Americans rejected the idea of totalitarianism, and the differences of opinion about its three manifestations increasingly narrowed. Though some might be legitimately charged with shortsightedness or moral failure, the guilt surely applied to representatives of all intellectual positions. Neither the political disagreements nor the moral failures were traceable to philosophical relativism or absolutism.

The third charge, that relativists were unable and unwilling to actively oppose Nazism after World War II had started, was also inaccurate and misleading. It implied that most relativists hoped to avoid war at all costs and failed to understand the evil dynamism of Nazism. It implied that those who held absolute values, who stood for universal moral principles, urged forceful action against Germany and were willing to go to war to end Nazi aggression. Neither of those implications was true. While all Americans defended democracy or condemned totalitarianism at least in the abstract, the practical question of participation in the war was an issue on which intellectuals divided sharply.

The total lack of correlation between philosophy and foreign policy revealed itself clearly in the national debate between September, 1939 and December, 1941. Sidney Hook and Mortimer Adler, the major antagonists at the Conference on Science, Philosophy, and Religion, both favored strong action against the Nazis. Robert M. Hutchins and his close friend and fellow Thomist, Stringfellow Barr, the president of St. Johns College, disagreed completely on foreign policy. Hutchins emerged as one of the major spokesmen for nonintervention, while Barr signed "A Summons to Speak Out," an interventionist statement appearing in June, 1940, that called for an immediate declaration of war against Germany. Two of the most outspoken relativists, Charles Beard and Max Lerner, equally disagreed. Beard allied with the Thomist Hutchins as an ardent noninterventionist, while Lerner agreed with the Thomist Barr that American involvement was necessary for the cause of freedom. Jerome Frank, one of the leading legal realists, found himself in agreement with the president of Fordham University, Robert I. Gannon, S.J., who had totally rejected realism. Both believed that the United States should stay out of the war, and both eventually repudiated their isolationism before Pearl Harbor. In May, 1940, five hundred American scientists signed a declaration urging the government to keep the country out of the war, but the next year over 90 per cent of 13,155 Catholic priests who responded to a questionnaire declared opposition to United States participation in any "shooting war" outside of the western hemisphere.[18]

On the questions of intervention and aid to England relativism had no discernible "debilitating" effect. A large number of relativists urged either participation in the war or massive assistance to Great Britain, which risked involvement. Hook, Lerner, Ralph Barton Perry, Carl Becker, Lewis M. Terman, Rexford G. Tugwell, Felix Frankfurter, Thurman Arnold, Harry D. Gideonse, Charles E. Merriam, William Allen Nielson, and T. V. Smith all urged American action to oppose aggression. Gideonse, one of the most vigorous anti-Thomists in American education, had been attacking isolationism and neutrality since 1937. "The price of peace is commitment to definite action in case of infringement by aggression," he insisted in 1940. "We have had enough moralizing sermons."[19] Acknowledging that his earlier isolationism had been a futile policy, Jerome Frank argued in early 1941 that the only way to save American democracy was "by rushing all possible help to those in Europe who are out to lick nazism and by being ready ourselves to lick it if they should fail." Fear that war would destroy free government was no excuse for isolationism, charged Felix Frankfurter, for "democracy in this country has expanded despite four wars."[20] The United States was already at war, Lerner declared in April, 1941, and democratic government itself "can be not only the product of winning the war but also the means for winning it."[21] Many who accepted some form of philosophical relativism were in the forefront of those who urged vigorous action to halt German aggression, and they accepted the idea of war as a necessary evil.

A number of relativists opposed intervention or large-scale aid to England, but their ideas on foreign policy were not the result of any unwillingness to commit themselves or inability to take a firm moral stand. Beard, for example, remained irreconcilably opposed to American involvement because he was convinced that powerful economic interests and misguided persons were leading the country into war against the national interest. Though Beard had emphasized the relativism of historical knowledge, he based his determined isolationism on a confident and certain interpretation of American history.[22] Harry Elmer Barnes, another relativist noninterventionist, continually referred to the failure of American efforts in World War I and believed that efforts to defend Europe would fail and at the same time imperil the United States. "Our intervention in Europe's war would not save the American way of life in Europe," he declared in late 1940, "but it would rudely and precipitately destroy it in our own country."[23]

Franz Boas, the elder statesman of American anthropology, strikingly exemplified the moral commitment of naturalists who opposed intervention. Boas's opposition to intervention had a special poignancy, too, since for thirty years he had devoted himself to the repudiation of racism. After 1933 he had continually attacked the "absurd falsity" of Nazi racial doctrines.[24] Under his inspiration a number of scholars elaborated a thorough scientific critique of racist ideas. The biological and anthropological evidence against racist doctrines helped provide a scientific basis for opposition to Nazism, and in the thirties and early forties such naturalists as Ruth Benedict, M. F. Ashley Montagu, Jacques Barzun, and Paul Radin took up the task of discrediting Nazi science.[25] In December, 1938, both the American Anthropological Association and the American Psychological Association adopted similar resolutions, declaring in the words of the former that "anthropology provides no scientific basis for discrimination against any people on the grounds of racial inferiority, religious affiliation nor linguistic heritage."[26]

In 1938 Boas, with the aid of his Columbia University colleague Wesley C. Mitchell and others, recruited the support of 1,284 physical and social scientists for a manifesto that unequivocally asserted the primacy of intellectual freedom and its direct connection with political democracy. "The present outrages in Germany," Boas commented, "have made it all the more necessary for American scientists to take a firm anti-fascist stand."[27] After war broke out, Boas had to come to a difficult decision. "Unavoidably war brings with it suppression of freedom of action and of the free expression of thought, which are recovered with difficulty when peace is secured," he decided. "Therefore we must not become involved in the war."[28] Moral and intellectual commitment to human freedom was foremost in his mind, but he concluded that war would produce results more harmful than would noninvolvement. On December 21, 1943, while attending a luncheon at the Men's Faculty Club of Columbia University, the eighty-five-year-old Boas was struck with a fatal heart attack. As he lay dying on the floor, he urged his colleagues in his last words to carry on the struggle against racism in all its forms.[29]

As foreign policy issues divided those who shared a relativist philosophy, they did the same with absolutists. Barr, Adler, William Y. Elliott and others urged American support for Great Britain and even entry into the war. At the same time another large group including Hutchins, his supporter Alan Valentine, and such Jesuit scholars as Wilfred Parsons and Francis P. Le Buffe opposed involvement. Since America was not really democratic, either in its economic structure or its philosophy, Hutchins maintained, it was not capable of democratizing the world. America's goal should be to establish a truly democratic and humane society which could inspire the world by its example. If the country entered the war that possibility would be lost, and the United States itself would likely become totalitarian. "War, for this country, is a counsel of despair. It is a confession of failure," he argued in early 1941. "It is national suicide."[30] Victory for either side was "not worth the sacrifice of one American life," Le Buffe declared in 1940. The "greatest danger to this country is not from Europe but from the irreligion and atheism here today."[31]

The strength of the churches in general was largely on the side of nonintervention. The Committee on International Peace of the Central Conference of American Rabbis recommended as late as 1935 that the organization "stand opposed to all wars." By 1936 no such proposals were presented, but it was not until 1939 that the conference demanded a major revision of the neutrality laws as a preparation for actual American involvement.[32] In 1934 over 60 per cent of 21,000 Protestant ministers replying to a poll in the *World Tomorrow* pledged that they would never, as individuals, sanction a future war. In 1936, 56 per cent of 13,000 respondents to another poll reaffirmed that total rejection. Though opposition to such pacifism, and support for involvement, grew after 1939, the Ministers No War Committee of 1941 still included more prominent leaders of American Protestantism than did any of the interventionist groups.[33] "Two paramount objectives command the devotion of the people of the United States in relation to the European war," declared the *Christian Century* in May, 1940. "One is to keep this country out of the conflict, the other is to bring every influence to bear to stop the war."[34] Protestant and Jewish pacifism had gained enormous strength in the twenties, and only the start of the war and then the bombing of Pearl Harbor could break its power.

Catholic opposition to intervention was perhaps even stronger than that of the Protestants. After war broke out in September, 1939, the three major Catholic periodicals, *Commonweal*, *Catholic World*, and *America*, demanded a total embargo on trade with all the belligerent nations.[35] "Needless to say," explained *America*, "this Review aligns itself with those who hold that it is impossible at this moment to justify on moral grounds American participation, direct or indirect, in any war in Europe."[36] In 1940 and 1941 active interventionists believed that Catholics were the group in the United States most opposed to involvement and began concentrating special efforts on lessening that hostility. The Catholic church, declared the prominent interventionist Herbert Agar, who had himself joined in the attack on naturalism, was "the strongest and steadiest force for appeasement in the country."[37] As with the Protestant pacifists, Catholic opposition continued through 1941. "Americans can still reflect that the best means for them to oppose Nazism everywhere is not by surrendering to war," a *Commonweal* editorial reiterated in April, 1941. "We can oppose the succeeding steps down this desperate line without weakening our opposition to the spiritual, political, and economic evils of national socialism."[38]

Needless to say, the attitudes of Catholics, Protestants, and Jews were as varied as those of any other group in the country. A number of leaders of all three faiths began urging aid to Britain and even American entry into the war during the months after the invasion of Poland. President Roosevelt himself secured the support of Cardinal Mundelein of Chicago, the most prominent Catholic churchman in the midwest, in his effort to revise the neutrality laws in late 1939.[39] In early 1941 a number of influential Protestants, led by Reinhold Niebuhr and Henry Sloane Coffin, established *Christianity and Crisis*, a journal devoted to attacking pacifism and nonintervention. Still, however, many more religious spokesmen, especially Protestants and Catholics, opposed American intervention than advocated it.

There was thus no correlation whatever between philosophy as such and foreign policy. Both scientific naturalists and rational absolutists divided sharply over the problems of war and held a wide variety of opinions. Absolutists and religious leaders provided as confused and varied counsels as did those who adhered to scientific naturalism. Relativism, even granted its existence as a monolithic category, produced no special or unique response to the practical foreign policy issues of the thirties and forties.

Those who opposed intervention, whether relativists or absolutists, did so from a range of motives that bore no explicit or necessary relationship to their philosophies. Whatever the moral or intellectual failures of the thirties may have been, they were shared equally by adherents of all philosophical positions.

The strong opposition to American intervention came from other sources. The revulsion against the barbarities of World War I weighed heavily on all Americans and drove many to a complete rejection of war and others to an opposition that only the Nazi conquest of Europe could reverse. Discovery of the Allied propaganda efforts during the earlier war and disclosures of the economic interests apparently forcing American entry in 1917 confirmed that rejection and strengthened the resolve of many. During the thirties, too, the depression seemed the greatest problem facing the United States, and it led intellectuals to down-play the significance of events in Europe and to focus their efforts on economic recovery and reform. An ideological commitment to unilateralism, ethnic hostility and loyalty, religious ties with various European countries, and anger over the repudiation of the World War I debts all helped contribute to the desire of various Americans to remain out of the new war.[40]

The charge of "debilitating relativism" that anti-naturalists and interventionists popularized in the late thirties seriously distorted the actual situation. It misinterpreted the lines of the political debate by suggesting that there was an operative philosophical difference between the interventionists and the noninterventionists which in fact did not exist. Relativism had led to no special foreign policy or moral failing. Additionally it almost completely ignored the intellectual difficulties that confronted ethical theory. People did not consciously choose to become "relativists," but rather were led to their conclusions by the intellectual developments of the preceding half century. Modern critical philosophy had developed a powerful critique of traditional theories of prescriptive ethics, and the foes of relativism failed to rehabilitate them or to generate any intellectually convincing alternative. Finally, the attack gave the subsequent impression that the intellectual attitudes of the twenties and thirties were important mainly in their relationship to the events that led up to World War II. The intellectual crisis grew out of those attitudes, but the war neither caused their disappearance nor circumscribed their importance. Instead, those attitudes continued to have a major impact on American thought and to dominate its course. The assumptions of scientific naturalism, as they were modified and given specific political form by the international conflicts of the thirties and forties, shaped American attitudes for the following two decades.

Crucial to the formation of postwar attitudes, the debate over foreign policy and then the wartime unity that followed seemed in fact to confirm two basic assumptions of the relativist theory of democracy. First, they demonstrated that absolute philosophies provided no clear guide to practical politics and that philosophical unity was unnecessary for democratic success. The experience seemed to disprove the whole absolutist argument. "It soon becomes apparent," declared the political scientist J. Roland Pennock after the war, "that rival ethical theories often lead to identical judgments of relative values." [41] Second, it confirmed the relativist belief that cultural and social conditions, not philosophies, were the bases of democratic success. "Their common belief in peace and their common support of our side in the war," Joseph Ratner commented on the members of a symposium on world peace, "seems to me to refute their partisan arguments on behalf of some one religious, cultural, philosophical, or ethical basis for enduring peace." [42] Cultural agreement was crucial, scientific naturalists agreed, but it could arise only in a philosophically relativistic and socially pluralistic society that allowed freedom and cherished diversity. Such a culture was the ideal basis of democracy. Both of those assumptions would underlie the social and political thought of the postwar decades.

IV

The Resolution
of Democratic Theory

13

Relativist Democratic Theory
& Postwar America

Much of the turmoil of the forties and early fifties tended to obscure the major developments that were taking place among American intellectuals. The resounding democratic affirmations—often couched in absolute terms —the vocal attacks on relativism and excessive empiricism, the apparent disappearance of pragmatism as a philosophical movement, the so-called religious revival of the fifties, and the reassertion of natural law theory accompanied by the emergence of a new philosophical conservatism, all seemed to indicate a significant reorientation in American thought. Indeed there was a reorientation occurring, but it was not a general movement from empiricism and relativism to philosophical absolutism or religious transcendentalism. Instead, pragmatic and naturalistic attitudes continued generally to dominate the thought patterns of intellectuals, who at the same time were undergoing a subtle but fundamental shift in their political orientation.

During World War II and the cold war that followed, a number of American intellectuals defended the ideal of democracy in absolutist terms, but most accepted no absolutist philosophy to justify their assertions. The attack on a "debilitating relativism" flourished during and immediately after the war, but gradually receded during the fifties, failing to overcome the pervasive naturalism. Many of those who employed for a time the language of natural law were referring not to any clear theoretical position, but merely to the need for broad and humane cultural norms. Those involved in a serious attempt to develop a coherent philosophy based on natural law—exclusive of Catholics—numbered only a handful. Few thoughtful Americans disagreed with the contention that such values as political freedom and personal dignity were crucial, but the great majority maintained that they could be defended within a naturalistic framework.

235

Pragmatism as an identifiable and aggressive philosophical movement did begin to fade from view, but not because the absolutists had routed it. Instead pragmatism blended into the broader naturalism that dominated American thought. Many who were predominantly concerned with philosophy as such moved toward language analysis or some version of logical positivism when those approaches revealed numerous technical and linguistic problems in pragmatism. Another group, more concerned with actual social reform, continued to rely on a general pragmatism and devoted their energies to practical politics. Some of those thought it unnecessary to engage in further abstruse philosophical battles, while others consciously added new qualifications to their social philosophy but kept them within an essentially pragmatic framework. Social scientists passed beyond the cruder formulations of the thirties as they developed more sophisticated statistical and mathematical techniques and began to search for a more comprehensive and abstract empirical social theory. The aggressive, confident, and reform-oriented pragmatism that John Dewey had so long symbolized thus declined, but the major epistemological assumptions behind his pragmatism remained vividly alive. Pragmatism had not been rejected, but superseded.

The innumerable factors, intellectual and social, that had fostered scientific naturalism before World War II continued to operate after it. Government, foundations, and private industry increased spectacularly their support of research activity throughout both the physical and social sciences. Expansion continued at a dizzying rate. There were more doubts about the old idea of progress and a greater recognition of the problems caused by expanding technology, but American intellectuals continued to believe that science was the most reliable and useful method of studying human, as well as physical, phenomena. Neither religious transcendentalism nor philosophical absolutism could induce them to abandon their naturalistic world view.

One of the major reasons they retained their faith in naturalism was the success of the relativist democratic theory that had been clearly formulated and widely accepted during the late thirties and early forties. Most American intellectuals were convinced that theoretical absolutism logically implied political authoritarianism. Most too were convinced that a philosophical relativism implied, in practice if not in strict logic, an open and democratic political structure. Those naturalists who remained skepti-

236

cal of the logical precision of the relativist theory still found its general argument persuasive.

In addition to being a prescriptive logic, however, the relativist theory of democracy was also an empirical theory of politics. It spread through the social sciences not just because it provided a naturalistic ethical basis for democratic theory, but also because it suggested a fascinating range of problems and hypotheses that seemed to be empirically testable. Whereas rival approaches, such as that of natural law, seemed largely barren of empirical leads, the relativist theory seemed extraordinarily rich. What was the empirical relationship between individual values and various political structures? What were the social, psychological, and cultural sources that led to the adoption of an absolutist or relativist political attitude? Were certain types of people specially drawn to absolute value systems and absolutist political movements? How much diversity, and of what kinds, could a society tolerate and still remain stable? What types of social and cultural institutions provided the most reliable basis for democratic political forms? How much consensus was actually necessary for a stable society, and on what levels must that consensus exist? At a time when the American Political Science Association was growing from 3,200 members in 1944 to 15,000 in 1966, the empirical possibilities suggested by the relativist theory of democracy were of signal professional importance. To a large extent it provided for two decades after the war the major research paradigm for political science and for the newly developing and related fields of political sociology and political psychology. It provided hypotheses, problems, and criteria of judgment.

Such scholars as Leo Strauss and John Hallowell continued into the sixties to argue that democracy demanded a commitment to absolute values and natural law, but the relativist theory of democracy continued to spread, either in a highly developed logical form or more commonly in a pervasive belief in the democratic virtues of a philosophical as well as social pluralism.[1] In 1960 the Rockefeller Brothers Fund published a special studies project on the nature of democratic government, which revealed the extent to which the relativist theory had triumphed. "Experience shows that men can be equally loyal to democratic ideals even though they give different ultimate reasons for their loyalty," the report maintained. Signed by such diverse figures as Laurance S. Rockefeller, Adolph A. Berle, Jr., Lucius D. Clay, Theodore M. Hesburgh,

Henry R. Luce, Richard P. McKeon, Charles H. Percy, Dean Rusk, Edward Teller, Charles Frankel, and Pendleton Herring, the report summarized and accepted much of the contemporary academic thinking about democracy. "As the religious wars of the sixteenth and seventeenth centuries and the ideological purges in contemporary totalitarian societies indicate, the effort to impose unity of belief in matters of religion and ultimate philosophy, far from unifying a society, can lead to extraordinary bloodshed and brutality."[2]

The postwar dominance of the relativist theory of democracy was intimately connected with the onset of the cold war in the late forties. On the one hand, the conviction that Russia was a totalitarian state, and its emerging conflict with the United States, kept the theoretical problem of democracy in the forefront of American thought. The relativist theory retained the political relevance it had acquired in the late thirties. On the other hand, the absolutist-relativist dichotomy prepared the terms in which American intellectuals would perceive the nature of the conflict with the Soviet Union. By analyzing politics in the fundamental epistemological terms to which they were deeply committed intellectually, they smothered the possibility of distinguishing between Nazi Germany and Soviet Russia and assumed their almost complete theoretical identification. Ironically, too, some came close to accepting the autonomy of ideas in much the same way that many of their critics had in the thirties. Absolutist philosophies, such as Marxism, inevitably led to totalitarianism, regardless of the other political and social institutions of a society. Hence they assumed that Marxism, by itself, would necessarily lead to totalitarianism and hence could never contribute to beneficent political change in the United States or elsewhere.

The absolutist-relativist dichotomy induced intellectuals to perceive the cold war as a struggle between a relativist and an absolutist society. "Once involved in the struggle for political power, the ethical absolutist is confronted by the most serious temptation," the political scientist Gabriel A. Almond declared in 1954. The temptation was, of course, to impose his philosophy on society by totalitarian means. "The Leninists seized this temptation and let loose forces which swept them beyond humane anchorage."[3] As the Soviet Union represented absolutism, so the United States then must represent relativism, reflected in the concomitant forms of social pluralism and ethical diversity. "If there is a multiplicity of such groups," commented another political scientist in 1952, "so is there a multiplicity of ethical systems."[4] Believing that the United States was totally different from Soviet Russia, intellectuals came to assume that its most significant characteristics must be a variety of freely competing groups and a broad ethical diversity. The absolutist-relativist dichotomy thus provided an interpretive device with which intellectuals could understand the emerging world conflict, while at the same time the conflict itself strengthened their commitment to the dichotomy by personifying the split between democracy and totalitarianism, between relativism and absolutism. Relativist democratic theory and the cold war were mutually reinforcing.

The relationship between the two helped explain a major transformation that took place in American thought during the two decades after American entry into World War II. The political and social assumptions of American intellectuals helped lead them to a strongly nationalistic stance in international affairs and to a fundamentally status quo orientation in domestic politics. The transformation was the result of the relative success of the New Deal in creating a "balanced" society, together with the threat of totalitarianism before and after the war; both phenomena helped form and, in turn, were interpreted by the relativist assumptions of American intellectuals. Through its various reforms the New Deal seemed to have established a viable form of social and economic pluralism in the United States, the kind of institutional relativism that most intellectuals saw as the necessary empirical basis of democratic society. With their threat of totalitarian conquest, Nazism and then Soviet communism personified in most vivid forms the danger of philosophical absolutism and its attendant monolithic social structure. Hence intellectuals were led to believe in the democratic success of America and the totalitarian threat of Russia, both of which were explained—and initially perceived—in terms of the relativist theory of democracy.

Of greatest importance, American perceptions were thereby distorted by the built-in ambiguity of the relativist theory. For that theory was from the start both descriptive and prescriptive. It was an empirical description of the social consequences of philosophical relativism and absolutism, which implied an explanation of the social and intellectual conditions that supported democratic and authoritarian governments. At the same time, the relativist theory of democracy was an ethical logic meant to justify democratic or relativist societies and to reject totalitarian or absolutist societies. Thus the central ambiguity, or double implication of the theory, meant that in describing the United States and Russia in terms of the absolutist-relativist dichotomy, intellectuals were automatically praising the one and condemning the other. And conversely, as the other half of the reciprocal relationship, when they supported on a conscious level the American political system against the Russian, they were assuming implicitly that the United States was in fact a pluralist society and that the Soviet Union was in fact monolithic. Thus the descriptive assumptions that American intellectuals shared were themselves implicitly prescriptive, while the conscious prescriptive judgments they made concerning the cold war carried with them, often unrecognized, an automatic descriptive assumption. Those reciprocal assumptions led American intellectuals to pursue, with some justification, a strongly anti-Soviet foreign policy, but it also induced them, with considerably less justification, to accept fundamentally complacent domestic politics. It was thus not the opponents of naturalism who directly altered the political tone of the postwar years, but rather the new political content infused into the theoretical assumptions of the naturalists themselves.

Three additional factors helped ally social scientists especially with those emerging political attitudes. First, still reacting to the earlier charges that their scientific orientation had made them insensitive to values, many were determined to head off such criticism a second time. Social scientists could be as committed to the defeat of totalitarianism as anyone, they reasoned, and they would not be charged with failure again. Second, during and after the war the professional context within which social scientists worked tended to draw them toward the status quo. Growing economic affluence, the continued professional desire for status as scientists, availability of lucrative research grants, opportunities to serve as government consultants, and their increasingly well defined institutional roles all helped create the social conditions that filtered out the more unpleasant aspects of American society and accentuated the pleasant. Third, one of the major changes in social science theory between the thirties and the fifties was the decline of strict objectivism.[5] Behavioralism —an empirical functionalism that eschewed many of the metaphysical implications of the earlier behaviorism and claimed to study human actions merely because such an approach was useful—came to dominate political science and strongly influence other fields, but few social scientists would any longer claim that complete value neutrality was a practical possibility. Recognizing the theoretical need for guiding values, therefore, many were induced to openly proclaim their values. Almost inevitably, they proclaimed the value of democracy.[6]

Finally, the surprising and frightening rise of Senator Joseph McCarthy of Wisconsin in the early fifties provided the major domestic catalyst that transformed the assumptions behind the relativist theory into an explicitly conservative social philosophy. Indiscriminately attacking communists, socialists, New Dealers, and intellectuals, McCarthy ruined the careers of honorable men, disrupted the workings of the federal government, and seriously impaired, directly or indirectly, the constitutional rights of many Americans. During his triumphant years McCarthy exerted a broad influence over the conduct of American politics and seemed to possess a widespread and fanatical popular support. In 1950 and 1952 he opposed the reelection of eight fellow senators, including two successive Democratic majority leaders, and all eight met defeat. Though later research indicated that McCarthy had only a peripheral influence on the elections, they were widely regarded at the time as evidence of his mass following.[7]

To some extent McCarthy drew on the hostility between naturalist intellectuals and religious spokesmen that had intensified in the thirties. The argument that naturalism led to totalitarianism easily translated in the early fifties into the argument that naturalism led to communism. "We are beginning to recognize as a nation," Father Robert I. Gannon, the president of Fordham University, had declared in 1942, "that the real enemy of democracy is atheism, whether it be adorned with a black swastika, a red star or a Ph.D."[8] As anti-communism became synonymous with Americanism, many religious leaders seized the opportunity once again to equate Christianity with democracy in an attempt to discredit their naturalist enemies. As many Catholics gave strong support to McCarthy, they reconfirmed for themselves their own Americanism and reconfirmed for the naturalists their logical connection with absolutist political beliefs.[9]

McCarthyism represented a dangerous and unprincipled threat to the democratic procedures that underlay American government, and intellectuals quickly began to search for an explanation of its success. Such prominent scholars as Richard Hofstadter, Daniel Bell, David Riesman, Seymour Martin Lipset, and Talcott Parsons, guided by the assumptions behind the relativist theory of democracy, agreed that McCarthyism was an example of political absolutism that drew its strength from those who were psychologically and emotionally unable to accept the relativist,

241

pluralistic structure of the United States. Americans had a great talent for practical political compromise, those intellectuals argued, but Americans equally had a highly moralistic outlook. Democratic success had resulted from the practice of reserving such absolute judgments, in most cases, to the realm of private morals while allowing politics to operate on a generally pragmatic basis. "To the extent that moral indignation—apart from its rhetorical use in political campaigns—played so small a role in the actual political arena," Bell explained, "the United States has been able to escape the intense ideological fanaticism—the conflicts of clericalism and class—which has been so characteristic of Europe." McCarthyism, however, seizing upon the psychological and emotional anxieties found predominantly in lower class and poorly educated groups, threatened a new "tendency to convert politics into 'moral' issues."[10]

Perceiving the issue in terms of the absolutist-relativist dichotomy, with its prescriptive-descriptive ambiguity, intellectuals were bound to interpret McCarthyism as absolutist since they thought it profoundly evil. McCarthyism thus represented to them moralism, ideology, religious fundamentalism, intellectual oversimplification, and irrationalism. Established social institutions, as the other half of the contrast, inevitably appeared good. They represented practical compromise, pragmatism, "market decisions," intellectual complexity, and structural rationality. McCarthyism helped give the assumptions behind the relativist theory a status quo orientation because it forced many intellectuals to look to established and presumably pluralistic institutions as bulwarks against the threat of a feared absolutist, mass movement.

Additionally, when applied to McCarthyism, relativist theory created a new admiration for elites, highly educated and socially prominent groups, as opposed to the psychologically discontented and poorly educated masses. Since a sophisticated relativism would most likely only be found among better educated groups, they alone could fully understand the nature of democratic politics. Ever concerned with the social bases of democracy, many intellectuals concluded that elites, with their sophisticated world views and stable social position, were the most reliable source of democratic values. Basing democratic theory on social elites, intellectuals made it profoundly conservative. As with the cold war, relativist theory and McCarthyism reinforced one another and led toward an acceptance and praise of the domestic status quo.[11]

Two of the most significant and distinct proponents of the relativist theory were the theologian Reinhold Niebuhr and the historian Daniel Boorstin. Markedly dissimilar intellectually, politically, and temperamentally, Niebuhr and Boorstin shared the assumptions behind the relativist theory, demonstrating both their variety and their persistence. Widely read and highly respected, they helped establish from very different perspectives the prominence of the relativist theory in postwar thought.

It was paradoxical, which was only appropriate for Niebuhr, that the foremost theologian of twentieth century America also became a leading advocate of the theory of democracy whose source lay in the predominantly naturalistic attitude of American intellectuals. It was perhaps even more paradoxical that Niebuhr's theology, which emphasized the transcendence of God, the sinfulness of man, and the authority of the Bible, was in its social implications a Christian restatement of William James's pragmatism. For although Niebuhr drew on the Bible and European theologians for his central concepts, he consistently interpreted them along Jamesian lines. His pragmatism, too, ran far deeper than his concern for a hard-headed, practical attitude toward political issues. It lay at the very foundation of his thought, and when Niebuhr outlined his version of neo-orthodoxy he produced a biblical version of James's open universe.

"I stand in the William James tradition," he once wrote a friend. "He was both an empiricist and a religious man, and his faith was both the consequence and the presupposition of his pragmatism." [12] Niebuhr, like James, attempted to unite a religious world view with a tough-minded empiricism. But most important, Niebuhr, like James, retained a firm conviction in the indeterminateness of the universe and in the relativity of all human knowledge. "God, though revealed, remains veiled; his thoughts are not our thoughts nor his ways our ways," he wrote in 1937 when he was just beginning to develop his mature theology. "The worship of such a God leads to contrition; not merely to a contrite recognition of the conscious sins of pride and arrogance which the human spirit commits," he maintained, "but to a sense of guilt for the inevitable and inescapable pride involved in every human enterprise." God existed, and hence absolute truth existed as well as an absolute basis for human hope and human morality. But God's transcendence placed that truth beyond human reach, and man's inescapable finitude meant that God's absolute truth, though it stood in judgment over the world, could never completely become man's truth. "Every revelation of the divine is relativised by the finite mind which comprehends it."[13] Hence, like James, Niebuhr maintained that truth existed, but that no one could ever know how much of it he possessed.

Human finitude precluded any full understanding of God's truth, and man's unavoidable self-interest further deflected his quest for knowledge. All human thought was influenced by cultural orientations, economic and social interests, and personal desires and fears. "Knowledge of the truth is thus invariably tainted with an 'ideological' taint of interest, which makes our apprehension of truth something less than knowledge of *the* truth and reduces it to *our* truth."[14] As with James, truth was necessarily personal, and such subjectivity was unavoidable.

The problem with man, however, was that he was continually tempted to proclaim his personal truths as universal. Man's reason, and his spiritual power to partially transcend his personal experience, consistently led him into the vain belief that he was the master of the universe. That inherent vanity was in fact the sinful nature of man. "Man, in other words, is a sinner not because he is one limited individual within a whole but rather because he is betrayed by his very ability to survey the whole to imagine himself the whole."[15] Even the noblest and purest of men—Niebuhr said especially the noblest and purest—were tempted to set up their own beliefs as absolutes and in fact repeatedly did so. "The truth, as it is contained in the Christian revelation, includes the recognition that it is neither possible for man to know the truth fully nor to avoid pretending that he does."[16]

By understanding the revelation of the Bible men could recognize as valid their partial transcendence of experience and achieve fuller insight into their relationship with God. At the same time they could recognize their human finitude and realize that complete fulfillment and understanding lay only in a realm beyond human experience. "The test of how well this paradox of the gospel is comprehended and how genuinely it has entered into human experience, is the attitude of Christians toward those who differ from themselves in convictions which seem vital to each," he declared in 1943. "The test, in other words, is to be found in the issue of toleration."[17] Thus, Niebuhr emphasized the transcendence of God, and interpreted its meaning in a Jamesian sense of indeterminateness. In a practical, human sense, there were no valid absolute truths. Whereas most Americans who shared a naturalistic world view condemned human absolutes as totalitarian, Niebuhr condemned them as sin. Though his language and his world view differed from theirs, his argument in terms of political theory was identical.

Niebuhr made that political theory explicit in 1944 when he published what was perhaps, with the possible exception of *Moral Man and Immoral Society*, his most widely influential book, *The Children of Light and the Children of Darkness*. In it Niebuhr set out specifically to defend democratic government and to elaborate its theory. The central problem with humanistic thought, he argued, lay in its excessive faith in the goodness and rationality of man. The Children of Light, those who believed in a moral ideal beyond the individual will and hoped to create a more just world, rejected the idea of the inherent sinfulness in man and hence in themselves. They were thus unable to cope with the Children of Darkness, those who recognized no law beyond their own wills and who shrewdly played upon human irrationality and egotism. Additionally, because the Children of Light ignored the idea of sin, they fell victim to vain belief in their own righteousness and often attempted to impose their ideals of justice on their fellow men by force. If the Children of Light were ever to establish a humane and stable society, they had to abandon their optimism and recognize the sinfulness, self-interestedness, and paradoxical nature of man. Such a full vision was attainable only on the basis of the truths of the Bible.

As Niebuhr interpreted his theology in terms of Jamesian indeterminateness, so he equated it with the moral and intellectual foundations of democratic theory. "The reason this final democratic freedom is right, though the reasons given for it in the modern period are wrong," he argued, "is that there is no historical reality, whether it be church or government, whether it be the reason of wise men or specialists, which is not involved in the flux and relativity of human existence; which is not subject to error and sin, and which is not tempted to exaggerate its errors and sins when they are made immune to criticism."[18] As many naturalist intellectuals had done, Niebuhr continually criticized the Catholic church for its absolutist position. By proclaiming an absolute authority to interpret God's truth, the church manifested the sin of pride and the threat of social authoritarianism. "This reveals the chasm between the presuppositions of a free society and the inflexible authoritarianism of the Catholic religion."[19] Instead of such absolutist convictions, democracy demanded a knowledge of the paradoxical meaning of God's transcendence and man's finitude, both of which required a religious commitment to toleration and humility. "It is interesting to observe that the preservation of democratic mutuality between class groups finally depends upon the same quality of religious humility which is a prerequisite of ethnic and cultural pluralism in a democracy."[20] Niebuhr insisted that only a biblical faith could provide the depth of insight and strength of perseverence that could maintain such an attitude, yet his logic itself was based on the same assumptions that characterized the naturalistically oriented relativist theory of democracy.

The great influence Niebuhr exercised in the decades after World War II was thus itself paradoxical. Although many intellectuals praised and seemed to accept his theological insights into the nature of human evil, they were drawn to his work fundamentally because its essential argument remained relativistic. The idea of original sin seemed compelling after fascism and Stalinism, World War II, and the full disclosures of the Nazi death camps, but there were after all many spokesmen for the doctrinal varieties of original sin. Niebuhr appealed to American intellectuals not because he proclaimed the sinfulness of man or the supremacy of Christianity, but because he added the profound consideration of human evil to a fundamentally pragmatic and relativistic social theory.[21] Because of Niebuhr's Jamesian interpretation of theology, American intellectuals could accept his insights and his analysis of democratic theory without significantly altering their naturalistic world view.

Coming from a background of socialism and pacifism and remaining committed to the needs of reform, Niebuhr represented the left wing of the relativist consensus. Throughout his life he remained actively involved in domestic reform activities ranging from vigorous support of labor unions to an unswerving devotion to the cause of ethnic minorities. In the late forties Niebuhr helped form the liberal, anti-communist Americans for Democratic Action, and continued to insist that political action was necessary to combat the numerous injustices in American society.

At the same time, however, he just as firmly advocated a strong anti-communist foreign policy and during the forties came to believe that America, in spite of its flaws, represented a fundamentally correct approach to social justice. In fact, perhaps much against his intent, Niebuhr helped to dramatize and, in a sense, even glorify American action in the cold war. By continually emphasizing the painful responsibility, the loss of "innocence," and the moral perplexities entailed in practical international actions, he added an outlook that later degenerated into the "agony of decision" approach to foreign policy. Applying the relativist-absolutist dichotomy to the cold war, Niebuhr became ever more critical of Marxism. By the early fifties he asserted that Russia had become a "holy land," and that communism was a "dogma," a "noxious creed," and an "official theory," in addition to being a "monstrous evil" and the "essence of sin." It was, in short, absolutist. "The Marxist dream is distinguished from the liberal dream," he maintained in 1952, "by a sharper and more precise definition of the elite which is to act as surrogate for mankind, by more specific schemes for endowing this elite with actual power; by its fanatic certainty that it knows the end toward which history must move; and by its consequent readiness to sacrifice every value of life for the achievement of this end."[22] Relativist theory underlay each point but was perhaps most clearly revealed in his use of the word "consequent." Absolute philosophies necessarily led to political authoritarianism.

Conversely, the United States, though not perfect, was "a refutation in parable of the whole effort to bring the vast forces of history under the control of any particular will, informed by a particular idea." In spite of America's proclaimed bourgeois values, the country had managed to down-play ideology and deal realistically with social problems. "Our actual achievements in social justice," Niebuhr explained, "have been won by a pragmatic approach to the problems of power, which has not been less efficacious for its lack of consistent speculation upon the problems of power and justice." The practice of American politics was much more flexible than its rhetoric might suggest, and that flexibility and practicality helped minimize the battle of dogmas and allowed for meaningful social reform. "We have managed to achieve a tolerable justice in the collective relations of industry by balancing power against power and equilibrating the various competing social forces of society."[23] Though he never tired of pointing out the shortcomings of American society, Niebuhr had come to believe that its pluralist capitalism was the most reliable basis for preserving human freedom.

While Niebuhr was framing neo-orthodox theology in terms of the absolutist-relativist dichotomy, Daniel Boorstin was working toward an explanation of the whole course of American history in the same terms. After graduating from Harvard, Boorstin studied law at the Inner Temple in London and then at the Yale Law School, where he received his Doctor of the Science of Laws degree in the late thirties. Learning from the experiences of the depression the need for political reform and seeing the status quo implications of the American legal system, Boorstin was drawn toward the realist approach to the study of jurisprudence. During his stay at Yale he worked with Myres McDougal and Walton Hamilton, both ardent realists, while preparing his dissertation on Sir William Blackstone's *Commentaries*.

The Mysterious Science of the Law, published in 1941, subjected Blackstone's legal philosophy to a sharp, but not wholly unsympathetic, realist critique. Law, Boorstin believed, was a social instrument, and legal philosophy was a method of justifying the interests the legal system served. There was no such thing as abstract reason, and no such thing as an impartial legal theory. Rather, all thought served, consciously or unconsciously, to defend the values that the author assumed to be good. "This book attempts to indicate how the ostensibly impartial processes of reason," Boorstin wrote, "are employed by the student of society to support whatever social values he accepts." [24] Legal logic, as the realists had suggested, represented a rationalization of social interests.

Although Boorstin admired Blackstone's achievement, he insisted on its conservative meaning. "We will attempt to see how he used the prevailing ideas and assumptions of his day so as to prevent questioning of the existing social arrangements, and to demonstrate the acceptability of the society in which he believed." [25] Since Blackstone had been the principal source for transferring the common law from England to the United States, Boorstin's political message was clear. The American legal system had been formed, not on the basis of an objective or even consistent legal theory, but on the basis of a highly conservative and property-conscious social philosophy. Unable to resist the opportunity, Boorstin suggested that in the future the work of the anti-realist American Law Institute, which was attempting a "restatement" of American law, might well be compared to Blackstone's "mysterious science." [26]

Boorstin, though he shared many of the realists' assumptions, exhibited a special concern with the problem of moral values. Blackstone had not been wrong or dishonest in constructing a legal system that defended his social values, for the essential purpose of every man's reason was to understand and explain the values he held. "If man is to be self-conscious, to know the limits and understand the purposes of his critical faculty," Boorstin declared, "he must therefore be aware that his reason is serving a preconceived and desired purpose." Moral values and social preferences thus preceded conscious thought, and the task of human reason was to clarify and propagate them. "The function of reason is in a sense sub-ordinate."[27] Though he implied a pragmatic criterion of judgment, Boor-stin's belief in the priority of moral beliefs to reason raised consciously the fundamental question of the source and nature of human values. He was unable to avoid that problem.

As he began searching for the basis of human values and especially, in the world of the forties, for the basis of democratic values, Boorstin was led to the study of American history. And what better place to start than with the greatest spokesman for democracy in his country's past? "If we can improve our definition of the original Jeffersonian world of ideas," Boorstin explained in 1948, "we will have gone a long way toward achiev-ing a self-consciousness in American culture, toward discovering the perils of the way of thought which we have inherited from the Jeffersonians, and hence toward strengthening the philosophical foundations of a moral so-ciety in our day."[28] Those philosophical foundations, he hoped, would answer the question his earlier study, and World War II, had suggested.

What Boorstin discovered in the thought of Jefferson and his circle was to become the basis for his later interpretation of American history, but in the forties he was still too concerned with philosophy itself to give it the kind of enthusiastic approval that would characterize his subse-quent work. Because of the absence of feudal institutions and the presence of a vast, open continent, Boorstin argued, Jeffersonian thought had been empirical, pragmatic, and activist, devoted to spreading a healthy new society across the land. Operating in an amazingly fortunate physical en-vironment, the Jeffersonians were untroubled "by the ultimate questions of ethics," and accepted on faith their belief that a republican society was ordained by nature. Because of the conviction they shared in the existence of a benevolent Creator, their pragmatism retained an intellectual hu-mility and a concern for individual rights and human equality. The com-bination of unreflective practicality and religious humility marked a distinctive American attitude in contrast to the metaphysical theorizing that characterized much of European history. "The Jeffersonian approach to political thought had the great virtue of immunizing the American republican against such doctrinaire schemes of government as those which plagued his French contemporaries."[29]

Boorstin shared with most of his own contemporaries a disdain for such social absolutes, but he did not in the late forties equate all philoso-phy with dogma. In fact, his major disappointment was that Jeffersonian thought, admirable and sophisticated in many ways, had concealed major philosophical confusions. Its inordinate emphasis on the practical and its assumption of a natural harmony between man and nature had "fostered a philosophic vagueness which has profoundly affected American political thought," and deprived it of clarity and depth.[30] Jeffersonian practicality was itself a variety of dogmatic absolutism. The fortunate correspondence between the physical environment and the republican ideal might disappear, and then "a naturalistic philosophy might no longer provide a foundation for a moral society."[31] Indeed, Boorstin pointed out, such a "happy coincidence" had begun to fade in the late nineteenth century, and the twentieth had almost completely destroyed it. Man now seemed separated from nature, and his technical mastery invited him to control not only his physical environment but also his fellow man. Jefferson's emphasis on the practical, when divorced from his benevolently ordered world view and armed with the revolutionary powers of modern science, posed the threat of social oppression. "Against these perils only the most vigorous speculation, the broadest and most energetic search for foundations in metaphysics and theology of the tenets of behavior, can be an antidote."[32]

In his call for clear philosophical thinking Boorstin was not hoping for abstract system-building but for a more critical and morally oriented pragmatism. "The more conscious we become of the philosophical assumptions underlying our action, the more do we see the ways in which philosophy can give us freedom."[33] He was seeking a middle way between the "dogmatic activism" of the Jeffersonian tradition and the doctrinaire abstracts of Europe. Most significant, he seemed to find the key to that middle road in the humility the Jeffersonians had derived from their belief in a Creator, who had also given them an implicit criterion of judgment that sustained their republican principles. Since "it is surely not in our power to live any more within the Jeffersonian world of ideas," that humility and moral criterion had to come to twentieth century man from sources other than religious faith.[34]

During the next few years Boorstin began to recognize a usable substitute for Jefferson's Creator. Under the pressure of the cold war he, along with most of his contemporaries, began to feel ever more sharply the evil of the Soviet Union and the relative goodness of the United States. America, compared with Soviet communism and the earlier fascist and Nazi movements, was a great democratic success. If the Jeffersonians and other spokesmen for American democracy had been unreflective and pragmatic, then such an attitude must be largely responsible for America's success. Clearly the European totalitarians were theoretical dogmatists and absolutists. "The characteristic tyrannies of our age—naziism, fascism, and communism—have expressed precisely this idolatry," he declared. "They justify their outrages because their philosophies require them." [35] Drawing on his pragmatic background and his belief in the nontheoretical nature of American thought, Boorstin began to interpret both democracy and America in terms of the relativist-absolutist dichotomy. The logic of the relativist theory of democracy seemed to supply the answers to his problems, for it combined a method of sharply distinguishing American politics from European, of justifying the existence of democratic government, and of supplying the humility Jefferson's Creator had inspired.

The prescriptive-descriptive ambiguity in the relativist theory revealed itself even more clearly in Boorstin's work than it had in Niebuhr's. When Boorstin began to interpret America in terms of the relativist-absolutist dichotomy, he began to equate social and philosophical pluralism not only with the empirical basis of democracy and with its ethical justification, but with the existing structure of American society itself. From a critical analysis of the ethical ambiguities in American thought, he came to accept that very ambiguity as the foundation of democracy and American society itself as the democratic norm. Unreflective practicality became ethically good when he saw it in the context of the relativist theory rather than in the context of a logical analysis of political theory.

By 1953 Boorstin was ready to equate all philosophy with dogmatism and to praise the unreflective pragmatism he had earlier questioned. American history, he decided, had been characterized by a sense of givenness, a pervasive belief that the country had been blessed with a set of values and institutions that automatically defined and secured the morally ideal social life. Americans felt a moral continuity with their past and a moral consensus in their present, both of which enabled them to ignore the need for any explicit political or ethical theory. That consensus underlay the strength of American life and saved the country from the kind of ideological warfare that had racked Europe. Any attempt at formulating a clear theory of American democracy could only produce dissension, for American democracy lay in its historical tradition and the unconscious attitudes of its people.

251

Though Boorstin's philosophical mind initially made him slightly condescending toward the inarticulate American consensus, by the late fifties he was hailing it as a social ideal. In *The Americans: The Colonial Experience*, which he published in 1958, Boorstin with unqualified enthusiasm adopted the absolutist-relativist dichotomy as the central theme in American history. The environment of the new world "thawed the categories of thought" and forced men to become practical, empirical, and undogmatic.[36] The first settlers learned that knowledge came from action, that reality superseded dogma, and that metaphysical systems were dangerous burdens. That specially American characteristic explained "the difference between Washington and Napoleon; between Roosevelt, Truman, and Eisenhower on the one hand and the garret-spawned European illuminati like Lenin, Mussolini, and Hitler."[37] Issues of any kind could only be reasonably settled by facts not theories, and only a slow organic evolution could produce the kind of consensus that united and stabilized a society. "To say that a society can or ought to be 'unified' by some total philosophic system—whether a *Summa Theologica*, a Calvin's *Institutes*, or Marx's *Capital*—is to commit oneself to an aristocratic concept of knowledge: let the elite know the theories and values of the society: they will know and preserve for all the rest."[38] Philosophical relativism was logically democratic in theory and inevitably democratic in practice.

America was distinct from Europe, for "political life there is the world of ends and absolutes." Hence, Europe was by its very nature threatened with totalitarianism. As long as Americans remained practical and untheoretical, they would avoid that danger. "If we have learned anything from our history," he maintained, "it is the wisdom of allowing institutions to develop according to the needs of each particular environment; and the value of both environmentalism and traditionalism as principles of political life, as ways of saving ourselves from the imbecilities, the vagaries, and the cosmic enthusiasms of individual men."[39]

Boorstin had thus returned to the position he held two decades earlier —values were prior to reason and arose unreflectively from experience. Reason was capable of defending those values, he assumed, as he had in 1941, but also of disrupting them through dangerous speculation and ideology. But during those two decades he had developed conscious criteria of judgment for both values and the uses of reason. The relativist theory of democracy, with its dichotomy between relativism and absolutism and its emphasis on cultural consensus, provided those criteria.

Metaphysical theories, abstract systems, and "blueprints" for social change were bad. Compromise, unreflective practicality, and slow social evolution were good. The former were totalitarian; the latter democratic. Understanding that, one could critically evaluate human history, distinguish between the desirable and the undesirable, and defend the genius of American politics. By the late fifties Boorstin had become an American Blackstone.

As Boorstin and Niebuhr moved in their different ways toward a greater acceptance and even praise of the structure of American society, they characterized the spreading status quo orientation that marked social thought during the two decades after World War II. That fundamental change in attitude was not simply the result of the cold war, the success of the New Deal, or the threat of McCarthyism. Rather it was the result of all of those forces together activating the conservative implications that were inherent in the general assumptions of the relativist theory of democracy.

First, the anti-absolutist attitude led American intellectuals to distrust all comprehensive theories of social reform and to believe that an emphasis on moral isues in politics tended to weaken democratic processes. By the early fifties many, like Boorstin, were equating all broad moral and social theories with ideology, pejoratively used to mean an unrealistic, moralistic absolutism that by its very nature endangered social tranquility. By discrediting ideology and morally based pleas for social change, they tended to equally discredit any call for a significant restructuring of American society.

That anti-absolutism helped inspire a widespread interest in the psychological roots of political behavior, guided by the assumption that there was an absolutistic or authoritarian personality type. Through interviewing techniques and various psychological scales much evidence was produced to indicate that such a type did exist and that it was easily distinguished from a more tolerant and democratic personality type. "The authoritarian predispositions," summarized two scholars, "would seem to be more closely linked with the reactionary and radical positions than with an overall ideological continuum from liberalism to conservatism."[40] Hence radicals of the left and right tended to be psychologically authoritarian, and liberals and conservatives of the center tended to be tolerant. Such findings easily translated into the belief that the middle represented a kind of emotional maturity and that major social criticism of any kind

253

was the result of psychological displacement or even derangement. Such studies revealed the extent to which the relativist-absolutist dichotomy had been accepted. Identifying the extreme left and extreme right as absolutists, scholars assumed that they would have similar personality structures.[41]

Second, thinking in terms of the relativist-absolutist dichotomy, by which they interpreted the differences between the United States and the Soviet Union, intellectuals assumed that American society was essentially relativistic and therefore pluralistic. "Power in America seems to me situational and mercurial," commented the sociologist David Riesman, "it resists attempts to locate it." Because of its pluralistic social structure, the United States was characterized by "indeterminacy and amorphousness in the cosmology of power."[42] The country had thus largely succeeded in the fundamental democratic task of balancing power. "A closely related characteristic of democratic orders—or at least of the American democratic order—is a wide dispersion of power," agreed V. O. Key, one of the most influential political scientists of the postwar decades. Effective power was so dispersed that "the locus of power may shift from question to question and even from time to time on the same question."[43] Given that accomplishment, any serious disruption of the balance, any reform movement that went outside established institutions, could only be harmful to the country's democratic achievement.

The belief that American society was pluralistic led to a revival in the fifties of the group theory of politics. Drawing inspiration from Arthur F. Bentley's 1908 classic, *The Process of Government*, and readily recognizing the approach as a relativistic alternative to Marxist class determinism, political scientists and sociologists analyzed American politics in terms of the interactions of a large number of competing groups.[44] Looking for group conflict, they easily found it. Believing that pluralistic groups were necessary to democracy, they assumed that their presence necesarily meant that a successful democracy existed. Equating group conflict with a dispersal of political power, they concluded that power in America was in fact widely dispersed.

Third, the moral emphasis on tolerance in the relativist theory easily translated into an acceptance of the institutional status quo. While clearly admirable in itself, the central concern with toleration, in a nation where civil liberties were guaranteed by law, made the relativist theory of democracy an essentially defensive doctrine. It emphasized civil liberties, but minimized the problems of social and economic inequality. Belief in the primacy of toleration and compromise readily led to the assumption, most useful to determined defenders of the status quo, that broad demands for political and economic change were actually irresponsible. The assumption that a "reasonable" compromise was always possible within the given social structure made an opposition to established institutions appear politically illegitimate.[45]

It is quite likely that the renewed concern for civil liberties for all and civil rights for minorities that flourished in the postwar decades developed partially out of the assumptions behind the relativist theory. The relativist emphasis on toleration supported the moral necessity of both. At the same time, both were clearly issues that could be resolved, at least legally, within the existing structure of American society. Interest in civil liberties and civil rights could well have helped reform-minded intellectuals overlook the fundamental status quo orientation of their theory by providing them with sharp demands that preserved for them a partially critical stance toward American society. Invariably, when speaking of the country's essential democratic success, social scientists would point to either or both as examples of weaknesses that needed to be remedied. Civil liberties and civil rights were justified by their theory and at the same time institutionally conservative.

Fourth, the emphasis on cultural agreement that lay behind the relativist theory led to the assumption that America enjoyed an underlying political consensus that stabilized the society. "It was not the consensus of ideology" or any other erratic phenomenon, declared Benjamin F. Wright of Harvard. "It was rather the consensus rooted in the common life, habits, institutions, and experience of generations." As Boorstin and many others were doing, Wright accepted the relativist-absolutist dichotomy and used it not only to interpret the nation's past, but to comment on its present. "History contains so many examples of an absolute conviction of self-righteousness being founded on fanaticism and ignorance, of eternal principles which were no more than transitory policies," he declared in 1958, "that the tolerant humility of Franklin seems the way of maturity and wisdom."[46] The belief in the existence of a cultural consensus inspired the work of many political scientists and sociologists, as they tried to discover its precise range and nature. In spite of considerable disagreement on particulars, there was a broad agreement on its existence; by the fifties the country's intellectuals were in the midst of a dedicated Tocqueville renaissance. Most important, the great majority viewed the consensus as morally good. If Americans did enjoy such cultural agreement and if it was the basis of the nation's democratic tradition, then its rejection courted destruction of democracy. Political action that was to be both rational and effective had to be carried out within the terms of that cultural agreement. Those assumptions narrowed sharply the limits of legitimate political discourse.

The emphasis on cultural consensus was doubly important. Not only did it assume a healthy unity which automatically defined major change as disruptive, unwarranted, and destructive, but it also tended to downplay the significance of economic inequality. If the real bases of democracy were cultural consensus, intellectual diversity, and group competition, then the economic structure itself was of only subsidiary importance. No longer did vast economic inequality seem the grave threat to democratic society that many earlier Americans had considered it. As long as the economic system seemed roughly congruent with the cultural consensus, corporate concentration and maldistribution of income posed no major threat. And of course the economic system was fully congruent with the cultural consensus because the consensus itself was defined in practice as largely an acceptance of that very economic system.

Finally, and of greatest significance, the relativist theory led intellectuals to assume that American society was not only good, but that it was itself a normative phenomenon. Accepting the relativist-absolutist dichotomy, they perceived America as pluralistic. The very idea of a science of society contained a normative implication; for, when social scientists thought they had discovered the social and cultural prerequisites for democracy, those prerequisites became a kind of norm—the conditions that must be present in order to sustain a democracy. Assuming that America was pluralistic, they assumed that it fulfilled those conditions. Inheriting the prescriptive-descriptive ambiguity of the relativist theory, they came to assume that the country's pluralism represented both the empirically necessary foundation for democratic government and at the same time the institutionalization of the ethical relativism that justified democracy in theory. Under the pressure of the cold war and the unconscious conceptual fusion of the prescriptive and the descriptive, American society gradually emerged as an empirical and a moral norm for democratic government.

Clearly the great majority of intellectuals did not consciously develop all of the logical implications of the relativist theory. That lack of conscious consideration, however, was precisely the reason why the prescriptive-descriptive ambiguity went largely unnoticed and was widely accepted. American intellectuals did consciously accept the relativist-absolutist dichotomy, applied both to philosophies and societies, the belief that a relativist culture was the empirical basis of democracy, and the conviction that the United States represented such a relativist culture. Those explicit beliefs developed into the implicit assumption that American society was a norm for democracy, both empirically and morally. That fundamental, but largely covert, assumption lay at the heart of the status quo orientation of the postwar decades. It was implied in the various conservative implications of the relativist theory of democracy and in turn explained their widespread acceptance. If American society was unconsciously accepted as normative, then critical theory could only be peripheral and major change unthinkable. By what other standard could American society be judged?

Even before the war Ralph Barton Perry, a philosopher at Harvard whose major field was ethical theory, suggested the identification that would take place between the existent and the normative. The ends of the various social "modes of organization," of law, politics, economics, and morals, he wrote in 1939, all shared the common end of achieving practical agreement amidst social diversity. "This common end of practical agreement I propose to designate as the moral end," he declared. "When these modes of organization are considered as enduring through a replacement of the human beings which compose them, they constitute moral institutions." [47] Hence, the institutions of a society, at least of a relativistic society, were themselves the criteria of social ethics. Assuming a relativistic culture, the areas of institutionalized agreement defined the limits of morality.

Similarly, the most significant change in Boorstin's thought between the late forties and the early fifties was from a sensitive theoretical and political criticism of the dominant tendencies of American thought to an almost unqualified praise of their virtues. Without ever quite explicitly saying it, Boorstin began to treat American culture as functionally normative, and as properly so. "Aspects of experience which are elsewhere sharply distinguished," he wrote approvingly, "here seem to merge into each other: the private and the public, the religious and the political, even—as I have suggested—the 'is' and the 'ought,' the world of fact and the world of fancy, of science and of morals." In fact, Boorstin explicitly saw the growth of a normative existent as the essence of the American experience, as the explanation of the country's genius. "We can see the growing sense of 'giveness,' the growing tendency to make the 'is' the guide to the 'ought,' to make America as it was (or as they had now made it) a criterion of what America ought to be."[48] Boorstin was referring specifically to the Puritans, but his statement was even more applicable to the attitudes of intellectuals in the postwar decades.

The traditional "grand alternatives" of social thought, two Yale social scientists wrote in 1953, had become "increasingly difficult for thoughtful men to find meaningful." Most western societies were by and large in agreement on the utility of a social pluralism and on the ends they sought; disagreement came only over the techniques of reaching those ends. "In economic life the possibilities for rational social action, for planning, for reform—in short, for solving problems—depend not upon our choice among mythical grand alternatives but largely upon choice among particular social techniques."[49] Rationality meant that all "ideologies" were mythical and had to be abandoned. The agreement on common problems meant that men should devote themselves to working out efficient techniques for reaching those values upon which there was a broad consensus. The existing social structure was the criterion of political rationality.

Few intellectuals explicitly affirmed the equation between the American given and the democratic norm, but that unarticulated assumption was widely prevalent in the postwar decades. It revealed itself most clearly in the directly related fields of political theory and comparative politics. In both, scholars tried to examine the empirical foundations of democracy, and in both they tended to equate the theory with the American achievement. "We have made the Enlightenment work in spite of itself, and surely it is time we ceased to be frightened of the mechanisms we have devised to do so," declared the political scientist Louis Hartz. "We have implemented popular government, democratic judgment and the equal state on a scale that is remarkable by any earthly standard."[50] The earthly standard turned out, by and large, to be the American standard.

Accepting many of the empirical discrepancies between theory and practice that scholars in the twenties and thirties had discovered, political theorists moved in the direction suggested by Pendleton Herring in 1940. The classical theory of democracy was clearly idealistic and impractical. Attempts to implement it led to disruption and inefficiency. Instead of presenting an unattainable ideal, political theorists in the postwar decades reasoned, democratic theory should be practical and realistic. It should, in short, be descriptive of the way democracy actually worked. When empirical behavior contradicted the theory, the latter not the former should be questioned. Discrepant behavior was often, in fact, functionally stabilizing and hence a positive practical good.

The major weaknesses of the classical theory, most of its critics agreed, were its overly optimistic view of the average citizen and its failure to understand the role of elites. Detailed empirical studies of American voting behavior made it clear that a very high percentage of citizens had little accurate knowledge of issues, that they failed to participate or even vote, and that their decisions were generally the result of prejudices, group affiliations, or simple habit rather than rational reflection.[51] Additionally, studies of the practice of American politics showed that only a relatively small number of citizens actually tried to influence the decisions of government. Though participation was open to all, only a few had the actual interest and ability necessary to engage in politics. "The democratic method," declared Joseph A. Schumpeter, "is that institutional arrangement for arriving at political decisions in which individuals acquire the power to decide by means of a competitive struggle for the people's vote."[52] Democracy was an institutionalized conflict between elites for political power, rather than any system of actual popular participation in the classical sense.

Rather than perceiving such empirical discoveries as bad, political theorists tended to accept them as given and to examine their functional utility. Large-scale nonparticipation and apathy was socially beneficial, since it helped preserve democratic stability by providing a large uninvolved mass that acted as a balancing force. "The apathetic segment of America," declared one group of researchers, "probably has helped to hold the system together and cushioned the shock of disagreement, adjustment, and change."[53] Elites, too, were seen as good, since democracy needed their special abilities and greater energy. More important, political scientists began to discover that the consensus necessary for democratic success did not reside in the people as a whole as much as with social elites. Because of their education, commitments, and established roles, elite groups tended to underwrite the political consensus of a democratic society, and protect it from the sporadic assaults of the ill-informed and dangerous.[54] Additionally, because of the open nature of American society,

259

the range of elites represented, at least potentially, all social interest groups. "Our political activists are distributed among social groups in such a way," concluded Robert E. Lane, a political scientist at Yale, "as to open up channels of influence for every group."[55] Elites would, in fact, represent the interests of each group much more adequately than could its members as a whole. Group theory thus served another function, reconciling an elitist orientation with popular values. As long as elites could form freely, social scientists argued, they would represent all groups and hence all individuals.

Perhaps the most influential and persuasive advocate of a more realistic democratic theory was the political scientist Robert A. Dahl. In *A Preface to Democratic Theory*, published in 1956, Dahl rejected the descriptive accuracy and logical consistency of theories based on constitutional checks and balances as well as on unrestricted popular sovereignty. Assuming the primacy of cultural conditions as the basis of democracy, he argued that America had succeeded because it combined a unique cultural consensus with a widespread number of competing minorities. Dahl developed a lucid and highly sophisticated version of the relativist theory and concluded that American government was characterized by neither majority rule nor minority rule, but rather by "minorities rule." Its society was pluralistic, and that pluralism was the empirical basis of democracy and an ethical good. "To assume that this country has remained democratic because of its Constitution seems to me an obvious reversal of the relation," he maintained; "it is much more plausible to suppose that the Constitution has remained because our society is essentially democratic."[56] Concerned principally with making his theory descriptively accurate as well as operationally explicit and hence empirically verifiable, Dahl assumed that American practice was the criterion for democratic theory itself.

Five years later he applied his "polyarchal" theory of democracy to a study of city government in New Haven, Connecticut. Confirming the inaccuracies of classical theory, he pictured the average citizen as uninvolved and unconcerned with New Haven politics.[57] Effective control resided in fluid and competing groups of elites. The elites, however, were largely self-selected, since the political system was open and flexible. "The political stratum is easily penetrated by anyone whose interests and concerns attract him to the distinctive political culture of the stratum."[58] Political power was widely fragmented, and no group was able to dominate the decisions of government. New Haven, Dahl continued, confirmed both the need and general accuracy of a more realistic theory of democracy, but equally confirmed the belief that American politics represented the fulfillment of democratic ideals as far as they were practicable.

The belief that the United States had institutionalized democratic procedures in a realistic manner led to a central concern among social scientists with the problem of stability. One of his major interests, Dahl acknowledged, was "to predict the stability of a democratic system and perhaps even to design rules to guarantee its stability."[59] Under the pressure of the cold war as well as the pressure for useful research, sociologists and political scientists transformed the problem of the cultural bases of democracy into the problem of the cultural bases for American stability. There was an essential, if not always obvious, difference between the two. The first was broader and more dynamic; the second narrower and more static. "The great political task now as in the past," the political scientist David B. Truman declared in 1951, "is to perpetuate a viable system."[60] Assuming that the United States had already succeeded in its democratic goal, social scientists were more concerned with the problem of conservation than of creation. As they devoted more and more research to the problem of stability, that stability took on the value of an end in itself.

Needless to say, most of those who attempted to develop a realistic theory were not simple apologists for the status quo. Most were quite concerned with various reforms and often adopted "liberal" positions on social issues. In fact, one of their major goals was to defend democracy and to show that it was a workable and sound political ideal. In doing that, however, they were forced to show that a successful democratic government actually existed, and hence to identify the ideal with the existent. The very concept of a "realistic" democratic theory implied that "reality," not an ethical ideal, was the primary criterion of both theoretical validity and legitimate political action. Hence the American given, assumed to be pluralistic and therefore good—or, conversely, good and therefore pluralistic—tended to create a fundamentally complacent attitude among intellectuals, to deprive democratic theory of its traditional moral, critical function, and to gloss over the glaring discrepancies of wealth and power that existed in American society.[61]

The transformation of the existent into the normative in political theory was supported by the general movement in the postwar decades toward creating a wholly empirical social theory. Led by such scholars as the sociologist Talcott Parsons and the political scientist David Easton, social scientists came to believe that the role of theory was to provide an abstract and comprehensive framework which could systematically organize empirical findings. Theory, in other words, was to be wholly descriptive, and its purpose a systematic classification of the existent. Parsons's elaborate and, for a time, widely influential approach reduced theory to the problem of creating generalized categories for classifying social phenomena. In attempting to develop a theory that was descriptive and comprehensive, he treated societies as wholes, emphasizing their self-maintenance as systems and their efforts at collective goal-attainment. As a result, Parsons's theory minimized conflict, inequality, and all intra-societal power relations. Society was a smooth-running and collectively satisfying system. The generalized nature of his theory left it devoid of dynamism. Its wholly descriptive focus deprived it of any basis for social criticism. Its analysis of society as an integrated whole seemed to assume that the existing social order was therefore such an integrated, collectively satisfying system. That empirical focus, together with its purposive rejection of prescriptive theory, led in practice to a descriptive acceptance of the limits of American society and confirmed the assumption that the structure was basically good. Empiricism itself was not necessarily conservative, but in the context of the cold war and with concepts that were implicitly prescriptive, it led almost inevitably toward a wholesale acceptance of the existent social structure.[62]

Since American intellectuals began with the relativist perception of American society, which was implicitly prescriptive, realism as a criterion meant the existent as the criterion. Since ethical and empirical theory were conceptually though unconsciously fused, reality became the standard not only of systematic analysis but also of ethical behavior. That ambiguity created a fundamental reversal of roles. On an ethical level, reality became the standard to evaluate ideals, rather than ideals the standard by which to judge reality. It was almost as if many social scientists had purposely accepted an operationalist theory of meaning: democracy was defined as the way American government worked in practice.

While American pluralism was becoming the norm for democratic theory, students of comparative politics were making it the norm for their analysis of governments throughout the world. The international political situation in the postwar decades fostered an exceptionally rapid expansion in the field of comparative politics and gave it a new prestige and significance. "This is an era of nation building," declared the political scientist Lucien W. Pye. "Since the end of World War II, half a billion people have become citizens of newly independent countries, and nearly a billion more are citizens of old countries striving to become modern nations."[63] As the United States became involved in the cold war and in the internal development of nations throughout the world, interest in and demand for knowledge about the politics of other countries quickly accelerated. By the end of the fifties comparative politics was perhaps the most dynamic field in the social sciences.[64]

In 1956 Gabriel A. Almond, then teaching at Princeton University, published an essay on "Comparative Political Systems" which established many of the theoretical guidelines that dominated the study of comparative politics for the next decade. Drawing on the systematic categories developed by Talcott Parsons and certain new approaches from anthropology and psychology, Almond proposed the idea of political culture as the central analytical concept for the comparison of political systems. "Every political system is embedded in a particular pattern of orientations to political action," he explained. "I have found it useful to refer to this as the *political culture*."[65] Political culture was broader than such concepts as political system or ideology. It was narrower than the concept of culture itself. It represented the culturally determined ways in which individuals perceived and conceived their national political system and their own relationship to it. Political culture was the whole set of culturally derived attitudes that underlay the operation of any particular political structure.

Though it was intended as an objective tool for social science, and clearly represented a significant theoretical advance, Almond's concept itself was another version of the relativist theory of democracy with its attendant prescriptive-descriptive ambiguity. When he turned to his classification and analysis of the various types of political culture, he sharply distinguished the relativist culture from the various other forms. The United States and England had both developed a "secular" political culture. "By a secular political culture I mean a multi-valued political culture, a rational-calculating, bargaining, and experimental political culture," he explained. "It is a homogeneous culture in the sense that there is a sharing of political ends and means." Many intellectuals, especially continental European ones, scorned such a political culture for its lack of logical clarity; they missed its practical, dynamic logic of democratic accommodation. "Actually the logic is complex and is constantly referred to reality in an inductive process," Almond commented, sounding very much like Boorstin. "It avoids the kind of logical simplism which characterizes much of the Continental European ideological polemic." Perhaps exaggerating his case for the sake of clarity, he pictured the secular political culture as analogous to a series of scientific experiments. "The secularized political process has some of the characteristics of a laboratory; that is, policies offered by candidates are viewed as hypotheses, and the consequences of legislation are rapidly communicated within the system and constitute a crude form of testing hypotheses." In questions of power, too, that political culture was wholly pluralistic. "The Anglo-American type of political system is one in which there is a diffusion of power and influence." [66]

The three other types he outlined—the preindustrial, the totalitarian, and the continental European—were widely divergent. They shared, however, two common characteristics: they lacked the relativistic consensus of the Anglo-American type and they possessed, in varying degrees, absolutist elements. The preindustrial, for example, partially retained "supernatural sanctions" which made it susceptible to "charismatic" political movements. The continental European was marked by the failure "to carry through a thorough-going secularization," which left it with strong Catholic and communist political influences. "In other words, these systems have a totalitarian potentiality in them." [67]

Almond's basis of distinction among these types was thus the relativist-absolutist dichotomy. The implicit prescription in that basis revealed itself throughout. Continental European political culture, not being wholly secularized, was "fragmented"; it had developed "by an uneven pattern"; its attitude toward parliamentarianism was "not appropriately oriented." The totalitarian political culture was, of course, dominated by force, instability, and central control. As a result it was largely, though not completely, "non-consensual." The preindustrial type was not "non-Western" but rather "pre-Western." [68] In spite of the originality and richness of his hypotheses, they assumed that American relativistic, pluralistic culture was the moral and empirical norm for democratic government throughout the world.

During the next few years Almond's concept of political culture became central to comparative politics and was soon employed throughout the social sciences. In 1963, together with his Stanford colleague Sidney

Verba, he refined and elaborated the concept in a massive five-nation comparative study. Almond and Verba judged the classical theory of democracy a "myth" and maintained that cultural orientation was the foundation of any stable political system. "Unless the political culture is able to support a democratic system," they declared, "the chances for the success of that system are slim." The specific democratic foundation, the "civic culture," was the ideal of political development throughout the world. The clearest models of the "civic culture," Almond and Verba declared, were Great Britain and the United States, "the two relatively stable and successful democracies."[69]

Together with such scholars as Lucien W. Pye, Edward S. Shils, and James S. Coleman, they developed a provocative model of the bases of democratic politics. Starting from their assumptions, it was not surprising that their model of political "modernization" and "development" was cast in the image of relativistic, pluralistic America. "It is clear from this list of attributes," Coleman wrote in 1960, "that the Anglo-American polities most closely approximate the model of a modern political system."[70] It was certainly not at all surprising, either, since the model itself had originally been drawn from the assumed characteristics of those very polities. The United States and England were not only democratic models, but they represented the "modern" system, which was the goal of "development." Social scientists continued to use objective words, but their meanings were consistently prescriptive.

When students of comparative politics discussed political development, they were often consciously aware of using the United States as a model. While it was one thing to judge the growth of clearly undemocratic or poverty-stricken nations by certain achievements of the United States, it was quite another matter to assume that America was broadly normative for the ideal of democratic government itself. Intellectuals in the postwar decades did just that, occasionally in an explicit manner, but more often implicitly or even unconsciously.

The New Deal, the cold war, and McCarthyism all helped shape, and were in turn shaped by, the relativist assumptions of American intellectuals. The pressure of those events transformed the prescriptive-descriptive ambiguity of their assumptions into an implicit equation of the American existent with the moral and empirical norms for democratic government. Given that equation, intellectuals produced a social analysis that assumed the institutional structure of the United States as the basis of political

265

rationality. Relativism and pluralism stood for the broad middle ground against the totalitarianism of both the left and the right. "Pluralism is conservative by contrast with revolutionary extremism," Shils declared in 1956, "pluralism is liberal by contrast with reactionary extremism."[71] It was revealing that intellectuals in the fifties chose to define themselves in relation to a similar absolutism they saw in both the left and the right.

As the relativist theory had helped resolve the crisis of democratic theory in the late thirties and early forties, so it helped form the political attitudes of the postwar decades. Clearly the New Deal, the cold war, and McCarthyism were crucial in pressuring intellectuals toward the status quo, but their theoretical assumptions were also determinant in three ways. First, the framework of the relativist-absolutist dichotomy interpreted those events and helped to determine their theoretical meaning from the start. Intellectuals had come to perceive world politics in terms of that dichotomy, and hence, limited by their specific viewpoint, they found it difficult and even irrational to interpret events in any other way. Second, the relativist theory was conceptually ambiguous, and readily lent itself to the implicit merger of the existent and the normative. Once that fusion had taken place, it tended to deprive social theory of its critical cutting edge and supported the assumption that American society was normatively democratic. Third, there was a logic in the assumptions behind the relativist theory that produced conclusions supportive of the status quo. Those conclusions were not logically necessary, as indeed no practical policy follows from broad theoretical premises according to strict logical necessity. In another context those assumptions could have produced different conclusions. But in the context of the political events and theoretical ambiguity of the postwar decades, the conservative logic was the persuasive logic. The crisis of democratic theory ended in the early fifties with the creation of a broad political-intellectual unity among American intellectuals.

14

America as
a Normative Concept

The relativist theory of democracy dominated American political thought during the two decades following the Second World War, but in the late fifties it began to provoke increasing criticism. By the mid-sixties the criticism became a swelling chorus that sought to repudiate the intellectual-political consensus on which the relativist theory rested. Though approaching the issue from a variety of directions, the critics focused their attacks on the accuracy of "pluralism" as a description of American society as well as on the ideological and apologetic nature of the relativist theory itself.[1] As the debate of the late thirties had forced intellectuals to confront fundamental questions, so too did the new debate of the late sixties. The consensus forged during the late thirties and forties no longer existed.

By the mid-sixties American society had begun to look significantly different to many citizens. The dashing of hopes created by the Kennedy enthusiasm, an increased awareness of poverty and racism, the sharpening identification of a military-industrial complex, ever growing governmental mendacity, and an apparently endless, pointless, and destructive war all combined to create a profound disillusion with the realities of America. As social dissent crystallized, organized, and expanded, social scientists and a broader but vaguer intellectual establishment loomed ever more inviting as targets and ever more plausible as culprits.

Intellectually, new perspectives were available that seemed to support the attack and point to new possibilities of social analysis. Historians, animated by the growing sense of disillusion and enjoying a broader perspective on the events of the thirties and forties, could see more clearly the stultifying impact of totalitarianism on American thought and evaluate more fully the failures and unfortunate consequences of the New Deal in addition to its achievements. Philosophers made the idea of an objective social science increasingly untenable, and pointed to the unproven assumptions that underlay all systems of knowledge. In a widely influential book Thomas S. Kuhn argued that even the "hard" physical sciences were based not simply on empirical facts but more fundamentally on professionally defined assumptions about the nature of the physical universe, which were themselves both unprovable and subject to radical change.[2] If such largely unrecognized assumptions determined the course of even physics and chemistry, many intellectuals reasoned, then surely similar fundamental, and value-laden, assumptions must underlie any social theory.

In spite of the widening attack on the postwar consensus, the new critics paid little attention to the theoretical problem of the moral basis of democracy. To a large extent that was due to a preoccupation with what seemed the more immediate need for practical social change itself. Perhaps, too, most shared a general belief in the futility of prescriptive political philosophy in an age still dominated by the general assumptions of scientific naturalism. Additionally, most of the new critics accepted the democratic ideal, and hence debate centered not on the problem of the rational justification of that ideal but on the issue of its practical interpretation and implementation.

Possibly, too, many of the critics would accept the basic argument of the relativist theory as a logic. Since the rationalist and religious counterattack had failed and since most of the new critics operated on naturalistic assumptions, the new debate of the late sixties was carried on largely within a naturalistic framework. In that context the logical, prescriptive argument behind the relativist theory still appeared the most persuasive and intellectually viable defense of democratic government available. In fact, the relativist theory could potentially be redirected toward broad reform purposes. Considered as a prescriptive political logic, for example, it strongly pointed toward the need for the widespread sharing of effective political power, decentralization of economic decision-making, and a fundamental commitment to meaningful and broad individual freedoms. If democracy depended on intellectual diversity, then attempts to smother dissent or to enforce some form of political orthodoxy were dangerous and destructive. If democracy depended on economic pluralism, then a true pluralism was necessary, one that decentralized the major economic institutions of American society rather than rationalized a continuing centralization and narrowing elite control. If democracy depended on a social pluralism, then a pluralism was necessary that in fact included all groups in the country and gave each a meaningful control over its own future. The relativist theory could solve no political problem, nor did it necessarily lead to any particular set of policies. As a logic, however, it could provide a reasonable and critical democratic theory with which to analyze contemporary society.

But if it were theoretically possible to use the relativist theory to suggest the need for social and economic change, the fact was that in the decades after the Second World War it served the opposite purpose. Just as the theory possessed reform implications, so too it possessed implications that tended to support the status quo. More important, the prescriptive-descriptive ambiguity that marked the theory in its crucial formative years deprived it of critical clarity and helped induce its proponents to equate the existent with the norm. Finally, of course, the entire psychological experience of the late thirties led intellectuals into a profound reaffirmation of American society and values that provided the emotional impetus to ensure that the relativist theory would take shape as a defense of the existent.

The major problem with the theory was not its prescriptive logic but its identification of America with the democratic ideal. Though some form of pluralism might theoretically provide a strong basis for democracy, that did not mean that the United States was actually pluralistic in the same theoretical sense. Even a partially successful pluralism did not mean that a fuller democracy was either impossible or impractical. Cultural consensus may well have been necessary for social stability as well as for a successful democracy, but clearly a cultural consensus might underlie any variety of political system; medieval society was apparently characterized by a considerable degree of cultural agreement. To the extent that relativist theory accepted America as the great democratic success, its argument rested on a redefinition of democracy and not on a persuasive analysis of American society. To the extent that it was critically conceived, it suggested a considerable gap between the ideal and the actual.

The political form that relativist theory took confirmed one of the most common criticisms of philosophical pragmatism, on which the relativist theory was based. The test of "what works" was essentially delusive and circular, for practical efficacy was not an objective criterion. Utility as a rationale demanded an answer to two questions: useful for what? and what was the justification of that purpose? Pragmatism required a broad

269

set of social values that would provide the criteria both for what ought to be done and what was actually successful. Without a clear and critical political analysis, and with a fundamental prescriptive-descriptive confusion, pragmatically based relativist theory easily accepted the existent as its set of validating social ideals. Its analysis was thus essentially circular: it started with assumptions about the nature of pluralistic-consensualist America and ended by appealing to those assumptions to show that the theory, and American politics, actually worked. The relativist theory allowed pragmatism and naturalism to survive triumphant into the postwar years, but it also left American intellectuals bereft of any independent critical theory and dependent upon the official assumptions of an increasingly corporation-dominated, producer-oriented, administratively controlled political and social structure.

Beyond the determining historical events that surrounded World War II, the status quo orientation of the relativist theory grew out of, and reinforced, two broader characteristics of American thought: the tendency to view America as embodying the most ideal form of human society ever established, and the correlative tendency to translate existing social institutions into political and moral norms. The tendency to see America as an ideal appeared continuously through the nation's history. In the seventeenth century the country was to be a city on a hill; in the eighteenth, the bastion of the Laws of Nature and of Nature's God; in the nineteenth, the last, best hope of man; and in the twentieth, quite simply, the great democratic success. In earlier centuries Americans keenly felt the duty that their "experiment" imposed on them, and often they felt even more keenly the inevitable tension that existed between the national ideal and its practical achievement. On most occasions, however, they found some way to reconcile the ideal with the reality, either by asserting that the ideal had in fact been fulfilled or by promising that fulfillment was rapidly approaching.[3]

The twentieth century pushed Americans to their most determined affirmations of positive fulfillment. The appearance of a mass, industrialized society meant that America's unique opportunity—free land, an open continent, the chance for a fresh start—lay in the past. The nation had presumably either fulfilled its promise or had failed for all time. If the ideal had not been realized by the twentieth century, then America had become merely one nation among many that struggled in the same way with the same problems as did all the others. While history was thus

270

threatening to catch up with the national mythology, the twentieth century also hurled up the challenge of foreign aggression and foreign ideologies. Uniting for war and cold war, Americans were forced to cling ever more firmly to their inherited values and affirm ever more fervently their national success. When America as the city on a hill and the last, best hope of man was replaced by America the great democratic success, challenge and tension had given way to enforced complacency.

America in the minds of many thus tended to become more and more a norm in itself, standing for practical democratic achievement and the fulfillment of that last, best hope. Often the dynamism that propelled the normative transformation came from people who were indeed fortunate and satisfied, some acting with sincerity and good faith and others in a consciously designing manner. But most Americans, not just the wealthy and powerful, tended to accept the normative concept, and it pervaded American social and political thought on all levels. Ralph Waldo Emerson, Perry Miller explained, "understood as well as any in what the difficult ordeal consists, that magnificent but agonizing experience of what it is to be, or to try to be, an American."[4] People were not simply born Americans—they had to become Americans. The process of becoming was intensely ideological, and it increasingly centered around the acceptance of American society as a normative existent.

The tendency to see the actual as the good generated the profoundly ideological tone of American politics, for there must always be tension, however repressed, between an existent and an ideal. Americans never abandoned the democratic ideal, and hence conflict continually erupted. Since the ideal remained, and since there were always some who dissented, the actuality was frequently attacked in the name of the ideal. As dissenters formed their attack in moral terms based on the ideal, their opponents were continually led to idealize the existent. What indeed caused the angry attacks of dissenters—especially in the mid-twentieth century—was not a commitment to Marxism or some irrational political messianism, but rather a real belief in and commitment to the very ideals they had been brought up as Americans to believe in. For when the ideal was juxtaposed to the reality, the existent appeared sadly lacking. The most bitter disillusionment and hostility thus grew, not just because there was a gap between the ideal and the reality, but because that imperfect reality was itself turned into a norm.

When intellectual and political leaders idealized the existent, when they made terms that were analytically confused but morally coercive —patriotism, Americanism, free enterprise system, mission, and, most grossly, "we're number one"—into central points of political debate and orthodoxy, they were being intensely ideological. The crucial point, therefore, was not a lack of ideology in America, but the lack of clarity, fullness of vision, and organized social analysis in the particular ideology around which debate raged. It was not that Americans were unreflective and therefore nonideological, but rather that they were unreflective and therefore unclear about the nature of their ideology. Seldom, if ever, were they nonideological.

By identifying ideology with abstract, a priori rationalism and comprehensive, authoritarian systems of thought, the relativist theory blinded itself to the fact that the theory itself—pragmatic, empirical, pluralistic— had in fact become an ideology. The general assumptions of political debate in America—unreflective, easily manipulable, and biased toward corporate power—also represented an ideology. Given the ideological blindness of the first, it was no surprise that it became a sophisticated version of the second.

The broad desire of many intellectuals to defend naturalism had led them to link it with the existing institutions of American society, while belief in the scientific nature of their theory obscured its partisan function. The relativist theory, with its prescriptive-descriptive ambiguity, provided the logical passageway that allowed the normative concept of America to walk in and take over most of academic social and political thought. It also helped explain why so many scholars—themselves intelligent, honest, humane, and democratic—could accept an ideology that in fact served to justify a quite imperfect status quo.

Notes

1. Scientific Naturalism in American Thought

1. Mortimer J. Adler, "The Chicago School," *Harper's Magazine*, 183 (September, 1941), 385.

2. *Daily Maroon* (University of Chicago), June 6, 1934.

3. Ibid., June 7, 1934.

4. Adler, "The Chicago School," 385–86.

5. *Daily Maroon*, October 21, 1936.

6. For the growth of universities in the late nineteenth century see *The Statistical History of the United States from Colonial Times to the Present* (Stamford, Conn., 1965), 210–13; Richard Hofstadter, "The Revolution in Higher Education," in *Paths of American Thought*, ed. Arthur M. Schlesinger, Jr. and Morton White (Boston, 1970 [1963]), 269–90; Hofstadter and C. DeWitt Hardy, *The Development and Scope of Higher Education in the United States* (New York, 1952); Lawrence R. Vesey, *The Emergence of the American University* (Chicago, 1965); William C. DeVane, *Higher Education in Twentieth Century America* (Cambridge, Mass., 1965); Frederick Rudolph, *The American College and University: A History* (New York, 1965 [1962]); Hugh Hawkins, *Pioneer: A History of the Johns Hopkins University, 1874–1889* (Ithaca, New York, 1960); John S. Brubacher and Willis Rudy, *Higher Education in Transition: An American History: 1636–1956* (New York, 1958); and for a different view, Henry Wilkinson Bragdon, *Woodrow Wilson: The Academic Years* (Cambridge, Mass., 1967).

7. Richard Hofstadter, "The Revolution in Higher Education," in *Paths of American Thought*, ed. Schlesinger and White, 276.

8. Hawkins, *Pioneer*, 90, 293–305.

9. Rudolph, *The American College and University*, 432–33.

10. Richard Hofstadter and Walter P. Metzger, *The Development of Academic Freedom in the United States* (New York, 1955), 363.

11. William Graham Sumner, "Sociology," in *Social Darwinism: Selected Essays of William Graham Sumner*, ed. Stow Persons (Englewood Cliffs, N. J., 1963), 14, 21, 10.

12. William Graham Sumner, *Folkways: A Study of the Sociological Importance of Usages, Manners, Customs, Mores, and Morals* (New York, 1940 [1906]), 41.

13. John Dewey, *The Influence of Darwin on Philosophy and Other Essays in Contemporary Thought* (New York, 1951 [1910]), 8–9.

14. William Graham Sumner, "Some Natural Rights," in *Social Darwinism*, ed. Stow Persons, 65–69.

15. Charles E. Merriam, *American Political Ideas: Studies in the Development of American Political Thought, 1865–1917* (New York, 1920), 470.

2. Naturalism & Objectivism in the Social Sciences

1. Leo F. Stock, "List of American Journals Devoted to the Humanistic and Social Sciences," *Bulletin of American Council of Learned Societies*, 8 (October, 1928), 18–20.

2. Hornell Hart and Dorothy Hankins, "Three New Books on Social Research," *Social Forces*, 8 (March, 1930), 449.

3. Horace M. Kallen, "Behaviorism," *Encyclopaedia of the Social Sciences* (New York, 1930), 2:497.

4. Quoted in Bernard Crick, *The American Science of Politics; Its Origins and Conditions* (Berkeley, 1967), 101.

5. Albert Somit and Joseph Tanenhaus, *American Political Science, a Profile of a Discipline* (New York, 1964), 66.

6. Charles E. Merriam, *New Aspects of Politics* (Chicago, 1925), 214.

7. For Watson's early work see J. B. Watson, "Psychology as the Behaviorist Views It," *Psychological Review*, 20 (March, 1913), 158–77; "The Place of the Conditioned-Reflex in Psychology," *Psychological Review*, 23 (March, 1916), 89–116; *Behavior: An Introduction to Comparative Psychology* (New York, 1914).

8. Albert Paul Weiss, *A Theoretical Basis of Human Behavior* (Columbus, Ohio, 1925), 7.

9. Walton Hamilton, "The Institutional Approach to Economic Theory," *American Economic Review*, 9 (Supplement, March, 1919), 316.

10. Wesley C. Mitchell to John M. Clark, August 9, 1928, reprinted in Stuart A. Rice, ed., *Methods in Social Science: A Case Book* (Chicago, 1931), 678.

11. Wesley C. Mitchell, *Business Cycles* (Berkeley, 1913); Mitchell, *Business Cycles: The Problem and Its Setting* (New York, 1927); Walton H. Hamilton and Helen R. Wright, *The Case of Bituminous Coal* (New York, 1926); John R. Commons, *Legal Foundations of Capitalism* (New York, 1924).

12. Robert E. L. Faris, *Chicago Sociology, 1920–1932* (San Francisco, 1967), 37.

13. Robert E. Park and Ernest W. Burgess, *Introduction to the Science of Sociology* (Chicago, 1921), 45.

14. Faris, *Chicago Sociology*, 120, 135–40.

15. G. A. Lundberg, *Social Research: A Study in Methods of Gathering Data* (New York, 1929), 25.

16. Franz Boas, "The Limitations of the Comparative Method of Anthropology," reprinted in *Race, Language and Culture* (New York, 1966 [1940]), 270–80.

17. Clark Wissler, *Man and Culture* (New York, 1923), 251.

18. George W. Stocking, Jr., *Race, Culture, and Evolution: Essays in the History of Anthropology* (New York, 1968), 300.

19. C. Judson Herrick, "The Limitations of Science," *Journal of Philosophy*, 26 (March 28, 1929), 187.

20. Forest E. Clements, "Quantitative Method in Ethnography," *American Anthropologist*, n.s. 30 (April–June, 1928), 296.

21. L. L. Bernard, "Sociological Research and the Exceptional Man," *Papers of the American Sociological Society*, 27 (1932), 4.

22. Howard Becker, *Systematic Sociology on the Basis of the Beziehungslehre and Gebildelehre of Leopold Von Wiese* (New York, 1932), 7.

23. Read Bain, "Scientist as Citizen," *Social Forces*, 11 (March, 1933), 413.

24. William F. Ogburn, "Three Obstacles to the Development of a Scientific Sociology," *Social Forces*, 8 (March, 1930), 347.

25. Lundberg, *Social Research*, 30.

26. F. H. Giddings, "The Scientific Scrutiny of Societal Facts," *Journal of Social Forces*, 1 (September, 1923), 509.

27. Gladys Bryson, "Sociology Considered as Moral Philosophy," *Sociological Review*, 24 (January, 1932), 36.

28. Read Bain, "The Concept of Social Process," *Papers of the American Sociological Society*, 26 (1931), 17.

29. Rexford G. Tugwell, "Human Nature in Economic Theory," *Journal of Political Economy*, 30 (June, 1922), 320.

30. Herbert Blumer, "Science without Concepts," *American Journal of Sociology*, 36 (January, 1931), 530.

31. L. L. Bernard, "Sociology and Psychology," in William Fielding Ogburn and Alexander Goldenweiser, eds., *The Social Sciences and Their Interrelations* (New York, 1927), 360.

32. Joseph Jastrow, "Psychology," *Encyclopaedia of the Social Sciences* (New York, 1934), 12:593.

33. Robert E. Park, "Human Nature and Collective Behavior," *American Journal of Sociology*, 32 (March, 1927), 735; "Sociology and the Social Sciences," *American Journal of Sociology*, 27 (July, 1921), 21.

34. Stocking, *Race, Culture, and Evolution*, 203. See also 230–33.

35. Clark Wissler, "Opportunities for Co-ordination in Anthropological and Psychological Research," *American Anthropologist*, n.s. 22 (January–March, 1920), 3.

36. Quoted in Allen F. Davis, *Spearheads for Reform: The Social Settlements and the Progressive Movement, 1890–1914* (New York, 1967), 29.

37. Samuel Haber, *Efficiency and Uplift: Scientific Management in the Progressive Era, 1890–1920* (Chicago, 1964), 54–55, 97–98, 116; Barry D. Karl, "Presidential Planning and Social Science Research: Mr. Hoover's Experts," in Donald Fleming and Bernard Bailyn, eds., *Perspectives in American History* (Cambridge, Mass., 1969), 3:347–409.

38. William E. Leuchtenburg, "The New Deal and the Analogue of War," in John Braeman, Robert W. Bremner, and Everett Walters, eds., *Change and Continuity in Twentieth-Century America* (New York, 1966), 87–91; Karl, "Presidential Planning," 350–51.

39. "War and Re-orientation," *Encyclopaedia of the Social Sciences* (New York, 1930), 1:189.

40. Clark Wissler, "Opportunities for Co-ordination in Anthropological and Psychological Research," *American Anthropologist*, n.s. 22 (January–March, 1920), 7.

41. William F. Ogburn and Alexander Goldenweiser, "The Field of the Social Sciences," in Ogburn and Goldenweiser, *The Social Sciences and Their Interrelations*, 7.

42. George E. G. Catlin, *A Study of the Principles of Politics: Being an Essay towards Political Rationalization* (London, 1930), 49.

43. Loren Baritz, *The Servants of Power* (Middletown, Conn., 1960), especially 199. For a different view of the attitudes of another group of social scientists see Richard S. Kirkendall, *Social Scientists and Farm Politics in the Age of Roosevelt* (Columbia, Mo., 1966).

44. For a discussion of the impact of institutional changes on intellectuals in the late nineteenth and early twentieth centuries see R. Jackson Wilson, *In Quest of Community: Social Philosophy in the United States, 1860–1920* (New York, 1968), especially 29–31, 51–52; Barry D. Karl, *Executive Reorganization and Reform in the New Deal: The Genesis of Administrative Management, 1900–1939* (Cambridge, Mass., 1963), 40–42; Stocking, *Race, Culture, and Evolution*, Chapter 11, especially 303–6;

Roy Lubove, *The Professional Altruist: The Emergence of Social Work as a Career, 1880–1930* (Cambridge, Mass., 1965), especially Chapters 2 and 6; and Robert H. Wiebe's more general, and vaguer, *The Search for Order, 1877–1920* (New York, 1968), especially Chapters 5 and 6.

45. Quoted in Karl, "Presidential Planning," 376.

46. Frederick Paul Keppel, *Philanthropy and Learning, with Other Papers* (New York, 1936), 23.

47. John Higham, *History: The Development of Historical Studies in the United States* (Englewood Cliffs, N. J., 1965), 117–18.

48. A. F. Kuhlman, "The Social Science Research Council: Its Origin and Objects," *Social Forces*, 6 (June, 1928), 583–85.

49. Ibid., 585.

50. Morris R. Cohen, "Method, Scientific," *Encyclopaedia of the Social Sciences* (New York, 1933), X, 389.

51. Merriam, *New Aspects of Politics*, 231.

52. See John Dewey, "Social Science and Social Control," *New Republic*, 67 (July 29, 1931), 276–77; *The Quest for Certainty: A Study of the Relation of Knowledge and Action* (New York, 1960 [1929]).

53. Stuart Chase, *The Tyranny of Words* (New York, 1938), 360.

3. Methodology & Morals

1. Leonard D. White, "The Local Community Research Committee and the Social Science Research Building," in T. V. Smith and Leonard D. White, eds., *Chicago: An Experiment in Social Science Research*, (Chicago, 1929), 25.

2. Robert E. Park, "The City as a Social Laboratory," ibid., 15.

3. Quoted in Lawrence A. Cremin, *The Transformation of the School: Progressivism in American Education, 1876–1957* (New York, 1961), 185.

4. See Allen F. Davis, *Spearheads for Reform: The Social Settlements and the Progressive Movement, 1890–1914* (New York, 1967), 68, 85, 96–98, 133–35, 170–73, 209.

5. Shelby M. Harrison, "Development and Spread of Social Surveys," in Shelby M. Harrison and Allen Eaton, *A Bibliography of Social Surveys: Reports of Fact-Finding Studies Made as a Basis for Social Action; Arranged by Subjects and Localities* (New York, 1930), xvii–xxiv, xxvi–xxix.

6. Cremin, *Transformation of the School*, 186–87.

7. Quoted in Daniel J. Kevles, "Testing the Army's Intelligence: Psychologists and the Military in World War I," *Journal of American History*, 55 (December, 1968), 570.

8. Karl Pearson, *The Grammar of Science* (London, 1911), 150.

9. Eric Roll, *A History of Economic Thought* (Englewood Cliffs, N. J., 1958), 458–59, 510–11.

10. Ibid., 515–16; Joseph A. Schumpeter, *History of Economic Analysis*, edited from manuscript by Elizabeth Boody Schumpeter (New York, 1954), 876.

11. Mordecai Ezekiel, "Correlation," *Encyclopaedia of the Social Sciences* (New York, 1931), IV, 443.

12. For samples of the new literature see Stuart A. Rice, "The Quantitative Approach to Sociology," *Social Forces*, 4 (March, 1926), 639–42; Rice, "Book Notes,"

Political Science Quarterly, 42 (March, 1927), 157–59; Rice, "Methodology," *Forces*, 5 (June, 1927), 671–73.

13. Stuart A. Rice, "Foreword," in *Statistics in Social Studies*, ed. Stuart A. Rice (Philadelphia, 1930), viii.

14. Stuart A. Rice and W. Wallace Weaver, "The Verification of Social Measurements Involving Subjective Classification," *Social Forces*, 8 (September, 1929), 16.

15. John Candler Cobb, "Quantitative Restating of Sociological and Economic Problems," *American Journal of Sociology*, 32 (May, 1927), 921.

16. Read Bain, "Sociology as a Natural Science," *Social Forces*, 11 (January, 1933), 293. See also Floyd N. House, *The Development of Sociology* (New York, 1936), 422–23.

17. Edward S. Robinson, *Law and the Lawyers* (New York, 1935), 49.

18. Walton Hamilton, "The Institutional Approach to Economic Theory," *American Economic Review*, 9 (supplement, March, 1919), 316.

19. Arthur Meier Schlesinger, "History," in *Research in the Social Sciences: Its Fundamental Methods and Objectives*, ed. Wilson Gee (New York, 1929), 233–37; Andrew Fish, "Psychology," *Commonwealth Review*, 11 (October, 1929), 66–88.

20. "War and Re-orientation," *Encyclopaedia of the Social Sciences* (New York, 1930), I, 194.

21. Rexford G. Tugwell, "Human Nature in Economic Theory," *Journal of Political Economy*, 30 (June, 1922), 332.

22. Stuart A. Rice, "The Behavior of Legislative Groups: A Method of Measurement," *Political Science Quarterly*, 40 (March, 1925), 60.

23. Horace M. Kallen, "Behaviorism," *Encyclopaedia of the Social Sciences* (New York, 1930), 2:498.

24. John M. Clark, "Recent Developments in Economics," in E. C. Hayes, ed., *Recent Developments in the Social Sciences* (Philadelphia, 1927), 259.

25. Stuart A. Rice, "Units and Their Definition in Social Science," *Social Forces*, 9 (June, 1931), 476.

26. F. Stuart Chapin, "Measurement in Sociology," *American Journal of Sociology*, 40 (January, 1935), 480.

27. L. L. Bernard, "The Objective Viewpoint in Sociology," *American Journal of Sociology*, 25 (November, 1919), 298.

28. L. L. Bernard, "The Concept of Progress: III. The Scientific Phase," *Social Forces*, 4 (September, 1925), 36.

29. L. L. Bernard, *Instinct: A Study in Social Psychology* (New York, 1924), 513–14. See David L. Krantz and David Allen, "The Rise and Fall of McDougall's Instinct Doctrine," *Journal of the History of the Behavioral Sciences*, 3 (October, 1967), 326–38.

30. L. L. Bernard, "Sociology and Psychology," in William F. Ogburn and Alexander Goldenweiser, eds., *The Social Sciences and Their Interrelations* (New York, 1927), 352–53.

31. L. L. Bernard, "Social Psychology Studies Adjustment Behavior," *American Journal of Sociology*, 38 (July, 1932), 6.

32. Bernard, "Sociology and Psychology," 348.

33. Percy W. Bridgman, *The Logic of Modern Physics* (New York, 1927), 5.

34. Percy W. Bridgman, *The Nature of Physical Theory* (Princeton, N. J., 1936), 41. See also A. Cornelius Benjamin, *Operationalism* (Springfield, Ill., 1955), 20–22.

35. See Benjamin, *Operationism*, 44–54; Harry Pelle Hartkemeier, "Relativity in the Social Sciences," *Social Science*, 9 (January, 1934), 24–29; Arthur F. Bentley, "The Positive and the Logical," *Philosophy of Science*, 3 (October, 1936), 472–85.

36. George A. Lundberg, "Quantitative Methods in Social Psychology," *American Sociological Review*, 1 (February, 1936), 44.

37. George A. Lundberg, "Public Opinion from a Behavioristic Viewpoint," *American Journal of Sociology*, 36 (November, 1930), 395, note 20.

38. William F. Ogburn, "Limitations of Statistics," *American Journal of Sociology*, 40 (July, 1934), 12–20; Walton Hamilton, "Methods in Social Science: Three Reviews of the Rice Book," *Journal of Political Economy*, 39 (October, 1931), 633–37.

39. Barry D. Karl, "Presidential Planning and Social Science Research: Mr. Hoover's Experts," in Bernard Bailyn and Donald Fleming, eds., *Perspectives in American History*, (Cambridge, Mass., 1969), 3:388–404.

40. Charner M. Perry, "Inductive vs. Deductive Method in Social Science Research," *Southwestern Political and Social Science Quarterly*, 8 (June, 1927), 66–74; John Dewey, "Social Science and Social Control," *New Republic*, 67 (July 29, 1931), 276–77.

41. Charles A. Beard, "Limitations to the Application of Social Science Implied in *Recent Social Trends*," *Social Forces*, 11 (May, 1933), 505–10; Charles A. Ellwood, "Recent Developments in Sociology," in E. C. Hayes, ed., *Recent Developments in the Social Sciences*, 1–49.

42. See for example A. L. Kroeber, "History and Science in Anthropology," *American Anthropologist*, n.s. 37 (October–December, 1935), 539–69; Paul Radin, *The Method and Theory of Ethnology: An Essay in Criticism* (New York, 1933).

43. Stuart A. Rice, "What Is Sociology," *Social Forces*, 10 (March, 1932), 323.

44. Edward A. Lincoln and Fred J. Shields, "An Age Scale for the Measurement of Moral Judgment," *Journal of Educational Research*, 23 (March, 1931), 193.

45. Bernard, *Instinct*, 513.

46. L. L. Bernard, *An Introduction to Social Psychology* (New York, 1926), 398.

47. Bernard, "Social Psychology Studies Adjustment Behavior," *American Journal of Sociology*, 38 (July, 1932), 7.

48. Harry Elmer Barnes, "Leading Trends in Sociology since Herbert Spencer," *Social Science*, 3 (August, September, October, 1928), 360.

49. T. V. Smith, "Philosophical Ethics and the Social Sciences," *Social Forces*, 7 (September, 1928), 22.

50. John Dewey, "Valuation and Experimental Knowledge," *Philosophical Review*, 31 (July, 1922), 325–51; "Values, Liking, and Thought," *Journal of Philosophy*, 20 (November 8, 1923), 617–22; "Value, Objective Reference, and Criticism," *Philosophical Review*, 34 (July, 1925), 313–32; "The Meaning of Value," *Journal of Philosophy*, 22 (February 26, 1925), 126–33; "The Determination of Ultimate Values or Aims through Antecedent or A Priori Speculation or through Pragmatic or Empirical Inquiry," *The Thirty-Seventh Yearbook of the National Society for the Study of Education*, ed. Guy Montrose Whipple, Part II: "The Scientific Movement in Education" (Bloomington, Ill., 1938).

51. Paul T. Homan, "An Appraisal of Institutional Economics," *American Economic Review*, 22 (March, 1932), 10–17; Homan, "Economic Theory-Institutionalism: What It Is and What It Hopes to Become," *American Economic Review*, 21

(Supplement, March, 1931), 134–41; T. N. Carver, "The Behavioristic Man," *Quarterly Journal of Economics*, 33 (November, 1918), 195–200.

52. Frank H. Knight, "Fact and Metaphysics in Economic Psychology," *American Economic Review*, 15 (June, 1925), 247.

53. Frank H. Knight, "Round Table Conference on the Relation between Economics and Ethics," *American Economic Review*, 12 (supplement, March, 1922), 193.

54. Frank H. Knight, "Ethics and the Economic Interpretation," *Quarterly Journal of Economics*, 36 (May, 1922), 480. See also Knight, "Fact and Metaphysics in Economic Psychology," *American Economic Review*, 15 (June, 1925), 247–66; "Economic Psychology and the Value Problem," *Quarterly Journal of Economics*, 39 (May, 1925), 372–409; and various essays collected in *The Ethics of Competition and Other Essays* (New York, 1935).

55. For background on Pi Gamma Mu see Leroy Allen, "A New Journal," *Social Science*, 1 (November, 1925), 60–61, and "Origin and Progress of Pi Gamma Mu," *Social Science*, 1 (November, 1925), 63–66.

56. R. M. MacIver, "Is Sociology a Natural Science?" *Papers of the American Sociological Society*, 25 (1930), 25–35. For Sorokin's earlier views see his *Contemporary Sociological Theories* (New York, 1928) and "A Survey of the Cyclical Conceptions of Social and Historical Process," *Social Forces*, 6 (September, 1927), 28–40; for his later views see "Recent Social Trends: A Criticism," *Journal of Political Economy*, 41 (April, 1933), 194–210, and Charles A. Ellwood, *Methods in Sociology: A Critical Study* (Durham, N. C., 1933), 130, note 1.

57. Charles A. Ellwood, "Scholarship in the Social Sciences," *Social Science*, 7 (January, 1932), 39; Ellwood, "Are Physical Scientists Becoming Sane?" *Social Science*, 7 (October, 1932), 426.

58. Charles A. Ellwood, "The Struggle over Method in the Social Sciences," *Social Science*, 5 (February, March, April, 1930), 139.

59. Charles A. Ellwood, "Emasculated Sociologies," *Social Science*, 8 (April, 1933), 110.

60. Charles A. Ellwood, "Scientific Method in Sociology," *Social Forces*, 10 (October, 1931), 18.

61. Ibid., 19. See also Ellwood, "Scientific Method in Sociology—Continued," *Social Forces*, 11 (October, 1932), 44–50.

62. Ellwood, *Methods in Sociology*, 131.

63. Ibid., 142.

64. Ibid., 142.

65. See Ellwood, *Methods in Sociology*, 134–36; Ellwood, "Scientific Methods of Studying Human Society," *Journal of Social Forces*, 2 (March, 1924), 329; Ellwood, "Scientific Method in Sociology—Continued," *Social Forces*, 11 (October, 1932), 49; Ellwood, "Social Evolution and Cultural Evolution," *Journal of Applied Sociology*, 11 (March–April, 1927), 308–14.

4. Non-Euclideanism: Logic & Metaphor

1. Charles Sanders Peirce, "The Fixation of Belief," *Essays in the Philosophy of Science*, ed. Vincent Tomas (New York, 1957), 20.

2. For example, see John Dewey, *Reconstruction in Philosophy* (Boston, 1962 [1920]), Chapter 1.

3. C. K. Ogden and I. A. Richards, *The Meaning of Meaning: A Study of the*

Influence of Language upon Thought and of the Science of Symbolism (London, 1923), 225.

4. See John Passmore, "Logical Positivism," in Paul Edwards, ed., *The Encyclopedia of Philosophy* (New York, 1967), V, 52–55; R. W. Ashby, "Verifiability Principle," ibid., VIII, 240–47; Ashby, "Logical Positivism," in *A Critical History of Western Philosophy*, ed. D. J. O'Connor (London, 1964); Moritz Schlick, "The Future of Philosophy," in College of the Pacific, *Publications in Philosophy*, 1 (1932), 45–62; Schlick, "A New Philosophy of Experience," in ibid., 1 (1932), 107–22; Rudolph Carnap, "Testability and Meaning," *Philosophy of Science*, 3 (October, 1936), 419–71 and 4 (January, 1937), 1–40; and Herbert Feigl's personal and revealing essay, "The Wiener Kreis in America," in Donald Fleming and Bernard Bailyn, eds., *Perspectives in American History*, vol. 2, *The Intellectual Migration: Europe and America, 1930–1960* (Cambridge, Mass., 1968), 630–73.

5. Ogden and Richards, *The Meaning of Meaning*, 228.

6. Stuart A. Rice, "What Is Sociology?" *Social Forces*, 10 (March, 1932), 324.

7. For the development of non-Euclidean geometry see Stephen F. Barker, "Geometry," in Paul Edwards, ed., *The Encyclopedia of Philosophy*, 3:285–90; Barker, *Philosophy of Mathematics* (Englewood Cliffs, N. J., 1964); E. T. Bell, *Men of Mathematics* (New York, 1937), Chapters 16 and 26; Raymond L. Wilder, *Evolution of Mathematical Concepts: An Elementary Study* (New York, 1968); Morris Kline, *Mathematics in Western Culture* (New York, 1953).

8. The literature on relativity is immense. For an introduction see Bernard Jaffe, *Outposts of Science: A Journey to the Workshops of Our Leading Men of Research* (New York, 1935); Rudolph Carnap, *Philosophical Foundations of Physics* (New York, 1966); Bertrand Russell, *The ABC of Relativity* (New York, 1958); Albert Einstein, *Relativity: The Special and General Theory* (New York, 1961).

9. Russell, *ABC of Relativity*, 84–85.

10. A. S. Eddington, "Gravitation and the Principle of Relativity," *Nature*, 101 (March 14, 1918), 36.

11. Sir Joseph Thompson, "The Reflection of Light by Gravitation and the Einstein Theory of Relativity," *Scientific Monthly*, 10 (January, 1920), 84, 85.

12. Comment by Sir Frank Dyson in Thompson, "The Reflection of Light by Gravitation and the Einstein Theory of Relativity," *Scientific Monthly*, 10 (January, 1920), 81.

13. Albert Einstein, "Preface," in Erwin Freundlich, *The Foundations of Einstein's Theory of Gravitation*, trans. Henry L. Brose (Cambridge, Eng., 1920), v.

14. Albert Einstein, *Sidelights on Relativity*, trans. G. B. Jeffery and W. Perrett (London, 1922), 30.

15. Henri Poincaré, *The Foundations of Science* (New York, 1929), 65.

16. A. d'Abro, *The Evolution of Scientific Thought from Newton to Einstein* (New York, 1927), 38.

17. Morris R. Cohen, "The Subject Matter of Formal Logic," *Journal of Philosophy*, 15 (December 5, 1918), 688.

18. Quoted in Bede Rundle, "Russell and Whitehead," in "History of Logic," ed. A. N. Prior, in *The Encyclopedia of Philosophy*, ed. Paul Edwards, IV, 556.

19. Morris R. Cohen, "The Subject Matter of Formal Logic," *Journal of Philosophy*, 15 (December 5, 1918), 679.

20. Gilbert N. Lewis, *The Anatomy of Science* (New Haven, Conn., 1926), 72.

21. Albert E. Blumberg, "Demonstration and Inference in the Sciences and Philosophy," *Monist*, 42 (October, 1932), 578.

22. Charles Parsons, "Foundations of Mathematics," in Edwards, *The Encyclopedia of Philosophy*, 5:207.

23. E. R. Hedrick, "Tendencies in the Logic of Mathematics," *Science*, 77 (April 7, 1933), 338.

24. Alfred North Whitehead, *Adventures in Ideas* (New York, 1933), 196; C. I. Lewis, "Alternate Systems of Logic," *Monist*, 42 (October, 1932), 481–507; F. S. C. Northrop, "An Internal Inconsistency in Aristotelian Logic," *Monist*, 38 (April, 1928), 193–210; Henry Bradford Smith, review of *An Introduction to Logic and Scientific Method* by Morris R. Cohen and Ernest Nagel, *Philosophy of Science*, 1 (October, 1934), 488–91; Oliver L. Reiser, "Aristotle, Galileo, and the Leaning Towers of Science," *Philosophy of Science*, 3 (October, 1936), 545–48.

25. Oliver L. Reiser, "Modern Science and Non-Aristotelian Logic," *Monist*, 46 (July, 1936), 308.

26. Paul Weiss, "Relativity in Logic," *Monist*, 38 (October, 1928), 539.

27. Oliver L. Reiser, "Non-Aristotelian Logics," *Monist*, 45 (January, 1935), 113.

28. For a brief discussion of complementarity see Barbara Lovett Cline, *The Questioners: Physicists and the Quantum Theory* (New York, 1965), 210–12.

29. Bede Rundle, "Post," in "History of Logic," ed. A. N. Prior, in *The Encyclopedia of Philosophy*, ed. Paul Edwards, 4:559.

30. See C. I. Lewis and Cooper Harold Langford, *Symbolic Logic* (New York, 1932).

31. C. I. Lewis, "Alternate Systems of Logic," *Monist*, 42 (October, 1932), 505.

32. Sterling P. Lamprecht, "Editor's Introduction," in Lewis and Langford, *Symbolic Logic*, page 4 of unnumbered introductory pages.

33. C. I. Lewis, "Alternate Systems of Logic," *Monist*, 42 (October, 1932), 483, 500, 507.

34. John Lange, "The Late Papers of C. I. Lewis," *Journal of the History of Philosophy*, 4 (July, 1966), 235–45.

35. Dewey, *Reconstruction in Philosophy*, 25.

36. Cassius J. Keyser, *The Pastures of Wonder: The Realm of Mathematics and the Realm of Science* (New York, 1929), 99.

37. Cassius J. Keyser, *Thinking about Thinking* (New York, 1926), 67.

38. Eric Temple Bell, *Debunking Science* (Seattle, Wash., 1930), 39.

39. Ibid., 14.

40. Eric Temple Bell, *The Search for Truth* (New York, 1934), 17.

41. Ibid., 254 and Chapter 14.

42. Ibid., 214.

43. Keyser, *Thinking about Thinking*, 91.

44. Rudolph Carnap, "Logic," in Harvard Tercentenary Publications, *Factors Determining Human Behavior* (Cambridge, Mass., 1937), 114.

45. Charles A. Beard and John D. Lewis, "Representative Government in Evolution," *American Political Science Review*, 26 (April, 1932), 236.

46. Francis G. Wilson, "A Relativistic View of Sovereignty," *Political Science Quarterly*, 49 (September, 1934), 409.

47. George H. Sabine, "Political Science and the Juristic Point of View," *American Political Science Review*, 22 (August, 1928), 556, 558.

48. John M. Clark, "The Socializing of Theoretical Economics," in R. G. Tugwell, ed., *The Trend of Economics* (New York, 1924), 86.

49. Ibid., 101. See also John M. Clark, "Soundings in Non-Euclidean Economics," *American Economic Review*, 11 (Supplement no. 1, March, 1921), 132–43.

50. Jerome Frank, "Mr. Justice Holmes and Non-Euclidean Legal Thinking," *Cornell Law Quarterly*, 17 (June, 1932), 572.

51. Ibid., 571.

52. Alfred Korzybski, *Science and Sanity* (Lakeville, Conn., 1958 [1933]), 7.

53. Ibid., 52.

54. Ibid., 46.

55. Charles C. Alexander, *Nationalism in American Thought 1930–1945* (Chicago, 1969), 121–23; Stuart Chase, *The Tyranny of Words* (New York, 1938).

56. Jacques Rueff, *From the Physical to the Social Sciences: Introduction to a Study of Economic and Ethical Theory*, trans. Herman Green (Baltimore, 1929), 2.

57. Ibid., 84.

58. Ibid., 78.

59. Ibid., 153.

60. Ibid., 95.

61. George A. Lundberg, "The Logic of Science," *Social Forces*, 8 (March, 1930), 448.

62. George E. G. Catlin, review of *From the Physical to the Social Sciences* by Jacques Rueff, *Political Science Quarterly*, 45 (June, 1930), 301.

63. "War and Reorientation," *Encyclopaedia of the Social Sciences* (New York, 1930), 1:203.

64. Horace M. Kallen, "Morals," *Encyclopaedia of the Social Sciences* (New York, 1933), 10:643.

65. Robert H. Lowie, *Primitive Society* (New York, 1970 [1920]), 13.

66. Franz Boas, "The Limitations of the Comparative Method of Anthropology," reprinted in *Race, Language and Culture* (New York, 1966 [1940]), 280. See also Marvin Harris, *The Rise of Anthropological Theory: A History of Theories of Culture* (New York, 1968), 253–58.

67. Harris, *Rise of Anthropological Theory*, 314.

68. Franz Boas, "Some Problems of Methodology in the Social Sciences," reprinted in *Race, Language and Culture*, 268.

69. Franz Boas, "History and Science in Anthropology: A Reply," reprinted in *Race, Language and Culture*, 311. See also Harris, *Rise of Anthropological Theory*, 272–82; Claude Levi-Strauss, *Structural Anthropology*, trans. Claire Jacobson and Brooke Grundfest Schoepf (New York, 1967), 6–11.

70. Franz Boas, *Anthropology and Modern Life* (New York, 1928), 201.

71. See for example Franz Boas, *The Mind of Primitive Man* (New York, 1913) and "The Methods of Ethnology," reprinted in *Race, Language and Culture*, 281–82.

72. Robert H. Lowie, review of *History, Psychology and Culture* by Alexander Goldenweiser, *American Anthropologist*, n.s. 36 (January–March, 1934), 115.

73. Lowie, *Primitive Society*, 5–6.

74. See Harris, *Rise of Anthropological Theory*, 270, 343, 336–37, 325–27, 353–54; Alexander A. Goldenweiser, "Evolution, Social," *Encyclopaedia of the Social Sciences* (New York, 1931), V, 656–62; Goldenweiser, "A New Approach to History," *American Anthropologist*, n.s. 22 (January–March, 1920), 26–47.

75. Franz Boas, "The Methods of Ethnology," reprinted in *Race, Language and Culture*, 285.

76. Paul Radin, *The Method and Theory of Ethnology: An Essay in Criticism* (New York, 1966 [1933]), 185.

77. Paul Radin, *Crashing Thunder: The Autobiography of a Winnebago Indian* (New York, 1926).

78. Radin, *Method and Theory of Ethnology*, 185.

79. A. L. Kroeber, "History and Science in Anthropology," *American Anthropologist*, n.s. 37 (October–December, 1935), 562.

80. Alexander A. Goldenweiser, *Early Civilization* (New York, 1922), 18.

81. Franz Boas, "Report on the Academic Teaching of Anthropology," *American Anthropologist*, n.s. 21 (January–March, 1919), 42.

82. Clark Wissler, "The Culture Area Concept as a Research Lead," *American Journal of Sociology*, 33 (May, 1928), 885.

83. John Dewey, "Human Nature," *Encyclopaedia of the Social Sciences* (New York, 1932), VII, 536.

84. Margaret Mead, *Sex and Temperament in Three Primitive Societies* (New York, 1962 [1935]), 206.

85. Clark Wissler, *Man and Culture* (New York, 1923), 356.

86. Lowie, *Primitive Society*, 439.

87. Alexander A. Goldenweiser, *History, Psychology, and Culture* (New York, 1933), 410.

88. Ruth Benedict, *Patterns of Culture* (New York, 1960 [1934]), 53.

89. Ibid., 227–28.

90. Ibid., 51.

91. Robert H. Lowie, *Culture and Ethnology* (New York, 1929), 41.

92. A. L. Kroeber, *Anthropology* (New York, 1923), 506.

93. Mead, *Sex and Temperament*, 226.

94. Ibid., 226.

5. The Rise of Legal Realism

1. For the creative ferment in American law at the beginning of the nineteenth century see Morton J. Horwitz's excellent essay "The Emergence of an Instrumental Conception of American Law, 1780–1820" in Donald Fleming and Bernard Bailyn, eds., *Perspectives in American History*, Vol. 5, *Law in American History* (Cambridge, Mass., 1971), 287–326. For discussions of the formalistic attitude toward law that characterized the later period see Karl N. Llewellyn, *The Common Law Tradition: Deciding Appeals* (Boston, 1960), 35–45; Calvin Woodward, "The Limits of Legal Realism: An Historical Perspective," *Virginia Law Review*, 54 (May, 1968), 699–701, 710–18; Roscoe Pound, "Mechanical Jurisprudence," *Columbia Law Review*, 8 (December, 1908), 605–23; Pound, "The Theory of Judicial Decision," *Harvard Law Review*, 36 (May, 1923), 802–25 and (June, 1923), 940–59; Edwin W. Patterson, *Jurisprudence: Men and Ideas of the Law* (Brooklyn, N. Y., 1953), 465–66; and Wilfred E. Rumble, Jr., *American Legal Realism: Skepticism, Reform, and the Judicial Process* (Ithaca, N. Y., 1968), 49–51.

2. Charles W. Bacon and Franklyn S. Morse, *The Reasonableness of The Law: The Adaptability of Legal Sanctions to the Needs of Society* (New York, 1924), iii, 145.

3. John M. Zane, "German Legal Philosophy," *Michigan Law Review*, 16 (March, 1918), 338.

4. Karl N. Llewellyn, "Case Method," *Encyclopaedia of the Social Sciences* (New York, 1930), 3:251–54; James Willard Hurst, "Legal Elements in United States History," in Fleming and Bailyn, *Law in American History*, 60–61; and Robert Stevens, "Two Cheers for 1870: The American Law School," ibid., 435–41, 467–68.

5. Oliver Wendell Holmes, Jr., *The Common Law* (Boston, 1949), 1.

6. Oliver Wendell Holmes, Jr., "The Path of the Law," in *The Mind and Faith of Justice Holmes*, ed. Max Lerner (New York, 1943), 72, 74, 76.

7. John Chipman Gray, *The Nature and Sources of the Law* (Boston, 1963 [1909]), 99–101, 168–73.

8. Robert E. Cushman and Robert F. Cushman, *Cases in Constitutional Law* (New York, 1958), 580.

9. Roscoe Pound, "Mechanical Jurisprudence," *Columbia Law Review*, 8 (December, 1908), 609.

10. Roscoe Pound, "The Scope and Purpose of Sociological Jurisprudence," *Harvard Law Review*, 25 (April, 1912), 514.

11. Benjamin N. Cardozo, *The Nature of the Judicial Process* (New Haven, Conn., 1962 [1921]), Lectures 2 and 3.

12. Nineteen of the twenty-three were taken from Karl Llewellyn's initial identification of those whom he considered leading realists. (Llewellyn, "Some Realism about Realism—Responding to Dean Pound," *Harvard Law Review*, 44 [June, 1931], 1222–64). The nineteen are Underhill Moore, Herman Oliphant, Charles E. Clark, Llewellyn, Jerome Frank, Walter Wheeler Cook, Thomas Reed Powell, Leon Green, Max Radin, William O. Douglas, Hessel E. Yntema, Edwin W. Patterson, Arthur L. Corbin, Wesley A. Sturges, Leon Tulin, Joseph F. Francis, Joseph W. Bingham, E. G. Lorenzen and Joseph C. Hutcheson. Biographical material was unavailable for one of Llewellyn's original twenty (Samuel Klaus). Four other scholars (Walter Nelles, Thurman Arnold, Robinson, and Felix S. Cohen) have impressed me as significant contributors to realism and have been added for that reason. The list does not include such younger realists as Myres McDougal or Fred Rodell. Brief biographical material on most of the realists is available in Association of American Law Schools, *Directory of Teachers in Member Schools* (St. Paul, Minn., 1922–1941).

13. For the two preceding paragraphs I am indebted to Jerold S. Auerbach's excellent study "Enmity and Amity: Law Teachers and Practitioners, 1900–1922," in Fleming and Bailyn, *Law In American History*, 551–601. See also Robert Stevens, "Two Cheers for 1870: The American Law School," ibid., 405–548.

14. Benjamin N. Cardozo, "Jurisprudence" in *Selected Writings of Benjamin Nathan Cardozo*, ed. Margaret E. Hall (New York, 1947), 8.

15. "Address of Elihu Root in Presenting the Report of the Committee," American Law Institute, *Proceedings*, 1 (Part 2, 1923), 48, 49, cited in Rumble, *American Legal Realism*, 156. On the growth of case law, see also Benjamin N. Cardozo, *The Growth of the Law* (New Haven, Conn., 1924), i, 3–5, 16.

16. Grant Gilmore, "Legal Realism: Its Cause and Cure," *Yale Law Journal*, 70 (June, 1961), 1040–41.

17. Harlan F. Stone, "The Significance of a Restatement of the Law," *Proceedings of the Academy of Political Science in the City of New York*, 10 (1922–1924), no. 3, 311.

18. Committee on the Establishment of a Permanent Organization for the Im-

provement of the Law, "The Law's Uncertainty and Complexity," American Law Institute, *Proceedings*, 1 (Part 1, 1923), 66–76.

19. Herman Oliphant, "The Relation of Current Economic and Social Problems to the Restatement of the Law," *Proceedings of the Academy of Political Science in the City of New York*, 10 (1922–1924), no. 3, 324.

20. Karl N. Llewellyn, "A Realistic Jurisprudence—The Next Step," *Columbia Law Review*, 30 (April, 1930), 443.

21. Ibid., 453.

22. Ibid., 439.

23. Ibid., 444.

24. Karl N. Llewellyn, *The Bramble Bush* (New York, 1930), 3.

25. Llewellyn, "A Realistic Jurisprudence—The Next Step," *Columbia Law Review*, 30 (April, 1930), 464.

26. Karl N. Llewellyn, "Holmes," *Columbia Law Review*, 35 (April, 1935), 488.

27. Jerome Frank, *Law and the Modern Mind* (New York, 1963 [1930]), 136.

28. Ibid., 50.

29. Ibid., 109. See also 114–21.

30. Ibid., 159.

31. Ibid., 6.

32. Ibid., 19.

33. Ibid., 98.

34. Ibid., 65.

35. Ibid., 178.

36. Roscoe Pound, "The Call for a Realist Jurisprudence," *Harvard Law Review*, 44 (March, 1931), 697–711.

37. Llewellyn, "Some Realism about Realism—Responding to Dean Pound," *Harvard Law Review*, 44 (June, 1931), 1222–64. Although Llewellyn alone signed the article, he explained that it had been conceived and researched in cooperation with Frank. Because Llewellyn did the actual writing, Frank did not think he should receive credit as an author.

38. Robert M. Hutchins, "An Institute of Human Relations," *American Journal of Sociology*, 35 (September, 1929), 187–93; Hutchins, "Connecticut and the Yale Law School," *Connecticut Bar Journal*, 2 (July, 1928), 170.

39. Karl N. Llewellyn, "The Effect of Legal Institutions upon Economics," *American Economic Review*, 15 (December, 1925), 682.

40. A. A. Berle, Jr. and Gardiner C. Means, *The Modern Corporation and Private Property* (New York, 1932). See also Richard S. Kirkendall, "A. A. Berle, Jr.: Student of the Corporation, 1917–1932," *Business History Review*, 35 (Spring, 1961), 43–58.

41. Hessel E. Yntema, "Legal Science and Reform," *Columbia Law Review*, 34 (February, 1934), 222.

42. L. C. Marshall, "The Beginnings of Judicial Statistics," in *Statistics in Social Studies*, ed. Stuart A. Rice (Philadelphia, 1930), 109. See also C. E. Gehlke, "Statistical Studies of Crime and the Administration of Justice," in Stuart A. Rice, ed., *Statistics in Social Studies* (Philadelphia, 1930).

43. Frank, *Law and the Modern Mind*, 124.

44. Patterson, *Jurisprudence*, 548–52.

45. Edward S. Robinson, *Law and the Lawyers* (New York, 1935), 72.

46. See especially Underhill Moore and Gilbert Sussman, "Legal and Institu-

tional Methods Applied to the Debiting of Direct Discounts–VI. The Decisions, the Institutions, and the Degree of Deviation," *Yale Law Journal*, 40 (June, 1931), 1219–50.

47. Donald Slesinger and E. Marion Pilpel, "Legal Psychology," *Psychological Bulletin*, 26 (December, 1929), 682.

48. Felix S. Cohen, "Transcendental Nonsense and the Functional Approach," *Columbia Law Review*, 35 (June, 1935), 826.

49. Max Radin, "Legal Realism," *Columbia Law Review*, 31 (May, 1931), 827.

50. Herman Oliphant, "Facts, Opinions and Value Judgments," *Texas Law Review*, 10 (February, 1932), 136.

51. Herman Oliphant, "A Return to Stare Decisis," *American Bar Association Journal*, 14 (February, 1928), 74; and (March, 1928), 160.

52. Frank, *Law and the Modern Mind*, 125.

53. Joseph C. Hutcheson, Jr., "The Judgment Intuitive: The Function of the 'Hunch' in Judicial Decision," *Cornell Law Quarterly*, 14 (April, 1929), 285.

54. Max Radin, "Statutory Interpretation," *Harvard Law Review*, 43 (April, 1930), 881. See also Thomas Reed Powell, "The Logic and Rhetoric of Constitutional Law," *The Journal of Philosophy, Psychology and Scientific Methods*, 15 (November 21, 1918), 645–58.

55. Hessel E. Yntema, "The Hornbook Method and the Conflict of Laws," *Yale Law Journal*, 37 (February, 1928), 480, 476.

56. Walter Wheeler Cook, "Scientific Method and the Law," *American Bar Association Journal*, 13 (June, 1927), 304–5.

57. Felix S. Cohen, "Transcendental Nonsense and the Functional Approach," *Columbia Law Review*, 35 (June, 1935), 821.

58. Felix S. Cohen, "Modern Ethics and the Law," *Brooklyn Law Review*, 4 (October, 1934), 43.

59. Ibid., 43. Edward J. Bloustein, "Logic and Legal Realism: The Realist as a Frustrated Idealist," *Cornell Law Quarterly*, 50 (Fall, 1964), 24–33 makes the same distinction between logical reason and logically necessary reason in his perceptive essay on the realists.

60. Herman Oliphant, "A Return to Stare Decisis," *American Bar Association Journal*, 14 (March, 1928), 160.

61. Morris R. Cohen, "Positivism and the Limits of Idealism in the Law," *Columbia Law Review*, 27 (March, 1927), 244.

62. Walter Wheeler Cook, "Scientific Method and the Law," *American Bar Association Journal*, 13 (June, 1927), 305.

63. Underhill Moore, "Rational Basis of Legal Institutions," *Columbia Law Review*, 23 (November, 1923), 612.

64. Walter Nelles, review of *Ethical Systems and Legal Ideals* by Felix S. Cohen, *Columbia Law Review*, 33 (April, 1933), 767, 765, 766.

65. John Dickinson, "Legal Rules: Their Function in the Process of Decision," *University of Pennsylvania Law Review and American Law Register*, 79 (May, 1931), 833–68; Hermann Kantorowicz, "Some Rationalism about Realism," *Yale Law Journal*, 43 (June, 1934), 1240–53.

66. Morris R. Cohen, "Justice Holmes and the Nature of Law," *Columbia Law Review*, 31 (March, 1931), 357.

67. Mortimer Adler, "Legal Certainty," Part II of "Law and the Modern Mind: A Symposium," *Columbia Law Review*, 31 (January, 1931), 108.

68. Charles C. Miltner, "Law and Morals," *Notre Dame Lawyer*, 10 (November, 1934), 8.

69. Jerome Frank, review of *The Bramble Bush* by Karl N. Llewellyn, *Yale Law Journal*, 40 (May, 1931), 1121, note. For an example of the relationship between legal realism and political reform, see Jerome Frank, "Modern Trends in Jurisprudence," *American Law School Review*, 7 (April, 1934), 1063–69.

70. For the realist concern with legal reform see Herman Oliphant, "A Return to Stare Decisis," *American Bar Association Journal*, 14 (February, 1928), 71–76, 107; (March, 1928), 159–62; Jerome Frank, "Mr. Justice Holmes and Non-Euclidean Legal Thinking," *Cornell Law Quarterly*, 17 (June, 1932), 568–603; Hessel Yntema, "Legal Science and Reform," *Columbia Law Review*, 34 (February, 1934), 207–29; Charles E. Clark, "Fact Research in Law Administration," *Connecticut Bar Journal*, 2 (July, 1928), 211–31.

71. Herman Oliphant, "Facts, Opinions, and Value-Judgments," *Texas Law Review*, 10 (February, 1932), 137.

72. Felix S. Cohen, *Ethical Systems and Legal Ideals: An Essay on the Foundations of Legal Criticism* (New York, 1933), 227.

6. The New Study of Politics

1. Arnold Bennett Hall, "Introduction" in the "Reports of the National Conference on the Science of Politics," *American Political Science Review*, 18 (February, 1924), 119. See also Bernard Crick, *The American Science of Politics: Its Origins and Conditions* (Berkeley, Calif., 1967), 116–17.

2. Herman G. James, "The Meaning and Scope of Political Science," *Southwestern Political Science Quarterly*, 1 (June, 1920), 5.

3. A. Gordon Dewey, "On Methods in the Study of Politics—Part One," *Political Science Quarterly*, 38 (December, 1923), 638.

4. Charles E. Merriam, *New Aspects of Politics* (Chicago, 1925), 217.

5. Charles E. Merriam, *Political Power* (New York, 1964 [1934]), 21.

6. Harold D. Lasswell, *Politics: Who Gets What, When, How* (New York, 1958 [1936]), 13.

7. Harvey Pinney, "A Historical Quest: Henry Adams and Political Sequence," *Social Science*, 9 (January, 1934), 65.

8. George E. G. Catlin, *Preface to Action* (London, 1934), 310.

9. Leonard D. White, "Introduction," in Carroll H. Wooddy, *The Chicago Primary of 1926: A Study in Election Methods* (Chicago, 1926), 2.

10. E. E. Schattschneider, *Politics, Pressures and the Tariff: A Study of Free Private Enterprise in Pressure Politics, as Shown in the 1929–1930 Revision of the Tariff* (New York, 1935), 4. For examples of the use of group conflict analysis, see Wooddy, *The Chicago Primary of 1926*; E. Pendleton Herring, *Group Representation before Congress* (Baltimore, Md., 1929); Peter Odegard, *Pressure Politics: The Story of the Anti-Saloon League* (New York, 1928); Belle Zeller, *Pressure Politics in New York: A Study of Group Representation before the Legislature* (New York, 1937); Harwood L. Childs, *Labor and Capital in National Politics* (Columbus, Ohio, 1930); Frank R. Kent, *The Great Game of Politics: An Effort to Present the Elementary Human Facts about Politics, Politicians, and Political Machines, Candidates and Their Ways, for the Benefit of the Average Citizen* (Garden City, N. Y., 1923);

Kent, *Political Behavior: The Heretofore Unwritten Laws, Customs and Principles of Politics as Practiced in the United States* (New York, 1928).

11. Merriam, *New Aspects of Politics*, 216.

12. Arnold Bennett Hall, "Introduction" to the "Report of the Third Conference on the Science of Politics," *American Political Science Review*, 20 (February, 1926), 125.

13. Stuart A. Rice, "Some Applications of Statistical Method to Political Research," *American Political Science Review*, 20 (May, 1926), 313.

14. See Harold Foote Gosnell and Charles E. Merriam, *Non-Voting: Causes and Methods of Control* (Chicago, 1924); Gosnell, "Statisticians and Political Scientists," *American Political Science Review*, 27 (June, 1933), 392–403.

15. See Stuart A. Rice, *Farmers and Workers in American Politics* (New York, 1924); Herman C. Beyle, *The Identification of Attribute-Cluster Blocs* (Chicago, 1931).

16. L. L. Thurstone, "Multiple Factor Analysis," *Psychological Review*, 38 (September, 1931), 406–27.

17. For a brief summary of much of this work see Gosnell, "Statisticians and Political Scientists."

18. Roscoe C. Martin, "The Municipal Electorate: A Case Study," *Southwestern Social Science Quarterly*, 14 (December, 1933), 236.

19. Charles E. Merriam, *New Aspects of Politics*, 13. See also Merriam, "Progress in Political Research," *American Political Science Review*, 20 (February, 1926), 10, 12, and "The Significance of Psychology for the Study of Politics," *American Political Science Review*, 18 (August, 1924), 487–88.

20. Charles E. Merriam, "Recent Tendencies in Political Thought," in Charles E. Merriam and Harry Elmer Barnes, eds., *A History of Political Theories, Recent Times: Essays on Contemporary Development in Political Theory* (New York, 1924), 18.

21. John A. Fairlie, "Politics and Science," *Scientific Monthly*, 18 (January, 1924), 28; Horace M. Kallen, "Political Science as Psychology," *American Political Science Review*, 17 (May, 1932), 194; and Charles E. Gehlke, "Social Psychology and Political Theory," in Merriam and Barnes, *History of Political Theories*, 403–29.

22. L. L. Thurstone, "Roundtable on Politics and Psychology," *American Political Science Review*, 19 (February, 1925), 110–12; American Political Science Association, "Report of the Committee on Political Research," *American Political Science Review*, 18 (August, 1924), 593, 600.

23. William McDougall, *Is America Safe for Democracy?* (New York, 1921), v.

24. Ibid., 23.

25. Harvey O'Higgins, *The Secret Springs* (New York, 1920), 12. See also E. Boyd Barrett, S.J., *The New Psychology: How It Aids and Interests* (New York, 1925); Wilfred Lay, *Man's Unconscious Spirit: The Psychoanalysis of Spiritism* (New York, 1921); A. G. Tansley, *The New Psychology and Its Relation to Life* (New York, 1920). For general discussions of the impact of Freudianism see Hendrik M. Ruitenback, *Freud and America* (New York, 1966); Marie Jahoda, "The Migration of Psychoanalysis: Its Impact on American Psychology," in Donald Fleming and Bernard Bailyn, eds., *Perspectives in American History*, Vol. 2, *The Intellectual Migration: Europe and America, 1930–1960* (Cambridge, Mass., 1968), 420–45; and Nathan G. Hale, *Freud and the Americans: The Beginnings of Psychoanalysis in the United States, 1876–1917* (New York, 1971).

26. Gisella J. Hinkle, "The Role of Freudianism in American Sociology," (Ph.D. diss., University of Wisconsin, 1951), 165–79, 272–87, 289, 291, 295.

27. James Harvey Robinson, *The Mind in the Making: The Relation of Intelligence to Social Reform* (New York, 1921), 41.

28. Beardsley Ruml, "Recent Trends in Social Science," in *The New Social Science*, ed. Leonard D. White (Chicago, 1930), 101.

29. Alleyne Ireland, "Democracy and Heredity," *Journal of Heredity*, 10 (November, 1919), 363, 360–61.

30. Quoted in John Higham, *Strangers in the Land: Patterns of American Nativism, 1860–1925* (New York, 1963), 276. See also 272–75. For a general treatment of racist ideas in the period see Thomas F. Gossett, *Race: The History of an Idea in America* (New York, 1965), especially Chapter 15.

31. Harry Elmer Barnes, *History and Social Intelligence* (New York, 1926), 573–75.

32. Harry Elmer Barnes, "Some Contributions of Sociology to Modern Political Theory," in Merriam and Barnes, *History of Political Theories*, 373.

33. Harold F. Gosnell, "Some Practical Applications of Psychology in Government," *American Journal of Sociology*, 28 (May, 1923), 742.

34. Merriam, *New Aspects of Politics*, 83, 246–47.

35. Elton Mayo, "Civilization—the Perilous Adventure," *Harper's Monthly Magazine*, 149 (October, 1924), 595.

36. Elton Mayo, "The Irrational Factor in Human Behavior: The 'Night-Mind' in Industry," *Annals of the American Academy of Political and Social Science*, 110 (November, 1923), 123, 124.

37. Elton Mayo, "The Great Stupidity," *Harper's Monthly Magazine*, 151 (July, 1925), 227.

38. Harold D. Lasswell, *Propaganda Technique in the World War* (New York, 1927), 4, 5.

39. Harold D. Lasswell, *Psychopathology and Politics* (New York, 1960 [1930]), 183. See also 74–77.

40. Ibid., 194.

41. Elton Mayo, *The Human Problems of an Industrial Civilization* (New York, 1960 [1933]), 177. See also 1, 168.

42. Lasswell, *Psychopathology and Politics*, 197.

43. Elton Mayo, "The Great Stupidity," 229. See also Mayo, "Civilized Unreason," *Harper's Monthly Magazine*, 148 (March, 1924), 534.

44. Walter Lippmann, *Public Opinion* (New York, 1965 [1922]), 9.

45. Ibid., 10, 13.

46. Ibid., 55.

47. Ibid., 78, 79.

48. Ibid., 132, 133, 146.

49. Walter Lippmann, *The Phantom Public* (New York, 1925), 14.

50. Ibid., 41.

51. Ibid., 70–71.

52. John Dewey, "Public Opinion—a Review of Walter Lippmann's Book," *New Republic*, 30 (May 3, 1922), 288.

53. Stuart A. Rice, "Stereotypes: A Source of Error in Judging Human Character," *Journal of Personnel Research*, 7 (#7), 275.

54. Floyd H. Allport and D. A. Hartman, "A Technique for the Measurement

and Analysis of Public Opinion," *Papers and Proceedings of the American Sociological Society*, 20 (1925), 243.

55. Norman C. Meier, "Motives in Voting: A Study in Public Opinion," *American Journal of Sociology*, 31 (September, 1925), 210, 211, 212.

56. Gosnell and Merriam, *Non-Voting*, xi, x, 251–52.

57. Wooddy, *Chicago Primary of 1926*, 275.

58. John Dickinson, "Democratic Realities and Democratic Dogma," *American Political Science Review*, 24 (May, 1930), 288, 291, and *passim*.

59. Walter J. Shepard, "Democracy in Transition," *American Political Science Review*, 29 (February, 1935), 18–19, 20

60. William F. Willoughby, "A Program for Research in Political Science," *American Political Science Review*, 27 (February, 1933), 2.

61. B. F. Wright, Jr., "The Tendency Away from Political Democracy in the United States," *Southwestern Political and Social Science Quarterly*, 7 (June, 1926), 32.

62. See for example William Starr Myers, "The Meaning of Democracy," *Annals of the American Academy of Political and Social Science*, 169 (September, 1933), 153–58; Isidor Loeb, "Fact and Fiction in Government," *American Political Science Review*, 28 (February, 1934), 1–10.

63. Alpheus Thomas Mason, "Politics: Science or Art?" *Southwestern Social Science Quarterly*, 16 (December, 1935), 10.

64. See also T. V. Smith, "Equality—The Regulative Ideal for Political Science," *Southwestern Political and Social Science Quarterly*, 11 (June, 1930), 12–25; R. K. Gooch, "Governments as an Exact Science," *Southwestern Political and Social Science Quarterly*, 9 (December, 1928), 252–63.

65. Edward S. Corwin, "The Democratic Dogma and the Future of Political Science," *American Political Science Review*, 23 (August, 1929), 577, 591, 570.

66. William Y. Elliott, "Mussolini, Prophet of the Pragmatic Era in Politics," *Political Science Quarterly*, 41 (June, 1926), 164. See also Elliott, "The Pragmatic Politics of Mr. Laski," *American Political Science Review*, 18 (May, 1924), 251–75; "Sovereign State or Sovereign Group," *American Political Science Review*, 19 (August, 1925), 475–99; "The Metaphysics of M. Leon Dugiut's Pragmatic Philosophy of the Law," *Political Science Quarterly*, 37 (December, 1922), 639–54; and "The Political Application of Romanticism," *Political Science Quarterly*, 39 (June, 1924), 234–65.

67. William Y. Elliott, "The Pragmatic Politics of Mr. H. J. Laski," *American Political Science Review*, 18 (May, 1924), 257.

68. William Y. Elliott, *The Pragmatic Revolt in Politics* (New York, 1928), 250, 9. See also 3, 7, 14–15, 31, 41, 319, 337, 341–42, 495–96.

69. G. E. G. Catlin, review of *The Pragmatic Revolt in Politics* by W. Y. Elliott, *Political Science Quarterly*, 44 (June, 1929), 262.

70. Thurman Arnold, *The Symbols of Government* (New York, 1962 [1935]), 229.

71. Ibid., xiv.

72. Ibid., 17.

73. Ibid., 8, 17.

74. Ibid., 123.

75. Ibid., 98. See also 34.

76. Ibid., 10.

77. Ibid., 270–71.

78. Ibid., 46–47.

79. Elton Mayo, "An Open Letter to Robert W. Bruere," *Survey*, 54 (September 15, 1925), 644.

7. America & the Rise of European Dictatorships

1. Quoted in Merle Curti, *The Growth of American Thought* (New York, 1964), 677.

2. Christopher Lasch, *The American Liberals and the Russian Revolution* (New York, 1962), 27, 124–26; and Robert K. Murray, *Red Scare; A Study in National Hysteria, 1919–1920* (Minneapolis, Minn., 1955), 33–34. See also Peter G. Filene, *Americans and the Soviet Experiment, 1917–1933* (Cambridge, Mass., 1967), 22.

3. Lasch, *American Liberals*, 125. See also 59.

4. Ibid., 86 87, 107.

5. Clayton R. Lusk, "Radicalism under Inquiry," *American Review of Reviews*, 61 (February, 1920), 164.

6. Arthur W. Dunn, "The 'Reds' in America: From the Standpoint of the Department of Justice," *American Review of Reviews*, 61 (February, 1920), 164.

7. "Persecutions of the Russian Churches," *Outlook*, 133 (April 11, 1923), 641. See also Lasch, *American Liberals*, 130. Of the liberals and progressives who supported the bolsheviks, or looked favorably upon their experiment, most of them disliked and openly criticized the violence and political coercion that marked the bolshevik government. See Filene, *Americans and the Soviet Experiment*, 149–51, 241–42, 259, 271–73.

8. Louis Fischer, "Communist Puritans," *Nation*, 119 (September 3, 1924), 235. See also Herbert Wilton Stanley, "The Hoax of Bolshevism," *Atlantic Monthly*, 124 (July, 1919), 1; and William Adams Brown, Jr., "The Moral Issue in Russia," *Atlantic Monthly*, 124 (July, 1919), 88.

9. *Catholic World*, 117 (May, 1923), 260.

10. Edwin W. Hullinger, "The Death of Communism in Russia: What Has Taken Its Place," *Outlook*, 134 (June, 1923), 265.

11. W. Stephen Sanders, "The Bankruptcy of Communism in Russia," *Living Age*, 304 (January 10, 1920), 77.

12. Franklin H. Giddings, "Absolutist Communism," *Independent*, 103 (July 3, 1920), 13.

13. Quoted in Lewis Feuer, "American Travelers to the Soviet Union 1917–32: The Formation of a Component of New Deal Ideology," *American Quarterly*, 14 (Summer, 1962), 128. Feuer's excellent essay clearly indicates the extent and causes of the Soviet appeal to Americans during the twenties and early thirties.

14. Ibid., especially 136–44.

15. Quoted ibid., 122.

16. "Our Case against the Soviet Republic," *New Republic*, 19 (July 2, 1919), 266.

17. William Hard, "The Anti-Bolsheviks: Mr. Spargo," *New Republic*, 19 (July 9, 1919), 306.

18. Walter Lippmann, "Autocracy versus Catholicism," *Commonweal*, 5 (April 13, 1927), 627.

19. William C. Abbott, "Democracy or Dictatorship," *Yale Review*, 16 (October, 1926), 10.

20. John Booth Carter, "American Reactions to Italian Fascism, 1919–1933,"

(Ph.D. diss., Columbia University, 1953), 39. This dissertation contains much material on American opinion toward fascism for which I am indebted.

21. John P. Diggins, "Mussolini and America: Hero-Worship, Charisma and the 'Vulgar Talent,' " *Historian*, 28 (August, 1966), 559–85.

22. "The Italian Crisis," *Independent*, 109 (August 5, 1922), 45. See also Gino Speranza, "Fascismo," ibid., 109 (November 11, 1922), 258–59.

23. *New Republic*, 32 (November 8, 1922), 263.

24. Quoted in Carter, "American Reactions," 112.

25. "Rome and the New Italy," *Commonweal*, 5 (January 5, 1927), 231.

26. Quoted in Norman Hapgood, ed., *Professional Patriots* (New York, 1928), 62. See also Carter, "American Reactions," 245.

27. "If Mussolini Had Ruled Detroit," *Christian Century*, 46 (December 11, 1929), 1534.

28. Quoted in John P. Diggins, "Flirtation with Fascism: American Pragmatic Liberals and Mussolini's Italy," *American Historical Review*, 71 (January, 1966), 495. The essay details the extent and nature of the pragmatists' "flirtation" with Italian fascism.

29. John P. Diggins, "The Italo-American Anti-Fascist Opposition," *Journal of American History*, 54 (December, 1967), 579–98.

30. Ibid., 588; and Marcus Duffield, "Mussolini's American Empire: The Fascist Invasion of the United States," *Harper's Magazine*, 159 (November, 1929), 661–72.

31. "The League of Nations Faces the Test," *Nation*, 117 (September 12, 1923), 256; *Nation*, 118 (June 25, 1924), 722; "Mussolini Menaces Europe," *Nation*, 122 (February 17, 1926), 171; and Carter, "American Reactions," 383. For the special role of the *Nation* in American liberal thought see John P. Diggins, "Flirtation with Fascism: American Pragmatic Liberals and Mussolini's Italy," *American Historical Review*, 71 (January, 1966), 499–500.

32. John P. Diggins, "Mussolini and America: Hero-Worship, Charisma, and the 'Vulgar Talent,' " *Historian*, 28 (August, 1966), 569–70.

33. Marcus Duffield, "Mussolini's American Empire: the Fascist Invasion of the United States," *Harper's Magazine*, 159 (November, 1929), 661–72; "Does Mussolini Rule Millions Here?" *Literary Digest*, 103 (November 16, 1929), 14; and Carter, "American Reactions," 81–85.

34. Robert Dell, "The Menace of Mussolini and Harthy," *Nation*, 122 (March 3, 1926), 230. See also Carter, "American Reactions," 393. Carter does not emphasize the American fear of a new war, but he notes that public opinion seemed to grow less favorable to fascism in the later twenties.

35. William Y. Elliott, "The Case against Fascism," *Forum*, 75 (April, 1926), 490.

36. *New Republic*, 33 (January 3, 1923), 131.

37. "Is Democracy Doomed?" *Forum*, 75 (April, 1926), 483. See also Francesco Nitti, *Bolshevism, Fascism, and Democracy* (New York, 1927), especially Chapter 12.

38. William C. Abbott, "Democracy or Dictatorship," *Yale Review*, 16 (October, 1926), 2.

39. Ibid., 1.

40. "How the Principal Foreign Dictatorships Are Operated Today," *Congressional Digest*, 12 (November, 1933), 264–65.

41. T. R. Ybarra, "This Dictator Business," *Outlook and Independent,* 151 (February 13, 1929), 249.

42. Roger Shaw, "Dictators or Democrats," *Review of Reviews,* 82 (September, 1930), 69.

43. Struthers Burt, "The Future of Democracy," *Saturday Evening Post,* 200 (April 28, 1928), 27. For examples of the discussion before the rise of Nazism see "Can Democracy Survive," *Living Age,* 332 (June 15, 1927), 1060–64; Edward C. Lindeman, "A New Challenge to the Spirit of 1776," *Survey,* 57 (March 1, 1927), 679–82; Frankwood E. Williams, "The Significance of Dictatorship," *Survey,* 68 (May 1, 1932), 130–35; C. N. Bretherton, "Too Much Democracy," *North American Review,* 224 (December, 1927), 646–53; Lothrop Stoddard, "Why Dictators?" *World's Work,* 60 (January, 1931), 67–70; Jerome Davis, "The Challenge of Dictatorship," *Century,* 12 (Spring, 1930), 170–79; Arthur Spatz, "Democracy and Dictatorship," *Open Court,* 41 (June, 1927), 381–84; "Is Democracy Doomed?" *Forum,* 75 (April, 1926), 481–95.

44. Charles Maurras, "Is Democracy Bankrupt?" *Outlook,* 143 (June 2, 1926), 177.

45. Robert K. Gooch, "The Anti-Parliamentary Movement in France," *American Political Science Review,* 21 (August, 1927), 553.

46. Frank H. Simonds, "Parliamentary Breakdown in Europe," *American Review of Reviews,* 73 (March, 1926), 291, 294.

47. Claud Mullins, "Democracy—A Realist View," *Atlantic Monthly,* 141 (April, 1928), 561.

48. "Has Democracy Broken Down: A Debate," *Forum,* 81 (January, 1929), 37.

49. Will Durant, "Is Democracy a Failure?" *Harper's Magazine,* 153 (October, 1926), 565.

50. "The Day of the Dictator," *Nation,* 117 (September 26, 1923), 312.

51. "Analysis of Democracy," *Commonweal,* 16 (June 22, 1932), 201.

52. Quintus Quiz, "Those Strong Dictators," *Christian Century,* 48 (2), (October 7, 1931), 1233; Henry Cabot Lodge, Jr., *The Cult of Weakness* (Boston, 1932), 142; and Frank A. Vanderlip, "Is Democracy a Failure?" *Saturday Evening Post,* 205 (September 24, 1932), 3.

53. John P. Diggins, "Mussolini and America: Hero-Worship, Charisma and the 'Vulgar Talent,'" *Historian,* 28 (August, 1966), 573; Lewis S. Feuer, "American Travelers to the Soviet Union 1917–32; The Formation of a Component of New Deal Idealogy," *American Quarterly,* 14 (Summer, 1962), 136; Frank Warren, *Liberals and Communism: The "Red Decade" Revisited* (Bloomington, Ind., 1966), 64–65; Ralph L. Roy, *Communism and the Churches* (New York, 1960), 66–71; Daniel Aaron, *Writers on the Left: Episodes in American Literary Communism* (New York, 1961), 139, 151–60.

54. Frederic A. Ogg, "Does America Need a Dictator?" *Current History,* 36 (September, 1932), 645.

55. Henry Hazlett, "Without Benefit of Congress," *Scribner's Magazine,* 92 (July, 1932), 13, 14, 17–18.

56. Frederic A. Ogg, "Does America Need a Dictator?" *Current History,* 36 (September, 1932), 645.

57. Arthur M. Schlesinger, Jr., *The Crisis of the Old Order, 1919–1933* (Boston, 1964), 268.

58. James Truslow Adams, "Shadow of the Man on Horseback," *Atlantic Monthly*, 149 (January, 1932), 10.

59. John Palmer Gavit, "Through the Brandenburger Tor," *Survey Graphic*, 61 (February, 1929), 543.

60. Sidney B. Fay, "The Teutonic Countries," *Current History*, 33 (November, 1930), 295.

61. "The Religious War in Germany," *Commonweal*, 13 (April 8, 1931), 617.

62. Frank H. Simonds, "If Hitler Comes to Power," *Review of Reviews*, 85 (June, 1932), 36.

63. "Germany 'in Prospect,' " *Business Week* (December 7, 1932), 22.

64. "Dictator or Parliament," *Nation*, 131 (October 8, 1930), 365.

65. "Back to Barbarism," *Nation*, 136 (April 12, 1933), 388.

66. "The Church and Christian Totalitarianism," *Christian Century*, 51 (February 14, 1934), 215.

67. "The Terror in Germany," *Living Age*, 344 (May, 1933), 200.

68. George N. Shuster, *Strong Man Rules* (New York, 1934), 234.

69. *The Case of Civilization against Hitlerism* [Presented under the auspices of the American Jewish Congress at Madison Square Garden, New York, March 7, 1934] (New York, 1934), 103, 145.

70. For both widespread American knowledge of the Jewish persecution and the country's general failure to take what effective actions were possible see Arthur D. Morse, *While Six Million Died: A Chronicle of American Apathy* (New York, 1967); David S. Wyman, *Paper Walls: America and the Refugee Crisis 1938–1941* (Boston, 1968); and Henry L. Feingold, *The Politics of Rescue: The Roosevelt Administration and the Holocaust, 1938–1945* (New Brunswick, N. J., 1970).

71. H. L. Mencken, "The Library," *American Mercury*, 30 (December, 1933), 510.

72. Sigmund Neumann, "Germany: Battlefield of the Middle Classes," *Foreign Affairs*, 13 (January, 1935), 282.

73. Frederick L. Schuman, "Nazi Dreams of World Power," *Current History*, 39 (February 7, 1934), 536.

74. Ibid., 541. See also Frederick L. Schuman, "The Third Reich's Road to War," *Annals of the American Academy of Political and Social Science*, 175 (September, 1934), 42.

75. Alton Frye, *Nazi Germany and the American Hemisphere, 1933–1941* (New Haven, Conn., 1967), 38–39, 45, 51.

76. Albert Brandt, "Nazi International," *Catholic World*, 138 (January, 1934), 404.

77. Augustus Bauer, "The Threats to Hitler's Rule," *New Republic*, 78 (May 9, 1934), 357; Rudolf Breitscheid, "The Plight of Germany," *Contemporary Review*, 146 (October, 1934), 387; and Horace G. Alexander, "Whither Germany? Whither Europe?" *Contemporary Review*, 144 (December, 1933), 670.

78. "Ex Cathedra," *World Tomorrow*, 16 (February 15, 1933), 146.

79. "The End of National Socialism," *Christian Century*, 52 (March 13, 1935), 327.

80. Stanley B. Jones, "Democracy in the New Age," *Catholic World*, 137 (August, 1933), 513.

81. Lewis Einstein, "The Cult of Force," *North American Review*, 236 (December, 1933), 501, 503.

82. "American Institute of Public Opinion—Surveys, 1938–1939," *Public Opinion Quarterly*, 3 (October, 1939), 598. For American attitudes to the complex problems presented by the Spanish Civil War see F. Jay Taylor, *The United States and the Spanish Civil War, 1936–1939* (New York, 1956); Allen Guttmann, *The Wound in the Heart: America and the Spanish Civil War* (New York, 1962); and Richard Traina, *American Diplomacy and the Spanish Civil War* (Bloomington, Ind., 1968).

83. John P. Diggins, "Flirtation with Fascism: American Pragmatic Liberals and Mussolini's Italy," *American Historical Review*, 71 (January, 1966), 498; John P. Diggins, "Mussolini and America: Hero-Worship, Charisma, and the 'Vulgar Talent,'" *Historian*, 28 (August, 1966), 569–74; and Brice Harris, Jr., *The United States and the Italo-Ethiopian Crisis* (Stanford, Calif., 1964).

84. See especially John P. Diggins, "The Italo-American Anti-Fascist Opposition," *Journal of American History*, 54 (December, 1967), 588–90.

85. See especially Aaron, *Writers on the Left*, 312, 320, 337, 369–70. See also Norman Holmes Pearson, "The Nazi-Soviet Pact and the End of a Dream," in Daniel Aaron, ed., *America in Crises: Fourteen Crucial Episodes in American History* (New York, 1952), 327–48; Warren, *Liberals and Communism*, 177–215; and Roy, *Communism and the Churches*, 71–81.

86. Quoted in Lewis S. Feuer, "American Travelers to the Soviet Union 1917–32: The Formation of a Component of New Deal Ideology," *American Quarterly*, 14 (Summer, 1962), 148.

87. Robert C. Brooks, *Deliver Us from Dictators* (Philadelphia, 1935), 208.

88. Oswald Garrison Villard, "Issues and Men—The Strange German Character," *Nation*, 139 (July 18, 1934), 63. See also *Annals of The American Academy of Political and Social Science*, 180 (July, 1935) and 200 (November, 1938); *Social Research* (September, 1937); and Warren, *Liberals and Communism*, 182–92.

89. "Nazi Progress toward Totalitarianism," *Christian Century*, 50 (July 19, 1933), 924.

90. Prince Hubertus Lowenstein, "The Totalitarian State in Germany and the Individual," *Annals of the American Academy of Political and Social Science*, 180 (July, 1935), 26.

91. Sidney B. Fay, "The Nazi Totalitarian State," *Current History*, 38 (August, 1933), 610.

92. Oswald Garrison Villard, review of *Dictators and Democracies* by Calvin B. Hoover, *Public Opinion Quarterly*, 2 (April, 1938), 335.

93. Oran James Hale, "The Way of Social Science and History Teaching in Hitler's Germany," *Social Forces*, 12 (December, 1933), 187.

94. Calvin B. Hoover, *Dictators and Democracies* (New York, 1937), vii.

95. Ibid., 20.

96. Ibid., 10.

97. Ibid., 12.

98. George H. Sabine, *A History of Political Theory* (New York, 1937), 773, 764.

99. Hamilton Fish Armstrong, *We or They* (New York, 1937), 34, 103.

100. "Manifesto," *Nation*, 148 (May 27, 1939), 626. For a subsequent defense of the Soviet Union see "To All Active Supporters of Democracy and Peace," *Nation*, 148 (August 26, 1939), 228. The latter had the extreme misfortune of appearing in print two days after the announcement of the Nazi-Soviet pact.

8. Counterattack

1. Robert M. Hutchins, "Address of Dedication," in Leonard D. White, ed., *The New Social Science* (Chicago, 1930), 1–2.

2. Robert M. Hutchins, *No Friendly Voice* (Chicago, 1936), 87.

3. Milton S. Mayer, "Hutchins of Chicago," *Harper's Magazine*, 178 (March, 1939), 344–45.

4. Interview by the author with Mr. Robert M. Hutchins, Thursday, May 22, 1969, Santa Barbara, Calif.

5. Robert M. Hutchins, "The Law School Tomorrow," *North American Review*, 225 (February, 1928), 139, 135, 139.

6. Ibid., 139.

7. Robert M. Hutchins, "The Law and the Psychologists," *Yale Review*, 16 (July, 1927), 690.

8. Robert M. Hutchins, "Address Given to the Sixth Annual Dinner of the American Law Institute," *Proceedings of the American Law Institute*, 6 (July 1, 1927 to June 30, 1928), 600.

9. Robert M. Hutchins, "The Law School Tomorrow," *North American Review*, 225 (February, 1928), 137.

10. Robert M. Hutchins, "The Law and the Psychologists," *Yale Review*, 16 (July, 1927), 680. See also Robert M. Hutchins and Donald Slesinger, "Some Observations on the Law of Evidence—State of Mind to Prove an Act," *Yale Law Journal*, 38 (January, 1929), 283–98; "Some Observations on the Law of Evidence," *Columbia Law Review*, 28 (April, 1928), 432–40; "Some Observations on the Law of Evidence—Memory," *Harvard Law Review*, 41 (May, 1928), 860–73; and "Some Observations on the Law of Evidence—The Competence of Witnesses," *Yale Law Journal*, 37 (June, 1928), 1017–28.

11. Robert M. Hutchins, "Some Observations on the Law of Evidence—Memory," *Harvard Law Review*, 41 (May, 1928), 873.

12. Interview with Hutchins, May 22, 1969.

13. Robert M. Hutchins, "The University of Utopia," *Yale Review*, 20 (March, 1931), 456.

14. For an account of the university's attempts at educational reform before and during Hutchins's tenure see Chauncy Samuel Boucher, *The Chicago College Plan* (Chicago, 1935).

15. Robert M. Hutchins, "Hard Times and the Higher Learning," *Yale Review*, 22 (June, 1933), 716–17.

16. Robert M. Hutchins, "Prospects of Higher Education," *School and Society*, 37 (January 7, 1933), 3.

17. Robert M. Hutchins, "Education and the Public Mind," *School and Society*, 38 (August 5, 1933), 164, 165.

18. Interview with Hutchins, May 22, 1969.

19. Hutchins, *No Friendly Voice*, 46.

20. Ibid., 43–44.

21. Ibid., 44.

22. Ibid., 45.

23. Ibid., 42.

24. Ibid., 48.

25. Ibid., 48.
26. Robert M. Hutchins, *The Higher Learning in America* (New Haven, Conn., 1962 [1936]), 27.
27. Ibid., 94.
28. Ibid., 95, 97. See also 96.
29. Ibid., 98, 108, 97–98.
30. Ibid., 66, note 3.
31. Pearl L. Weber, "Universities and First Principles," *Education*, 60 (September, 1939), 45.
32. T. V. Smith, "The Chicago School," *International Journal of Ethics*, 46 (April, 1936), 384.
33. Anton J. Carlson, "So This Is the University?" *Bulletin of the American Association of University Professors*, 24 (January, 1938), 18.
34. John Dewey, " 'The Higher Learning in America,' " *Social Frontier*, 3 (March, 1937), 167; Dewey, "President Hutchins' Proposals to Remake Higher Education," *Social Frontier*, 3 (January, 1937), 104.
35. Mortimer J. Adler, "The Chicago School," *Harper's Magazine*, 183 (September, 1941), 384.
36. Alan Valentine, "No Middle Flight," *Yale Review*, 25 (Summer, 1936), 814.
37. James Feibleman, *Positive Democracy* (Chapel Hill, N. C., 1940), 233.
38. John T. Wahlquist, "The Dilemma of American Education," *Educational Forum*, 2 (May, 1938), 386.
39. Robert M. Hutchins, "Education and Social Improvement: The Cult That Destroys," *Vital Speeches of the Day*, 4 (June 1, 1938), 500.
40. "Dr. Hutchins Turns Scholastic?" *Modern Schoolman*, 11 (March, 1934), 53.
41. Walter Lippmann, *A Preface to Morals* (Boston, 1960 [1929]), 187.
42. Walter Lippmann, *An Inquiry into the Principles of the Good Society* (Boston, 1937), 31.
43. Ibid., 108–9.
44. Ibid., 380.
45. Ibid., 347.
46. Ibid., 346.
47. Ibid., 334.
48. Reinhold Niebuhr, *Leaves from the Notebook of a Tamed Cynic* (New York, 1964 [1929]), 62, 178.
49. See especially, Reinhold Niebuhr, "Intellectual Biography," in Charles W. Kegley and Robert W. Bretall, eds., *Reinhold Niebuhr: His Religious, Social, and Political Thought* (New York, 1961), 8–9. For a general discussion of Niebuhr's role in the thirties see Donald B. Meyer, *The Protestant Search for Political Realism, 1919–1941* (Berkeley, Calif., 1960), especially Chapters 13 and 14.
50. Reinhold Niebuhr, *Moral Man and Immoral Society* (New York, 1960 [1932]), xx, xiv.
51. Reinhold Niebuhr, *Beyond Tragedy: Essays on the Christian Interpretation of History* (New York, 1965 [1937]), 108.
52. Robert M. Hutchins, "What Shall We Defend? We Are Losing Our Moral Principles," *Vital Speeches of the Day*, 6 (July 1, 1940), 547.

53. Ibid., 547.
54. Ibid., 548–49.
55. Ibid., 549.

9. Crisis in Jurisprudence

1. John Chamberlain, "The Folklore of Reviewers," *Saturday Review of Literature*, 17 (March 12, 1938), 8.

2. Frederick K. Beutel, "Some Implications of Experimental Jurisprudence," *Harvard Law Review*, 48 (December, 1934), 178–79.

3. Edward S. Robinson, *Law and the Lawyers* (New York, 1935), 225. See also Robinson, review of *Legal Psychology* by Harold Ernest Burtt, *Yale Law Journal*, 41 (May, 1932), 1106.

4. Rufus C. Harris, "Idealism Emergent in Jurisprudence," *Tulane Law Review*, 10 (February, 1936), 174, 177, 182.

5. Philip Mechem, "The Jurisprudence of Despair," *Iowa Law Review*, 21 (May, 1936), 672, 692.

6. Morris R. Cohen, review of *Law and the Lawyers* by Edward S. Robinson, *Cornell Law Quarterly*, 22 (December, 1936), 177. See also Cohen, review of *The Symbols of Government* by Thurman Arnold, *Illinois Law Review*, 31 (November, 1936), 411–18; and "On Absolutisms in Legal Thought," *University of Pennsylvania Law Review and American Law Register*, 84 (April, 1936), 691.

7. Karl N. Llewellyn, "Foreword," in *The Bramble Bush: On Our Law and Its Study* (New York, 1951), 10.

8. Jerome Hall, "Nulla Poena since Lege," *Yale Law Journal*, 47 (December, 1937), 189. See also 175, 181–82, 186–88, 189–93.

9. Edgar Bodenheimer, *Jurisprudence* (New York, 1940), 316. See also ibid., 309–10.

10. Roscoe Pound, "The Future of Law," *Yale Law Journal*, 47 (November, 1937), 2.

11. Roscoe Pound, *Contemporary Juristic Theory* (Claremont, Calif., 1940), 1.

12. Ibid., 9. See also 1, 8–11.

13. Lon L. Fuller, review of *Readings in Jurisprudence* by Jerome Hall, *University of Pennsylvania Law Review and American Law Register*, 87 (March, 1939), 625. See also Fuller, review of *The Formative Era of American Law* by Roscoe Pound, *Illinois Law Review*, 34 (1939), 374 and "Williston on Contracts," *North Carolina Law Review*, 18 (1939), 13–15.

14. Lon L. Fuller, *The Law in Quest of Itself* (Boston, 1966 [1940]), 4.

15. Ibid., 5.
16. Ibid., 5.
17. Ibid., 11.
18. Ibid., 65.
19. Ibid., 89.
20. Ibid., 122.
21. Ibid., 122–27.
22. Ibid., 100–115.

23. Edgar Bodenheimer, review of *The Law in Quest of Itself* by Lon L. Fuller, *Georgetown Law Journal*, 29 (May, 1941), 1100, 1102.

24. Brendan F. Brown, review of *The Law in Quest of Itself* by Lon L. Fuller, *Iowa Law Review*, 26 (November, 1940), 175.

25. Miriam Theresa Rooney, "Law and the New Logic," *Proceedings of the American Catholic Philosophical Association*, 16 (1940), 217.

26. Clarence Manion, "The American Metaphysics in Law," *Proceedings of the American Catholic Philosophical Association*, 18 (1942), 132, 133–34.

27. Brendan F. Brown, "Natural Law and the Law-Making Function in American Jurisprudence," *Notre Dame Lawyer*, 15 (November, 1939), 10–11.

28. Walter B. Kennedy, "A Review of Legal Realism," *Fordham Law Review*, 9 (November, 1940), 363–69.

29. Miriam Theresa Rooney, "The Movement for a Neo-Scholastic Philosophy of Law in America," *Proceeedings of the American Catholic Philosophical Association*, 18 (1942), 185, 199; Brendan F. Brown, "Jurisprudential Aims of Church Law Schools in the United States," *Notre Dame Lawyer*, 13 (March, 1938), 165; and see the proceedings of the meetings of the American Catholic Philosophical Association, 1932–1942.

30. Brendan F. Brown, "Jurisprudential Aims of Church Law Schools in the United States," *Notre Dame Lawyer*, 13 (March, 1938), 188–89.

31. Miriam Theresa Rooney, "The Movement for a Neo-Scholastic Philosophy of Law in America," *Proceedings of the American Catholic Philosophical Association*, 18 (1942), 186.

32. "Introduction," *Notre Dame Lawyer*, 15 (November, 1939), 1.

33. John Thomas Connor, "Some Catholic Law School Objectives," *Catholic Educational Review*, 36 (March, 1938), 165, 170.

34. William F. Clarke, "The Problem of the Catholic Law School," *University of Detroit Law Journal*, 3 (May, 1940), 169.

35. Francis P. Le Buffe, S.J. and James V. Hayes, *Jurisprudence: With Cases to Illustrate Principles* (New York, 1938), v. See also Karl Kreilkamp, *The Metaphysical Foundation of Thomistic Jurisprudence* (Washington, D. C., 1939); William F. Obering, *The Philosophy of Law of James Wilson: A Study in Comparative Law* (Washington, D. C., 1938); and Miriam Theresa Rooney, *Lawlessness, Law and Sanction* (Washington, D. C., 1936).

36. Brendan F. Brown, "Natural Law and the Law-Making Function in American Jurisprudence," *Notre Dame Lawyer*, 15 (November, 1939), 23–24.

37. Dietrich von Hildebrand, "The Dethronement of Truth," *Proceedings of the American Catholic Philosophical Association*, 18 (1942), 9. See also 3–6.

38. Karl Kreilkamp, "Dean Pound and the End of Law," *Fordham Law Review*, 9 (May, 1940), 232.

39. Francis E. Lucey, S.J., "Jurisprudence and the Future Social Order," *Social Science*, 16 (July, 1941), 213, 214.

40. Francis E. Lucey, S.J., "Natural Law and American Legal Realism: Their Respective Contributions to a Theory of Law in a Democratic Society," *Georgetown Law Journal*, 30 (April, 1942), 498, 512, 533.

41. E. W. Simms, "A Dissent from Greatness," *Virginia Law Review*, 28 (February, 1940), 467, 482, 473–74.

42. Paul L. Gregg, S.J., "The Pragmatism of Mr. Justice Holmes," *Georgetown Law Journal*, 31 (March, 1943), 294.

43. John C. Ford, S.J., "The Totalitarian Justice Holmes," *Catholic World*, 159 (May, 1944), 115.

44. Charles C. Miltner, C.S.C., "The Philosophical Background of American Democracy," *Notre Dame Lawyer*, 15 (March, 1940), 186. See also William P. Steinber, "Natural Law in American Jurisprudence," *Notre Dame Lawyer*, 13 (January, 1938), 89–100.

45. See Mortimer J. Adler and Walter Farrell, O.P., "The Theory of Democracy," *Thomist*, 3 (July, 1941), 397–449; (October, 1941), 588–652; 4 (January, 1942), 121–81; (April, 1942), 286–354; (July, 1942), 446–522; (October, 1942), 692, 761; 5 (April, 1943), 49–118.

46. Patrick J. Roche, *Democracy in the Light of Four Current Educational Philosophies* (Washington, D. C., 1942), 12, 13, 14.

47. For examples see Moorehouse F. X. Millar, S.J., "The Origin of Sound Democratic Principles in Catholic Tradition," *Catholic Historical Review*, 14 (April, 1928), 104–26; "Scholastic Philosophy and American Political Theory," *Thought*, 1 (June, 1936), 112–36.

48. Wilfred Parsons, S.J., "Philosophical Factors in the Integration of American Culture," in *Phases of American Culture* (Worcester, Mass., 1942), 15, 20, 24.

49. William Franklin Sands, "What Is an American?" *Commonweal*, 33 (February 21, 1941), 438.

50. Raoul E. Desvernine, "Philosophy and Order in Law," *Proceedings of the American Catholic Philosophical Association*, 17 (1941), 135, 136.

51. Max Radin, "In Defense of an Unsystematic Science of Law," *Yale Law Journal*, 4 (June, 1942), 1275.

52. Karl N. Llewellyn, "On Reading and Using the Newer Jurisprudence," *Columbia Law Review*, 40 (April, 1940), 593, 603.

53. Edwin Patterson, "Foreword," in Edwin N. Garlan, *Legal Realism and Justice* (New York, 1941), viii.

54. Jerome Frank, *Fate and Freedom: A Philosophy for Free Americans* (New York, 1945), 295; see also ibid., 98–99, 259–60.

55. Jerome Frank, "Preface to Sixth Printing," *Law and the Modern Mind* (New York, 1963 [1948]), xx.

56. Karl N. Llewellyn, "On the Good, the True, the Beautiful, in Law," *University of Chicago Law Review*, 9 (February, 1942), 247.

57. Karl N. Llewellyn, "One Realist's View of Natural Law for Judges," *Notre Dame Lawyer*, 15 (November, 1939), 3, 8.

58. Karl N. Llewellyn, "On the Good, the True, the Beautiful, in Law," *University of Chicago Law Review*, 9 (February, 1942), 264, 257, 264.

59. Max Radin, "The Education of a Lawyer," *California Law Review*, 25 (September, 1937), 688.

60. Ibid., 688.

61. Max Radin, *Law as Logic and Experience* (New Haven, Conn., 1940), 156–58.

62. See also Max Radin, "In Defense of an Unsystematic System of Law," *Yale Law Journal*, 51 (June, 1942), especially 1270–75.

63. Walter Wheeler Cook, "My Philosophy of Law," in *My Philosophy of Law: Credos of Sixteen American Scholars* (Boston, 1941), 60.

64. Ibid., 60–61.

65. Ibid., 64.

66. Hessel E. Yntema, "Jurisprudence on Parade," *Michigan Law Review*, 39 (May, 1941), 1163.

67. Edwin W. Patterson, review of *The Law in Quest of Itself* by Lon L. Fuller, *Iowa Law Review*, 26 (November, 1940), 172–73.

68. Myres S. McDougal, "Fuller v. The American Legal Realists: An Intervention," *Yale Law Journal*, 50 (March, 1941), 840.

69. Fred Rodell, *Woe Unto You, Lawyers!* (New York, 1957 [1939]), 149.

70. Walter B. Kennedy, "My Philosophy of Law," in *My Philosophy of Law*, 151–52.

71. Roscoe Pound, "My Philosophy of Law," in *My Philosophy of Law*, 250.

72. Walter Wheeler Cook, "My Philosophy of Law," in *My Philosophy of Law*, 64.

10. Crisis in Social Science

1. Goetz A. Briefs, "The Crisis of Our Age," *Review of Politics*, 4 (April, 1942), 319.

2. Goetz A. Briefs, "Crisis of Democracy," *Review of Politics*, 2 (July, 1940), 351.

3. Charles C. Miltner, "Catholic Principles of Politics," *Review of Politics*, 3 (January, 1941), 118.

4. Francis J. O'Malley, "A Christian Society," *Review of Politics*, 2 (October, 1940), 489.

5. Leonard J. Eslick, "The Current Conception of Truth," *Proceedings of the American Catholic Philosophical Association*, 18 (1942), 28–29, 43.

6. Stephen F. McNamee, S.J., "Presidential Address," in *Phases of American Culture* (Worcester, Mass., 1942), 11, 12.

7. Max Ascoli, "On Mannheim's 'Ideology and Utopia,'" *Social Research*, 5 (February, 1938), 106.

8. Arnold Brecht, review of *Scholasticism and Politics* by Jacques Maritain, *American Political Science Review*, 35 (June, 1941), 545.

9. Herbert Martin, "Democracy and Morality," *Social Science*, 16 (October, 1941), 382.

10. Oscar Jaszi, "The Good Society," *Journal of Social Philosophy*, 3 (January, 1938), 154, 155, 157. For other examples see C. C. Smith, "Science and the Humanities," *Social Science*, 15 (January, 1940), 46–47; N. N. Alexeiev, "Modern Culture and the New European War," *Review of Politics*, 2 (January, 1940), 21–33; and Benjamin E. Lippincott, "The Bias of American Political Science," *Journal of Politics*, 2 (May, 1940), 125–39.

11. John Donaldson, "The Social Sciences: Scientific or Normative," *Social Science*, 15 (January, 1940), 20.

12. Howard W. Odum, "The Errors of Sociology," *Social Forces*, 15 (March, 1937), 342.

13. Mulford Q. Sibley, "Apology for Utopia: Part II," *Journal of Politics*, 2 (May, 1940), 183.

14. Albert Salomon, review of *Social Thought from Lore to Science*, Vols. I and II by Harry Elmer Barnes and Howard Becker, *Social Research*, 6 (February, 1939), 122. See also Albert Salomon, "Sociology and Sociologism," *Journal for Social Philosophy*, 3 (April, 1938), 210–22; and Allen G. Gruchy, "John R. Commons' Concept of Twentieth Century Economics," *Journal of Political Economy*, 48 (December, 1940), 823–48.

15. Charles A. Ellwood, "An Editorial Review: Naturalistic Sociology," *Social Science*, 18 (January, 1943), 34.

16. Charles A. Ellwood, "The Challenge of Today to Social Scientists," *Social Science*, 12 (April, 1937), 155.

17. Ludwig von Mises, "Social Science and Natural Science," *Journal of Social Philosophy and Jurisprudence*, 7 (April, 1942), 246.

18. A. B. Wolfe, "Thoughts on Perusal of Wesley Mitchell's Collected Essays," *Journal of Political Economy*, 47 (February, 1939), 29.

19. Claude C. Bowman, "Imagination in Social Science," *American Sociological Review*, 1 (August, 1936), 640.

20. Albert G. A. Balz, "The Challenge of Metaphysics to Social Science," *Journal of Social Philosophy*, 3 (January, 1938), 119.

21. Paul Kecskemeti, "Ethics and the 'Single Theory,' " *Social Research*, 2 (May, 1935), 221.

22. Emil Lederer, "Freedom and Science," *Social Research*, 1 (May, 1934), 221. See also 219–20.

23. Paul Kecskemeti, "Ethics and the 'Single Theory,' " *Social Research*, 2 (May, 1935), especially 218–21.

24. Max Wertheimer, "Some Problems in the Theory of Ethics," *Social Research*, 2 (August, 1935), 355 and passim.

25. Morris R. Cohen and Ernest Nagel, *An Introduction to Logic and Scientific Method* (New York, 1934), v. For another defense of Aristotelian logic see L. Kattsoff, "Concerning the Validity of Aristotelian Logic," *Philosophy of Science*, 1 (April, 1934), 149–62.

26. W. Y. Elliott, "The Pragmatic Revolt in Politics: Twenty Years in Retrospect," *Review of Politics*, 2 (January, 1940), 2, 9.

27. Pitirim A. Sorokin, "Declaration of Independence of the Social Sciences," *Social Science*, 16 (July, 1941), 226. See also Pitirim A. Sorokin, "Improvement of Scholarship in the Social Sciences," *Journal of Social Philosophy*, 2 (April, 1937), 237–45.

28. Pitirim A. Sorokin, *Social and Cultural Dynamics* (New York, 1937), 1:62.

29. Ibid., 64.

30. Ibid., 73.

31. Ibid., 72–73.

32. Ibid., 678–79.

33. Ibid., 2:475.

34. Ibid.

35. Ibid., 1:75.

36. Ibid., 2:6. For Sorokin's claim to represent the idealistic position as he defined it, see 1:x and 1:75, note 10. For his debt to Aristotle see Sorokin, "Pseudo Sociologos: A Reply to Professor Goldenweiser," *Journal of Social Philosophy*, 3 (July, 1938), 361.

37. Sorokin, *Social and Cultural Dynamics*, 2:475. See also 3:531–39.

38. Ibid., 2:512.

39. Pitirim A. Sorokin, *The Crisis of Our Age*, condensed for student discussion by Paul E. Johnson (New York, 1945), 3, 5.

40. Carl L. Becker, "Some Generalities That Still Glitter," *Yale Review*, 29 (June, 1940), 666.

41. E. T. Bell, *Men of Mathematics* (New York, 1937), 15.

42. See Alexander Goldenweiser, "Nature and Tasks of the Social Sciences," *Journal of Social Philosophy*, 2 (October, 1936), 5–34; Bronislaw Malinowski, *The Foundations of Faith and Morals: An Anthropological Analysis of Primitive Beliefs and Conduct with Special Reference to the Fundamental Problems of Religion and Ethics* (London, 1936), ix, 62; Malinowski, "A New Instrument for the Interpretation of Law—Especially Primitive," *Yale Law Journal*, 51 (June, 1942), 1247; Malinowski, "Culture as a Determinant of Behavior," *Scientific Monthly*, 43 (November, 1936), 447–49; Margaret Mead, "Shall Hitler Call Our Tune?" *Independent Woman*, 20 (January, 1941), 29.

43. Howard Becker, "Supreme Values and the Sociologist," *American Sociological Review*, 6 (April, 1941), 156, 164. For his critique of operationalism see Becker, "The Limits of Sociological Positivism," *Journal of Social Philosophy*, 6 (July, 1941), 362–69.

44. Harry Elmer Barnes, review of *The World's Need of Christ* by Charles A. Ellwood, *American Sociological Review*, 6 (April, 1941), 295–96.

45. Harold D. Lasswell, *Democracy through Public Opinion* (New York, 1941), 1, 2.

46. George E. G. Catlin, *The Story of the Political Philosophers* (New York, 1939), x.

47. Charles E. Merriam, *On the Agenda of Democracy* (Cambridge, Mass., 1941), 122. See also 123–26 and Merriam, *What Is Democracy?* (Chicago, 1941), 6–7.

48. Merriam, *What Is Democracy?* 91.

49. Charles E. Merriam, *The New Democracy and the New Despotism* (New York, 1939), 46. See also 11–12, 15–16, and 45.

50. Peter H. Odegard, review of *What Is Democracy?* by Charles Merriam, *Democracy in American Life* by Avery Craven, and *Aspects of Democracy*, ed. R. B. Huliman, *American Political Science Review*, 35 (December, 1941), 1161.

51. Francis O. Wilcox, "Teaching Political Science in a World at War," *American Political Science Review*, 35 (April, 1941), 327.

52. Ibid., 333.

53. Carl J. Friedrich, *The New Belief in the Common Man* (Boston, 1942), 30.

54. Charles W. Smith, Jr., "The Intelligence Factor in Public Opinion," *Journal of Politics*, 1 (August, 1939), 311. See also J. Salwyn Shapiro, review of *Victorian Critics of Democracy* by Benjamin G. E. Lippincott, *Political Science Quarterly*, 53 (December, 1938), 619–20.

55. E. Pendleton Herring, *The Politics of Democracy* (New York, 1965 [1940]), 25–26.

56. E. E. Schattschneider, review of *The Politics of Democracy* by E. Pendleton Herring, *American Political Science Review*, 34 (August, 1940), 788.

57. Maurice R. Davie, "Theory and Practice in Social Science," *Social Science*, 17 (January, 1942), 49.

58. Frank H. Knight, " 'What Is Truth' in Economics?" *Journal of Political Economy*, 48 (February, 1940), 3.

59. Robert M. MacIver, "Some Reflections on Sociology during a Crisis," *American Sociological Review*, 6 (February, 1941), 5.

60. Charles Beard, "Democracy and Education in the United States," *Social Research*, 4 (September, 1937), 394.

61. George H. Sabine, *A History of Political Theory* (New York, 1937), viii, vii, viii.

62. George H. Sabine, "What Is a Political Theory?" *Journal of Politics*, 1 (February, 1939), 13.

63. Ellsworth Faris, "Sociology and Human Welfare," *Social Forces*, 18 (October, 1939), 4.

64. Robert S. Lynd, *Knowledge for What? The Place of Social Science in American Culture* (Princeton, N. J., 1970 [1940]), especially 119–20, 143–49, 177–82, 200–201, 215–16, and 239–43.

65. Ellsworth Faris, "The Promise of Sociology," *American Sociological Review*, 3 (February, 1938), 8.

66. Peter H. Odegard, "The Political Scientist in the Democratic Service State," *Journal of Politics*, 2 (May, 1940), 159.

67. Charles E. Merriam, *The New Democracy and the New Despotism*, 8.

68. Robert S. Lynd, *Knowledge for What?* 191.

69. E. L. Thorndike, "Science and Values," *Science*, 83 (January 3, 1936), 2, 1.

70. Read Bain, "Freedom, Law and Rational Social Control," *Journal of Social Philosophy*, 4 (April, 1939), 235, note 4. See also Read Bain, "Sociology and Psychoanalysis," *American Sociological Review*, 1 (April, 1936), especially 211–16.

71. William Anderson, "Introduction" in Anna Haddow, *Political Science in American Colleges and Universities 1636–1900*, ed. William Anderson (New York, 1939), x.

72. J. R. Kantor, "Interbehavioral Psychology and the Social Sciences," *Journal of Social Philosophy*, 3 (October, 1937), 47. See also Luther L. Bernard, *An Introduction to Sociology: A Naturalistic Account of Adjustment to His World* (New York, 1942), especially vii–ix, and Bernard, *Social Control in Its Sociological Aspects* (New York, 1939), especially 480–87; Earle Edward Eubank, "Errors of Sociology," *Social Forces*, 16 (December, 1937), 178–201; L. L. Thurstone, "Psychology as a Quantitative Rational Science," *Science*, 85 (March 5, 1937), 227–32; and Thurstone, "Factor Analysis as a Scientific Method with Special Reference to the Analysis of Human Traits," in *Eleven Twenty-Six: A Decade of Social Science Research*, ed. Louis Wirth (Chicago, 1940).

73. Wesley C. Mitchell, "Science and the State of Mind," *Science*, 89 (January 6, 1939), 3. For his recognition of the personal element see Wesley C. Mitchell, "Feeling and Thinking in Scientific Work," *Social Science*, 15 (July, 1940), 229–32.

74. Wesley C. Mitchell, "Intelligence and the Guidance of Economic Evaluation," in Harvard Tercentenary Conference of Arts and Sciences, *Authority and the Individual* (Cambridge, 1937), 27.

75. George A. Lundberg, *Foundations of Sociology* (New York, 1939), 31. For continued interest in the objectivist viewpoint see George A. Lundberg, "What Are Sociological Problems?" *American Sociological Review*, 6 (June, 1941), 357–69; Walter C. Reckless, "The Implications of Prediction in Sociology," *American Sociological Review*, 6 (August, 1941), 471–77; Elio D. Monachesi, "An Evaluation of Recent Major Efforts at Prediction," *American Sociological Review*, 6 (August, 1941), 478–86; Stuart Carter Dodd, "A System of Operationally Defined Concepts for Sociology," *American Sociological Review*, 4 (October, 1939), 619–34; A. B. Hollingshead, "Behavior Systems as a Field for Research," *American Sociological Review*, 4 (October, 1939), 816–22; and Harry Alpert, "Operational Definitions in Sociology," *American Sociological Review*, 3 (December, 1938), 855–61.

76. Stuart A. Rice, "World Standards of Living," *Vital Speeches of the Day*, 4 (August 15, 1938), 665.

77. Percy W. Bridgman, *The Intelligent Individual and Society* (New York, 1938), 21. See also 3, 67, 112–17, 125–27, 140, 232–34.

78. George A. Lundberg, "Contemporary Positivism in Sociology," *American Sociological Review*, 4 (February, 1939), 51, 52.

79. "Editorial," *Journal of Social Philosophy*, 1 (October, 1935), 5.

80. Moses J. Aronson, "Editorial," *Journal of Social Philosophy*, 5 (October, 1939), 5.

11. Toward a Relativist Theory of Democracy

1. Roland L. Warren, "The Place of Values in Social Theory," *Journal of Social Philosophy and Jurisprudence*, 7 (April, 1942), 223.

2. Thomas I. Cook, review of *The Course of American Democratic Thought* by Ralph H. Gabriel, *American Political Science Review*, 34 (June, 1940), 562.

3. Thurman Arnold, *The Folklore of Capitalism* (New Haven, Conn., 1959 [1937]), 23.

4. Fred Rodell, "Fun into Fundamentals," *New Republic*, 93 (December 15, 1937), 175.

5. Leon Green, "Myths of Our Day," *Yale Review*, n.s. 27 (Spring, 1938), 624–25.

6. See Harold J. Laski, review of *The Folklore of Capitalism* by Thurman Arnold, *Brooklyn Law Review*, 7 (May, 1938), 535–37; Felix S. Cohen, review of *The Folklore of Capitalism* by Thurman Arnold, *National Lawyers Guild Quarterly*, 1 (March, 1938), 161–64; and Edward S. Corwin, review of *The Folklore of Capitalism* by Thurman Arnold, *American Political Science Review*, 32 (August, 1938), 745–46.

7. Sidney Hook, "The Folklore of Capitalism," reprinted in Hook, *Reason, Social Myths and Democracy* (New York, 1966 [1940]), 49, 45, 47.

8. Thurman Arnold, "The Folklore of Mr. Hook—A Reply," reprinted in ibid., 53, 56.

9. Sidney Hook, "Neither Myth Nor Power—A Rejoinder," reprinted in ibid., 56, 59, 61.

10. For attempts to produce a rational justification of democracy see Joseph A. Leighton, *Social Philosophies in Conflict: Fascism and Nazism, Communism, Liberal Democracy* (New York, 1937); Marie Collins Swabey, *Theory of the Democratic State* (Cambridge, Mass., 1937); W. T. Stace, *The Destiny of Western Man* (New York, 1942); and Arnold Brecht, "The Search for Absolutes in Political and Legal Philosophy," *Social Research*, 7 (May, 1940), 202; "Relative and Absolute Justice," *Social Research*, 6 (February, 1939), 75; "The Impossible in Political and Legal Philosophy," *California Law Review*, 29 (March, 1941), 312–31; "The Myth of Is and Ought," *Harvard Law Review*, 54 (March, 1941), 811–31; and "The Rise of Relativism in Political and Legal Philosophy," *Social Research*, 6 (September, 1939), 392–414.

11. George H. Sabine, review of *Theory of the Democratic State* by Marie Collins Swabey, *American Political Science Review*, 31 (December, 1937), 1144.

12. John Dewey, *Reconstruction in Philosophy* (Boston, 1962 [1920]), 61, 30, 65–66.

13. John Dewey, *Characters and Events: Popular Essays in Social and Political Philosophy* (New York, 1929), 2:725.

14. John Dewey, *The Public and Its Problems* (New York, 1927), 200, 201.

15. John Dewey, *Freedom and Culture* (New York, 1963 [1939]), 93–94.

16. John D. Lewis, "The Elements of Democracy," *American Political Science Review*, 34 (June, 1940), 477.

17. Jerome Frank, *Fate and Freedom: A Philosophy for Free Americans* (New York, 1945), 367.

18. Max Lerner, *Ideas Are Weapons: The History and Uses of Ideas* (New York, 1939), 188, 205; Lerner, "Face the War," *Saturday Review of Literature*, 22 (May 25, 1940), 23.

19. Marten Ten Hoor, "Medievalism in Contemporary Political Thought," *Journal of Social Philosophy*, 3 (July, 1938), 347.

20. Malcolm Sharp, "Positive Positivist," *Daily Maroon* (University of Chicago), November 14, 1940.

21. Howard Mumford Jones, "The Drift to Liberalism in the American Eighteenth Century," in Harvard Tercentenary Conference of Arts and Sciences, *Authority and the Individual* (Cambridge, Mass., 1937), 120; Frank H. Knight, "God and Professor Adler and Logic," *Daily Maroon*, November 14, 1940.

22. Hook, *Reason, Social Myths, and Democracy*, 76, 87.

23. Leo Lehmann, "The Catholic Church in Politics," *New Republic*, 97 (November 16, 1938), 34.

24. H. Rutledge Southworth, "The Catholic Press," *Nation*, 149 (December 16, 1939), 676. See also 675 and 677.

25. Edward C. Lindeman, "Introduction," in Conference on the Scientific Spirit and Democratic Faith, *The Scientific Spirit and Democratic Faith* (New York, 1944), ix.

26. Horace M. Kallen, "Freedom and Authoritarianism in Religion," in ibid., 10.

27. John Dewey, "The Democratic Faith and Education," in Conference on the Scientific Spirit and Democratic Faith, *The Authoritarian Attempt to Capture Education* (New York, 1945), 4 and passim.

28. Marten Ten Hoor, "Medievalism in Contemporary Political Thought," *Journal of Social Philosophy*, 3 (July, 1938), 344.

29. Dewey, *Freedom and Culture*, 102.

30. Horace S. Fries, "Science, Ethics, and Democracy," *Journal of Social Philosophy*, 6 (July, 1941), 321–22.

31. Hook, *Reason, Social Myths and Democracy*, 3–11, 283–97.

32. Jerome Nathanson, *Forerunners of Freedom: The Recreation of the American Spirit* (Washington, 1941), 151. For Hook see *Reason, Social Myths and Democracy*, especially Chapters 1 and 13.

33. Dewey, *Freedom and Culture*, 153–54.

34. Max Lerner, "Foreword," in *The Mind and Faith of Justice Holmes: His Speeches, Essays, Letters and Judicial Opinions*, ed. Max Lerner (New York, 1943), ix.

35. Felix S. Cohen, *The Legal Conscience: Selected Papers of Felix S. Cohen*, ed. Lucy Kramer Cohen (New Haven, Conn., 1960), 452.

36. T. V. Smith, *Beyond Conscience* (New York, 1934), 343, 335.

37. Ibid., 332, vii.

38. See T. V. Smith, *The Democratic Way of Life* (Chicago, 1939); Leonard D. White and T. V. Smith, *Politics and Public Service: A Discussion of the Civic Art*

in *America* (New York, 1939); T. V. Smith, *The Legislative Way of Life* (Chicago, 1940); T. V. Smith, *The Promise of American Politics* (Chicago, 1936); and T. V. Smith, *Lincoln, Living Legend* (Chicago, 1940).

39. T. V. Smith, *Creative Skeptics: In Defense of the Liberal Temper* (Chicago, 1934), 10.

40. T. V. Smith, *Creative Skeptics*, 226–27. See also 177–228, 256–65, and 231–47.

41. T. V. Smith, *Discipline for Democracy* (Chapel Hill, N. C., 1942), 124.

42. T. V. Smith, "Justice Holmes: Voice of Democratic Evolution," in *The Philosophy of American Democracy*, ed. Charner M. Perry (Chicago, 1943), 119.

43. Philipp Frank, "The Relativity of Truth and the Objectivity of Values," in Conference on Science, Philosophy and Religion in Their Relation to the Democratic Way of Life, Inc., *Science, Philosophy, and Religion, Third Symposium* (New York, 1943), 13.

44. Boyd H. Bode, *Democracy as a Way of Life* (New York, 1937), 48.

45. Dewey, *Freedom and Culture*, 13, 6. See also 11–12.

46. Ibid., 151, 6, 147.

47. Charles E. Merriam, review of *Freedom and Culture* by John Dewey, *American Political Science Review*, 34 (April, 1940), 339, 342.

48. Jacques Barzun, *Of Human Freedom* (Boston, 1939), 40. See also 10–11, 276.

49. Ibid., 21, 8.

50. See for example Francis G. Wilson, "Political Suppression in the Modern State," *Journal of Politics*, 1 (August, 1939), 237–57; Dorothy Fosdick, "Ethical Standards and Political Strategies," *Political Science Quarterly*, 57 (June, 1942), 214–28; and John D. Lewis, "The Elements of Democracy," *American Political Science Review*, 34 (June, 1940), 467–80.

51. Carl J. Friedrich, *Constitutional Government and Politics: Nature and Development* (New York, 1937), 35, 136, 301.

52. Carl J. Friedrich, "Democracy and Dissent," *Political Quarterly*, (October-December, 1939), 571–72, 573, 582. For references to Holmes see Ibid., 580 and Friedrich, "Democracy and Dissent," *Review of Politics*, 2 (July, 1940), 379. See also Friedrich, *Constitutional Government and Democracy: Theory and Practice in Europe and America* (Boston, 1941), vii–viii, and also his qualification, 586–89.

53. Carl J. Friedrich, *The New Belief in the Common Man* (Boston, 1942), 178, 181.

54. E. Pendleton Herring, *The Politics of Democracy: American Parties in Action* (New York, 1965 [1940]), 26, 63, 40.

55. Ibid., 47.

56. Ibid., 97.

57. Ibid., 305.

12. Theoretical Principles & Foreign Policy

1. Mortimer J. Adler, "God and the Professors," *Vital Speeches of the Day*, 7 (December 1, 1940), 100, 102.

2. Sidney Hook, "The New Medievalism," *New Republic*, 103 (October 28, 1940), 604, 605, 606.

3. "Spoiling a Good Case," *Christian Century*, 57 (December 18, 1940), 1576.

4. The bibliography on the prewar debate over foreign policy is immense. See especially William L. Langer and S. Everett Gleason, *The Challenge to Isolation, 1937–40* (New York, 1952); Wayne S. Cole, *Senator Gerald P. Nye and American Foreign Relations* (Minneapolis, Minn., 1962); and the same author's *America First: The Battle against Intervention, 1940–1941* (Madison, Wis., 1953); Walter Johnson, *The Battle against Isolation* (Chicago, 1944); Manfred Jonas, *Isolationism in America, 1935–1941* (Ithaca, N. Y., 1966); Donald F. Drummond, *The Passing of American Neutrality, 1937–1941* (Ann Arbor, Mich., 1955); Selig Adler, *The Isolationist Impulse: Its Twentieth Century Reaction* (New York, 1961); Mark Lincoln Chadwin, *The Warhawks: American Interventionists before Pearl Harbor* (New York, 1968); Alexander De Conde, ed., *Isolation and Security* (Durham, N. C., 1957); Robert A. Divine, *The Illusion of Neutrality: Franklin D. Roosevelt and the Struggle over the Arms Embargo* (Chicago, 1962); and the same author's edited collection *Causes and Consequences of World War II* (Chicago, 1969); William M. Tuttle, Jr., "Aid-to-the-Allies-Short-of-War Versus American Intervention, 1940: A Reappraisal of William Allen White's Leadership," *Journal of American History*, 56 (March, 1970), 840–58; John McVickar Haight, Jr., *American Aid to France, 1938–1940* (New York, 1970).

5. Franklin D. Roosevelt, "Message to Congress," *Vital Speeches of the Day*, 5 (January 15, 1939), 211.

6. Henry M. Wriston, "The Military and the Moral Initiative," *Vital Speeches of the Day*, 7 (December 15, 1940), 156, 157.

7. Alex A. Daspit, "Fascism, Communism, and Democracy: A Contrast," in *Aspects of Democracy*, ed. Robert B. Heilman (Baton Rouge, La., 1941), 23–24.

8. Allen Tate, *Reason in Madness: Critical Essays* (New York, 1941), ix, 5, 7. See also 3–8.

9. Mary M. Colum, "The Double Men of Criticism," *American Mercury*, 52 (June, 1941), 763.

10. Archibald MacLeish, *A Time to Speak* (Boston, 1941), 111.

11. Waldo Frank, "Our Guilt in Fascism," *New Republic*, 102 (May 6, 1940), 604.

12. Lewis Mumford, *Faith for Living* (New York, 1940), 331, 56. See also Lewis Mumford, "The Corruption of Liberalism," *New Republic*, 102 (April 29, 1940), 568.

13. Herbert Agar et al., *The City of Man: A Declaration on World Democracy* (New York, 1940), 14, 17, 19.

14. Hans Kohn, *Not by Arms Alone* (Cambridge, Mass., 1941), 8.

15. N. Clarence Nixon, review of *It Is Later Than You Think: The Need for a Militant Democracy* by Max Lerner, *Journal of Politics*, 1 (August, 1939), 317.

16. See for example Daniel Aaron, *Writers on the Left: Episodes in Literary Communism* (New York, 1961), 150–60; and the arguments defending the Soviet Union that appeared in the late thirties: Freda Kirchwey, " 'Red Totalitarianism,' " *Nation*, 148 (May 27, 1939), 605–6, and "To All Active Supporters of Democracy and Peace," *Nation*, 149 (August 26, 1939), 228. For an evaluation of the relatively more perceptive attitude of American pragmatists see John P. Diggins, "Flirtation with Fascism: American Pragmatic Liberals and Mussolini's Italy," *American Historical Review*, 71 (January, 1966), 504–6.

17. James A. Magner, "The Church and Fascism," *Commonweal*, 28 (September

2, 1938), 464. See also "The Balance of Justice," *Commonweal*, 24 (May 8, 1936), 31–32; and Francis X. Talbot, "Further Reflections on the Spanish Situation," *America*, 57 (May 1, 1937), 76–77.

18. *New York Times*, May 6, 1940, 16/7 and May 20, 1940, 6/1; Raymond H. Dawson, *The Decision to Aid Russia, 1941: Foreign Policy and Domestic Politics* (Chapel Hill, N. C., 1959), 265.

19. *New York Times*, January 23, 1940, 19/1.

20. *New York Times*, February 10, 1941, 10/4; June 19, 1941, 22/3.

21. *New York Times*, April 5, 1941, 7/5. For the change of many liberal intellectuals often associated with pragmatism from noninvolvement to interventionism, see Adler, *The Isolationist Impulse*, 270–72.

22. See for example Charles A. Beard, *A Foreign Policy for America* (New York, 1940); and *Giddy Minds and Foreign Quarrels* (New York, 1939). See also Jonas, *Isolationism in America*, especially 75–77; and Adler, *The Isolationist Impulse*, 237–88.

23. Harry Elmer Barnes, "Europe's War and America's Diplomacy," *Virginia Quarterly Review*, 16 (Autumn, 1940), 559–60.

24. Franz Boas, "Race Prejudice from the Scientist's Angle," *Forum and Century*, 98 (August, 1937), 94. See also Franz Boas, "Race and Progress," *Science*, 74 (July 3, 1931), 1–9; "The Effects of American Environment on Immigrants and Their Descendants," *Science*, 84 (December 11, 1936), 522–25; "Aryans and Non-Aryans," *American Mercury*, 32 (June, 1934), 219–23; "Science in Nazi Germany," *Survey Graphic*, 26 (August, 1937), 415–17; "Racial Purity," *Asia*, 40 (May, 1940), 230–34; and *Race, Language and Culture* (New York, 1966), passim.

25. Ruth Benedict, *Race: Science and Politics* (New York, 1940); M. F. Ashley Montagu, *Man's Most Dangerous Myth: The Fallacy of Race* (New York, 1942); Jacques Barzun, *Race: A Study in Modern Superstition* (New York, 1937); and Paul Radin, *The Racial Myth* (New York, 1934).

26. Quoted in Benedict, *Race*, 263.

27. *New York Times*, December 11, 1938, Section 1, 50/1.

28. *New York Times*, December 24, 1939, 8/1.

29. Marvin Harris, *The Rise of Anthropological Theory* (London, 1968), 291.

30. Robert M. Hutchins, "The Proposition Is Peace," *Vital Speeches of the Day*, 7 (April 15, 1941), 391. See also Hutchins, "The Path to War," ibid., 7 (February 15, 1941), 258–61; and "Dark Hours in Our History," ibid., 7 (July 1, 1941), 569–70.

31. *New York Times*, May 13, 1940, 10/1.

32. Adler, *The Isolationist Impulse*, 245–46.

33. Donald Meyer, *The Protestant Search for Political Realism, 1919–1941* (Berkeley, Calif., 1960), 351, 354, 374.

34. "On Saving Civilization," *Christian Century*, 57 (May 8, 1940), 598.

35. Divine, *Illusion of Neutrality*, 309.

36. "We Conscientiously Object," *America*, 61 (September 2, 1939), 493.

37. Quoted in Chadwin, *The Warhawks*, 147.

38. "Action and More Action," *Commonweal*, 33 (April 11, 1941), 611.

39. Divine, *Illusion of Neutrality*, 305–6.

40. See note 4, and especially Jonas, *Isolationism in America* and Adler, *The Isolationist Impulse*.

41. J. Roland Pennock, "Political Science and Political Philosophy," *American Political Science Review*, 45 (December, 1951), 1085.

42. Joseph Ratner, review of *Approaches to World Peace*, ed. Lyman Bryson, Louis Finkelstein, and Robert M. MacIver, *Journal of Philosophy*, 42 (April 26, 1945), 248.

13. Relativist Democratic Theory & Postwar America

1. For a sample of the natural rights argument see Leo Strauss, *Natural Right and History* (Chicago, 1953); Strauss, *What Is Political Philosophy?* (Glencoe, Ill., 1959); John H. Hallowell, "Politics and Ethics," *American Political Science Review*, 38 (August, 1944), 639–55; Hallowell, "Plato and His Critics," *Journal of Politics*, 27 (May, 1965), 273–89. For versions of the relativist theory see *Democracy in a World of Tensions: A Symposium Prepared by UNESCO*, ed. Richard McKeon (Chicago, 1951), especially 210 and 502; Leland DeWitt Baldwin, *Best Hope of Earth: A Grammar of Democracy* (Pittsburgh, Pa., 1948); Charner M. Perry, *The Philosophy of American Democracy* (Chicago, 1943), ix–xv; Hans Kelsen, "Absolutism and Relativism in Philosophy and Politics," *American Political Science Review*, 42 (October, 1948), 906–14; Richard Wollheim, "Democracy," *Journal of the History of Ideas*, 19 (April, 1958), 241; Pendleton Herring, "On the Study of Government," *American Political Science Review*, 47 (September, 1953), 961–74; Walter M. Simon, "John Locke: Philosophy and Political Theory," *American Political Science Review*, 45 (June, 1951), 395; Alan P. Grimes, "The Pragmatic Course of Liberalism," *Western Political Quarterly*, 9 (September, 1956), 633–40; David B. Truman, "The American System in Crisis," *Political Science Quarterly*, 74 (December, 1959), 486–91; Herman Finer, "Towards a Democratic Theory," *American Political Science Review*, 39 (April, 1945), 249–68; G. Watts Cunningham, "Reason, Morality, and Democracy," in Milton R. Konvitz and Arthur E. Murray, eds., *Essays in Political Theory Presented to George H. Sabine* (Ithaca, N. Y., 1948); Sidney Hook, *Political Power and Personal Freedom: Critical Studies in Democracy, Communism and Civil Rights* (New York, 1962), especially Chapters 1–5. Perhaps the most complete logical reformulation is in Thomas Landon Thorson, *The Logic of Democracy* (New York, 1962). One of the most recent restatements is Herbert J. Spiro, *Politics as the Master Science: From Plato to Mao* (New York, 1970), 14–18.

2. Sixth Report of the Rockefeller Brothers Fund Special Studies Project, *The Power of the Democratic Idea* (Garden City, N. Y., 1960), 17–18, 5.

3. Gabriel A. Almond, *The Appeals of Communism* (Princeton, N. J., 1954), 374, 375.

4. Earl Latham, "The Group Basis of Politics: Notes for a Theory," *American Political Science Review*, 46 (June, 1952), 397. For the spread of the totalitarian image of the Soviet Union see Les K. Adler and Thomas G. Paterson, "Red Fascism: The Merger of Nazi Germany and Soviet Russia in the American Image of Totalitarianism, 1930's–1950's," *American Historical Review*, 75 (April, 1970), 1046–64; and also the critical exchange concerning the essay, *American Historical Review*, 75 (December, 1970), 2155–64. In this context I believe it is important that Nazi Germany and Soviet Russia did not in fact present *identical* threats to the United States, but my purpose here is only to suggest 1) that the identification of Nazi Germany and the Soviet Union grew in part out of certain fundamental theoretical assumptions that American intellectuals shared and hence were crucial parts of a much broader pattern of thought, and 2) that all of these joined, often unconsciously, to induce many Americans to perceive their own nation in certain ethical and institutional terms, which help explain

American history in the postwar years and which were in themselves highly questionable.

5. See for example the essay of the widely respected Swedish sociologist, Gunnar Myrdal, "The Relation between Social Theory and Social Policy," *British Journal of Sociology*, 4 (September, 1953), 210–42; Gabriel A. Almond, "Politics, Science, and Ethics," *American Political Science Review*, 40 (April, 1946), 283–94; David Easton, "The Decline of Modern Political Theory," *Journal of Politics*, 13 (February, 1951), 36–58; David Easton, *The Political System: An Inquiry into the State of Political Science* (New York, 1953); Dwight Waldo, " 'Values' in the Political Science Curriculum," in Roland Young, ed., *Approaches to the Study of Politics* (Evanston, Ill., 1958), 96–111; Robert E. Lane, *The Liberties of Wit* (New Haven, Conn., 1961).

6. See especially Harold D. Lasswell and Abraham Kaplan, *Power and Society: A Framework for Political Inquiry* (New Haven, Conn., 1950), especially ix–xxiv; Daniel Lerner and Harold D. Lasswell, eds., *The Policy Sciences: Recent Developments in Scope and Method* (Stanford, Calif., 1951).

7. Richard H. Rovere, *Senator Joe McCarthy* (New York, 1963 [1959]), 36–37.

8. Robert I. Gannon, S.J., "What Are We Really Fighting?" *Fordham Law Review*, 11 (November, 1942), 254.

9. Michael Paul Rogin, *The Intellectuals and McCarthy: The Radical Spectre* (Cambridge, Mass., 1969 [1967]), 238–39; Richard Hofstadter, *The Paranoid Style in American Politics and Other Essays* (New York, 1967), 69–82; Hofstadter, *Anti-Intellectualism in American Life* (New York, 1963), 129–41.

10. Daniel Bell, ed., *The Radical Right: The New American Right Expanded and Updated* (New York, 1964), 64.

11. Rogin's *Intellectuals and McCarthy* is an excellent study of the relationship between McCarthyism and the growing conservative orientation of pluralist social theory. See also Peter Bachrach, *The Theory of Democratic Elitism: A Critique* (Boston, 1967), especially 29–35. Samuel A. Stouffer, *Communism, Conformity, and Civil Liberties: A Cross-Section of the Nation Speaks Its Mind* (New York, 1955), which produced empirical evidence to indicate that elites in fact did hold more sophisticated and "liberal" views on such questions as civil liberties, was widely influential among intellectuals in the fifties and early sixties. See, for example, Herbert H. Hyman, "England and America; Climates of Tolerance and Intolerance," in Bell, ed., *The Radical Right*, 269–306.

12. Quoted in June Bingham, *Courage to Change: An Introduction to the Life and Thought of Reinhold Niebuhr* (New York, 1961), 224.

13. Reinhold Niebuhr, *Beyond Tragedy: Essays on the Christian Interpretation of History* (New York, 1965 [1937]), 44, 45, 44.

14. Reinhold Niebuhr, *The Nature and Destiny of Man: A Christian Interpretation*, vol. 2, *Human Destiny* (New York, 1963 [1943]), 214.

15. Ibid., vol. 1, *Human Nature* (New York, 1964 [1941]), 17.

16. Ibid., 2:217.

17. Ibid., 2:219.

18. Reinhold Niebuhr, *The Children of Light and the Children of Darkness— A Vindication of Democracy and a Critique of Its Traditional Defense* (New York, 1960 [1944]), 70–71.

19. Ibid., 128. See also Niebuhr, *The Nature and Destiny of Man*, 1:201–2, 220–21, and 2:220–25.

20. Niebuhr, *Children of Light and Children of Darkness*, 150.

21. See Arthur Schlesinger, Jr.'s essay "Reinhold Niebuhr's Role in American Political Thought and Life," in *The Politics of Hope* (Boston, 1963), 97–125.

22. Reinhold Niebuhr, *The Irony of American History* (New York, 1952), 109, 19, 16, 21, 22, 122, 67.

23. Ibid., 79, 34, 31. See also Chapter 5.

24. Daniel J. Boorstin, *The Mysterious Science of the Law* (Cambridge, Mass., 1941), vii.

25. Ibid., 6.

26. Ibid., 198, note 57. For a general and somewhat different treatment of Boorstin see David W. Noble, *Historians against History: The Frontier Thesis and the National Covenant in American Historical Writing since 1830* (Minneapolis, Minn., 1965), 157–75.

27. Boorstin, *Mysterious Science of the Law*, 191.

28. Daniel J. Boorstin, *The Lost World of Thomas Jefferson* (Boston, 1963 [1948]), xi–xii.

29. Ibid., 200.

30. Ibid., 8.

31. Ibid., 246. For Boorstin's doubts and criticism concerning the thought of the Jeffersonian circle see ibid., 7–8, 29, 123, 130–31, 136–39, 163–66, 169–71, 193, 198, 216–17, 224–25.

32. Ibid., 112.

33. Ibid., 170–71.

34. Ibid., xi.

35. Daniel J. Boorstin, *The Genius of American Politics* (Chicago, 1962 [1953]), 3.

36. Daniel J. Boorstin, *The Americans: The Colonial Experience* (New York, 1958), 193.

37. Ibid., 154.

38. Ibid., 168.

39. Boorstin, *Genius of American Politics*, 184, 185–86.

40. Morris Janowitz and Dwaine Marick, "Authoritarianism and Political Behavior," *Public Opinion Quarterly*, 17 (Summer, 1953), 186.

41. See also T. W. Adorno et al., *The Authoritarian Personality* (New York, 1950); Morris Rosenberg, "Misanthropy and Political Ideology," *American Sociological Review*, 21 (December, 1956), 690–95; Herbert McClosky, "Conservatism and Personality," *American Political Science Review*, 52 (March, 1958), 27–45; David M. Levy, "Anti-Nazis: Criteria of Differentiation," in Alfred H. Stanton and Steward M. Perry, *Personality and Political Crisis: New Perspectives from Social Science and Psychiatry for the Study of War and Politics* (Glencoe, Ill., 1951), 151–227.

42. David Riesman with Nathan Glazer and Reuel Denney, *The Lonely Crowd: A Study of the Changing American Character* (New Haven, Conn., 1961 [1950]), 223.

43. V. O. Key, Jr., *Politics, Parties, and Pressure Groups* (New York, 1958), 9–10.

44. See especially David B. Truman, *The Governmental Process: Political Interests and Public Opinion* (New York, 1958), especially vii–xii and Chapter 2; and V. O. Key, Jr., *Politics, Parties, and Pressure Groups*, Chapters 1–6. A useful evaluation and bibliography of group theorists and their critics can be found in Darryl Basken, "American Pluralism: Theory, Practice, and Ideology," *Journal of Politics*, 32 (February, 1970), 71–95.

45. Rogin, *Intellectuals and McCarthy*, 277–78, argues the same point.

46. Benjamin F. Wright, *Consensus and Continuity*, 1776–1787 (New York, 1967 [1958]), 57, 39.

47. Ralph Barton Perry, "The Moral Norm of Social Science," *Journal of Social Philosophy*, 5 (October, 1939), 17.

48. Boorstin, *Genius of American Politics*, 175, 38. On this point see John P. Diggins, "Consciousness and Ideology in American History: The Burden of Daniel J. Boorstin," *American Historical Review*, 76 (February, 1971), 101–5 and *passim*.

49. Robert A. Dahl and Charles E. Lindblom, *Politics, Economics, and Welfare* (New York, 1953), 3, 6. For their use of the relativist criteria, see 25–28, 42–43.

50. Louis Hartz, "Democracy: Image and Reality," in W. N. Chambers and R. N. Salisbury, *Democracy in Mid-20th Century* (St. Louis, Mo., 1960), 29. Though Hartz accepted the contention that the United States was dominated by a unique and "liberal" consensus, and shared many of the assumptions behind the relativist theory, he was one of the few academic intellectuals to specifically emphasize the undesirable and even undemocratic aspects of American society. In fact, were it possible to discuss the critics of the dominant postwar attitudes, Hartz would be among the most suggestive. He saw clearly the oppressive and "absolutistic" qualities of the American consensus and criticized it in terms of the relativist theory itself. The "heart of the problem," he commented, resided in a unique kind of "American liberal absolutism." (See *The Liberal Tradition in America: An Interpretation of American Political Thought since the Revolution* (New York, 1955), 302 and *passim*.) Although Hartz was widely respected, his fellow social scientists did not fully understand, much less accept, the theoretical basis of his critique. As Marx had stood Hegel on his head, Hartz attempted almost as much with the dominant application of the relativist theory.

51. Bernard R. Berelson, Paul F. Lazarsfeld, and William N. McPhee, *Voting: A Study of Opinion Formation in a Presidential Campaign* (Chicago, 1963), especially Chapter 14; Robert E. Lane, *Political Ideology: Why the American Common Man Believes What He Does* (New York, 1962); Angus Campbell, Philip E. Converse, Warren E. Muller, and Donald E. Stokes, *The American Voter* (New York, 1960), especially Chapters 19 and 20.

52. Joseph A. Schumpeter, *Capitalism, Socialism and Democracy* (New York, 1962 [1942]), 269.

53. Berelson et al., *Voting*, 322.

54. V. O. Key, Jr., *Public Opinion and American Democracy* (New York, 1961), 556–58; David B. Truman, "The American System in Crisis," *Political Science Quarterly*, 74 (December, 1959), 481–97; Robert E. Lane, *Political Ideology*, 79–81; Robert A. Dahl, *Who Governs? Democracy and Power in an American City* (New Haven, Conn., 1961), 315–25.

55. Robert E. Lane, *Political Life: Why People Get Involved in Politics* (Glencoe, Ill., 1959), 348.

56. Robert A. Dahl, *A Preface to Democratic Theory* (Chicago, 1963 [1956]), 143. For an early critique of Dahl accompanied by a rejoinder see *American Political Science Review*, 51 (December, 1957), 1040–61. For Dahl's sympathetic, though not wholly convinced, view of the ethical logic of the relativist theory see "Political Theory: Truth and Consequences," *World Politics*, 11 (October, 1958), 100–101.

57. Dahl, *Who Governs?*, especially 224–25, 277–81.

58. Ibid., 91.

59. Dahl, *Preface to Democratic Theory*, 92.

60. Truman, *Governmental Process*, 524.

61. Lane Davis, "The Cost of Realism: Contemporary Restatements of Democracy," *Western Political Quarterly*, 17 (March, 1964), 37–45, is an excellent critique of realist theory on that point. Dahl himself was well aware of some of the evaluative problems in political science: see Robert A. Dahl, "The Evaluation of Political Systems," in *Contemporary Political Science: Towards Empirical Theory*, ed. Ithiel de Sola Pool (New York, 1967), 166–81. Pluralism never met with total acceptance. Some criticism appeared in the fifties, and by the middle sixties it was becoming quite common. See Rogin, *Intellectuals and McCarthy*; Bachrach, *Theory of Democratic Elitism*; Jack L. Walker, "A Critique of the Elitist Theory of Democracy," *American Political Science Review*, 60 (June, 1966), 285–95; Joseph LaPalombara, "Decline of Ideology: A Dissent and an Interpretation," *American Political Science Review*, 60 (March, 1966), 5–16; Darryl Basken, "American Pluralism: Theory, Practice, and Ideology," *Journal of Politics*, 32 (February, 1970), 71–95; Theodore Lowi, "The Public Philosophy: Interest-Group Liberalism," *American Political Science Review*, 61 (March, 1967), 5–24; and Theodore Lowi, "American Business, Public Policy, Case-Studies, and Political Theory," *World Politics*, 16 (July, 1964), 677–715. For restatements and revisions of pluralism see Robert E. Lane, "The Politics of Consensus in an Age of Affluence," *American Political Science Review*, 59 (December, 1965), 874–95; Seymour Martin Lipset, "Some Further Comments on the 'End of Ideology,'" *American Political Science Review*, 60 (March, 1966), 17–18; and Robert A. Dahl, "Further Reflections on 'the Elitist Theory of Democracy,'" *American Political Science Review*, 60 (June, 1966), 296–305.

62. For a representative sampling of Parsons's work see *The Social System* (New York, 1951); *Essays in Sociological Theory* (New York, 1954); and *The Structure of Social Action* (New York, 1937), 2 volumes. For Easton's work see *The Political System: An Inquiry into the State of Political Science* (New York, 1953); *A Framework for Political Analysis* (Englewood Cliffs, N. J., 1965); and *A Systems Analysis of Political Life* (New York, 1965). Easton has consistently been aware of the status quo problems with empirical systems theory: see especially *Political System*, Chapters 2 and 10 and *Framework*, Chapter 6. For analyses of the relationship between empiricism and social conservativism see Robert S. Lynd, *Knowledge for What? The Place of Social Science in American Culture* (Princeton, N. J., 1939), especially 119–22; C. Wright Mills, *The Sociological Imagination* (New York, 1959), especially Chapters 2 and 3; Herbert Marcuse, *One-Dimensional Man: Studies in the Ideology of Advanced Industrial Society* (Boston, 1964), especially Chapters 1 and 7; and Tom Bottomore, "Out of This World," *New York Review of Books*, (November 6, 1969), 34–39.

63. Lucian W. Pye, *Politics, Personality, and Nation Building: Burma's Search for Identity* (New Haven, Conn., 1962), 3.

64. See David B. Truman, "Disillusion and Regeneration: The Quest for a Discipline," *American Political Science Review*, 59 (December, 1965), 868–69; and Gabriel A. Almond, "Political Theory and Political Science," *American Political Science Review*, 60 (December, 1966), especially 876–78.

65. Gabriel A. Almond, "Comparative Political Systems," *Journal of Politics*, 18 (August, 1956), 396.

66. Ibid., 398, 400. For Almond's earlier acceptance of a pragmatic value theory see "Politics, Science, and Ethics," *American Political Science Review*, 40 (April, 1946), 283–94.

67. Gabriel A. Almond, "Comparative Political Systems," *Journal of Politics*, 18 (August, 1956), 401, 406, 408.

68. Ibid., 408, 406, 407, 403, 401.

69. Gabriel A. Almond and Sidney Verba, *The Civic Culture: An Analytic Study, Political Attitudes and Democracy in Five Nations* (Boston, 1965), 366, 338.

70. James S. Coleman, "Conclusion: The Political Systems of the Developing Areas," in Gabriel A. Almond and James S. Coleman, eds., *The Politics of Developing Areas* (Princeton, N. J., 1960), 533.

71. Edward A. Shils, *The Torment of Secrecy: The Background and Consequences of American Security Policies* (Glencoe, Ill., 1956), 225.

14. America as a Normative Concept

1. The critical literature has already grown to immense proportions. See, for example, Chapter 13, notes 50 and 61 and the following: Philip Green and Sanford Levinson, eds., *Power and Community: Dissenting Essays in Political Science* (New York, 1970); Noam Chomsky, *American Power and the New Mandarins* (New York, 1969); James J. Graham, *The Enemies of the Poor* (New York, 1971); Christopher Lasch, *The Agony of the American Left* (New York, 1969); Barton J. Bernstein, ed., *Towards a New Past: Dissenting Essays in American History* (New York, 1969); Gabriel Kolko, *The Triumph of Conservatism: A Reinterpretation of American History, 1900–1916* (New York, 1963).

2. Thomas S. Kuhn, *The Structure of Scientific Revolutions* (Chicago, 1962). Broad criticism and reinterpretation of Kuhn's approach appeared in Imre Lakatos and Alan Musgrave, eds., *Criticism and the Growth of Knowledge* (Cambridge, Mass., 1970) and Frederick Suppe, ed., *The Structure of Scientific Theories* (Urbana, Ill., 1971). For an especially revealing difference in interpretation compare David B. Truman, "Disillusion and Regeneration: The Quest for a Discipline," *American Political Science Review*, 59 (December, 1965), 865–73 and Gabriel A. Almond, "Political Theory and Political Science," *American Political Science Review*, 60 (December, 1966), 869–79 with the general use of Kuhn's approach in the essays in Green and Levinson, eds., *Power and Community*. For examples of the fundamental attack on the idea of the objectivity of human knowledge see Michael Polanyi, *Personal Knowledge; Towards a Post-Critical Philosophy* (Chicago, 1958); Max Black, *Studies in Method and Language* (Ithaca, N. Y., 1959); Floyd W. Matson, *The Broken Image: Man, Science and Society* (New York, 1964); J. J. Katz, *The Philosophy of Language* (New York, 1966).

3. See for example Loren Baritz, *City on a Hill: A History of Ideas and Myths in America* (New York, 1964) and Paul C. Nagel, *This Sacred Trust: American Nationality, 1798–1898*. For the kinds of ambivalence Americans felt about their new country see Henry Nash Smith, *Virgin Land: The American West as Symbol and Myth* (Cambridge, Mass., 1950); Leo Marx, *The Machine in the Garden: Technology and the Pastoral Idea in America* (New York, 1964); Howard Mumford Jones, *O Strange New World: American Culture: The Formative Years* (New York, 1964).

4. Perry Miller, *Nature's Nation* (Cambridge, Mass., 1967), 174.

A Note on Sources

It would be unwise and useless to list all of the individual works on which the present study is based. The most complete bibliography is contained in the footnotes of the various chapters. The following comments are intended only to indicate some of the more important sources on which I have drawn as well as to suggest useful introductions to the fields and problems discussed.

For the sake of convenience I have frequently used paperback editions. These are indicated in the notes by the inclusion of two publication dates, the first giving the date of the edition used, the second the date of the original publication.

All students of intellectual history are aware of such standard surveys as Merle Curti, *The Growth of American Thought* (New York, 1964), Henry Steele Commager, *The American Mind: An Interpretation of American Thought and Character since the 1880's* (New Haven, Conn., 1950), Stow Persons, *American Minds: A History of Ideas* (New York, 1958), and Ralph Henry Gabriel, *The Course of American Democratic Thought: An Intellectual History since 1815* (New York, 1956). The third edition (1964) of Curti's book contains an elaborate and expanded bibliography. David Noble, *The Progressive Mind, 1890–1917* (Chicago, 1970), Roderick Nash, *The Nervous Generation: American Thought 1917–1930* (Chicago, 1970), and Charles C. Alexander, *Nationalism in American Thought, 1930–1945* (Chicago, 1969) provide the most recent summaries of American thought in the twentieth century, though they suffer from rather artificial chronological divisions. All contain large and helpful bibliographies. *Perspectives in American History*, Vol. 2, *The Intellectual Migration: Europe and America, 1930–1960*, ed. Donald Fleming and Bernard Bailyn (Cambridge, Mass., 1968) sheds much light on an important but little studied aspect of American intellectual history. Laura Fermi presents a more personal account of the same migration in *Illustrious Immigrants: The Intellectual Migration from Europe, 1930–1941* (Chicago, 1968).

In *Social Darwinism in American Thought* (Boston, 1955) Richard Hofstadter traces the impact of Darwinian evolution on American intellectuals between the Civil War and World War I, while the essays collected in *Evolutionary Thought in America* (Hamden, Conn., 1968), edited by Stow Persons, discuss the influence of naturalism on a number of particular fields, including philosophy and some of the social sciences. Paul F. Boller, Jr., has written the most recent account of the same developments in *American Thought in Transition: The Impact of Evolutionary Naturalism, 1865–1900* (Chicago, 1969).

316

Much of the historiography has emphasized the liberal and reform attitudes of American intellectuals, noting the general problems of "relativism" and naturalism. David Noble, *The Paradox of Progressive Thought* (Minneapolis, Minn., 1958), Daniel Aaron, *Men of Good Hope: A Story of American Progressives* (New York, 1951), Eric F. Goldman, *Rendezvous with Destiny: A History of Modern American Reform* (New York, 1952), and Richard Hofstadter, *The Age of Reform: From Bryan to F.D.R.* (New York, 1955) have been among the most influential studies of reform intellectuals. Henry May's *The End of American Innocence: A Study of the First Years of Our Own Time 1912–1917* (Chicago, 1959) examines changing ideas in the years immediately before World War I. May focuses on artists and literary figures, but he deals to some extent with social theorists and his conclusions are framed in a broad context. Though restricted to five individuals—Beard, Carl Becker, Holmes, Veblen, and Dewey—Morton White's *Social Thought in America: The Revolt against Formalism* (New York, 1949) is excellent.

Emphasizing the social role of intellectuals, Christopher Lasch provides a series of provocative intellectual biographies in *The New Radicalism in America 1889–1963* (New York, 1965). Lasch's essay "The Cultural Cold War: A Short History of the Congress for Cultural Freedom," which appears in *Towards a New Past: Dissenting Essays in American History* (New York, 1969), edited by Barton J. Bernstein, applies his interpretation of the social role of intellectuals specifically to the cold war period. Lewis Coser, *Men of Ideas: A Sociologist's View* (New York, 1965) attempts a sociological analysis of the position of intellectuals with a special emphasis on twentieth century America. Tracing changing ideas throughout the period of the 1950s, Robert A. Skotheim's *American Intellectual History and Historians* (Princeton, N. J., 1966) gives attention to the impact of historical relativism and totalitarianism. Frank Warren, *Liberals and Communism: The "Red Decade" Revisited* (Bloomington, Ind., 1966) and Arthur A. Ekirch, *Ideologies and Utopias: The Impact of the New Deal on American Thought* (Chicago, 1971) examine the social ideas of a number of Americans during the thirties. Many of the essays in *Paths of American Thought* (Boston, 1963), edited by Arthur Schlesinger, Jr., and Morton White, are quite valuable. Michael Rogin deals particularly with social scientists in his excellent analysis of post-World War II social theory, *The Intellectuals and McCarthy: The Radical Spectre* (Cambridge, Mass., 1967). Rogin's study is an analysis of populism, an intellectual history of the fifties, and a moderate statement of the emergent participatory democratic theory of the sixties.

The Journal of the History of the Behavioral Sciences (Brandon, Vt., 1965–) provides one of the major sources for the history of the social sciences, though its articles tend to be somewhat narrowly conceived.

Floyd W. Matson's *The Broken Image: Man, Science and Society* (New York, 1964) makes a useful contrast, offering a broad interpretive study of social science theory from the eighteenth to the mid-twentieth century. Loren Baritz, *The Servants of Power: A History of the Use of Social Science in American Industry* (Middletown, Conn., 1960) and Richard S. Kirkendall, *Social Scientists and Farm Politics in the Age of Roosevelt* (Columbia, Mo., 1966) reach strikingly dissimilar conclusions about the political roles of two different groups of social scientists.

Peter L. Berger, *Invitation to Sociology: A Humanistic Perspective* (New York, 1964) is an excellent discussion of the philosophical problems of the social sciences, and his examination of *The Social Construction of Reality: A Treatise in the Sociology of Knowledge* (New York, 1966), written with Thomas Luckmann, outlines some of the central questions in the sociology of knowledge. Richard S. Rudner's *Philosophy of Social Science* (Englewood Cliffs, N. J., 1966) restates the empiricist position; Peter Winch develops an antiempiricist approach in *The Idea of a Social Science and Its Relation to Philosophy* (New York, 1965). Gunnar Myrdal's *Objectivity in Social Research* (New York, 1969) is a recent discussion of some of the main assumptions of contemporary social science.

There are a number of histories of the various social sciences, and the next few years should produce an increasing number of valuable contributions. *American Scholarship in the Twentieth Century* (Cambridge, Mass., 1953), edited by Merle Curti, is a convenient starting point. Edwin G. Boring, *A History of Experimental Psychology* (New York, 1957) is still the definitive source for its subject. Walter Bromberg, *The Mind of Man: A History of Psychotherapy and Psychoanalysis* (New York, 1954) covers another major area in the field's history. Robert Thomson, *The Pelican History of Psychology* (Middlesex, England, 1968) and A. A. Roback, *A History of American Psychology* (New York, 1964) provide broader overviews. Eric Roll, *A History of Economic Thought* (Englewood Cliffs, N. J., 1958) and Joseph A. Schumpeter, *History of Economic Analysis* (New York, 1954), edited from manuscript by Elizabeth Boody Schumpeter, are standard histories of economic ideas. Joseph Dorfman's sweeping work *The Economic Mind in American Civilization, 1606–1933*, 5 vols. (New York, 1946–1959) is the most comprehensive study of the field in the United States. Marvin Harris's perceptive work *The Rise of Anthropological Theory* (London, 1968) is one of the finest pieces of scholarship on the history of the social sciences available. The work devotes considerable attention to Boas and his students and includes a massive bibliography. *Culture: A Critical Review of Concepts and Definitions* (New York, 1963), edited by A. L. Kroeber and Clyde Kluckhohn, is a useful survey of anthropological writings, and George W. Stocking, *Race, Culture,* and *Evolution: Essays in the History of Anthropology* (New York, 1968) is perceptive and thoughtful. Bernard Crick's *The American Science of Politics: Its Origins and Conditions* (Berkeley, 1959) is still the best source available on the history of political science, though its scope is somewhat narrower than it might be. Albert Somit and Joseph Tanenhaus provide an interesting examination of political science as an established academic field in *American Political Science, a Profile of a Discipline* (New York, 1964). Maurice R. Stein, *The Eclipse of Community: An Interpretation of American Studies* (Princeton, N. J., 1960) discusses aspects of American sociology in the twentieth century, and Floyd N. House's *The Development of Sociology* (New York, 1936) is a useful contemporary view of the discipline's past. Pitirim A. Sorokin's *Contemporary Sociological Theories* (New York, 1928), though outdated in many ways, is still the most comprehensive analysis of the variety of sociological theories. John H. Madge, *The Origins of Scientific Sociology* (New York, 1962) and Howard W. Odum, *American Sociology: The State of Sociology in the United States through 1950* (New York, 1951) are helpful surveys of sociological developments in the twentieth century. Interesting material on Chicago's prestigious department is available in Robert E. L. Faris, *Chicago Sociology, 1920–1932* (San Francisco, 1967). Edwin Patterson's *Jurisprudence: Men and Ideas of the Law* (Brooklyn, N. Y., 1953) is a useful introduction by one of the leading realists. Perry Miller's thoughtful work *The Life of the Mind in America from the Revolution to the Civil War* (New York, 1965) contains an extended treatment of legal thought; *Perspectives in American History*, Vol. 5, *Law in American History*, ed. Donald Fleming and Bernard Bailyn (Cambridge, Mass., 1971) contains a variety of essays relating to the law. Karl Llewellyn's *The Common Law Tradition: Deciding Appeals* (Boston, 1960) is somewhat technical but nevertheless very suggestive to the historian. Eugene V. Rostow discusses twentieth century legal thought in *The Sovereign Prerogative: The Supreme Court and the Quest for Law* (New Haven, Conn., 1962), 3–44. Wilfred Rumble, Jr., attempts to analyze the legal doctrines behind realism in *American Legal Realism: Skepticism, Reform, and the Judicial Process* (Ithaca, N. Y., 1968).

There are a number of helpful works in the history of philosophy. Herbert W. Schneider, *A History of American Philosophy* (New York, 1963) and Joseph L. Blau, *Men and Movements in American Philosophy* (New York, 1952) are standard treatments. *A Critical History of Western Philosophy* (New York, 1964), edited by D. J. O'Connor, contains several good analyses of nineteenth and twentieth century philosophy in both the United States and Europe. *The Encyclopaedia of Philosophy*, 8 vols. (New York, 1967), edited by Paul Edwards, is helpful on innumerable problems.

Developments in American education are summarized in Lawrence A.

Cremin, *The Transformation of the School: Progressivism in American Education, 1876–1957* (New York, 1961); Isaac L. Kandel, *American Education in the Twentieth Century* (Cambridge, Mass., 1957); Edgar W. Knight, *Fifty Years of American Education* (New York, 1962); and William Clyde De-Vane, *Higher Education in Twentieth-Century America* (Cambridge, Mass., 1965). Frederick Rudolph, *The American College and University: A History* (New York, 1962) and *Higher Education in Transition: An American History: 1936–1956* (New York, 1958) by John S. Brubacher and Willis Rudy are broader surveys. Lawrence R. Vesey's *The Emergence of the American University* (Chicago, 1965) is a perceptive study of the transition decades at the end of the nineteenth century. For a discussion of conflicting educational philosophies, the most recent edition of Merle Curti's *The Social Ideas of American Educators* (Paterson, N. J., 1963) is valuable and enlightening.

For political theory itself, George H. Sabine, *A History of Political Theory* (New York, 1961) is the most comprehensive and perceptive introduction, while Sheldon M. Wolin's *The Politics of Vision: Continuity and Innovation in Western Political Thought* (Boston, 1960) is stimulating and insightful. In his *Contemporary Political Thought: A Critical Study* (Homewood, Ill., 1967) Eugene J. Meehan analyzes the political ideas of a number of twentieth century intellectuals, focusing on various groups of social scientists. Arnold Brecht's massive and closely argued *Political Theory: The Foundations of Twentieth-Century Political Thought* (Princeton, N. J., 1959) is the most sophisticated analysis of the problems presented to traditional democratic theory by the "relativism" and scientific naturalism of the twentieth century. Thomas Landon Thorson has attempted the most sustained recent effort to establish the theoretical and moral foundations of democratic theory from a scientific naturalist viewpoint in *The Logic of Democracy* (New York, 1962). Henry Mayo, *An Introduction to Democratic Theory* (New York, 1960) contains useful accounts of many of the basic problems of democratic theory, while Peter Bachrach, *The Theory of Democratic Elitism: A Critique* (Boston, 1967) provides both a summary and analysis of elite democratic theory. Theodore J. Lowi has critically and provocatively examined American political assumptions since the New Deal in his book *The End of Liberalism: Ideology, Policy, and the Crisis of Public Authority* (New York, 1969).

Index

absolutism, philosophical, as basis of totalitarianism, 200–205; as cultural force, 212

absolutism, opposition to and status quo orientation, 253–54

absolutist-relativist dichotomy, 202, 210, 238, 240, 242, 247, 251, 252, 254–56, 266. *See also* relativist theory of democracy

Adams, James Truslow, 127

Addams, Jane, 25

Adler, Mortimer J., 3, 92, 141, 145, 150, 151, 169, 176, 202, 203, 218–19, 225, 228

Agar, Herbert, 222, 229

Allport, Floyd H., 97, 107, 204

Allport, Gordon, 97

Almond, Gabriel A., 238, 263–65

America, 229

American Anthropological Association, 227

American Bar Association, 78, 79

American Catholic Philosophical Association, 165

American Economic Association, 28

"American Friends of Italian Freedom," 123

American Jewish Congress, 130

American Law Institute, 80, 248

American Liberty League, 171

American Political Science Association, 17, 28, 190, 237

American Psychological Association, 227

American Sociological Society, 28

American Statistical Association, 33

Americans, The: The Colonial Experience (Daniel Boorstin), 252

Americans for Democratic Action, 246

anti-democratic thought, 100–101, 117, 126–27

Anti-Fascist Alliance of North America, 123

Anthropology (Albert L. Kroeber), 21

anthropology, 16, 20–21; and non-Euclideanism, see chapter 4

Aquinas, 145, 149

Aristotelian logic, attack on, 56–64

Aristotelianism, see neo-Aristotelianism

Aristotle, 56, 60, 61, 63, 145, 149

Armstrong, Hamilton Fish, 137

Arnold, Thurman, 80, 93, 11–14, 159–60, 167, 175, 177, 197–99

Aronson, Moses J., 196

Ascoli, Max, 133, 181

Ashley-Montagu, M. F., 20, 227

Association of American Law Schools, 78–79

Atwood, Harry Fuller, 100

Augustine, 155

"Authoritarian Attempt to Capture Education, The," 204

authoritarian personality, 253–54

Babbitt, Irving, 100

Bain, Read, 19, 22, 23, 26, 34, 194

Baldwin, James Mark, 16

Balz, Albert, 183

Barden, John P., 4

Barnes, Harry Elmer, 42, 100–101, 189, 227

Barr, Stringfellow, 150, 225, 228

Barth, Karl, 155

Barzun, Jacques, 213, 216, 227

Beard, Charles A., 17, 40, 62, 64, 123, 191, 192, 225

Beard, Mary, 130

Becker, Carl L., 188

Becker, Howard, 19, 22, 189

behavioralism, 240

behaviorism, 18, 34–38, 194–96. *See also* objectivism; scientific naturalism

Bell, Daniel, 241, 242

Bell, Eric Temple, 59–61, 188

Benedict, Ruth, 20, 70, 227

Bentley, Arthur F., 17, 39, 137, 194, 254

Berle, A. A., Jr., 19, 39, 86, 237

Bernard, Luther L., 19, 22, 23, 26, 36–38, 39, 40–41, 194

Beutel, Frederick K., 160

Beyle, Herman C., 97

Beyond Conscience (T. V. Smith), 208

Binet, Alfred, 32

Bliven, Bruce, 204

Blumberg, Albert E., 55

Blumer, Herbert, 19, 23

Boas, Franz, 20, 24, 40, 67, 69, 71, 100, 227–28

Bode, Boyd M., 210
Bodenheimer, Edgar, 161, 164
Bohr, Niels, 57
bolshevism, 117–21, 201. See also communism; Soviet Union
Bolyai, Farkas, 50
Boole, George, 54
Boorstin, Daniel, 243, 247–53, 257–58
Borgese, Guiseppe, 133
Boring, Edwin G., 98
Brandeis, Louis D., 76, 167
Brecht, Arnold, 181
Brest-Litovsk, treaty of, 118
Bridgman, Percy W., 38, 137, 195
Briefs, Goetz, 179
Brigham, Carl C., 100
Brooks, Van Wyck, 222
Brown, Brendan, 164, 165, 166
Buchanan, Scott, 150
Bullard, Arthur, 118
Burbank, Luther, 6
Burgess, Ernest W., 19
Business Cycles and Unemployment (Wesley Mitchell), 33
Business Week, 129
Butler, Nicholas Murray, 126

Cahan, Abraham, 130
Cardozo, Benjamin N., 74, 77, 167
Carlson, Anton J., 3, 150, 204
Carmichael, Oliver C., 149
Carnap, Rudolph, 48, 61
Carnegie, Andrew, 7
Carnegie Corporation of New York, 28
Carver, Thomas Nixon, 7
case law, growth and legal realism, 79–80
case method, 75
Catholicism, 60, 164–71, 179, 203–4, 224–25, 229, 241, 245
Catholic World, 119, 131, 229
Catlin, George E. G., 26, 65, 95, 96, 97, 111, 189
Chaddock, Robert E., 33
Chapin, F. Stuart, 34, 36, 39, 97
Chase, Harry Woodburn, 130
Chase, Stuart, 29
Chicago, University of, 3, 7, 16, 17, 19, 31, 139, 142, 149–51, 156
Children of Light and the Children of Darkness, The (Reinhold Niebuhr), 245
Christian Century, 122, 130, 132, 135, 219, 228
Christianity and Crisis, 229

churches, and World War II, 228–29
Clark, Charles E., 80, 93, 142, 149
Clark, John M., 19, 35, 62
Clarke, William F., 166
Clay, Lucius D., 237
Cobb, John Candler, 34
Coffin, Henry Sloane, 229
Cohen, Felix S., 80, 87, 89, 90, 93, 94, 172, 177, 207
Cohen, Morris R., 28, 53, 55, 90, 92, 161, 172, 177, 184
Colby, Bainbridge, 130
cold war, 235, 246–47, 253, 261, 265–66; and relativist theory of democracy, 238–40
Coleman, James S., 265
Common Law, The (Oliver Wendell Holmes, Jr.), 76
Commons, John R., 19, 86
Commonweal, 122, 126, 129, 229
communism, 117–21, 134, 210, 224; as absolutist, 119, 247; identification with fascism and Nazism, 133–37
complementarity, principle of, 57
Comstock, Ada L., 222
Conklin, Edwin Grant, 100
Conner, James Thomas, 166
Contemporary Juristic Theories (Roscoe Pound), 162
control, idea of, in social science, 26
Cook, Walter Wheeler, 80, 89, 91, 174–76, 178
Cooley, Charles Horton, 16
Copeland, Morris A., 18
Cornell, Ezra, 7
Corwin, Edward S., 110
Cram, Ralph Adams, 100
Crisis of Our Age, The (Pitirim Sorokin), 188
Croly, Herbert, 123
Crommelin, A. C., 51
culture, concept of, 24; as analogous to geometry, 70–73, 186–88; as basis of political system, 205, 251, 255–56, 263–65; and relativist theory of democracy, 210–16; and status quo orientation, 261
Cunningham, H. E., 99

Dahl, Robert A, 260–61
Daily Maroon, 4
Darwin, Charles, 15, 31
Darwinism, 5–8, 9–10, 23, 75
Daspit, Alex A., 220

Langdell, Christopher C., 75
Langford, C. H., 57
Lashley, K. S., 18
Lasswell, Harold D., 17, 31, 35, 95, 107, 114; and commitment to scientific naturalism, 193; and concept of power, 96; and political psychology, 97, 102–4; and reaffirmation of democracy, 189
Law and the Lawyers (Edward S. Robinson), 160
Law and the Modern Mind (Jerome Frank), 83, 173
Law in Quest of Itself, The (Lon L. Fuller), 162
law of the excluded middle, 57
Le Bon, Gustave, 99
Le Buffe, Francis P., S.J., 166, 228
Lederer, Emil, 184
Legal Foundations of Capitalism (John R. Commons), 86
legal realism, see chapter 5, 140–41, 145–47, chapter 9, 247–49
Lerner, Max, 203, 207, 225
Lewis, Clarence Irving, 56–59
Lewis, Gilbert N., 55
Lewis, John D., 202
Lewis, Sinclair, 127
Lindeman, Eduard C., 204
Lippmann, Walter, 108, 112, 113, 114, 203, 207; and critique of democracy, 104–7; and disillusion with scientific naturalism, 152–54; and fascism, 121; as interventionist, 222; and political psychology, 100
Lipset, Seymour Martin, 241
Living Age, 130
Llewellyn, Karl N., 80, 81–82, 85, 86, 91, 172, 173–74
Lobachevski, Nickolai, 50, 60
logic, as formalistic, 55; multi-valued, 57–61
Logic of Modern Physics, The (Percy W. Bridgman), 38
logical positivism, 48
Lowell, A. Lawrence, 17
Lowie, Robert H., 20, 66, 68, 70, 71, 137
Luce, Henry R., 238
Lucey, Francis E., S.J., 168
Lukasiewicz, Jan, 57, 59, 60
Lundberg, George A., 19, 20, 22, 39, 65, 195–96
Lusk, Clayton R., 118
Lynd, Robert S., 193, 194

McCarthy, Joseph, 241
McCarthyism, 241–42, 253, 265–66
McCormack, John, 131
McDougal, Myres S., 176, 248
McDougall, William, 37, 98
MacFadden, Bernarr, 127
MacIver, Robert M., 44, 191, 192
McKeon, Richard P., 238
MacLeish, Archibald, 221, 222
McNamee, Stephen F., S.J., 180
Malinowski, Bronislaw, 188
Man and Culture (Clark Wissler), 20
Manion, Clarence, 164
Margenau, Henry, 204
Maritain, Jacques, 180
Marsh, O. C., 6
Marshall, Leon C., 86
Martin, Everett D., 100
Martin, Herbert, 181
Marx, Karl, 56
Marxism, 29–30, 247
Mason, Alpheus T., 109
Mateotti, Giacomo, 124
mathematics, as formalistic, 55–56
Maurras, Charles, 126
Mayo, Elton, 101–2, 103, 104, 107, 114
Mead, Margaret, 20, 70, 72, 188
Meaning of Meaning, The (Charles Ogden and I. A. Richards), 47
Means, Gardiner C., 86
Mecham, Philip, 161
Mein Kampf (Adolph Hitler), 65
Melby, Ernest O., 149
Mencken, H. L., 100, 131
Menger, Karl, 48
Merriam, Charles E., 10, 17, 31, 95, 101, 102, 108, 212; and commitment to scientific naturalism, 193; and concept of power, 96; and method, 28; and political psychology, 35, 97; and quantification, 34; and reaffirmation of democracy, 189; and reform, 39
metaphysics. See neo-Aristotelianism
method, in social science after 1910, 28–30, 39–40
Methodist Student Movement, 188
Michael, Jerome, 141
Millar, Moorehouse F. X., 170
Miller, Perry, 271
Miltner, Charles C., 92, 168
Ministers No War Committee of 1941, 228
Minkowski, Herman, 51
Mises, Ludwig von, 183

249–53, 255–56; and concept of elites, 242; as critical theory, 268–69; impact of World War II on, 231; and Mc-Carthyism, 241–42; as political paradigm, 237; and pragmatism, 200–202, 205–7, 211–12, 269–70; and status quo, 239–40, 253–66, 269. See also absolutist-relativist dichotomy

relativity, theory of, 51–52

religious revival of the fifties, 235

"restatement" of the law, and legal realism, 80

Review of Politics, 179

Rice, Stuart A., 33, 35, 36, 39, 49, 97, 107, 194, 195

Richards, I. A., 47, 63

Riemann, Georg, 50, 51

Riesman, David, 241, 254

Robinson, Edward S., 34, 80, 86, 87, 160

Robinson, James Harvey, 99

Roche, Patrick J., 170

Rockefeller, Laurance S., 237

Rockefeller Brothers Fund, 237

Rockefeller, Laura Spelman, Foundation, 27, 31

Rodell, Fred, 176, 198

Rome-Berlin axis, 132, 133

Roosevelt, Franklin D., 134–35, 220, 229

Roosevelt administration, 219–20

Root, Elihu, 79

Ross, Edward A., 16, 134

Rueff, Jacques, 64–65

Ruml, Beardsley, 28, 99

Rusk, Dean, 238

Russell, Bertrand, 55, 62

Ryan, John A., 134

Sabine, George, 62, 137, 191 ,192, 199

Sage, Russell, Foundation, 32

St. John's University, 166

Salomon, Albert, 182

Sanders, W. Stephen, 119

Sands, William Franklin, 171

Sapir, Edwin, 20

Schattschneider, E. E., 96, 190

Schlesinger, Arthur M., 35

Schlick, Moritz, 48

Schneider, Herbert W., 123, 204

Schuman, Frederick L., 131

Schumpeter, Joseph A., 259

science, as analogous to democracy, 206–7; as cultural force, 212–13; and faith in after World War II, 236. See also scientific naturalism

Science and Sanity (Alfred Korzybski), 63

scientific naturalism, 3, 8–9, 10–12, 39, 47, 49, 53–54, 268; advocates divided, 172–75, 191–95, 198–99, 225–28; attack on, 5, 11–12, 221–23, 235, chapters 8–10; challenges democratic theory, 11, 114, chapters 5 and 6; as conducive to totalitarianism, 110–11, 151–54, 156, 157–58, 163, 179, 181, 188, 218, 241; and Catholicism, 60–61, 164–71, 179–80, 203–4, 241; criticism of early social science, 16–17; as "debilitating," see chapter 12; and ethical theory, 40–46, chapter 4; and interventionism, 226; and legal theory, see chapter 5; movement away from in thirties, 152–56; and non-interventionism, 226–27; persistence of among intellectuals, 175–78, 191–96, 197, 216–17, 223–24, chapter 13, 268; as philosophy of democracy, see chapters 11 and 13; and political science, 95–98; and reformulation of democratic theory, see relativist theory of democracy; theoretical emphasis after 1910, 21–24; and World War II, see chapter 12

Search for Truth, The (Eric Temple Bell), 60

Silvemini, Gaetano, 133

semantics, 63–64

Sharp, Malcolm, 203

Shephard, Walter J., 108

Shils, Edward S., 265, 266

Shuster, George N., 130

Sign, 204

Simon, Theodore, 32

Simonds, Frank H., 129

Sisson, Edgar, 118

Skinner, B. F., 18

Slesinger, Donald, 86, 87, 141, 149

Small, Albion, 16

Smith, Alfred E., 130

Smith, Henry Bradford, 56

Smith, T. V., 31, 42, 149, 150, 216; and relativist theory of democracy, 208–10

Social and Cultural Dynamics (Pitirim A. Sorokin), 185, 188

Social Research (George A. Lundberg), 20

Social Science, 44

social science, attack on, see neo-Aristotelianism, Catholicism; and bolshevism, 120; and consulting, 26,